Environmental Commo(
and Emissions Trading

Market-based solutions to environmental problems offer great promise, but require complex public policies that take into account the many institutional factors necessary for the market to work and that guard against the social forces that can derail good public policies. Using insights about markets from the new institutional economics, this book sheds light on the institutional history of the emissions trading concept as it has evolved across different contexts. It makes accessible the policy design and practical implementation aspects of a key tool for fighting climate change: emissions trading systems (ETS) for environmental control.

Blas Luis Pérez Henríquez analyzes past market-based environmental programs to extract lessons for the future of ETS. He follows the development of the emissions trading concept as it evolved in the United States and was later applied in the multinational European Emissions Trading System and in sub-national programs in the United States such as the Regional Greenhouse Gas Initiative (RGGI) and California's ETS. This ex post evaluation of an ETS as it evolves in real time in the real world provides a valuable supplement to what is already known from theoretical arguments and simulation studies about the advantages and disadvantages of the market strategy.

Political cycles and political debate over the use of markets for environmental control make any form of climate policy extremely contentious. Pérez Henríquez argues that, despite ideological disagreements, the ETS approach, or, more popularly, "cap-and-trade" policy design, remains the best hope for a cost-effective policy to reduce GHG emissions around the world.

Blas Luis Pérez Henríquez is Director of the Center for Environmental Public Policy, University of California, Berkeley, USA; Senior Visiting Fellow at the Grantham Research Institute on Climate Change and the Environment, London School of Economics and Political Science, London, UK; and Visiting Professor at the Center for Economic Research and Teaching (CIDE), Mexico City, Mexico.

Resources for the Future

About Resources for the Future *and* RFF Press

Resources for the Future (RFF) improves environmental and natural resource policy-making worldwide through independent social science research of the highest caliber. Founded in 1952, RFF pioneered the application of economics as a tool for developing more effective policy about the use and conservation of natural resources. Its scholars continue to employ social science methods to analyze critical issues concerning pollution control, energy policy, land and water use, hazardous waste, climate change, biodiversity, and the environmental challenges of developing countries.

RFF Press supports the mission of RFF by publishing book-length works that present a broad range of approaches to the study of natural resources and the environment. Its authors and editors include RFF staff, researchers from the larger academic and policy communities, and journalists. Audiences for publications by RFF Press include all of the participants in the policymaking process—scholars, the media, advocacy groups, NGOs, professionals in business and government, and the public.

Environmental Commodities Markets and Emissions Trading

Towards a low-carbon future

Blas Luis Pérez Henríquez

To David Vogel,

With great appreciation and friendship.

RFF PRESS
RESOURCES FOR THE FUTURE

This first edition published 2013
by RFF Press
Routledge 2 Park Square, Milton Park, Abingdon, Oxon, OX14 4RN

Simultaneously published in the USA and Canada
by RFF Press
Routledge 711 Third Avenue, New York, NY 10017

RFF Press is an imprint of the Taylor & Francis Group, an informal business

British Library Cataloguing in Publication Data
A catalogue record for this book is available from the British Library

Library of Congress Cataloging-in-Publication Data
Pérez Henríquez, Blas Luis.
Environmental commodities markets and emissions trading : towards a
low-carbon future / Blas Luis Pérez Henríquez.
p. cm.
Includes bibliographical references and index.
1. Emissions trading. 2. Carbon offsetting. I. Title.
HC79.P55P47 2013
363.738'746--dc23
2012024084

ISBN: 978-1-61726-094-0 (hbk)
ISBN: 978-1-61726-095-7 (pbk)
ISBN: 978-1-93633-191-8 (ebk)

Typeset in Bembo
by Integra Software Services Pvt. Ltd, Pondicherry, India

MIX
Paper from
responsible sources
FSC
www.fsc.org   FSC® C004839   Printed and bound by CPI Group (UK) Ltd, Croydon, CR0 4YY

Contents

List of illustrations

Figures

Tables

Preface

Climate policy and the carbon market are well understood by only a few. Diplomats, policy experts, and academics, as well as some in the carbon trading industry and the emerging environmental finance industry, currently have a monopoly on knowledge about the intricacies of what it takes to develop and implement emissions trading systems (ETS) for environmental control. This book seeks to weaken that monopoly. It will shed light on the institutional history of the concept of ETS as it has evolved across different contexts of implementation, and make accessible the policy design and practical implementation aspects of a key tool for fighting against man-made climate change.

Market-based environmental policy analysis requires taking into account all the institutional factors necessary for the market to function optimally as well as the social forces that work to shape a final environmental policy design. It is useful, therefore, to analyze the implementation patterns of past market-based environmental programs to extract policy implementation lessons from such experiences. *Ex post* evaluation of actual experiences provides a valuable supplement to what is already known from theoretical arguments and simulation studies about the advantages and disadvantages of the market strategy as it evolves in real time in the real world. Within political cycles at the national and regional level, debate over the use of markets for environmental control remains contentious. Despite recent ideological disagreements and political polarization, the ETS approach, in particularly the cap-and-trade design, remains the best hope for achieving a cost-effective and politically acceptable regulatory framework to reduce greenhouse gas emissions around the world.

As existing and emerging ETS systems take hold in national, regional, and multinational regulatory frameworks on different continents, the possibilities for the integration and exchange of environmental commodities across systems will expand. It took two decades for the first large-scale ETS addressing acid rain in the US to become operational and cost effective. It is taking another decade to "get it right" and to calibrate the policy design of the first multinational climate-related ETS developed by the European Union. Along with the evolution of the ETS concept and its policy design refinements across more and more complex contexts of implementation, the need for a global solution to the issue of climate change will in the future require legions of public officials around the world to learn about the history of this policy idea, its rocky start, and the policy design parameters that have helped make successful experiences workable and cost effective. Hence, this book.

Thanks to Paul Portney for encouraging me to undertake this project. Also, special thanks to my colleagues at the University of California, Berkeley: Eugene Bardach, Alex Farrell, Michael Hanemann, and Eugene Smolensky for strengthening this book with thoughtful comments and suggestions, and in particular to Lee Friedman for his careful review and valuable enhancements to this and previous versions of the manuscript. Thanks also to Tom Tietenberg who kindly reviewed and suggested important recommendations for enhancing this book. From the London School of Economics and Political Science's Grantham Research Institute on Climate Change and the Environment my gratitude goes to Sam Frankhauser and Dimitri Zenghelis, along with Alessandro Vitelli for their insights on the international aspects of this book, as well as to Rafael Calel for the useful discussions on environmental economics and the comparative institutional aspects of the project. At Resources for the Future, invaluable help on improving this book was granted by Joe Kruger, Richard Morgenstern, and Don Reisman. This project allowed me to meet many policy practitioners, academics, and experts on climate policy and carbon markets, many new friends, who throughout the years have provided me with ideas, suggestions, and encouragement to finish this project, among them: Linda Adams, Richard Baron, Juan Carlos Belausteguigoitia, Severin Borenstein, Henry Brady, Dallas Burtraw, Bruce Cain, Jan Corfee-Morlot, Simon Dietz, Jill Duggan, Dan Farber, Adrian Fernandez, Albert Fishlow, James Goldstene, Dan Kammen, Nancy Kete, David Kirp, Ray Kopp, Jennifer Macedonia, Michael Nacht, Mary Nichols, Judith Rees, Fernando Tudela, David Victor, David Vogel, Mark Wenzel, Peter Zapfel and John Zysman. From Mexico's Center for Research and Teaching in Economics, thanks to Enrique Cabrero and David Arellano for their support as I developed part of this project during my tenure as visiting professor there.

Finally, my infinite gratitude goes to a long list of graduate research assistants who supported my work during more than a decade at UC Berkeley's Center for Environmental Public Policy at the Goldman School. This project particularly benefited from Andrea Murphy, Laura Wisland and Dan Goncher who provided invaluable research support; from Sara Moore and Jean Spencer for their sharp editing skills; and from Nate Dewart, who formatted and organized the final manuscript and tables and performed other key tasks for the completion of this book. To those mentioned here, and those who I'm sure forgetting, thanks again for your generosity and support. I am responsible for any remaining mistakes and omissions.

List of acronyms

AAUs	Assigned amount units
AB 32	Assembly Bill 32 (California's Global Warming Solutions Act of 2006)
ACR	American Carbon Registry
AEIC	American Energy Innovation Council
AMS	Allowance Management System
AQMD	Air Quality Management District
AQMP	Air Quality Management Plan
AR	Assessment Report
ARP	Acid Rain Program
ATS	Allowance Tracking System
BAU	Business as usual
BSA	Burden-Sharing Agreement
CAA	US Clean Air Act
CA ETS	California Emissions Trading System
CAIR	Clean Air Interstate Rule
CAMD	Clean Air Markets Division
CAMR	Clean Air Mercury Rule
CAR	Climate Action Reserve
CARB	California Air Resources Board
CBE	Communities for a Better Environment
CBOT	Chicago Board of Trade
CBS	Clean Air Markets Division Business System
CCA	Climate Change Agreements
CCAR	California Climate Action Registry
CCC	Committee on Climate Change
CCL	Climate Change Levy
CDM	Clean Development Mechanism
CEMS	Continuous Emissions Monitoring Systems
CEQ	Council on Environmental Quality
CERs	Certified Emissions Reductions
CFC	Chlorofluorocarbon

CITL	Community Independent Transaction Log
CME	Chicago Mercantile Exchange
C-MAP	Clean Air Mapping and Analysis Program
CO_2	Carbon dioxide
CO_2e	Carbon dioxide equivalent
COP	Conference of the Parties
CRS	Congressional Research Service
CSAPR	Cross-State Air Pollution Rule
CT	Carbon Trust
DECC	Department of Energy and Climate Change
DEFRA	Department of Environment, Food, and Rural Affairs
DPs	Direct Participants
EC	European Community
EDF	Environmental Defense Fund
EEA	European Economic Area
EGUs	Electric-generation units
EIA	Energy Information Administration
EIT	Economies in transition
EPA	Environmental Protection Agency
ERC	Emission Reduction Credits
ERUs	Emission Reduction Units
ETG	Emissions Trading Group
ETS	Emissions Trading System(s)
EU	European Union
EUAs	European Union Allowances
EU ETS	European Union Greenhouse Gas Emissions Trading System
EUTL	European Union Transaction Log
FED	Functional Equivalent Document
FERC	Federal Energy Regulatory Commission
FIPs	Federal Implementation Plans
GAO	Government Accountability Office
GDP	Gross domestic product
GHG	Greenhouse gas
GIS	Geographic Information System
GNP	Gross national product
GSP	Gross state product
HFCs	hydrofluorocarbons
HCFC	hydrochlorofluorocarbon
IEA	International Energy Agency
IPCC	Intergovernmental Panel on Climate Change
IPP	Independent power producers
IPPC	Integrated Pollution Prevention and Control
IR	Industrial Rationalization
ISO	International Organization for Standardization

JI	Joint implementation
JISC	Joint Implementation Supervisory Committee
KP	Kyoto Protocol
MATS	Mercury and Air Toxics Standards
MDP	Missing Data Procedures
MLF	Multilateral Fund
MMBtu	Million Metric British Thermal Units
MOU	Memorandum of Understanding
MP	Montreal Protocol
MRV	Measuring, reporting, and verification
$MtCO_2e$	Metric Tons Carbon Dioxide Equivalent
NAAQS	National Ambient Air Quality Standards
NA ETS	North American Emissions Trading System
NAMAs	Nationally Appropriate Mitigation Actions
NAP	National allocation plans
NAPAP	National Acid Precipitation Assessment Program
NATS	Nitrogen Allowance Tracking Systems
NBP	NO_x Budget Trading Program
NBP ETS	NO_x SIP Call Federal Budget Trading Program
NEI	National Emissions Inventory
NEPA	National Environmental Protection Act
NESCAUM	Northeast States for Coordinated Air Use Management
NF_3	Nitrogen trifluoride
NMM	New Market Mechanisms
non-EGUs	Non-electric generating units
NO_x	Nitrogen oxides
N_2O	Nitrous oxide
NSR	New Source Review
NYMEX	New York Mercantile Exchange
O_3	Ozone
ODS	Ozone-depleting substances
OECD	Organisation for Economic Co-operation and Development
OTAG	Ozone Transport Assessment Group
OTC	Over-the-counter
OTC	Ozone Transport Commission
Pb	Lead
PFC	Progressive Flow Control
PFCs	Perfluorocarbons
$PM_{2.5}$	Fine particulate matter with an aerodynamic diameter of up to 2.5 μm
R&D	Research and development
RACT	Reasonably Available Control Requirements
RATA	Relative accuracy test audits
RECLAIM	Regional Clean Air Incentives Market

RFF	Resources for the Future
RGGI	North East Regional Greenhouse Gas Initiative
RMU	Removal unit
RTC	RECLAIM Trading Credits
SCAQMD	South Coast Air Quality Management District
SF_6	Sulfur hexafluoride
SIP	State implementation plan
SO_2	Sulfur dioxide
SO_x	Sulfur oxides
TCE	Transaction cost economics
TCP	Transaction-cost politics
UK ETS	United Kingdom Carbon Emissions Trading Scheme
UN	United Nations
UNEP	United Nations Environment Program
UNFCCC	United Nations Framework Convention on Climate Change
US	United States
UV-b	Ultraviolet rays
VCS	Verified Carbon Standard
VOCs	Volatile organic compounds
WCI	Western Climate Initiative

Chapter 1

Introduction

Make no mistake, climate policy is energy policy. If we are to preserve our planet and make it sustainable indefinitely for future generations, then we must transform our energy systems and make the transition to a low-carbon economy. Energy is a necessity in all of the world's societies. Thus it is not surprising that energy policies are often crucial for a country's leaders—when successful resulting in an ample and affordable supply and when unsuccessful leading to conflict, war, and tragedy. Now we have discovered that even the peaceful burning of fossil fuels to create energy threatens to devastate our planet in another way—through the threat of climate change caused by the accumulation of greenhouse gases in the atmosphere.

Regulation is not enough to push the transition to a low-carbon, green economy. Rather, a systems approach is needed, one that is mutually supportive of government, business, and civil society action on climate change. Energy conservation, expansion of renewable sources, and increased energy efficiency are some of the complementary programs and measures that should be implemented to lower worldwide greenhouse gas (GHG) emissions. These efforts will require major investments and will have long-term implications, particularly in the developing world if these countries are to avoid the historical carbon-intensive development patterns of industrialized countries. Alternative growth strategies for emerging nations will require enhancing the flow of capital and developing new technological pathways to make the concepts of green growth and a clean economy a reality. A mature, well-integrated global carbon market can assist in achieving these policy objectives.

This book introduces a review of the theory, practice, and future of emissions trading from the policy analysis perspective. It reflects on the most salient policy design and implementation lessons from the emission trading systems (ETS) implementation experience to date. It is a study based on the institutional development history of creating environmental commodities markets, first focusing on pioneering experiences implementing cost-effective air pollution regulation in the United States (US), and later looking at the European Union's (EU's) efforts to combat global climate change. In this later context, policies governing environmental commodities markets have proven to be one of the key policy mechanisms supporting the civil transition to a low-carbon economy.

While there is concern that regulating GHG is costly to the business sector, so too is the lack of certainty about the institutions to be developed to address climate change at the national and international level. Increasingly, a new paradigm for economic development is gaining favor among national, regional, and local governments based on three main ideas: First, climate action offers an opportunity for social and economic transformation towards a clean economy. Second, through ingenuity and innovation, new engines of prosperity from economy-wide transformation based on low-carbon growth development strategies will emerge. Third, the planet's natural assets will be conserved for future generations to enjoy—the essence of the concept of sustainability.

Laggard nations with large carbon footprints will eventually pay the price through the reduced competiveness of their economies. They will also become vulnerable on the energy security front if they continue to depend heavily on expensive and dirty sources of energy. The transition from conventional fossil fuels is going to take time—at least several decades. However, first movers in developing cost-effective regulatory frameworks for GHG emission reductions, like the multinational emissions trading system, and clean sustainable energy policy guidelines such as those devised by members of the EU are betting on the future benefits of the catalyzing effect of these policies and programs to their economies and the environment. Similar efforts are being implemented at the national and local level, for instance in Australia and California respectively, to introduce a price on carbon into their economies as well as to make the concept of sustainability an attractive—and profitable—business proposition. Rethinking energy policy as a basis for economic prosperity through green growth and clean energy technological developments is occurring voluntarily in emerging nations such as Brazil, China, India, Mexico, and South Korea even without a legal requirement under current international agreements. The emergence of a global carbon market creates the incentive for early action, as these efforts can be recognized under United Nations Framework Convention on Climate Change (UNFCCC) flexible policy mechanisms. Moreover, the multinational, regional, and local systems currently in place demand emission reduction projects as part of their cost-minimization strategies through the voluntary market for emission reduction credits.

Not only are there financial benefits to early action, but there are also avoided future costs. Early emission reductions may prove to be more valuable than those achieved at a later time. The Stern Review (2007) widely publicized the idea that if nations take "strong action now" the world can avoid, at a much reduced cost, the "serious impacts on growth and development" that climate change threatens to impose from necessary adaptation efforts in the future. Analysts, however, have pointed out the weaknesses of a top-down approach under the UNFCCC for global collective climate action. Popular buy-in will be needed to clear the key hurdles to advancing effective international climate and energy policy, which include: the disconnect between science and policy action, significantly higher damage and mitigation cost estimates than those put forth by the Stern Review, the threat of slowing economic growth, and the large fiscal transfers from the industrialized world to the developing world that a strong global climate action plan would require (Helm 2008).

Making the emerging United Nations (UN) compliance carbon market system efficient and effective will take time, as the multilateral process is slow, cumbersome, and complex. Nations will continue to debate how best to improve the UN system's performance in stabilizing GHG emissions as well as how to finance such efforts, as the discussions during the UN climate summit in Durban in 2011 on New Market Mechanisms (NMMs) attest. The goal is to increase the scale of the KP's Clean Development Mechanism (CDM), which allows for compliance credit to be given to developed nations that pay for emission-reduction projects implemented in developing countries. The next phase in the UNFCCC negotiations aims to enable advanced developing economies to gradually make the transition away from the current CDM path and to take on more ambitious emissions reduction targets either at the national level or by industrial sector through the NMMs and voluntary implementation of Nationally Appropriate Mitigation Actions.

Clear rules and standards will have to be devised to avoid market fragmentation as the market approach expands. But in the meantime, a transitional institutional development phase is required. This period of several decades will require a credible political commitment to a global carbon market by key governments beyond the EU in order to underpin this policy approach's capacity to support the greening of national economies around the world.

Whatever the preferred sequence of integration, a price on carbon emissions is the most practical solution to address the dangers and risks of climate change. A well-functioning global carbon market can provide the lowest cost solution to mitigate greenhouse gas emissions. But more importantly, it can provide regulatory certainty on the environmental goal while incentivizing managerial and technological innovations as well as the financial flows necessary for humanity to transit to a low-carbon future. Swift and decisive action is needed at the regional, national, and international level in order to enable the green economy concept. However, as Stavins (2000) suggests:

> No particular form of government intervention, no individual policy instrument—whether market-based or conventional—is appropriate for all environmental problems. Which instrument is best in any given situation depends upon a variety of characteristics of the environmental problem, and the social, political, and economic context in which it is being regulated. There is no policy panacea. Indeed the real challenge for bureaucrats, elected officials, and other participants in the environmental policy process comes in analyzing and then selecting the best instrument for each situation that arises.

Environmental economists have produced results showing that economic incentives for pollution control improve efficiency. Empirical studies have shown how to make incentive-based programs more efficient at controlling pollution.

Ultimately, more study will be necessary to find out how new emission trading mechanisms operate in the real world, in particular whether they deliver their theoretical efficiency gains.[1] With time, policy lessons will emerge from experimentation in increasingly diverse and complex contexts of implementation as we move toward a global carbon market. Because GHG are evenly distributed in the atmosphere, a cap-and-trade ETS is "especially well suited to addressing the problem of climate change."[2]

At the time when governments around the world started to experiment with market-based solutions for environmental control, policy analysts from the Organisation for Economic Co-operation and Development (OECD) argued that theoretical decision-making models for choosing among alternative policy instruments tend to be too abstract to function as a basis for making actual policy choices. In order to effectively implement a policy instrument, a more practical approach is needed, one that takes into account institutional concerns such as administrative and political feasibility. While the neoclassical economic framework underscores externalities, marginal costs, and marginal benefits of pollution abatement, an institutional perspective takes a more comprehensive approach to formulating policy (OECD 1997). Thus, it is useful to analyze the patterns of implementation of past market-based environmental programs to extract policy implementation lessons for future application. This book presents suggestions for developing efficient and cost-effective market policies to protect the environment and the global commons based on an examination of previous market experiences with air pollution emissions controls in the US, the EU, and elsewhere.

1.1 Research questions

The working hypothesis of this book is that policy analysts, policy entrepreneurs, and policy managers can design more effective control policies to improve current and future market-based environmental programs by paying attention to the expected interplay of interests in the design and implementation stage and to the findings of the historical review of use of the ETS concept through the lens of institutional economics. Policymakers designing market-based environmental programs should ask:

i)   *Are specific market design features (i.e., fine-tuning, contextual adaptation, market enhancing institutions, use of information technology, rates of policy participation among target population, etc.) necessary to make a market-based policy feasible?*

ii) *To what degree does the interaction of social and institutional factors (i.e., politics, lobbying, electoral cycles, etc.) interfere with or limit the efficiency potential of these mechanisms?*

iii) *How transferable is the policy know-how derived from actual implementation of environmental market-based programs, given that what works in one context may not work in another?*

1.2 Unit of analysis: emissions trading systems

This book seeks to examine what has worked and not worked in market-based air pollution control programs, in particular the ETS approach. Such decentralized programs are judged by the criteria of cost, as well as capacity to achieve the set of predetermined policy goals mandated by a federal legislature, state legislatures, or an international multilateral agreement. This book looks at programs that seek to control emissions at the national, sub-national, regional, and international level.

Joskow et al. (1998, 669), announced a triumph in the evolution of ETS programs when they concluded that the market created by the US Environmental Protection Agency (EPA) for sulfur dioxide (SO_2) emissions had "become reasonably efficient." However, when the 1990 US Clean Air Act Amendments (CAA) were enacted, its Title IV (also known as the Acid Rain Program or ARP)—designed to reduce acidic depositions by controlling emissions of SO_2, the main precursor of acid rain—proved difficult to implement. Almost two decades of experimentation and halfhearted attempts to jump-start environmental markets to support air pollution control policies had preceded this program.

The creation of allowances for SO_2—a kind of property rights for emissions—and the ability to trade those allowances, promised cost-minimizing opportunities in pollution abatement. Electric utilities burning fossil fuels produce 70 percent of US SO_2 emissions and are highly regulated. The ARP ETS introduced flexibility into their compliance with emissions regulations. However, these potential efficiency gains hinged on the establishment of a well-functioning, fluid market for SO_2 allowances. By achieving this milestone, the ARP initiated a new era in the use of incentive-based regulation.

In the early 1990s, it was not clear if or how the new market-based program was going to perform in the US institutional setting. For instance, Bohi and Burtraw (1991, 676) warned of potential "regulatory gridlock," given the structure of the electric utility regulatory framework, which is a patchwork of state and regional regulations.

The annual auctions for the permits held by the EPA provided valuable price information, and the financial markets rapidly acknowledged the potential of a secondary air pollution allowance market. By 1993 financial intermediaries had already standardized transaction procedures and developed financial instruments for inter-temporal market transactions such as options, futures, and "swaps" (Joskow et al. 1998, 683). Based on lessons from pioneering experiences developing environmental commodities exchanges, Sandor (2012) reminds us that: "Both standardization and the use of a central marketplace lowered transaction costs, leaving both buyers and sellers better off."[3]

The successful implementation of the ARP ETS established the US as the leader in market-based environmental policy. Introduced by the Republican President George H. Bush, the program was initially touted by business leaders as the most business-friendly approach to environmental protection and was also endorsed by important environmental groups. It was even presented as the American way to solve environmental problems since the market, not central commands or taxes, was the mechanism for achieving a clear environmental policy goal set by an emissions cap.

However, policy approaches and priorities are highly vulnerable to political cycles and politics. In the US, since the 2008 presidential election, the use of the ETS cap-and-trade design has fallen out of favor. Some conservative politicians campaigning against federal climate policy have described the ETS approach as a "cap-and-tax scheme"—and green taxes are notoriously difficult to introduce in the American policy formulation process.

It was the EU that decided to implement the first multinational ETS to address the issue of climate change. Ironically, the EU's ETS is largely based on the policy design parameters used in the US cap-and-trade model developed for the ARP. Politically, the EU is more amenable to environmental taxes than the US, and it also has a lower tolerance for risk because of a lack of policy action under a statutory requirement known as the precautionary principle. The EU and its Member States have taken the lead in market-based pollution design, giving their industries and citizens a head start in preparing for a carbon-constrained world. In doing so, they expect to gain a competitive edge by becoming more energy efficient and independent and by developing new clean, sustainable energy technologies.

1.3 Policy diffusion and accumulated policy know-how

The US historical experience developing emission trading systems for air pollution and the EU's ETS to reduce GHG emissions, along with the emergence of national, sub-national, regional, and sectoral ETS institutional developments in North America, the Asian-Pacific Rim, and in major developing countries provide us with a catalogue of lessons for designing and implementing decentralized global governance structures for environmental control using ETS and the commodities markets infrastructure. The experience from these programs is informing market-based environmental programs worldwide.

Other important precedents for market-based environmental programs were set by a US lead (Pb) trading program for gasoline and by the phasing out of chlorofluorocarbon emissions under the Montreal Protocol. The institutional limits to the market approach in environmental policy within the US were revealed by the failure to establish fluid emission allowance markets when regulatory "bubbles"[4] for air pollution control were created under the EPA's 1986 Emission Trading Policy Statement (Kete 1994).

Still, an increasing number of nations and private and public organizations are currently experimenting with emission trading programs, from the intra-firm, national, and sub-national, to the multinational level. In all cases, these trading programs eventually will require authorization or endorsement by federal government institutions to be part of a multilateral system such as the one called for by the UNFCCC. The executive powers and senates and parliaments of nations around the world would need to ratify treaties and agreements recognizing and validating each other's emission reduction efforts in order to enable international legally binding instruments.

If the top-down, all-or-nothing UNFCCC process continues to stall, as seems likely given that it is highly politicized and dominated by national interests, perhaps linking and expanding successful ETS programs under mutual recognition protocols may lead to a more practical, bottom-up development of ETS programs around the world. Such institutional developments may advance the establishment of a global carbon market through harmonization and mutual recognition of carbon allowances, emission reduction credits and offsets, and domestic and regional ETS and regulatory controls. However, a well-integrated international environmental commodities market, in particular the carbon market, will require a set of minimum policy design standards and a set of best practices recognized by all parties and enforced by a new integrity system supported by a technically based international carbon standard and subject to verification and validation by some coordinating agent akin to the ones established under the International Organization for Standardization (ISO).

In sum, this book seeks to:

- Introduce a method for improving market-based environmental policy analysis by taking into account both the necessary features for well-functioning markets and the inevitable political and social forces that shape policy design.
- Discuss ways to assess the transferability of policy experience in this field between different contexts of varying complexity to develop policy paths towards institutional harmonization, carbon allowance fungibility, and environmental commodities market integration.

International, market-based environmental policymaking will continue to grow in importance as a tool in combating climate change. Addressing implementation problems with these policies, whether social, political, or institutional, will only become more exigent as the negative environmental impacts compound. This book begins with lessons from the past and continues on to address the present-day debates between the developed and developing worlds around the burden of responsibility for CO_2 emissions. The international negotiations process is time-consuming, complicated, and thus far hobbled by the lack of buy-in from the US, other major industrialized nations, and some key emerging economies (Susskind 1994). Unfortunately, despite bringing together the largest-ever gathering of heads of state to address a global threat, the December 2009 Copenhagen Climate Change Conference—which was convened to unveil the successor of the KP, the implementation plan of the UNFCCC—was a failure. UN members were unable to agree on a new compliance period for such a system. They were also unable to induce emerging nations to participate in an equitable manner in the global effort to address climate change.

While the 2010 UNFCCC sixteenth session of the Conference of Parties (COP16) in Cancun, Mexico somewhat restored the credibility of the multilateral approach, reaching a consensus between both developed and developing countries that "climate change is one of the greatest challenges of our times," the KP has failed to reconcile all of the diverse interests of the international community with regard to climate change. The absence of the US—a major consumer per capita of energy—from the list of countries that have ratified the treaty reflects this weakness. Japan, which chaired the development of the protocol at the Kyoto COP3 in 1997, at COP16 rejected the possibility of extending Kyoto beyond its expiration date of 2012 given the lack of active participation by key players such as the US and China.

In the Durban, South Africa COP17 in 2011, negotiations concluded with the adoption of the Durban Platform, a road map to a global legal agreement applicable to all parties under the convention and expected to take effect in 2020. In the Doha, Qatar COP18 in 2012, the rules for a second commitment period under the legal framework for managing emissions based on the "Kyoto architecture" are to be set in place. It is likely that the UNFCCC diplomatic process will continue at its own pace.

The principle of common, but differentiated, responsibilities, which acknowledges the asymmetry in the financial, technological, and institutional capacity of nations, still guides these negotiations. However, a historic shift in the multilateral policymaking context has taken place: there is now almost universal agreement that enhancing mitigation efforts by both developed and developing countries is a policy priority as we are reaching dangerous levels of GHG in our atmosphere.

As the UNFCCC Secretariat pointed out after the renewed international commitment to climate action in Cancun:

> By agreeing on a maximum two degrees Celsius temperature rise, countries sent the strongest signal ever that there would be shift towards a low-carbon global economy. However, all pledges put forward by governments came to a combined total of only 60% of the emission reductions needed for a 50% chance of keeping temperatures below that goal.[5]

Therefore, in order to implement cost-effective, multilateral environmental programs, supplementary (or even alternative) equivalent and mutually recognized institutional-building processes should be considered in the next phases of the UNFCCC action plan to enable a real global effort.

1.4 Outline of the book

Chapter 2 presents a review of the theoretical principles behind the emissions trading model. It then suggests a more systematic analytic framework to improve environmental market-based policy design, using historical examples such as the ARP. The chapter examines "path dependency," in which history and economic and political frictions matter.[6] It also looks at alternate governance structures given the contextual characteristics of a particular institutional environment.

Chapter 3 reviews the evolutionary development of early commodities markets and its implications for environmental policy. It introduces an inventory of the institutional features to be considered by policy makers in implementing a workable environmental commodities market. In the case of emissions trading systems, the fundamental decisions of (1) determining the overall pollution emission limits, (2) establishing initial allocations of emission permits (or allowances) among market participants, and (3) codifying a basic structure of trading rules together represent the triad of fundamental components for the development of a functional environmental commodities market.

Chapter 4 shows how the attempt to develop market-based systems for air pollution control in the US during the 1970s and 1980s failed due to the violation of basic market development conditions. It focuses on the learning processes involved in the development by EPA of first-generation market-based instruments (i.e., offsets, bubbles, netting, and banking) in its emissions trading program.

Chapter 5 analyzes the development and implementation of the 1990 ARP. It is a case study of the evolution of the first large-scale "cap-and-trade" SO_2 ETS. This chapter identifies the specific market design features that made the SO_2 allowance cap-and-trade policy feasible as well as factors that might have negatively impacted its cost effectiveness and presents the policy lessons and management strategies that emerged from this policy process. This chapter also discusses exogenous factors, such as political cycles and technological advances in information technologies, which favored the emergence of the first large-scale experiment with emissions trading in the US. Strong political commitment to the emissions trading approach at the time, in combination with design and management strategies that took advantage of developments in information management and monitoring mechanisms while implementing the program, made this environmental markets creation experience successful.

Chapter 6 begins the analysis of the transferability of the cap-and-trade system to alternate contexts within the US. In particular, it reviews the case of the Regional Clean Air Incentives Market (RECLAIM), a program implemented by the Los Angeles South Coast Air Quality Management District to control urban smog pollution.

Chapter 7 analyzes the development of interstate cap-and-trade. In contrast to the federal ARP designed and operated at the federal level, and the local RECLAIM program, the emissions trading mechanisms analyzed in this chapter emerged from interstate collaboration efforts to reduce ozone in the Northeastern US. In implementing an integrated and workable cap-and-trade system for air quality management, these regional emissions markets have established positive precedents for coordinated, market-based environmental policymaking between independent political jurisdictions similar to the international institutional context. However, this experience also shows how regulatory uncertainty and litigation can negatively impact the development of environmental markets.

Chapter 8 examines the challenges of extrapolating environmental trading mechanisms to a global scale, such as with the EU ETS and the UNFCCC process. Then, it describes some issues to consider in adapting the cap-and-trade model to the UNFCCC process. This chapter also suggests a model for an evolving system that relies on strong domestic emissions trading programs. It proposes a multilateral governance regime that sets institutional thresholds (or accession protocols) for nations to participate in an international emissions market mechanism. Nations willing to participate must meet certain predetermined ETS design and performance standards for measuring, reporting, and verification, as well as compliance aspects sanctioned by a central international authority (such as the UNFCCC Secretariat) but supported by more technical independent institutions akin to the ISO. For instance, an International Carbon Standard can be based on the accumulated policy know-how of best practices from existing quality assurance programs such as the US Climate Action Reserve, The Climate Registry and the American Carbon Registry, which are supporting voluntary regional efforts towards the development of the North American carbon market, and from international programs such as the Verified Carbon Standard and global risk management companies such as Det NorskeVeritas Certification AS among others. Such a system can ultimately foster certainty, integrity, and credibility in the implementation of workable and cost-effective global environmental commodities markets. Moreover, policy exchange forums to share policy implementation lessons and to design innovations and new strategies to scale up the carbon market are important to build capacity for implementing market-based instruments. The historical institutional developments of the ETS approach, and the framework of environmental market creation parameters here presented, underscore the key policy design features needed for an operational, market-based international carbon governance structure.

Chapter 2

Theoretical foundations

This chapter introduces the methodological concepts underlying this book. It includes a brief review of concepts from both the environmental economics and institutional literature used to develop a more complete policy framework for improving the design of market-based policy instruments.

In general, policy analysis requires the careful evaluation of the consequences of alternatives on criteria that go beyond efficiency. However, there is currently no single framework that systematically leads the analyst through all of the relevant considerations needed to design and implement market processes for environmental control.

This book seeks to define a set of "decision" guidelines for analysts of environmental policy, based on real cases of market solutions for environmental problems and the principles of institutional design. These rules take into account the interactions between social, institutional, and political forces that bear on the quality of an air pollution trading mechanism's design. This framework was developed based on experiences among Organisation for Economic Co-operation and Development (OECD) countries with market-based solutions for air pollution such as the federal, state, and regional cap-and-trade systems developed in the United States (US), the United Kingdom Carbon Emissions Trading Scheme (UK ETS), the European Union Greenhouse Gas Emissions Trading System (EU ETS), and new, emerging emissions trading system (ETS) programs around the world. This book also offers some pragmatic policy design and implementation strategies to create a workable global greenhouse gas emissions trading mechanism under the United Nations Framework Convention on Climate Change (UNFCCC).

2.1 Research questions

Three general questions provide an outline to our research:

Are specific market design features (e.g., fine-tuning, contextual adaptation, market enhancing institutions, use of information technology, or rates of policy participation among a target population) necessary to make a market-based policy feasible?

To what degree does the interaction of social and institutional factors interfere with or limit the efficiency potential of these mechanisms?

How transferable is the policy experience derived from actual implementation of environmental market-based programs, given that what works in one context may not work in another?

The relative success of incentive-based environmental programs to achieve a predetermined set of policy goals in a cost-effective manner is a function of a series of institutional, organizational, technical, and political factors. It is important to identify the key institutional features that allow these types of programs to achieve their regulatory objectives through a flexible mechanism. Keeping in mind these research questions, this book identifies some of the specific key institutional and design parameters that create variation in the quality (e.g., cost-effectiveness) of market-based environmental programs designed to control air pollution by reviewing the history of emissions trading systems across different implementation contexts.

2.2 Review of theoretical principles

2.2.1 Environmental economics

2.2.1 (A) The uncertain extent of market failure

Markets serve society by organizing economic activity efficiently. However, the effectiveness of market allocation of many environmental assets and risks is constrained: often there is no market for environmental resources. The economics literature has thoroughly explored the most common causes of market failure for environmental goods: incomplete markets, externalities, non-exclusion, non-rival consumption, non-convexities, and asymmetric information. In particular, market failure theory suggests that market-based decisions based on faulty or missing prices do not generate an efficient allocation of resources. How society can address these failures is a major debate in public economics.

Ideally, in environmental protection program design we should know in advance the correct level of pollution control. However, the lack of markets for environmental assets makes this process complicated. From an economic perspective the most natural solution to the problem of control is to "patch" the market by correcting the price system. While the price system has many values, it also has limitations that should be taken into account in governance design.

The economic paradigm calls for comparing the benefits of decreased pollution with the cost of pollution control and sets controls at the level where the marginal benefits are equal to the marginal cost of control (Stavins and Hahn 1995). The more control exerted over pollution, the higher the marginal cost of that control and the lower the marginal benefit. If pollution controls are set to a level below the point where marginal benefit equals marginal cost of control, a dollar spent on control will yield more than a dollar's worth of benefit. In such a case, net benefit can be increased by increasing the level of control. Likewise, if pollution control is set above the point where marginal benefit equals the marginal cost of control, then a dollar spent yields less than a dollar's worth of benefit. In this case, benefits can be increased by lowering the level of control (Tietenberg 1998).

In theory, we know that weighing the marginal cost and benefit of pollution control gives us the efficient level of control. In practice, it is much harder: only in an ideal world can one do a complete assessment of the cost of environmental damage. In an imperfect world, we use proxy measures to calculate this cost. For example, differential expenditures on equivalent housing in less polluted areas relative to more polluted areas can serve as an input to the estimation of how consumers value the marginal benefit of a cleaner environment.[1] This indirect technique, while it assumes perfect information, relies on market observations to determine how much a community values a clean environment.

Researchers can also use surveys to elicit information from individuals. Participants are asked to respond to hypothetical situations about their maximum willingness to pay for a specific reduction in morbidity or their minimum willingness to accept a specific increase in morbidity. Another popular way to measure the value of a clean environment is to look at implicit and explicit trade-offs between conservation and development (i.e., the value of clean air from a forest versus the value of infrastructure built on the land where the forest stood). However, these studies may misrepresent preferences if an individual puts a high value on an environmental good and over-reports to increase the chances of receiving more of that environmental good.

To avoid the problem of misrepresentation of preferences, alternative methods suggest focusing on valuing changes in private health indicators rather than environmental risks. For instance, if health is a good that provides individuals with time to work and conduct leisure activities, then it is considered a source of satisfaction. Therefore, its loss is a disutility in economic terms. Air pollution constitutes an exogenous input that negatively impacts health. Medical care is an endogenous input to maintain health. This method predicts that changes in air pollution levels will cause individuals to increase consumption of medical care to minimize the loss of work or leisure time (Yang et al. 2005). The value of clean air could then be estimated from the behavioral response to the environmental change (e.g., pollution levels).

The search for empirical measures of the value of a clean environment has produced an abundant literature on direct and indirect valuation methods (see Fomler and Ierland 1989; Freeman 1993; Hanemann 1991; Hanley and Spash 1993). Still, we cannot know the true cost of environmental damage. This is as much a shortfall of economics as of physical science: the interdependence of ecosystems makes a full estimate of impacts elusive.

2.2.1 (B) Alternative environmental policy instruments

There are many ways to approach a pollution abatement problem. From a comparative institutions perspective, regulation by technological requirement or standards (e.g., command-and-control schemes) has often been criticized for being too costly

(Hanley 1997, 154). However, choices are made in a complex political environment in which many factors matter, and so sometimes command-and-control is selected as the preferred control mechanism.

Policy instruments are not ideologically neutral. Institutional and cultural environments affect choice. Whether one prefers administrative measures or economic incentives to control pollution seems to depend at least as much on philosophy and ideology as on the technical properties of the two approaches. Those who favor improving efficiency through pricing previously non-priced resources, such as air and water, naturally prefer market-oriented regulatory instruments, while those who oppose the encroachment of utilitarian principles on social life tend to oppose market solutions (Majone 1989, 166).

Weitzman suggests that it "is a fair generalization to say that the average economist in the Western marginalist tradition[2] has at least a vague preference toward indirect control through prices, just as the typical non-economist leans toward the direct regulation of quantities" (1974, 477). In some situations, incentive-based policies may be less expensive than a direct command regulatory scheme. However, a critical issue for achieving the regulator's objective efficiently is the cost of monitoring and enforcement. Two market-based policy tools to deal with technological externalities[3] that have received widespread support are marketable permits (Dales 1968) and emissions taxes (Pigou 1932). Both tools induce businesses to search for cheaper methods of achieving environmental standards.

These economic instruments stand in stark contrast to the popular command-and-control approach that relies on regulation (permission, prohibition, standard setting, and enforcement). Under highly restrictive conditions, it can be shown that both approaches share the desirable feature that any gains in environmental quality will be obtained at the lowest possible cost. However, from the regulator's viewpoint these are not equivalent policy instruments (Baumol and Oates 1993, 177). The tax approach requires that the regulator set a tax rate as the price, whereas the emissions-trading approach requires the regulator to set a quantity limit equal to the allowed number of tradable permits. Uncertainty (e.g., due to information asymmetry between the regulator and a regulated firm or industry) breaks down the formal identity or equivalence between prices (e.g., taxes) and quantities (permits) (Weitzman 1974, 480). A particular tax rate may turn out to be too high or too low to achieve a particular emissions level, and a given number of permits may lead to prices that are uncomfortably high (for industrialists) or uncomfortably low (for environmentalists).

These policy approaches may be classified as either Coasian or Pigouvian, based on the theoretical principles behind each mechanism. To attain Pareto optimality, the Pigouvian approach charges a polluter a fixed price (e.g., a tax) for each unit of pollution (Bohm and Russell 1985).[4] In theory, the charge encourages environmentally sound and efficient production and consumption through marginal-cost pricing.

Thus, the regulator's task is to set and enforce a financial penalty (e.g., tax) or level of emissions equal to the marginal social damages caused by the emissions associated with production. If the regulator is certain about the price at which marginal costs equal the marginal benefits of pollution control, then incorporating that price into the emitter's cost of doing business will achieve the socially optimal abatement objective. But, in reality the price is far from certain. Weitzman (1974) shows that the effectiveness of reducing pollution by charging a financial penalty for emissions will depend on the slopes of the cost and benefit curves and how far expected values deviate from reality.[5]

A green tax or charge provides price certainty. Once it is set by government, which can be a complex political task in itself, pollution abatement costs are visible to all. But one of the main limitations of putting a price on pollution is imperfect information. Scientific, spatial, and economic constraints preclude perfect monitoring of emissions and production.[6] Not even the polluters themselves are able to accurately account for the production they derive with each additional unit of pollution, much less the regulator.[7] The cost-minimizing logic of a pollution tax still applies whatever its level: those that can avoid polluting will do so in order to not pay the tax, leaving the limited assimilative capacity of the atmosphere for those who find it more economical to pay the tax. But if the price is set too low, pollution levels will continue to be excessive. With too high a price, production will fall by more than what the pollution damages justify. Either way there is a misallocation of resources. Because of the limited information available, as well as political constraints that limit the ability to adjust a tax rate once set, the regulator cannot accurately tune the price to remedy the environmental problem.

The chief alternative to financially penalizing pollution through taxes or other charges is to create an emissions market. In this approach the challenge is to clearly define property rights over pollution and have continuous negotiations, as modeled in the Coase theorem.[8] The Coase model is based on three key assumptions: (1) successful negotiations; (2) the enforceability of agreements; and (3) zero transaction costs. In an emissions market the regulator needs to establish the rules of the permit market, monitor the trades, and ensure that the producers selling permits actually reduce emissions. With a large number of producers, continuous monitoring and enforcement requirements can be expensive. However, if there are few participants in the trading system, there may not be enough competition in the system, and the market will be inefficient. In practice, allowances to pollute are issued by the regulator approximating the concept of a legal right over emissions. Although permits levels are granted based on a scientific assessment of pollution, the distribution of those permits is often more of a political negotiation than an economic process like a simple auction.

ETS came in to favor in the US due to a growing interest in reducing the cost of compliance with environmental laws during the passage of the 1977 Clean Air Act amendments (CAA). However, it was not until the 1990 CAA amendments that a full-fledged ETS became operational to mitigate acid rain (e.g., Acid Rain Program (ARP) ETS). More recently, and given failed efforts to pass a trading system, a tax on carbon dioxide (CO_2) emissions has been discussed in the US policy formulation process by some economists—and even some industry leaders and conservative think tanks—as a more straightforward and potentially more efficient means to set a price for carbon. A report by the US Congressional Research Service (CRS 2009) on the potential advantages of the carbon tax found that a fixed price ceiling on emissions or their inputs (e.g., fossil fuels) could lessen the effects of price volatility on energy prices. The relative economic efficiency of the carbon tax is contingent upon expected costs and benefits of climate change mitigation that the CRS report characterizes as "uncertain and controversial." Depending on its design, a carbon tax approach may offer "greater transparency, reduced administrative burden, and relative ease of modification."

In Europe, taxing producers for pollution has traditionally been the preferred mechanism because of its revenue-raising potential, although a trading-based climate policy emerged as the regional approach (i.e., EU ETS). At the national level, the UK recently introduced a carbon floor price of £16 in 2013 for coal and gas electricity generation plants that will gradually rise to £30 by 2020 in case the price of carbon under the regional approach collapses. Australia is implementing a national climate plan that will first set a fixed price on carbon at A$23 per ton in 2012 as an interim step toward implementing a full-fledged ETS in 2015. The Canadian province of British Columbia is currently experimenting with a revenue-neutral tax on carbon emissions as a mechanism to stimulate a shift to a low-carbon economy. In the developing world,[9] experimentation with both systems is ongoing.

Aside from the information burden to the regulator, which must set the right price for pollution, the primary disadvantage of a carbon tax, as stated by the CRS 2009 report, "is that it would yield uncertain emission control. ETS proponents argue that the potential for irreversible climate change impacts necessitates the emissions certainty that is only available with a quantity-based instrument (e.g., cap-and-trade)." Cap-and-trade does provide a single price per unit of emissions to all market participants. In contrast, the carbon tax could end up with rates that differ across industries (as is the case in Norway) depending on diverse political economy, influence, and financial factors. This can affect the overall cost-effectiveness of the environmental market-based policy approach.[10] As suggested by Stavins (2010), many of the economic and policy questions on how to best address global common issues through market-based mechanisms remain unsettled.

Besides the logistical challenges, emissions markets face political challenges domestically and in multilateral negotiations. Through the UNFCCC, chiefly OECD countries have pushed for a global environmental market for carbon emissions to address the issue of climate change in a cost-effective manner.[11] Until 2009, the US—the country that first experimented with a large-scale emissions trading mechanism to control air pollution—was the exception. During the eight years of the George W. Bush administration, which held regressive views on climate change, the US did not ratify the Kyoto Protocol (KP), and the US Congress continues to reject it. The KP includes flexible mechanisms such as emissions trading as part of its institutional design.

The first major economy to implement a voluntary economy-wide cap-and-trade system to address climate change was the UK in 2002. Then, in 2005, the EU implemented the first multinational approach in order to meet their greenhouse gas emission reduction commitments. This success demonstrated that at the multilateral level, flexibility and efficiency gains from the development of international environmental markets are realized only from learning-by-doing, cooperative behavior and joint problem solving that includes all relevant parties.

The UK and EU efforts, as well as those of other emerging national carbon markets such as Australia, China, Japan, South Korea, Switzerland, and New Zealand, combined with sub-national efforts from California and Quebec and other inter-state regional efforts in North America, are laying the foundations of the market infrastructure required to link these systems and create a global carbon market despite ongoing political controversy. While the election of Barack Obama signaled reengagement and support for co-operation to develop a workable international climate agreement, the concept became highly politicized in the US legislature and action slowed (*New York Times* 2010). The role of the US, with California jump-starting the effort, will be pivotal in the expansion and consolidation of global carbon markets in the years to come.

In either taxing or trading pollution, institutional capacity questions remain. Baumol and Oates (1993) remind us that in international environmental policy-making, agreements are unlikely unless there are some reordering activities (perhaps including side payments) that will make all national parties to the externality better off. Finding some institutional structure that can provide incentives to facilitate the appropriate agreements is the challenge. For instance, as agreed to at the Conference of Parties (COP16), held in 2010 in Cancun, Mexico, climate finance instruments such as the UN Green Climate Fund are now being advanced to support low-carbon projects and policies in developing nations. As part of the set of international institutions being developed to address climate change, a well-designed and regulated global environmental commodities market should also help both to protect the environment and to reduce the costs of working toward that goal. In 2011, at Durban, South Africa (COP17), parties agreed to adopt the Durban Platform—a roadmap to a global legal agreement applicable to all nations, not only the industrialized world. The challenge of equitable and cost-effective implementation remains.

2.2.1 (C) The case for pollution trading mechanisms

Crocker (1966) first introduced the idea of a market as the basis for structuring atmospheric pollution control systems. Dales (1968) later proposed that tradable property rights be defined for environmental resources and then sold to the highest bidder as a means of managing environmental quality. Later, Baumol and Oates (1971) and Montgomery (1972) formally developed the principles behind this approach.

Friedman suggests that traditionally taxing air pollution (a decentralized method) is seen as a more efficient method of environmental protection than a command-and-control approach that relies on regulatory standards (a more centralized method). He warns us that "[t]he 'solution' is derived without taking explicit account of the information and transaction costs that create the problem and how to overcome them" (2002, 641). In the 1980s, when emissions trading was still a theoretical proposition, Friedman suggested that "[a] policy of marketable pollution permits (which blends centralized and decentralized processes) is more promising than either taxes or standards" (1984, 562).

2.2.1 (D) The emissions trading model

As noted above, in designing an ETS, the regulator needs to establish the rules of the permit market, monitor the trades, and ensure that the producers selling permits actually reduce emissions. To initiate the market, the regulator would issue a limited number of permits for the discharge of a pollutant (i.e., a cap on pollution). The permits would then be bought by producers with a higher need to pollute than the permit holders, who would have found ways to reduce their emissions more efficiently. As supply and demand for these permits develop, market-clearing prices would indicate the opportunity cost of emissions. Since all emitters would face the same price for a permit, and therefore the same marginal price of reducing emissions, cost-minimizing behavior would result. Thus, the trading system can promote emissions control at a minimum cost. Figure 2.1 illustrates the advantages of trading as described in Tietenberg (2006, 31).

In this figure, we see that two emitters are each emitting 15 units of uncontrolled emissions, but have received different allowances (one allowance equaling one unit of emissions). Emissions Source 1 received seven allowances, so has to reduce emissions by eight units. Emissions Source 2 received eight allowances, so it has to reduce emissions by seven units.

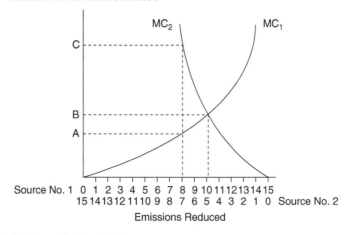

Figure 2.1 Emissions Trading Model
Source: Tietenberg (2006)

As illustrated in Figure 2.1, both firms have an incentive to trade. The marginal cost (MC_2) of the last unit of control for Source 2 (C) is substantially higher than that for the first (A). Source 2 could lower its costs if it could buy one permit from Source 1 at any price lower than C. Meanwhile, the first source would be better off if it could sell a permit for any price higher than A. Because C is greater than A, and Source 2 has more than five allowances, there are grounds for a trade. An allowance transfer would take place until Source 1 had only five units left (and controlled ten units), while the second source had ten permits (and controlled five units). At this point, the permit price would equal B (the marginal value of that permit to both sources), and neither source would have any further incentive to trade. The permit market would be in equilibrium, yielding the most cost-effective emissions reduction.

A key point is the need to issue the appropriate number of permits (15 was chosen arbitrarily to illustrate this model). This process exempts the regulatory agency from determining the tax for pollution to achieve cost-effective allocations. Emissions are reduced, but flexibility is given in how emissions are reduced, so emissions are reduced at the lowest possible cost.

Despite almost 30 years of the theoretical promise of efficiency gains, it was not until the last two decades of the twentieth century that environmental managers have actually experimented with blending regulation and economic incentives to address the issue of environmental degradation. It is now acknowledged by policymakers that even under a market failure scenario, "[i]t still may be relatively efficient to allow individual economic agents *some* discretion to influence or to govern partially, through a market process of engaging in voluntary transactions, how resources are allocated" (Friedman 1984, 561). However, some believe that there are only a few specific areas of environmental management that may be improved by this approach.

In summary, a system of tradable permits is the main alternative to taxes as an efficient mechanism for pollution control. Assuming full enforcement, permit trading guarantees limiting emissions to the target level and avoids the challenges of government putting an upfront price on pollution. Instead, it allows the market to determine the price later on. In the US, tradable pollution permits have been allocated for free at the outset of a trading system ("grandfathering in" pre-existing levels of pollution), with the exception of the launch of a cooperative effort of Northeast and Mid-Atlantic states known as the Regional Greenhouse Gas Initiative (RGGI) in September 2008. (The RGGI began full operation on January 1, 2009, and is the first market-based, mandatory cap-and-trade program to reduce greenhouse gases from the power sector in the US. This program is discussed in Chapter 8.) Grandfathering has helped to make the ETS politically feasible, avoiding the large transfer payments between industry and government associated with taxing pollution. More recently, the experiences of the UK, California and EU in developing their ETS programs have shown growing support from potential participants for using auctions as a fair instrument for allowance allocation. Finally, the permit approach is a less dramatic change than taxation, as compared with more conventional regulatory methods, and thus easier to implement.

2.2.2 An institutional perspective for emissions permit trading systems

As May and Neustadt (1986, 2) suggest, policymaking can be improved by conducting a careful analysis of the history, issues, individuals, and institutions involved. After more than two decades of implementation, the OECD (1997, 10–11) suggests that it is valuable to do *ex post* evaluation of economic instruments in environmental policy. In market theory, one assumes frictionless transactions, but this is not often the reality of policy implementation. Institutional constraints are often a considerable barrier.

Majone offers a broad typology of these institutional constraints, which include: "laws, regulations, norms, and decision-making procedures" (1989). Hahn emphasizes the need for "more careful analysis of the regulatory status quo, underlying beliefs about property rights, and how political choices are actually made in different countries" (1989, 111). Latin contends that the literature on market incentives "reflects an excessive preoccupation with theoretical efficiency, while it places inadequate emphasis on actual decision-making, costs, and implementation concerns" (1985, 1270–1271). Latin's central argument is the following:

> A system for environmental regulation must function despite the presence of pervasive uncertainty, high decision-making costs, and manipulative strategic behavior resulting from conflicting private and public interests. Under these conditions, the indisputable fact that uniform standards are inefficient does not prove that any other approach would necessarily perform better. In a "second best" world, the critical issue is not which regulatory system aspires to ideal "efficiency" but which is most likely to prove effective.
>
> (1985, 1270–1271)

Dwyer (1992, 59) also argues that the advantages of the emissions trading mechanism over command-and-control are its theoretical goals: greater efficiency and increased incentives to develop new control technologies. He warns policy makers that the market approach, as any other regulatory approach, faces an array of concerns about implementation, institutional hurdles, political feasibility, effective monitoring, and enforcement: in his opinion, the most serious obstacles to successful market-based regulation. Dwyer (1993, 104) also points out that a legislative body may be slow to concede clear authority for market-based regulations, and regulators may be hostile to the new approach. As a result, market-based programs may be burdened with severe regulatory restrictions. Industrial firms, distrusting regulators' intentions and the ability of the market to produce emissions credits in the future, may withhold credits from the market. However, this could be resolved by auctioning permits to new entrants into the market.

Dwyer (1992, 59) adds that policymakers must evaluate proposed regulatory schemes under real-world conditions of scientific uncertainty, large information costs, limited administrative resources, and non-economic behavior. To mitigate these concerns, a market-based environmental management system should judiciously combine regulation with economic instruments. For policy analysts the question remains: *What is the correct formula for combining regulatory and incentive instruments to achieve cost-effective environmental goals given diverse institutional environments?*

Hanley et al. (1997) point out that evidence suggests the cost-savings potential of emissions permit systems cited by early studies was exaggerated. They attribute the lack of cost savings to the institutional design of actual permits (principally the specific trading rules), problems associated with market power, and sluggish information flow. Institutional design issues must be addressed as a central part of market-based environmental policy.

2.3 Improving market-based environmental policy analysis

Market-based environmental policy analysis must take better account of the institutional features of a well-functioning market and the social forces that shape policy design. *Ex post* evaluation of past and current air pollution trading systems provides insight into the advantages and disadvantages of market-based strategies. The structure of this interdisciplinary approach is based on linking elements of the traditional policy analysis decision-making criteria to a series of relevant theoretical concepts developed by the institutional economics literature. The present study of the international experience implementing air pollution markets pairs the policy and institutional theoretical parameters, introduced in this chapter, with the market elements required to develop an efficient environmental commodities markets, introduced in Chapter 3.

2.3.1 Criteria selection

Careful attention should be given *ex ante* to the expected interplay of social, political, and economic interests in the design and implementation stages in order to develop more effective environmental market-based programs. It may be helpful to review the comparative advantages of alternative policy approaches to solve specific problems in a particular institutional environment. A systematic methodology that incorporates institutional concerns at the design stage will enable market-based environmental policy instruments to pass the effectiveness, political, and legal feasibility hurdles essential for proper policy implementation. The basic criteria for market-based environmental policy analysis include:

- *Exchange Efficiency*: Potential gains from incentive-based solutions over command-and-control.
- *Dynamic Efficiency*: Capacity to provide good incentives to induce technological innovation and progress toward reducing pollution emissions.
- *Market Transaction Efficiency*: Degree to which institutional means reduce non-governmental costs not included in price incentives.
- *Administrative Efficiency*: Expected potential reduction of governmental administrative, implementation, and monitoring costs.

- *Equity*: Distributive effects of implementing alternative policy instruments.
- *Political Feasibility*: Policy design features that reduce the pressures that are likely to arise in the process of gaining legislative approval for program implementation.
- *Certainty of Satisficing*: Degree of assurance that the system is capable of meeting the predetermined environmental objective.

It is important to identify the design features that are key to the successful implementation of environmental market-based programs or, in Herbert Simon's terms, policies that "satisfice," or produce satisfactory results. The *satisficing* condition is one that demonstrates a mechanism's ability to achieve, in practice, a predetermined pollution reduction goal (Williamson 1995).

Scarce resources inform the definition of policy goals. If goals are vague because of scarce resources and outcomes difficult to measure, the policy instrument becomes more important. Therefore, instruments cannot be neatly separated from goals. The choice of means determines the criteria under which the policy instrument will be evaluated.

Unlike theorists, policy analysts must consider how policy instruments are constrained by political, administrative, and other institutional factors, as well as by self-interested actors. It is through the perspective of institutional economics that the role of social, political, and economic organizations is viewed as a determinant of economic efficiency (Majone 1989, 117).

2.3.2 Economic institutional analysis

The New Institutional Economics incorporates what Davis and North describe as the "institutional environment" and the "institutional arrangements" (1971, 5–6). An institutional environment consists of the fundamental, political, social, and legal ground rules that establish the basis for production, exchange, and distribution. An institutional arrangement as defined by Williamson (1985, 211) is a relationship between economic units that governs the way in which these units can cooperate or compete. Other institutional factors that need to be accounted for in market-based environmental policy design are path dependence (history matters) and economic and political frictions (transaction costs). Dixit explains:

> Policymaking is constantly influenced by the legislature, the executive and its agencies, the courts, various special-interest lobbies, the media and so on. The legislature may fail to enact the economist's desired policies [which was the case for market-based environmental programs in the United States for many years]; the administrative process may fail to implement the legislated policies in the intended manner. The outcomes may fail to correct market failures and may instead introduce new costs of their own.
>
> (1996, 10)

Therefore, the analysis begins with the assumption that "[s]ystematic pressures within governmental systems sometimes work against achieving an efficient allocation of resources," as established in Williamson (1985, 426).

Given the many ways institutional factors can inhibit the effectiveness of market-based environmental programs, it is helpful to assemble a set of good or best practices from past programs. Unfortunately, the examples of programs that meet or nearly meet expectations are few. In their absence, we can look at institutional theory for guidance on best practices.

Arrow (1971) introduces a framework to classify organizations by the kind of operating instructions they issue and their rules for enforcing these operations.[12] He focuses on the degree of centralization of these rules and instructions. Typically, centralized rules are enforced as simple "yes/no" compliance questions. Decentralized market allocation introduces a "more or less" decision on how to achieve environmental standards efficiently and is usually enforced by incentives that reward for "more" and penalize for "less." From such a perspective, the trading mechanism for air pollution control combines centralized regulatory commands through setting overall limits on pollution emissions in a specific air basin and in setting the trading rules themselves. However, it relies upon decentralized coordination by providing discretion to the regulated parties (e.g., industry) in deciding their own individual quotas (or allowances) of pollution emissions (e.g., CO_2 or sulfur dioxide) and how to achieve them.

An interesting aspect of emissions trading is that the regulator has a "yes/no" enforcement task (are actual emissions within the limits allowed by the permits owned?) and the "more or less" decision of the firm about the number of permits to hold is enforced purely by the firm's own self-interest (its profit function).

For organizations characterized by Arrow (1971, 48), transaction cost economics (TCE) also offers a useful perspective since it addresses the issue of "the costs of running the economic system." Stavins (1995, 143), identifies three potential sources of transaction costs in tradable emissions markets: (1) search and information; (2) bargaining and decision; and (3) monitoring and enforcement. All costs are due to lack of complete information.

Tirole (1988, 4) argues that information flows between members of an organization are limited because of incentive compatibility and the cost of communicating. For instance, as Friedman puts it, regulatory and incentive-based environmental policies (e.g., taxes, subsidies, and trading mechanisms) "involve the 'appointment' of the government as a centralized bargaining agent to represent interests in pollution avoidance. This reflects a trade-off: a loss of allocative efficiency (the bargaining agent does not know the exact preferences of individuals or countries for clean air) in order to gain transactional efficiency" (2002, 648). This absence of information, for instance, is costly and has an impact on the efficiency gains introduced by implementing a decentralized environmental policy mechanism.

Arrow (1971) warns that the latter issue is peculiarly subject to the potential hazards of opportunism. For instance, a member of an organization keeps information private when he or she would suffer from its becoming public. Such is the case of industrial agents not wanting to disclose information to the regulatory agency about their polluting processes (and control methods) for fear of incurring costs and sanctions derived from future regulatory compliance and inspection. Tietenberg

(1998, 32) further explains that because the degree to which polluting plants would be regulated depends on control cost information, it is unrealistic to expect managers to transfer unbiased information to the government.

As previously stated, firms (and nations) have different capabilities and thus some can reduce emissions more easily and at less cost than others. Information about this is important to the functioning of the system, and in some cases, also for the diffusion of new capabilities (e.g., techniques) to reduce emissions. Thus, the management of such information and the rules of the system can increase the costs of implementing a program for the regulatory agency. In short, as suggested in Friedman "[i]nformation and transaction costs play important roles in determining the relative efficiency of any governance structure for a specific activity" (1984, 561).

2.3.3 Historical relevance and transaction costs

It is useful to analyze institutional implementation patterns to identify key policy design features of emissions trading systems in actual settings. For instance, those individuals involved in the design and implementation of these policies are an important source of valuable information, as they have developed deep knowledge about market-based programs for environmental management. The story of their successes and failures reflected in the policy patterns of implementation of the trading mechanism provides valuable lessons that suggest "practices which, if made routine, could at least protect against common mistakes," as first introduced in Neustadt and May (1986, 2).

Based mainly on the work of Coase, North, and Williamson, TCE not only subscribes to the proposition that "history matters" but relies on it to explain the differential strengths and weaknesses of alternative forms of governance. The entire institutional environment (laws, rules, conventions, norms, etc.) within which the institutions of governance are embedded is the product of history. While the social conditioning that operates within governance structures is reflexive and often intentional, it too has accidental and temporal features. TCE focuses on remediable inefficiencies, that is, those conditions for which feasible alternatives can be described that, if introduced, would yield net gains. As pointed out in Williamson (1995, 236), this is to be distinguished from hypothetical net gains, where the inefficiency in question is judged by comparing an actual alternative to a hypothetical ideal. The focus is on the evolution of governance structures and their ability to cope with transaction costs.

Dixit (1996) uses a framework known as transaction-cost politics (TCP), which was first introduced by North (1990), in an effort to apply these concepts to policy contexts. The TCP framework underscores the importance of politics, history, and institutions, and applies the institutional perspective to the case of economic policymaking. An important difference between TCP and TCE is the following: The TCE framework assumes that capitalist institutions and organizations seek to achieve efficiency by minimizing costs since their objective function (profit maximization) is clear. In contrast, the TCP framework assumes the political forces of institutional selection and evolution—elections, changes in party membership and platforms, and so forth—to be weaker and slower than capitalist institutions. Thus, the presumption is that demands for efficiency through political institutions will receive a weaker, slower response as governments face competing goals in a multi-tasking (and ideologically diverse) institutional environment (Dixit 1996, 31).

Guided by these general conceptual frameworks, this study identifies periods in time when the theoretical blackboard market-based solution (i.e., assuming perfect information and zero transaction costs) concedes theoretical frictionless optimality in exchange for implementation feasibility in a given institutional environment. Developing a timeline of the implementation history of actual environmental trading mechanisms enables identification of the contextual institutional, organizational, technical, and political factors that cause variation in the implementation costs of such programs. This methodological approach therefore highlights important market design parameters for emissions trading mechanisms by observing what happens during implementation. The template framework to analyze ETS implementation patterns is:

Blackboard Theory → Implementation Processes → Degree of Efficiency

Coase (1960) and Stavins (1995) advise that real (imperfect) governments should not be compared with a theoretical market ideal. Demetz (1969) also objects to comparisons of real markets with idealized governments. However, the idealized versions provide benchmarks against which imperfect alternatives can be compared. If imperfect system A is 80 percent efficient and the efficiency of imperfect system B is only 70 percent (for the same economic task), then A is more efficient than B. Furthermore, such benchmark measures lead one to wonder whether there is an imperfect alternative C that can improve upon A. The blackboard–implementation–efficiency template focuses on historical, political, and market transaction cost considerations as the barriers and frictions that cause departures from the ideal market. Transaction costs are the counterpart of administrative costs in command-and-control systems. Stavins (1995, 144) suggests that both need to be considered in market-based policy analysis.

2.3.4 Policy design and implementation considerations

The common sense assumption is that better design, proper implementation, and institutional vision make for better outcomes. However, real-world transaction costs will have to be paid. Therefore, it is important to identify and, to the extent possible, quantify deviations from the original policy goals caused either by unanticipated implementation complexities or by intentional sacrifices made to build political support for the idea.[13] Thus, a central policy question is: *How significant can abatement cost reductions be in the face of the required administrative and political processes within a democratic system for an environmental market-based mechanism to become an efficient and effective public policy program?*

As stated previously, the institutional environment is where idealism meets reality. Expected efficiency gains may be reduced to a level that would make the market-based solution less cost-effective than existing regulations. As argued by Yandle (1989, preface), lack of efficiency is directly related to the interplay of politics, economics, and the institutions that order our lives. Hahn emphasizes that a mechanism "with wonderful efficiency properties, but which ignores political concerns is likely to remain a theoretical curiosity" (1990, 18).[14] In adapting to institutional barriers, the fine-tuning process of the implementation learning curve is critical to ensure the proper functioning of the market as a policy tool.[15] In the US it took a number of attempts to introduce market-based environmental regulatory systems before some success was achieved at the national level.

The development of a global carbon market through the UNFCCC poses even greater design, co-operation, and implementation challenges. As suggested by Shelling, "nations will not make sacrifices in the interest of global objectives unless they are bound by a regime that can impose penalties if they do not comply" (2002, 6–8). While there is almost no historical precedent for such a governance structure for global environmental problems (with the exception of some measures included in the Montreal Protocol), there have been international regimes that have been able to divide the benefits and burdens of multilateral processes. For instance, the Marshall Plan established a system of reciprocal multilateral scrutiny that compared the relevant criteria (e.g., protocols) developed by each nation to access the limited aid for reconstruction. In 1951–1952, the North Atlantic Treaty Organization underwent the same process in its burden-sharing exercise to reduce the level of US aid for military equipment and infrastructure. Reciprocal scrutiny and harmonization of relevant criteria constituted the framework created to reach an operational agreement among diverse nations that also took their comparative advantages into consideration. World Trade Organization negotiations show that lengthy international negotiations may reach agreements that satisfy the diverse national interests of participating countries.

In order to implement global environmental commodities markets, a set of global performance and design standards should be set as various trading schemes continue to emerge at the international, national, and sub-national levels. Emissions trading systems alone are not the silver bullet to address the risks of climate change. They represent a flexible and cost-effective approach within a portfolio of measures that should be implemented for the foreseeable future as we transition to a low-carbon economy. The vision of an emergence of green economies (i.e., clean and energy efficient) around the world should also include as a goal sustaining fast economic growth rates in poor and middle-income nations to enhance their levels of human development.[16]

The KP reflects developed countries' principles of equity and common (though differentiated) responsibilities: given their relatively greater resources and higher historical level of emissions, developed countries are taking leadership on reducing greenhouse gas emissions. However, some developing countries with high growth rates are becoming significant greenhouse gas emitters and should therefore take constructive action to contribute to the global effort to stabilize these emissions. The current system that allows for trading between the developed and the developing world, the Clean Development Mechanism, initiated a process of engagement and action but requires to be scaled up through policy innovation. This mechanism still needs to be more streamlined and harmonized for large developing countries to effectively participate. For instance, pragmatic suggestions such as the inclusion of some economic sectors (e.g., energy, cement, or steel) within large developing countries as part of the EU ETS compliance mechanisms (and eventually a global system) are currently being explored. Consideration of the inclusion of sectoral mitigation efforts from the developing world, known as Nationally Appropriate Mitigation Actions (NAMAs), to be supported by the developed world in aspects of finance, technology, and capacity building began during the 2007 Bali UN climate summit. At the 2010 COP16, a decision was made to establish a framework for measuring, reporting, and verification (MRV) mechanisms for NAMAs and "new market mechanisms." Additionally, a registry of projects began to be developed that could be matched with the necessary support instruments. Market-based instruments are expected to play a key role in financing these types of projects.

As we begin to develop a comprehensive and integrated global system to regulate greenhouse gas emissions, policymakers around the world should examine best practices in the design of environmental markets. Compatibility among the emerging national and regional ETS programs will enhance the capacity to mitigate emissions as well as encourage economic efficiency. Linking these systems through design protocols can enhance the cost-minimizing opportunities of the market approach and avoid design features that reduce the overall efficiency of the system. For instance, Hepburn and Stern state that "[d]ifficulties may arise in trading emissions with countries with low price ceilings or with overly generous allocations and correspondingly lower carbon prices," as well as "in trading goods with countries which have not adopted strong measures against climate change," and there is a need to "ensure consistency of definitions and units of account" among existing ETS programs (2008, 272). Without any doubt the institutional environment for international market-based policymaking presents huge challenges, but our knowledge of the use of markets for environmental control continues to expand. For the first time both developed and developing countries agreed to take action to reduce global emissions at COP16, and at COP17 both agreed to work towards a legal instrument to enforce commitments. The development of appropriate institutions and frameworks for financing and MRV of actions will support the future expansion of emissions trading along with other key policy measures to help address the risks and dangers of climate change.

Now that we have set out the policy design concerns regarding institutional environments, we need to address the institutional market design features necessary for the development of properly functioning and economically efficient emissions trading systems.

Chapter 3

Creating efficient environmental commodities markets

Environmental finance is a fast-growing field due to the need to develop innovative financial instruments to help protect the environment. Central to this process is the emergence of environmental commodities markets, in particular the carbon market. This environmental market is transforming the energy sector while at the same time shifting paradigms in economic development, including the practice of pricing carbon emissions for use in regulatory permit markets, rewards for voluntary action to reduce greenhouse gases, advances in energy efficiency, and the rise of new environmentally friendly energy sources.

Despite the potential of these developments, they will take decades to take hold in the mainstream and will not be exempt from complications. For example, consolidation to a global market mechanism, such as an emissions trading system (ETS) to curb greenhouse gases and foster environmentally sound economic development, will require strong market infrastructure development and unprecedented international co-operation, political will, and institutional coordination. A primary concern in creating an environmental commodities market is clearly defining the commodity, which in the case of carbon means specifying the amount of emissions allowed in a set period of time (i.e., the cap or emissions budget) to ensure that participants' rights and obligations are well understood and monitored (OECD 1997, 22–23).

Adoption of best practices in ETS design and implementation will enable current and new ETS to be compatible in order to allow future market integration. The integration or linking of existing and emerging ETS around the world will in turn enhance flexibility and cost-minimizing opportunities by scaling the systems up. Along with this institutional evolutionary process, environmental commodities markets will need to be supplemented with the appropriate national and international regulatory compliance mechanisms. Strengthening the credibility and transparency of emerging ETS through adequate measuring, reporting, and verification (MRV) standards can enable harmonization and coherence in the development of a global commodities market infrastructure.

A set of institutional features key to a successful ETS, taking knowledge and political will into account, is presented herein as a template for developing environmental commodities markets. However, before talking about successful environmental commodities markets, we need to examine what makes any commodities market successful.

3.1 The evolution of efficient commodities markets

There are four essential stages for the development of an efficient commodities market:

- defining the commodity;
- establishing an organized spot market;[1]
- establishing a futures market;[2] and
- establishing an options market.[3]

First, let's briefly review the history of traditional markets. Sandor (1992) describes the evolution of early commodities markets. In general, clear trading rules are essential to the development of efficient markets. Ancient history presents some examples of active commodities markets emerging since 1200 BC. However, it was not until medieval European fairs, most prominently in Champagne, France, that merchant codes and the "fair letter" (a de facto bill of exchange) were developed. These trade fairs and first financial instruments facilitated trade by "defining a transaction, thereby implicitly giving meaning to a commodity" (Sandor 1992, 154).

Bakken (1966) summarizes the four aspects of organized markets that were regulated by early financial institutions: agreements, transfers, payments, and warrantees. These elements define a commodity. Based on an historical analysis of the evolution of early commodities markets, including rice trading in Osaka during the seventeenth and eighteenth centuries, stock trading in Amsterdam during the seventeenth century, and grain trading in Chicago in 1849, Sandor concludes that markets which function well share these four common elements.

Commodities: A commodity is a good or act that is useful, has real value, and can be turned into a commercial product or other gain. Commodities traded on the spot market are required to have four features: *standardized grades*, *price bases*, *delivery mechanisms*, and *trading units*. Standards help to expand mutually beneficial trading by allowing trade to focus on price negotiation. Participants in many markets worldwide have developed futures markets to improve trading efficiency and provide a tool for securing future transaction prices (Sandor 1992, 154). An environmental commodity is not a tangible good; it represents an intangible asset that, in the case of air pollution markets, represents emission permits granted by a government's ETS regulatory measures, which cap emission levels. An environmental commodity can also be a commoditized voluntary emission mitigation effort or credits for generating renewable energy or implementing efficiency practices.

Sandor suggests that a successful environmental commodities market requires the "issuance of a stock of standard instruments corresponding to the target emissions levels" (1992, 154). He also suggests that political jurisdictions (i.e., at the national, regional, and sub-national level) should learn from efficient private sector structures when creating environmental commodities markets, such as including "international linkages, workable trading rules, reporting, and regulatory requirements, trade clearing and financial integrity" (1992, 154).

Futures and options markets: Commodity prices are based on supply and demand, and prices are volatile because of uncertainty. To minimize risk, the private financial sector has developed derivatives (or hybrid) instruments whose value depends on that of another asset such as futures and options. Futures are obligations to buy or sell a commodity on a specific future day for a preset price, while options are the right to buy or sell a specific item for a preset price during a specified period of time (Morris and Siegel 1993, 124). These instruments can be understood as side bets on the value of the underlying asset, also called hedging—taking one risk to offset another (Brealey and Meyers 1996, 711). All of these products could be sold in an environmental commodities market and represent the last stages in developing an efficient commodities market.

When developing environmental commodities markets, the policy objective is to lower the costs of limiting emissions (i.e., cost-effectiveness) by encouraging reductions by the emitters most efficient in the process of reducing emissions. The ability to sell emission allowances (available for sale because of emission reductions) encourages efficiency and enhances flexibility compared with regulatory compliance. Barriers to selling allowances discourage market efficiency. Organized exchanges aid the process by lowering the cost of finding a buyer or seller and by lowering administrative costs, making entitlement prices publicly known. Price signaling helps to guide emitters to the most cost-effective strategy for complying with emissions limits (Sandor 1992, 153).

3.2 Market elements for environmental commodities trading

New environmental commodities markets require "a streamlined infrastructure and simple rules and mechanisms which function in a transparent and efficient manner" (OECD Mar. 1998, 8). In other words, these new markets should be well crafted.

In order to commoditize an environmental good, as explained above, grading and standardization are essential. Environmental commodities (e.g., one ton of carbon dioxide (CO_2) emissions or carbon equivalents, sulfur dioxide (SO_2) or nitrous oxides) are based on environmental standards. To facilitate standardization, allowances should be issued by a single agency that also verifies compliance with environmental goals (e.g., an annual emissions budget reconciliation—comparing allowances held with emissions produced in one year). Information technologies can assist in the effective monitoring of tasks, as was observed in the United States (US), which implemented Continuous Emissions Monitoring Systems (CEMS) (see Chapter 5). Tracking of allowances should be recorded to perform clearinghouse activities (i.e., guarantee the performance and settlement of transactions) and consolidate emissions accounts for compliance. For example, the US Environmental Protection Agency (EPA) has developed an electronic registry called the Allowance Management System and developed software for electronic submission of plans and data assurance such as the Emissions Collection and Monitoring Plan System (see chapters 5 and 7). In the European Union Emissions Trading System (EU ETS), allowances traded were initially held in Member States' registries and overseen by a central administrator at the EU level. In 2012 the EU ETS began transitioning to a centralized system, the European Union Transaction Log, which checks each transaction for any irregularities (see Chapter 8).

Delivery and issuance information should also be maintained in the contract market. Electronic exchanges and online market transactions reduce transaction costs. However, all modern information management systems are vulnerable to hacking and manipulation, as demonstrated by the scandals in the EU ETS program over allowance thefts and tax fraud in 2010 and 2011. Therefore, strong cyber-security measures in allowance trading should constantly be maintained. In general, the private sector is well suited to assume the role of market-maker, provided there are appropriate oversight institutions and regulations.

3.2.1 Structure of an emissions trading system

Desirable features in an ETS include: environmental benefits achieved through a stringent cap on emissions that is agreed upon in the policy process and is set based on the best scientific knowledge and other technical assessments; abatement cost minimization (facilitated by wide participation and coverage of controlled substances); clear rules for changing the overall emission limit (as knowledge on the pollutant and its effects improves) and the entry of new participants; equity; ease of implementation; monitoring, verification, and reporting (to help ensure confidence in the market); and political feasibility. While all of these features are desirable, there are inevitable trade-offs between them (OECD 1997). These elements are consistent with the criteria set forth earlier in Chapter 2.

An appropriate governance structure is basic to the success of an ETS. As stated previously, the institutional environment is a determinant of the design of an ETS. Successful ETS should be streamlined with simple rules and transparent mechanisms: reducing regulatory compliance costs is a paramount goal. Any added complexity should serve the purpose of reducing emissions (i.e., through centralized intervention). A transparent mechanism will also increase confidence among potential participants. It is important to design ETS well, since the design "will determine the transaction costs as well as the uncertainty and risk inherent in the trading system" (Tietenberg 1998, 3).

Emissions trading systems have taken one of two forms: credit trading or allowance trading. Credit trading allows emissions reductions above and beyond pre-specified legal requirements to be certified as tradable credits. These types of programs tend to focus on specific emitters or projects. The credits acquired through emissions reductions can later be sold to new emitters entering the market as the more efficient pollution sources reduce their pollution emissions beyond regulatory standards. In contrast, the implementation of allowance trading starts by defining an aggregate emissions cap.

After the cap is set, the emissions authorized by this cap are then allocated to eligible parties. Tietenberg et al. review these two types of ETS and conclude, "[c]redit trading systems have proved to be less secure environmentally and to create higher transaction costs and greater uncertainty and risk compared to allowance trading, leading to reduced trading" (1998, 3). The generic structural and efficiency variations of each of these governance arrangements for ETSs are covered in chapters 4 and 5.

3.2.2 Defining the regulatory scope of ETS

The number and type of sources covered by the program, the substances that the program regulates, and the geographic area where the cap would be enforced need to be determined by the regulator. The scope of the system is the first aspect that policymakers must confront in the creation of an ETS. It is interesting that this is not usually discussed in the economics literature: the extent of the market is simply assumed.[4] The choice of which emissions and which emitters will be regulated is key, and will have political consequences. Defining what and who fall under the market-based regulatory regime requires not only the input of scientists but also of interest groups (e.g., businesses, environmentalists, etc.) through formal (e.g., Congressional hearings and stakeholders dialogues) and informal (e.g., advisory groups and the media) forums. For instance, in the case of climate policy developments around the world, Hobbs, Bushnell, and Wolak (2010) remind us that "there are continuing debates over where in the supply chain to impose Greenhouse Gas (GHG) limits. Proposals range from far upstream at the sale of fossil fuels to far downstream at the purchase of manufactured products and energy by ultimate consumers."

3.2.2 (A) Science as the basis for defining the scope of an ETS

Environmental programs should be based on the best available scientific and economic knowledge about the impacts of emissions on human health and welfare, as well as the ability to control and reduce them. An accumulating body of academic and scientific literature presents evidence of negative health and productivity impacts from environmental degradation, particularly from air and water pollution (Brown 2001). According to specialists and other observers, current trends in environmental problems will only worsen, especially in the developing world. Developing countries face difficult trade-offs between reducing pollution and advancing economic development. Some argue that there cannot be a push for a cleaner environment without stable economic growth and higher income levels (Grossman 1991). Understanding of environmental problems is still fragmentary, and a large degree of uncertainty exists about technological solutions.

An early example of a state's action to control transboundary air pollution is the Montreal Protocol, which entered into force in 1989. International precedent was set by the application of international law's precautionary principle: taking action, despite uncertainty, because of the potential irreversibility of pollution's effects. The Montreal Protocol was given impetus in part by the growing credibility of the scientific evidence: the depletion of the ozone layer was verified by the National Aeronautics and Space Administration (NASA) in 1988. NASA's findings confirmed those of the Nobel Laureates Curtzer, Molina, and Rowland,[5] who reported a significant decline in the ozone layer in 1971 and 1974. As recorded by Doolittle:

> Now, ozone depletion is a scientific certainty, and discussion of ozone depletion has entered the mainstream. *Time Magazine* reports on the effects of ozone thinning, the *NBC Evening News* discusses the causes of depletion, and the *McNeil/Lehrer News Hour* analyzes potential solutions. With this recent attention has come seemingly decisive action to deal with ozone depletion on an international scale. On January 1, 1989, the terms of the Montreal Protocol on Substances that Deplete the Ozone Layer went into effect
>
> (Doolittle 1989, 407).

Under similar circumstances, and also based on the precautionary principle, the United Nations Framework Convention on Climate Change (UNFCCC) was negotiated and its implementation continues to be decided in Conferences of the Parties (COP) rounds following the Rio Earth Summit in 1992. The following are some of the key agreements reached during the UNFCCC climate summits so far:

- Berlin 1995 (COP1) was known as the Berlin Mandate to take climate action while acknowledging "common but differentiated responsibilities" for developed and developing countries.
- Geneva 1996 (COP2) acknowledged scientific findings on climate change.
- Kyoto 1997 (COP3) introduced the compliance mechanism known as the Kyoto Protocol (KP), which set binding commitments for signatories from the industrialized world.
- Buenos Aires 1998 (COP4) put in place the work plan to address design issues of the "international emissions trading regime" such as the nature and scope of the mechanisms; the criteria for project eligibility; compatibility with sustainable development; auditing and verification criteria; institutional roles, principles, and guidelines; and so forth. During this meeting the US became the 60th country to sign the KP, but the US Congress did not ratify this agreement.
- Bonn 1999 (COP5) set an implementation timetable for the KP and its flexible mechanisms (i.e., emissions trading).

- The Hague 2000/Bonn 2001 (COP6) agreed on introducing flexible mechanisms for compliance and introduced climate finance mechanisms.
- Marrakech 2001 (COP7) produced the Marrakech Accords that enabled the operation of emissions trading.
- New Dehli 2002 (COP8) focused on enabling technology transfers to the developing world.
- Milan 2003 (COP9) resulted in an agreement supporting adaptation efforts of developing countries.
- Buenos Aires 2004 (COP10) produced an action plan based on an assessment of ten years spent developing a multilateral system to regulate greenhouse gases under the UNFCCC.
- Montreal 2005 (COP11) began to look at commitments beyond the KP's compliance period of 2012.
- Nairobi 2006 (COP12) enhanced the Adaptation Fund to support developing nations.
- Bali 2007 (COP13) produced a now forgotten action plan known as the "Bali Roadmap," and a new subsidiary body, the Ad Hoc Working Group on Long-term Cooperative Action, was created to accelerate implementation of the convention.
- Poznan 2008 (COP14) resulted in a preliminary agreement on funding mechanisms for the developing world.
- Copenhagen 2009 (COP15) reached no formal agreement on the continuation of the KP commitment period (2008–2012) despite the historic gathering of 115 heads of state. The conference succeeded only in issuing a political agreement statement asserting the signatories' "strong political will to urgently combat climate change" along with pledges for climate action by some nations that were captured in a non-official document known as the Copenhagen Accord of which parties "took note" at the end of the COP.
- Cancun 2010 (COP16) revitalized the multilateral process by reaching consensus in support of global climate action and assessing the conditions to extend the KP compliance period beyond 2012. COP16 incorporated as part of the UNFCCC some of the political agreements reached by the so-called Copenhagen Accord. In particular, it enabled climate finance mechanisms such as the UN Green Climate Fund and recognized individual pledges to reduce GHG emissions by both developing and developed countries.
- Durban 2011 (COP17) resulted in an agreement to establish a successor to the KP, consisting of another legal instrument or process with legal force under the UNFCCC that would be "applicable to all parties." The Durban Platform sets a 2015 deadline for an agreement to take effect in 2020.
- Doha 2012 (COP18) and beyond will continue multilateral work on developing a cost-effective approach to addressing climate change by stabilizing GHG concentrations in the atmosphere, while enabling development paths for a clean and prosperous economic future. The future rounds towards a new agreement present an opportunity to be creative, to learn from past experiences, and to

implement innovative demonstration programs and measures (i.e., learn-by-doing). Ultimately, the post-Kyoto international legal instrument agreed upon should achieve meaningful global climate action. Climate scientists continue to increase the degree of certainty and confidence in their findings about the sources, effects, and potential dangers of global warming. It would be risky to enter a third decade of negotiations without starting to effectively stabilize global GHG emissions to minimize the risks and dangers of climate change. The stakes are high.

In 1995, an Intergovernmental Panel on Climate Change (IPCC) created by the UNFCCC recommended policy action to curb GHG emissions (Bruce et al. 1996). The IPCC is constituted of a group of climate change experts from around the world representing all relevant disciplines, as well as users of IPCC reports, in particular representatives from governments. The challenge now is for nations to establish a credible, equitable, cost-effective, and predictable international regulatory system on climate change going forward. Preliminary conclusions in the initial IPCC reports stated that the balance of evidence suggests that there is a discernible human influence on global climate. The IPCC qualifies each scientific finding based on a framework for the treatment of uncertainties across the different working groups that assesses the amount and quality of data and the likelihood of the findings.

The most recent report in 2007 confirmed "the warming of the climate system is unequivocal, as is now evident from observations of increases in global average air and ocean temperatures, widespread melting of snow and ice, and rising global average sea level." (Pachauri and Reisinger, 2007, 30) The report confirms, for instance, that global GHG emissions due to human activities have grown since pre-industrial times, with an increase of 70 percent between 1970 and 2004. Carbon dioxide emissions, the most important man-made GHG, have grown by 80 percent during the same period. The general conclusion of the IPCC 2007 assessment report, communicated widely through the press and electronic media, was that "global warning was 'very likely' [greater than 90 percent probability] man-made and would bring higher temperatures and a steady rise in sea levels for centuries to come regardless of how much the world slows or reduces its greenhouse gas emissions." Amidst controversy about research methods and the resulting inaccuracies in the 2007 IPCC that have captured some media attention (Harvey 2010, *New York Times* 2010), the international scientific body is currently working on its Fifth Assessment Report (AR5) which will be finalized in 2014.

The existence of environmental costs is widely acknowledged by the literature. As acknowledged earlier, quantifying environmental costs is difficult. Current pollution abatement and control costs as a percentage of gross domestic product (GDP) among Organisation for Economic Co-operation and Development (OECD) nations range from 0.7 to 2.2 percent (Pasurka 2008). These costs are expected to increase, given the huge challenges that climate change presents. Governments at all levels are interested in finding policy alternatives to reduce the cost of achieving environmental goals. While some political and business leaders, as well as conservative groups and think tanks, still question current scientific evidence on the dangers and risks of climate change, many governments around the world are working on realizing the vision of a green economy that sustains high economic growth while enabling a low-carbon future.

Countries of the OECD have preferred market-based approaches for environmental control since the 1970s.[6] Since the creation of the Environment Committee in 1970, the OECD has regularly carried out and promoted work on the use of economic incentives in environmental policy. Following two recommendations of the annual meetings of the OECD ministerial council in 1972 and 1974 on the "polluter pays" principle, the potential usefulness of economic instruments has been analyzed in numerous reports, publications, and meetings by this organization (OECD 1991). ETS is one of these regulatory tools that nations have available to reduce the impacts on energy-intensive and trade-exposed industries and to smooth the transition to a low-carbon economy.

3.2.2 (B) Defining the scope of an ETS as a political process

As stated above, groups experiencing different impacts from the implementation of the ETS approach will use political avenues to influence the design of the regulatory framework (Majone 1989). Implementation of environmental regulatory standards raises the issue of competitiveness. As the economy becomes increasingly globalized, trade regulations have become increasingly harmonized and tariffs within many sectors and regions have been reduced. World markets are expected to become more efficient and productive as transaction costs and misallocated resources are reduced through harmonized and reduced regulations. Environmental regulation is commonly characterized as contrary to development, insofar as it incurs new costs. Environmentalists warn of downward harmonization of environmental regulations in the interest of development or "eco-dumping" (i.e., minimizing or creating lax environmental protections). Any environmental regulatory program must be evaluated for its impact on development (Low 1992). Industries to be affected commonly suggest that environmental measures impose a severe handicap on exporters that is certain to have adverse effects on the state's balance of payments, employment levels, and GDP (Baumol and Oates 1993).

The economic power of the business sector has allowed it, in some cases, to capture the regulatory process (Lindblom 1977). For example, it may control the political agenda during the policymaking process by influencing public opinion, deploying lobbyists, or leveraging expensive technical and expert information not easily available to other stakeholders. Also, the business sector has representatives on public advisory councils created specifically to influence regulation.

At the same time, there exists a modern vision from the corporate management perspective, suggested by Porter (1991), that "the conflict between environmental protection and economic competitiveness is a false dichotomy. It stems from a narrow view of the sources of prosperity and a static view of competition." In this article, Porter also put forward the idea that "strict environmental regulations do not inevitably hinder competitive advantage against foreign rivals; indeed, they often enhance it." With the introduction of the concept of product value chain, Porter (1998) established that firms gain competitive advantage from continuous "improvement, innovation and upgrading" in organization and performance. Under this perspective, pollution is considered waste that results from mismanagement and lack of appropriate technologies and processes to minimize or eliminate it. Therefore innovation is required to address this management challenge. Well-designed environmental public policies can create the incentives for firms to address the environmental quality challenge. The environmental dimension has therefore emerged as an element of a business' competitive advantage. In the global industrial restructuring processes that the world is currently witnessing, "a company's environmental performance will be increasingly central to its competitiveness and survival" (Needham and Dransfield 1994) For instance, the Sarbanes-Oxley Act of 2002, which regulates corporate governance in the US, implicitly compels companies to pay attention to their environmental exposure.

This shift is complemented by the public's increasing vigilance about the environmental impacts of trade and economic development (Vogel 1996, 1997, and Zaelke, Orbuch, and Housman 1993). The 1990s brought about the rise of an integrated, international non-governmental organization movement to oppose environmental degradation caused by trade globalization. More recently, natural disasters perceived to be caused by global climate change have fueled ever-growing interest in managing the risks of the relationship between human economic activity and environmental degradation. For instance, Hurricane Katrina in the US prompted public concern in 2005, and in 2012 the largest hurricane on record, Sandy, over the connection of such events and climate change.[7] Moreover, the April 20, 2010, explosion of the Deepwater Horizon offshore oil rig and the resulting oil spill in the Gulf of Mexico made clear the challenges that lie ahead in achieving energy security while protecting the environment. However, the transition to a low-carbon economy can bring major opportunities for economic growth as we transform the $5 trillion dollar energy industry, as well as other major infrastructure sectors such as transportation and urban development.

To some observers, we are already beyond the time frame for effective action to stabilize GHG emissions (Gelbspan 1998). Scientists seem to constantly generate reports ringing alarms that in some areas we are reaching the tipping point of irreversible effects on the planet and human livelihood.

Examples of accelerated dangers and tipping points include:

- A 2009 announcement by top climate scientists states that sea levels could rise twice as much as previously projected (Olsen 2009).
- Research reports published in late 2008 show that ocean acidification is speeding up much faster than expected, with the tipping point expected to come at a much lower level of atmospheric CO_2 levels than predicted by the IPCC (Nogrady 2008).

Some argue that it is paramount to develop effective communication, public outreach, and education strategies that foster policy, collective action, and behavioral changes in the face of climate change (Moser and Dilling 2007). However, this process can encounter resistance from directly affected interest groups. Gelbspan, in a speech at Brandeis University in April 2008 also argued for effectively informing the public of the reality of global warming to promote action. However, he suggested that "the carbon lobby has mounted a successful campaign of deception and mis-information." He added that "the coal influence has muted the press." Gelbspan also denounced the oil industry's public denial of global warming as one of the biggest obstacles to change (Channon 2008).

In 2007, the Nobel Peace Price was awarded jointly to the IPCC and to Al Gore Jr. "for their efforts to build up and disseminate greater knowledge about man-made climate change, and to lay the foundations for the measures that are needed to counteract such change." The mainstreaming of the dangers of climate change is now being supported by mass media efforts to better inform the public on this issue. Examples of these efforts include CNN's TV productions, *Planet in Peril* 2007 and 2008, which examine the environmental conflicts between growing populations and natural resources; the BBC's TV series *Planet Earth* and *Frozen Planet*, which raise awareness on the effects of climate on biodiversity and the Arctic and Antarctic, respectively; and an endless array of comprehensive climate web portals, blogs, and other new media outlets.

Meanwhile, in this context of political debate over scientific findings during the policy formulation process, intergovernmental and multilateral agreements are being created in an attempt to effectively address global commons problems such as stabilizing greenhouse gases to minimize the dangers to humanity as well as to preserve the earth's biodiversity. However, the *pacta sunt servanda* principle of inter-national law—the duty of states to keep their promises—is the only assurance that commitments will be honored (Pennock et al. 1964, 669).

Unfortunately, history shows that national sovereignty interests defined by domestic politics can cause countries to override or ignore decisions made by international enforcement mechanisms, such as the International Court of Justice in The Hague, the Netherlands; regional dispute resolution mechanisms such as the North American Free Trade Agreement Commission for Environmental Co-operation; and policy and economic commitments to international organized efforts. Thus, the executive power of a nation may commit to participate in an international program or accept a decision by a supranational governance structure (e.g., a recognized inter-national mechanism or organization). However, domestic politics can later cause the legislature to reject or not ratify the negotiated agreement (or resolution) at the congressional or parliamentary level. Therefore, credible commitment devices should be developed so that international market-based governance structures can function properly. Without agreement about binding targets, the goal of stabilizing greenhouse gases in the atmosphere to avoid potentially catastrophic climate events remains elusive.

Trustworthy measuring, verification, and reporting mechanisms are a critical component of a credible international climate action plan. China in particular opposed such components of an enhanced climate treaty, claiming national sover-eignty, and maintained its position as a non-Annex I nation unwilling to compromise its economic development goals for the benefit of the global commons. However, the talks in Copenhagen actually succeeded in raising the profile of the issue to the level of heads of state, so that the more than 100 of them who were in attendance worked with their peers on trying to reach a climate deal. Doubtless, climate change is now a higher profile issue to presidents and prime ministers around the world.

These negotiations are about the right of nations to emit carbon into the atmosphere in an equitable manner and without endangering humanity. While the UNFCCC process recognizes the differentiated historical responsibilities and capabilities of nations to address this issue, it is clear that the industrialized world alone cannot stabilize GHG emissions. However, if 450 ppm is the safety level of carbon dioxide equivalent (CO_2e) storage capacity in the atmosphere, as suggested by the IPCC, and industrialization so far has used almost 72 percent of this capacity (380 ppm), this situation leaves the developing world with a much reduced storage capacity in the face of huge economic development needs.

Effective future climate negotiations are urgently needed to conclude the institution building and reactivate the negotiation process toward actual implementation under the so-called 2008 Bali Roadmap's decisions (COP13). From the ETS design and implementation perspective, only transparent and harmonized MRV mechanisms can enable a workable international system. COP15 also concluded with a substantial climate finance commitment from the industrialized world to assist developing countries in following low-carbon economic growth paths. In order to secure the level of resources needed to meet those commitments, capital will have to be raised from the private sector and the carbon market. Governments will find it politically very difficult to achieve the stated goals in the Copenhagen Accord with public finance resources only, a reality that the Cancun and Durban rounds made clear. Industrialized nations have been impacted in one way or another by the 2008 global economic downturn, and climate policy remains on the backburner of most national political agendas. Leaders are reframing the issue, presenting the transformational effort that will be required to create a green global economy to their constituents as a technological revolution that will create jobs and clean economic growth. While currently highly politicized, particularly in the US, the ETS approach can minimize regulatory compliance costs while enhancing the level of climate financing available for real climate action around the world.

3.2.2 (C) Applicability of market-based systems as a technical decision

Criteria for instituting an ETS differ by context. As stated above, the scope of regulation—who and what to regulate—needs to be defined first. These choices include a technical assessment of administrative feasibility. In the US, whose institutional context is discussed further in Chapter 5, politics influenced the choice of emitters to be regulated by the Acid Rain Program (a trading mechanism for SO_2 allowances). While the US Congress wanted to show its commitment to environmental goals by targeting all major emitters, the proposed trading program was only going to be feasible among a small number of

SO_2 emitters which the EPA required to install CEMS, enabling electronic data collection and transmission. This demonstrated that implementing a market-based approach for air pollution control requires a core group (or critical mass) of emitters that can readily employ trading mechanisms (i.e., market readiness). An emitter's capability to control and also account for its emissions should be taken into consideration when discussing potential participants in an ETS (US EPA 1997).

In conclusion, technical, scientific, and political arguments inform environmental policy action. As mentioned earlier, multiple criteria guide the choice of policy instruments: static and dynamic efficiency, transaction and administrative costs, equity, income distributional effects (fairness), sensitivity to underestimation of environmental damage, the presence of irreversible effects, etc. Diverse environmental problems call for a combination of policy instruments including ordinary regulations, subsidies, taxes, charges, and tradable emissions permits. Understanding how to choose from the menu of instruments to address these issues is no simple task. This process requires a detailed understanding of environmental, social, and economic contexts (Sterner 1992). The following section presents a review of the technical aspects of designing cost-effective environmental policies by taking advantage of market incentives.

3.2.3 Design parameters of environmental markets as determinants of regulatory efficiency

Environmental economics theory, policy analysis, and accumulated policy design and implementation experiences around the world provide a catalogue of key market design parameters for the development of a cost-effective ETS. Below, we will look at the array of functions that these design features have to perform.

3.2.3 (A) Environmental commodities

As stated earlier, the first stage in the creation of an environmental commodities market is to define the tradable environmental commodity. Several aspects have to be considered in commoditizing air pollution emissions:

Select the substance(s) to regulate: The first step is to reach an agreement on the substances that will be subject to control by the trading system. Among OECD countries, the most prominent experiences at the national level are the experience of the US in SO_2 allowances trading to address acid rain and the experience of the UK in creating the first carbon-related ETS to address Europe's KP emission reduction commitments. At the multilateral level a global mechanism for GHG emissions trading is envisioned under the UNFCCC flexible mechanisms. An interim step toward that goal is the EU ETS, the first multinational, regional effort to curb CO_2 emissions using a cap-and-trade system as well as other emerging national, sub-national, and regional carbon ETS. The six greenhouse gases originally specified in the KP are:

1. Carbon dioxide (CO_2)
2. Methane (CH_4)
3. Nitrous oxide (N_2O)
4. Hydrofluorocarbons (HFCs)
5. Perfluorocarbons (PFCs)
6. Sulfur hexafluoride (SF_6)

Approximately 25 other gases, such as chloroform and carbon monoxide, qualify as climate-changing greenhouse gases, but only the above-mentioned six are released in sufficient quantities to justify regulation under Kyoto. Water vapor is a very important GHG, but it is not controllable by human intervention.

Define the extent of the entitlement: Defining the legal status of allowances as property rights over air pollution emissions is controversial. However, in order for an efficient market to emerge, the entitlement needs to be assumed at least as quasi-property. Therefore, legal rights over the tradable units of emissions or allowances should be clearly defined, and governments must show a credible commitment to the policy of using environmental markets. In the case of international trading systems, these entitlements must be harmonized with participant nations' legal frameworks as well as international legal principles. As a practical matter, entitlements can be imposed at any stage in the life cycle of a unit of pollution—the extraction (e.g., carbon content permits on fuels), production (e.g., permits on outputs or inputs of production), consumption (e.g., permits or user fees), or emission (e.g., tradable emissions allowances).

Create a homogeneous unit: The unit of trade needs to be of a clearly specified type. Units of trade should be standardized to be fully exchangeable (OECD Aug. 1998). For instance, in the case of greenhouse gases, a ton of carbon dioxide is the unit of trade.

Establish exchange ratios: Ideally units of trade should be standardized so that they are fully exchangeable, but where that is not possible, exchange ratios could theoretically be established. This practice was introduced in 2005 to improve performance of the US SO_2 allowances trading program. In this case, local air basins that had been treated as homogenous were recognized as heterogeneous; they contained "hot spots" for certain gas emissions—localized levels of pollution that exceeded safe standards within a larger air basin. The exchange ratio could adjust for this by using a weighting index to translate units from different geographical regions into equivalent tradable units. However, scientific uncertainty over equivalent values makes this less practicable than standardizing units of trade. Uniform mixing of CO_2 in the atmosphere makes it uniquely suited for establishing an equivalent metric (CO_2e) that provides a universal standard of measurement against which the impacts of releasing (or avoiding the release of) different greenhouse gases can be evaluated.

Establish duration: It is important for regulators to state the program's duration at the onset to enhance certainty. Firms need to know the length of time that allowances will be valid. For instance, the US SO_2 allowances trading program is considered by regulators to be permanent, while an earlier trading mechanism designed to reduce lead content in gasoline had an expiration date after which all gasoline became unleaded. Both programs have proven to be cost-effective.

Set a baseline: The granting of allowances should be based on existing or future acceptable levels of national or global emissions (Sandor 1992). The two key decisions here are the number of permits allowed in the system and their distribution. Stakeholders will more readily accept these decisions if equity considerations are addressed in this process. Baselines should take into account historic responsibility for existing pollution levels, economic impact to particular social sectors, and the differences in technical capabilities among potential participants. Baselines are the most politically contentious of all the market design parameters. For example, several years ago almost all countries used 1990 as the baseline for GHG emission reductions, but more recently it has become politically popular to use 2005 so that the percentage reduction promised sounds bigger than from the 1990 level.

3.2.3 (B) Emissions trading system development

In order to implement a workable ETS, the overall pollution emissions limits, allowances, procedures for initial allocation of emission permits (or allowances), and trading rules must be determined.

Emission targets: Most practical attempts to use markets for environmental control use target abatement levels that are politically determined. Binding emissions limits create incentives for allowance trading. However, flexibility to change the emissions limits might also be required, for example, in the presence of new knowledge about the effects of emissions or with changes in the scope of the system. This in turn reduces incentives to trade: the less strict (or certain) the limits, the lower the value of tradable emission units. To minimize uncertainty, clear rules should be established from the outset regarding changes to an environmental trading mechanism (OECD 1997, 8–9).

Initial allocation: Permits may be issued in two ways: (1) by giving them away for free to increase the political feasibility of the program, perhaps *pro rata* with existing emissions ("grandfathering"); and (2) by selling them, typically via an auction. Selling them at auction implies an additional financial cost to firms, namely the initial payment they will make for permits. Program participants are then allowed to trade these permits. Rules for introducing new pollution sources (after the program's implementation date) should be clearly specified. For instance, Deason and Friedman (2010) focus on the problem of GHG reduction over time.

Determine program participants: Participation rates determine the degree of efficiency gains that can be attained. The magnitude of predicted saving depends on the abatement cost differentials (i.e., cost heterogeneity) across sources, the number of pollution sources trading, and the cost-effectiveness of the base to which trading is compared (US Congress 1995). There is a large potential for cost savings with wide participation in an environmental market-based program. To encourage participation, "the trading system should be kept simple" (OECD 1997, 10).

Trading rules: Rules governing trade must be determined. The use of trading rules responds mainly to the concern that trading mechanisms may produce overly high concentrations of pollutants in some places and to the need for regulators to monitor and enforce emissions reductions subject to trades. There is a tension between the need for high levels of state oversight to ensure that credit trades are legitimate and the high transaction costs of this oversight. Therefore, designing efficient governing procedures for emissions trading is critical to maintaining a balance between cost-effectiveness and environmental integrity. A general principle should be that anyone may trade. Also, there should be no restrictions on the proportion of allowances that participants can trade as long as they comply with their compliance period emissions limit. The choice of compliance period is also an important trading rule which typically is set as a one-year period but can be extended to enhance performance of the ETS.[8] Therefore, participants could freely negotiate their trades and only be accountable for matching their allowance holding with their emission limits at the date set by the regulatory agency. Bank rules provide a safe haven for unused allowable tradable emissions units. Allowing early reductions to be banked for future use provides flexibility for participants to exceed their emissions limit in early periods of time if it is cost-effective for them to do so, and to save these extra emission reductions to offset future increases in emissions. Allowing emissions units to be borrowed from the future to meet current emissions limits also increases the flexibility of the system. This could lower the economic cost of emission reductions: Borrowing allows participants to mitigate pollution emissions at a lower cost if abatement costs turn out to be lower in future periods. Borrowing may present the drawback of the potential bankruptcy of participants who may find themselves unable to meet future commitments. Also, this feature may cause a reduction in market liquidity if all participants were to borrow against their own future emissions allocations rather than trade. Possible solutions to these issues include requiring greater future reductions to offset the borrowed emission units and limiting the amount of emission units that can be borrowed (OECD 1997). Also, permits could be time-delimited in use (e.g., only for that year and the year after the issue date).

In summary, a primary concern in creating a new environmental commodities market is clearly defining the commodity and specifying the amount of emissions allowed for a set period to ensure that participants' rights and obligations are well understood and monitored.

3.2.3 (C) Market governance infrastructure

A well-functioning environmental commodities market requires several types of infrastructure, including those described below.

Clearinghouse: A centralized location for entitlement transactions must be created.

Spot Market: An organized spot market plays an important role as a vehicle for efficient transactions (Sandor 1992).

Organized Exchanges: These institutions, such as the environmental market services of the Chicago Board of Trade and the New York Mercantile Exchange or the Intercontinental Exchange (ICE) and the Carbon Trade Exchange among others, match willing buyers and sellers, improve market liquidity, and provide information on prices.

Leasing: If allowed by the system, leased entitlements may be transferred to a new owner for a fixed, pre-specified period of time. However, this design feature is not relevant in state-of-the-art cap-and-trade ETS where participants can simply sell a discrete ton as part of the program. Leasing is important if the right to emit is defined as continuous flow over time, in order to allow someone else to use that flow for a specified period of time.

Information Services: Information services (such as web-based electronic bulletin boards quoting prices and quantities of emission units sold) assist the market by facilitating price convergence and providing greater certainty over the value of the environmental commodity.

Brokerage Activities: Brokers (middlemen who match buyers and sellers) may help participants make bilateral trades or trade on an exchange.

Standardized Procedures: Standard documentation—such as emission unit transfer forms, confirmation notices, and other accounting documents—facilitates trading.

3.2.3 (D) Program implementation parameters

To be successful, the implementation of the ETS approach needs to negotiate contextual realities and a diverse set of demands from stakeholders. In particular, certainty and credibility should be established through the following parameters:

Monitoring and Reporting Mechanisms: It is important to establish adequate mechanisms for monitoring (preferably using state-of-the-art information management technologies) that collect accurate and timely emissions data in order to ensure compliance (i.e., environmental integrity) with the allowance trading system. This will entail costs for emitters.

Emissions Inventories: User-friendly emissions data electronic inventories should be created.

Political Jurisdiction: An agency to monitor and administer the entitlement system should be defined by political jurisdiction.

Reporting Mechanisms: Modern electronic communication systems should be used to promote and facilitate emissions self-reporting on the part of program participants.

Transparency: Interested persons and groups should have online access to monitoring data in order to supplement official enforcement.

Inspection and Certification: In some cases, oversight and accreditation bodies may be required to certify monitoring mechanisms, institutions, and exchanges.

Enforcement: The regulatory agency must define the enforcement regime according to the institutional environment of implementation (i.e., local, federal, or international). Also, it should develop means for public awareness of noncompliance. Moreover, it is important to create legal mechanisms to hold entities accountable (e.g., implement a set of sanctions) and create an enforceable regulatory framework that allows action to be taken against non-compliant entities. Finally, processes for filing and publicizing independent monitoring activities and complaints by individuals and stakeholder groups should be developed.

3.2.4 Dynamic aspects of implementation

Institutional dynamics are an ongoing challenge in the crafting of new trading mechanisms. For instance, the implementation sequence of the design parameters may matter, or a particular time and context may be essential for making a program work.

In other words, analysis of the dynamics of institutional design and implementation requires that one decide *which* features should be placed into the system, in *what* order or sequence they will be implemented, and *when* to do so. The lessons from the emergence of early commodities markets illustrate the evolutionary path to be followed: Once a spot market is in place, they provide a proven sequence to be followed for prompting the emergence of an efficient market. Thus, the market provides substantiated reasons for why A (e.g., defining the commodity) should be done before B (e.g., allowing futures trade), or C (e.g., allowing broker intermediation).

Coupling market performance with environmental regulatory goals requires attention to other aspects of institutional dynamics analysis such as speed of implementation. This is particularly true in the case of innovative policy approaches in which, for instance, attitudes toward a new regulatory framework develop and learning processes occur. Tietenberg et al. argue for gradual implementation of an emissions trading program: "As long as the initial steps are consistent with the evolution of a cost-effective and equitable system, a slow-moving process can be an advantage rather than a disadvantage" (1998, 135).

The rationale behind this idea is that starting small gives both the institutions and the parties a chance to adjust and become familiar with the system. Since most initial efforts will set precedent, their development will be slow. Once the precedents have been established, however, the process will become smoother, quicker, and better able to handle a larger number of participants, emissions, and entitlements. Therefore, perhaps as the policy implementation process unfolds, Step A might be deferred until some generalized "later" or pushed up to some generalized "earlier."

Technical and political reasons can sometimes determine the necessary speed of implementation.

In some cases, the technically efficient sequence conflicts with the sequence that political momentum prescribes. As institutional behavior changes through experience, institutional design should expect to be influenced by lessons from history and routines that guide change in governance structures and organizations. Moreover, the use of information technologies helps institutions and organizations adapt and meet their goals more efficiently.[9] Next, we will look at a series of US case studies of environmental market-based policymaking and examine the issues confronted in the creation and implementation of the first generation of US market-based air quality management programs.

Chapter 4

The first generation of air pollution trading systems

A competitive environmental commodities market requires three conditions: (1) an adequate number of buyers and sellers so that none possess significant market power (the ability to influence market prices by a firm's own actions); (2) sufficient incentives to buy and sell credits or allowances; and (3) moderate transaction costs. An environmental commodities market must be able to function with minimal transaction costs in order to be efficient and competitive. Regulation is necessary to ensure the environmental integrity of the system, but compliance costs should not impede competitiveness. A successful emissions market also depends on the availability of information: information management systems should be efficient and transparent (Liroff 1986, 3). This chapter shows how the attempt to develop market-based systems for air pollution control in the United States (US) during the 1970s and 1980s failed due to an inadequate number of market participants, insufficient incentives to buy and sell credits, and, in particular, high transaction costs, attributed to fragmented markets.

4.1 The institutional environment of US air quality management

The US Clean Air Act (CAA), the congressional mandate given to the US Environmental Protection Agency (EPA), established the regulatory framework for the first US emissions trading system (ETS). The system faced competing social demands and constant organizational adaptation. Traditionally, social demands on air quality regulation design come from environmentalists, industry, and regulators. As suggested in Hahn and Hester (1987), conflicting political pressures surrounding the introduction of the market approach to air pollution regulation derived not only from concerns about measurable outputs, such as costs and environmental quality, but also from competing underlying values.

4.1.1 Evolution of the clean air management regulatory framework

The explosion of car ownership after World War II is thought to have pushed California to create the first clean air legislation in the US (1947), beginning this country's struggle to combat factory and auto emissions (Warren 2003). US federal government involvement in managing air quality began with the Air Pollution Control Act of 1955, since renamed the Clean Air Act.[1]

4.1.1 (A) Politically decentralized early legislation: 1955–1970

Based on a legacy of meager regulatory provisions derived from the 1955 Air Pollution Control Act, which did not provide for any enforcement, the states were largely left to implement their own air quality controls. In 1967, the Air Quality Act introduced a mandate for federal management of the US air mantle for the first time.[2] Until then, Congress had strongly opposed setting national air pollution standards, although it funded studies of the issue (Yandle 1989, 66). Only in the case of regional environmental emergencies would the federal government get involved or coordinate regional efforts.

Cook described the relaxed position the government held with regard to air pollution during the 1950s and 1960s: "On the whole, then, the relationship with industry and the federal government was at most self-regulatory, perhaps even laissez-faire, but certainly not adversarial, a far cry from what was to come in 1970" (1988, 38–39). As environmental problems became more evident, and as other social movements were taking shape, the government was pressed to take a harder line on air pollution.

4.1.1 (B) Federal air pollution control: 1970–1976

The wave of new social regulation that emerged in the 1960s, and the ideas proposed at the first Earth Day conference in 1969, transformed environmental policy development into a more adversarial process.[3] Polls at the time showed support for stronger regulation. Congress, attentive to public opinion, chartered the EPA in 1970, during the administration of President Richard Nixon.

The EPA was mandated to implement a regulatory regime that imposed stringent air quality goals, compressed deadlines, and clearly enforced mechanisms. Congress also enacted the 1970 CAA as the regulatory framework for air quality management in the US. The stated policy goals of this statute are "to protect and enhance the quality of the nation's air resources so as to promote the public health and welfare and the productive capacity of its population" (US CAA 1970). The 1970 CAA sought to utilize strict regulations to force the rapid development of new pollution control technologies. Industry, the US Commerce Department, and labor unions kept the EPA's activities under constant watch, fearing the obstruction of economic development.

Congress gave little heed to concerns about the new air pollution program's compliance costs. In fact, the statute prevented regulators from considering costs in setting ambient quality standards. Dwyer suggests that the enactment of the 1970 CAA "evinced Congress' deep distrust of industry and regulators" (1992, 60). The underlying argument at the time was that the health of the American people and the environment could not be compromised by concerns about reduced corporate profits (Dwyer 1993, 106).

Despite the ongoing debate about compliance costs, the EPA followed the mandate to establish an intricate system of National Ambient Air Quality Standards (NAAQS).[4] The congressional directive empowered the EPA to set allowable concentration levels for each pollutant and required the agency to incorporate an adequate margin of safety based on the scientific and technical knowledge available at that time. This presented a formidable research challenge with wide discretionary limits and great potential for error in setting standards and enforcement procedures.

The EPA's next step was to develop its own federal plan for attaining national environmental goals. The resulting plan gave state governments nine months to prepare state implementation plans (SIPs) in which the state would describe how the initial ambient air quality standards would be met by the statutory deadline of mid-1975. SIPs were to be developed for the 247 planning areas or "air quality control regions" into which the US was divided. To illustrate how unrealistic these programmatic goals were, Liroff states:

> In theory, to devise a cost effective plan for each region, a state would need perfect knowledge about all emission sources in the region, about the relationships between emissions from those sources and ambient air quality in the region, and about the costs of control and technologies available for reducing emissions. The state could then have processed that information and devised economically efficient programs for achieving ambient standards in each region.
>
> (1986, 21)

In Liroff's words, "reality was far from the ideal" (1986, 21). Critics of the CAA agreed, noting that the institutional capacity required to implement such an ambitious plan simply did not exist (Roberts and Farrell 1978, 156). The most serious problems were the lack of technically qualified staff and readily available data. Consequently, regulators grossly misjudged what was needed to reduce ambient pollution of stationary sources. As a result, controls on many individual pollution sources were tighter and more costly than was necessary to achieve the ambient standards while controls on other pollution sources were looser than what was needed (Liroff 1986, 23). Thus, imperfect information and limited institutional capacity seriously weakened the new clean air plan.

4.1.2 The US Environmental Protection Agency

As mentioned above, President Richard Nixon and the US Congress established the EPA in 1970. Congress gave the new agency the statutory responsibility to create federal pollution standards in order to improve environmental quality. Its main responsibilities include allocating control responsibilities among pollution sources, designing the corresponding regulations, and enforcing the regulations.[5] Environmental regulations at the state and local level are based on federal EPA guidelines.[6]

Stringent regulation by the CAA and EPA was effective and resulted in environmental gains. Kraft and Vig report that between 1970 and 1996 total emissions of regulated air pollutants decreased by 32 percent while the US population grew by 29 percent, the gross domestic product rose by 104 percent, and vehicle miles traveled increased by 121 percent. However, while regulated pollutants were reduced, the level of nitrogen oxides (NO_x), a component of smog, increased by 8 percent (1999, 20). Meanwhile, environmental progress from this strict and centralized regulatory approach resulted in high costs for compliance, monitoring, and enforcement—costs that were sometimes prohibitive to local economies.

4.1.3 Conventional policy instruments for air pollution control

The EPA's traditional regulatory approaches, also known as command-and-control policies, distribute control responsibility at points of discharge by setting specific standards across polluters. Commonly, two command-and-control policy designs are used as regulatory tools:

Technology-Based (or Design) Standards: This approach requires the use of specific mandatory technologies (e.g., smokestack scrubbers) to decide what the allowable emissions rate should be. It can also regulate the production of a particular product or pollutant for instance (e.g., no lead in gasoline, low-carbon fuels, and a phase-out of ozone-depleting substances).

Performance-Based Standards: This approach specifies an acceptable pollution level and gives polluters latitude in meeting this target. Performance standards provide greater flexibility than technology-based standards and support a more decentralized system (Tietenberg 1998, 5).

Although these policy instruments can lead to environmental gains, they can also come at a high cost to industry—a cost that is passed on to society. They do not address the problem that costs of controlling emissions can vary greatly among, and even within, firms. A centrally directed system tends to generate inefficiencies for firms (Tietenberg 1998, 5). Inefficiencies result mainly from the fact that a highly centralized approach generally fails to take advantage of important information. Under command-and-control, the EPA establishes separate standards for each point of discharge (e.g., stacks, vents, or storage tanks). Given that an industrial plant will typically contain several pollutant discharge points, each with its own unique standard, the amount of information the control authority needs in order to define cost-effective standards is staggering. Industrial plant managers, not regulators, have the detailed knowledge about pollution control costs that is crucial to identifying the least-cost technology (Liroff 1986). However, regulated parties have no incentive to share information with the EPA about their industrial processes. Private incentives unquestionably limit information flows. Industries may minimize information sharing with the government in order to avoid, among other things, stiffer regulation in the future (Tirole 1998, 49).

The 1970 CAA relied on command-and-control regulatory approaches, putting a burden on industry and taxpayers that some called excessive (Bollier and Claybrook 1986). As the emission limits deadline of 1975 approached, it was evident that many air control regions would not meet the standards. Regulators began to search for more cost-effective control strategies. Policymakers now joined academics in supporting a market-based regulatory alternative.[7] After repeated failed efforts to introduce policy instruments based on overt pricing such as green charges to control air pollution, emissions trading became the most politically feasible alternative.[8]

4.1.4 Demand for air pollution regulatory reform

The 1973 oil embargo contributed to a downturn in the economy, and this in turn contributed to a move toward finding more cost-effective environmental policies. In 1974, the quest to make NAAQS compliance politically feasible at the local level provided the stimulus for experimentation with the first broadly implemented market-based environmental regulatory mechanism.

The so-called "growth ban" provision included in the 1970 CAA had implications for economic development, specifically that areas of the country that did not attain all the NAAQS by the mandated deadlines "would not be permitted to accept new or substantially expanded existing sources of pollution that would add to emissions already exceeding one or more of the standards" (Liroff 1986, 23). As reported in Cook, "Not surprisingly, an environmental law preventing economic growth in numerous areas of the country, especially major urban areas experiencing economic decline, was a political hot potato no one wanted to handle. Regulators and legislators scrambled to find ways around the growth ban" (1988, 45). Conventional regulation of air pollution sometimes imposes uniform regulatory standard requirements in situations where they do not make sense. This leads to what Bardach and Kagan (1982) characterize as a pattern of "regulatory unreasonableness."

The 1975 deadline came, and dozens of urban areas were still exceeding federal air quality standards. With the growth ban coming into effect for these areas, and with high compliance costs for those trying to reduce emissions, economic development was clearly being hampered by environmental regulation. A 1975 US Senate report identified the most significant deficiencies of the air pollution control regulatory system: (1) a lack of clearly defined objectives; (2) difficulties relating to individual emitters' responsibility for environmental effects; (3) poor mechanisms for stimulating technological development; and (4) a tendency toward perpetual delay (Cook 1988, 35). The underlying argument was that only regulatory relief from the stringent CAA framework through a market-based regulatory approach would permit the US to avoid growth stagnation. However, the EPA stood by its regulations. Environmentalists saw proposals for trading air pollution as a way for industries to keep polluting. Meanwhile, industry—the potential beneficiary of a more flexible system—was ambivalent about regulatory reform using market instruments. Industry preferred the devil it knew (costly but familiar regulatory burdens) to the devil it did not know (an innovative regulatory mechanism). Moreover, regulatory costs acted as a barrier that kept potential competitors from entering the market.

Regulators' opinions were also divided on market-based regulatory mechanisms (Kelman 1981). Within the EPA, supporters portrayed the market-based approach as an opportunity to help balance environmental goals with demands for economic development. Detractors pointed out that expanding the sphere of the market to the realm of environmental regulation would cause a shift in the culture of the agency. Regulators would be departing from the conventional approach of using rule enforcement and sanctions to achieve an environmental goal and turning toward less certain, flexible mechanisms (Martinez and Jusmet 1998–1999, 93).

Table 4.1 Political economy of market-based environmental policymaking in the US

Players	Main concerns	Political positions
Environmentalists	Improve environmental quality	*Clear: strongly against change from status quo (i.e., command-and-control regime).* • Environmental quality should not be sacrificed for economic efficiency. • As a moral principle, clean air is an inalienable right not for sale at any price.
Industry	Reduce compliance costs	*Mixed reaction: flexibility vs. regulatory uncertainty.* • Flexible policies could provide regulatory relief. • Certainty provided in conventional environmental regulation is preferred.
Regulators	Execute congressional mandate	*Mixed reaction: untested policy approach vs. a means to balance environmental goals with economic development demands.* • Reform could provide regulators a means to solve the political problem derived from the growth ban imposed by the CAA. • A controversial approach would become a target for public attacks from environmental groups. • Federal and state environmental agencies differed in institutional capabilities (e.g., staff, modeling, monitoring, etc.) to attain the required information for the system to work. • Not all regulatory staff was convinced, or perhaps even understood, why implementing a trading system would be more cost-effective.

To the economist's eye, it was obvious that regulatory cost-heterogeneity among the different legal types of polluting sources presented many cost-saving opportunities if a trading mechanism could be implemented.[9] However, as pointed out by Hanley et al., "While economists can promote economic incentives as a cost-effective tool to increase pollution control, it is the regulator who must face the winners or losers of any proposed incentive system. The push and pull of these countervailing forces will determine the political feasibility of the proposed incentive system" (1997, 97). Table 4.1 above summarizes the position of the social forces influencing environmental reform proposals during the mid-1970s and the 1980s.

The economic and ideological debate between the social forces involved in clean air politics set the stage for the introduction of the first market-based mechanisms to control air pollution. The political economy of air pollution policy development during the 1970s and 1980s impeded the implementation of many of the necessary market elements to develop an efficient air pollution trading mechanism.

4.2 Institutional development of the emissions trading system

The failed implementation of the 1970 CAA was mainly due to elevated regulatory compliance costs that made the air quality program economically unfeasible. Additionally, the CAA was politically impeded because of the negative economic implications of its growth ban. Conventional regulations had set economic and environmental goals in opposition, producing paralysis. The policy alternative was to harness, rather than obstruct, market forces. Market-based approaches promised to "help break political logjams and facilitate real progress in environmental protection," reducing emissions at a lower aggregate cost to society than traditional mechanisms (Stavins 1989, 58). However, because of the legacy of institutional constraints and the stiff ideological opposition to market-based environmental regulation, the EPA had to take a gradual approach, supplementing rather than replacing old mechanisms with market-based approaches, creating a hybrid system which was inadequate to fully take advantage of the market to reduce the cost of regulatory compliance and spur technological innovation.

What began to unfold was the establishment of a two-track regulatory system. While the strong regulatory element provided in the CAA would ensure the environmental integrity of the program, a series of market-based features would gradually introduce flexibility to make the air quality management system more cost-effective. However, the innovative policy design of emissions trading did not run as expected during the first 15 years of actual experimentation by local air control management regions or districts. Some argue that, because the CAA was structured under the strict compliance model of enforcement, it was difficult to introduce flexibility into the air pollution control system.[10] Most likely, weak political support at the federal level was what most hindered the performance of the new mechanism.

4.2.1 Emissions trading system components

The EPA emissions trading program consisted of four separate components: netting, offsets, bubbles, and banking (Tietenberg 1985; Hahn 1989; Stavins 1998). The various program elements began independently in the mid- to late-1970s and were revised several times. The program was called "controlled trading" under the Carter administration and "emissions trading" under the Reagan administration. Below are detailed descriptions of the four distinct elements of the emissions trading program based mainly on Hahn and Hester (1987) and Hahn (1989).

Netting: Netting was introduced in 1974. It allows a firm that creates a new source of emissions in a plant to avoid the stringent emissions limits that would normally apply by reducing emissions from another source in the same plant. Thus, net emissions from the plant do not increase at all. A firm using netting is only allowed to obtain the necessary emissions credits from its own sources. This is also called internal trading because the transaction involves only one firm: credits obtained through external trades may not be used in netting. Netting is subject to approval at the state, not the federal, level (Hahn 1989, 99).

Offsets: The CAA specified that no new emissions sources would be allowed in non-attainment areas after the original 1975 deadlines for meeting air quality standards had passed (a non-attainment area is a region that has not met a specified ambient standard). Concern that this prohibition would stifle economic growth prompted the EPA to institute the offset rule. This rule specified that new sources would be allowed to locate in non-attainment areas but only if they "offset" new emissions by reducing emissions from existing sources by even larger amounts. The offsets could be obtained through internal trading, just as with netting. However, they could also be obtained from other firms, thus introducing the concept of external trading.

Bubbles: Bubbles allow existing sources to create and trade emissions reduction credits. Though considered by the EPA to be the centrepiece of emissions trading, they were not allowed until 1979. The name derives from the concept of placing an imaginary bubble over a plant, with all emissions exiting from a single point in the bubble. A bubble allows a single firm to sum the emissions limits from individual sources (stacks) of a pollutant in a plant, and to adjust the levels of control applied to different sources as long as this aggregate limit is not exceeded. The policy allows for both internal and external trades. A plant receives credits by reducing the sum below the aggregate limit established in a bubble. Emission reductions beyond pre-established targets create an asset to sell. However, firms must search for buyers of their excess emission reduction credits (ERCs). Moreover, regulators must authorize these transactions. Firms can use netting only when they are modifying an existing source, whereas firms with existing sources can use bubbles (Hahn and Hester 1989, 136). Initially, every bubble had to be approved at the federal level as an amendment to a SIP. In 1981, the EPA approved a generic rule for bubbles in New Jersey that allowed the state to give final approval for bubbles. Since then, the EPA has allowed other states to do likewise.

Banking: The fourth element of emissions trading was developed in conjunction with the bubble policy. Banking allows firms to save emissions reduction credits above and beyond permit requirements for future use in emission trading. While EPA action was initially required to allow banking, the development of banking rules and the administration of banking programs has subsequently been left to the states (Hahn 1989, 100).

The federal offset program introduced the feature of firms being able to trade the emission credits between distinct economic entities. In essence, firms that reduced emissions below the level required by law received credits usable against higher emissions elsewhere. Firms could employ the netting and bubble features to trade emission reductions among pollution sources within the firm as long as total emissions did not exceed an aggregate limit. Regulated entities that more than met their reduction targets could trade their credits on the open market. The theoretical incentives to participate were being allowed to reduce pollution in the most economical way and the potential to accumulate assets through emissions reductions by way of emission credits. However, the institutional and political hurdles faced by regulators during the design and implementation of the first-generation emissions trading programs limited the implementation of key design features necessary to foster a marketplace for the ERCs.

4.2.2 Limited creation of environmental market conditions: 1974–1989

This ERC trading program was created without many of the conditions required for the successful performance of an environmental commodities market.

4.2.2 (A) Environmental commodities: defining the tradable environmental commodity

Selecting the Controlled Substance: The first pollutant substances selected for controls by the EPA were sulfur oxides (including SO_2), particulate matter, and hydrocarbons, and then later photochemical oxidants (i.e., nitrogen oxides and lead).

Clarity about which substances are targeted under environmental control regulation provides certainty for both regulators and industry. Perhaps this is one of the most important contributions of the 1970 CAA towards constructing an emissions trading mechanism. However, defining an ERC exacerbated the debate over the introduction of market-based instruments to regulate particular industries with an untested mechanism.[11] Eventually, curbing acid rain through commoditizing SO_2 became the first real attempt to implement an ETS in the

US. This attempt was embroiled in political stalemate and controversy from 1974 to 1989.

Define the Extent of the Entitlement: The main policy implication of the ideological debate and controversy about the use of the trading mechanism for air quality control was the hindrance of this key institutional building block for market creation: establishing legal certainty about any environmental market-based program.

A key element in the institutional development of any market approach is a clear definition of the nature and distribution of property rights. Without clearly defined property rights to the tradable environmental good to be allocated among program participants, there were few incentives for free exchange in private markets under the ERC system.

Create a Homogeneous Unit: Under the CAA, SO_2 emissions are measured and reported in tons. The unit of trade could be specified as one ton of SO_2. However, in the ERC system (i.e., a case-by-case crediting approach), the exchangeability of pollution substances in tradable emissions transactions from different participating sources (e.g., steel smelters and electric utilities) becomes an issue that affects the environmental integrity of the program. For instance, regulators lack the technical capacity to assess the comparable environmental effects of each pollutant (and their mixing) in a timely manner.

Establish Exchange Ratios: Under the first bubble policy program, regulators had to decide what procedures emitters must follow to demonstrate that the combinations of increases and decreases proposed under this instrument will not harm the environment or endanger human health. Liroff points to the issue of the cost of assessing the risk of airborne pollution concentrations:

> Regulators' decisions on such technical matters will determine how great an administrative burden will be placed on polluters. The heavier the burden of proof, the costlier the demonstrations of equivalence, the more substantial the monitoring requirements—all these will reduce the cost savings available through trading and, hence, its attractiveness.
>
> (1986, 17)

Past experience shows the need to assess the environmental locational equivalence of proposed trading mechanisms. Some pollutants (for example, the organic compounds that contribute to smog) add to a regional air quality problem but without identifiable effects in a small local area. For these pollutants, regulators usually do not need to demand sophisticated modeling of air quality impacts, so trades may be relatively easy to execute. However, for pollutants that have significant localized effects, such as SO_2 and particulates, the impact on air quality must be modeled to assure that individuals downwind from the points of increase are not subject to significantly higher or more harmful levels of emissions.

In the case of SO_2 emissions standards, the EPA established a primary (i.e., for protection of health) NAAQS average of 80 µg/m^3 (0.03 ppm), and for a 24-hour period an average of 365 µg/m^3 (0.14 ppm). The secondary standard (i.e., for protection of welfare) was set for a three-hour average at 1300 µg/m^3 (0.50 ppm). In general, air in regions distant from major pollution sources contains low concentrations of SO_2. In urban areas, concentrations are typically ten times higher than in rural areas. Also, in the vicinity of industrial sources with adequate controls by the standards, the levels are sometimes nearly 1000 times greater than the NAAQS for periods per hour, creating hot spots.[12] Substantial modeling may be required where points involved in trades are very far apart and where the heights of the points involved in the trades differ. Therefore, localized impacts require a sensible approach to defining an air basin district or air quality region. For regions with multiple sources, it makes economic sense to link with other basins to trade and take advantage of additional cost minimization opportunities. However, a hot spot can be created by only one source. Exchange ratios, as in the case of international trade and monetary exchange rate, allow some level of equivalence between pollution intensity of an emission and the tradable environmental commodity of an emissions trading system (ETS). Therefore, trading between an intra-air basin hot spot source and the rest of the market participants could be managed through a well-designed exchange-ratio or equivalence system.

Establish Duration: One of the main failures of the early emissions trading mechanisms was not being able to provide certainty about the duration of the ERCs. There was considerable uncertainty about the value of ERCs given sudden changes in regulatory behavior. Among industry representatives there was a constant fear that regulators would confiscate permits or reduce their value to adjust to immediate political needs rather than satisfying the long-term goal of fostering the emergence of an environmental commodities market. A lack of certainty about the duration of the entitlements over an environmental commodity reduces the incentives to participate in trading between distinct economic entities.

Set a Baseline: One of the most disputed matters in the design of the trading mechanism was the definition of the baseline from which to calculate decreases in emissions—whether it should be an existing administrative requirement, a variation on that requirement, or an emitter's historic emissions level.

An important factor that complicated the merging of trading policies into the conventional regulatory system was the difficulty that existed in determining what emission decreases should qualify for ERCs. Disagreements over calculating credits were a major component of the conflict between those in favor of reduced bureaucratic oversight of an environmental market and those who believed in a strict set of rules to limit participants' opportunistic decision making within an ETS. The account of such debate is covered in Liroff:

> Critics say that selecting an inappropriate baseline might have adverse environmental consequences, because credits might be given at one point for emission reductions that exist only on paper, thereby allowing otherwise forbidden emissions elsewhere and squandering an opportunity to clean the air. For example, a state plan might assume a plant operates at full capacity and allows some point to emit 100 tons per year. But, if the plant has never operated at full capacity and has never emitted more than 80 tons per year at the point, the 20-ton difference might be used by the plant owner to avoid cleaning up 20 tons of actual emissions from another point. In such a case, actual emissions from the plant would increase as a result from of the trading opportunity. The baseline issue also arises in a second context. A state plan might require a plant owner to install a pollution control device to meet a 60-ton-per-year emission limit, even though the regulators and the plant owner expect that the device will never emit more that 40 tons a year. The extra 20-ton-per-year reduction not developed in response to the trading opportunity but having occurred in response to conventional regulations might be used by the plant owner to avoid a 20-ton-per-year abatement obligation at another point. Critics contend that if this extra 20-ton-per-year reduction beyond requirements occurred as a result of standard industry pollution reduction practice, no credit should be given to it, and it should not be used to avoid control requirements elsewhere.
>
> (1986, 15–16)

Proponents contended that even if using a particular baseline would permit avoidance of otherwise applicable requirements, trades should be approved when their baselines are consistent with existing administrative rules. Nevertheless, the core of the problem hinged on determining the appropriate baseline to use for allocating emissions rights. As summarized by Hahn and Hester, measuring actual emissions is "technically difficult, legally contentious, and politically sensitive" (1987, 52). It may also be expensive.

4.2.2 (B) Emissions trading system development

Emission Targets: Under the first generation of emissions trading mechanisms, there was no overall target of abatement, only the individual bubble targets for a given air basin.

Initial Allocation: ERCs were issued for those emission reductions beyond the preset standards for each particular industry on a case-by-case basis.

Determine Program Participants: ERC holders were eligible participants. However, in the credit trading policy, the scope of the program (i.e., who was covered and who could trade) was unclear for those outside the EPA.

The case-by-case approach multiplied the information needed to manage air quality above the cost-effective level, in particular because the understanding of environmental problems was still fragmentary. Moreover, the applicability criterion required identifying a core group of pollution sources that would be affected by the new rules. However, experience shows that a critical mass of participants should be comprised of pollution sources that can most readily employ trading mechanisms. A key element is to be able to account for their emissions. During the implementation of the early trading program, there was low institutional and technical capacity to assess emissions. Moreover, an overriding concern at the time was the environmental implications of allowing the exchangeability of different types (or grades) of emissions entitlements.

Trading Rules: The lack of legal certainty about the market rules was perceived by regulated entities as a lack of a credible commitment from regulators to such a system.

The rules governing trading can have a dramatic impact on the efficiency and equity characteristics of the market (Hahn and Noll 1982; Franciosi 1993). For instance, the fact that states were not legally required by federal law to use the controlled trading program in combination with uncertainties about its future course seems to have made firms reluctant to participate in the controlled trading system. In contrast, critics contended at the time that unless the rules governing trading were fairly strict, they would only enable industries to "game" regulators. In other words, industries would use trading opportunities to exploit weaknesses in state plans. Critics of decentralized control mechanisms used information from the first proposed trades as evidence of a need to tighten existing regulations and to deny industries that proposed trades any benefits from them. Liroff characterized these critics as the "expansionists"—those seeking greater and more specified federal directives—and their opponents as the "minimalists"—those in favor of introducing decentralized mechanisms (1986, 12).

The expansionists might have conceded at the time that, by urging the disapproval of many trades proposed by industry, they might discourage trading. However, rather than lamenting the loss of prospective trades, expansionists more likely would view the denial of trades as the curtailment of abusive efforts by emitters to take advantage of the system's flaws. Expansionists claimed that they only wanted to make sure that the EPA did not unintentionally encourage emitters to misuse trading by acceding to industry requests. In contrast, minimalists responded that, if the EPA structured its trading policy so that limits were placed on the rewards industries could reap through trading, or that industries going forward with new proposals ended up with even tighter regulatory requirements, industry proposals to participate in the program would dry up. The result would be that increased cost-effectiveness, improved SIPs, and other benefits from trading would be destroyed.

Expansionists agreed with minimalists that it was useful to provide industries with incentives for developing cost-effective abatement techniques, but expansionists were much less forthcoming with such incentives than minimalists. The expansionist position tended, for example, to oppose giving industries rewards for emissions reductions that would have happened anyway for business reasons. Especially in areas that had not attained the national ambient standards, expansionists supported only trades that promised to produce new reductions in emissions, as opposed to mere adjustments of emissions reduction requirements on paper. Expansionists viewed these adjustments on paper—labeled "paper credits"—as methods for avoiding controls that actually might be needed to attain ambient standards (Liroff 1986, 12).

Emissions banking, a key institutional feature for the proper functioning of an environmental commodities market, took several years to emerge. This design parameter eventually provided an easily accessible storehouse of credits available for future use or sale for emission reductions achieved in excess of applicable air quality standards. Furthermore, banking was expected to evolve into the means to facilitate trades when demand and supply of credits was not synchronized (Tietenberg 1992, 39). When the offset policy was being designed, banking was perceived to be in conflict with achieving ambient standards in non-attainment areas. After 1977, banking was introduced under rules that would not allow attainment limits to be exceeded (Tietenberg 1985, 9). With a low volume of trading, the emissions banking rules remained idle. More importantly, a lack of clear property rights over the emission credits inhibited their development as explained below. Furthermore, given the limited nature of the emissions trading model, other advanced market-based policy design features such as information services, futures markets, and standardized procedures were not developed.

4.2.2 (C) Market governance infrastructure

Clearinghouse: The ERC trading policy design required local air quality management districts to serve as transaction brokers and market makers as well as environmental control enforcers. This caused conflict, impeding the development of a spot market where ERCs could be freely traded in an open exchange.

4.2.2 (D) Program implementation parameters

Monitoring and Enforcement: With the case-by-case approach, emitters' trading plans would place great administrative burdens on regulatory personnel. The early ETS did not harness market forces to reduce the information burden on regulators, instead relying heavily on oversight over transactions.

Emitters' trading plans required considerable scrutiny because they included operating procedures with which regulators were unfamiliar and which were developed ad hoc for a particular type of industry. Critics of the first bubbles worried that, by allowing dischargers to seek additional compliance time to develop their bubble proposals for problem facilities, recalcitrant polluters would be given the opportunity to delay abatement. However, proponents argued "that, rather than undermining the integrity of the regulatory system by making enforcement more difficult, trading proposals can help disclose information useful to strategies for achieving ambient standards in an area" (Tietenberg 1992, 16). This latter characteristic of the emissions trading policy approach is perhaps its most valuable characteristic as a regulatory tool.

Enforcement and Penalties: The Clean Air Act provides both enforcement powers and penalties. The conventional regulatory elements contained in the US air quality program foster effective compliance under any market-based emissions control system. A penalty for each violation could result in fines of up to $25,000 a day and imprisonment for up to one year (Bryner 1995, 101). The CAA authorizes the EPA to seek injunctions to halt emissions that endanger public health. Also, citizens can file lawsuits against firms that fail to take non-discretionary actions or knowingly violate provisions of SIPs.

Political Jurisdiction: Trading proposals raise important issues about intergovernmental relations and interstate equity.

(1) *Decentralization*: One issue is how free state regulators should be from the EPA's guidance and review in their efforts to implement trading. As mentioned earlier, critics wary of the ETS approach sought to maintain considerable federal oversight of trades approved by states, while proponents pushed to reduce such oversight because it can be cumbersome to the system (Liroff 1986, 17–18).

(2) *Standard harmonization:* Another concern is the possibility that trade involving new and modified sources would reduce the uniformity among states that nationally established technology-based standards are intended to provide. Opponents of the trading system, and many state officials, have stressed the importance of uniform emissions standards, so that states will not use lenient environmental requirements as a means of competing for new industry. But proponents of early ETS noted that "many of such standards are set on a case-by-case basis and, even where the standards are uniform, states may have widely varied but not readily documentable attitudes about how strictly such standards will be enforced" (Liroff 1986, 17–18).

(3) *Institutional capacity at the state level:* As pointed out earlier, a major focus of disagreements in the initial stages of designing the emissions trading program was the amount of flexibility states should have, subject to EPA oversight, in developing and revising SIPs to attain the ambient standards. These plans require industries to reduce their emissions. A related source of controversy is the credibility of the plans, including those that have received EPA approval. SIPs are only as good as the assumptions underlying them, and considerable room exists for technical disagreements about the assumptions. Liroff's minimalists acknowledged that state plans are problematic. But the minimalists contended that the requirements of EPA-approved plans should be deemed appropriate bases for trading until the EPA formally reversed its decision and determined that state plans were, in fact, inadequate. Expansionists were often

reluctant to approve trades, even when they were consistent with EPA-approved state plans for attaining national ambient standards. They frequently argued that the plans were flawed and that the ambient standards would not be met the way states were projecting. Minimalists, by contrast, tended to assign greater credibility to the state plans. Arguing that EPA-approved state plans are the recognized legal basis for abatement obligations, minimalists suggested that as long as trades are consistent with state plans they should be acceptable, even if they (1) are mere paper adjustment requirements or (2) reflect abatement actions that industries would have taken in the absence of the trading opportunity (Liroff 1986, 12–13).

Now that we have reviewed each of the key market parameters developed under early emissions trading programs, let us now look at how these features, or the failure to introduce them, affected the market development requirements posed at the beginning of this chapter.

4.2.3 Failure to foster an emission reduction credits market

Fabozzi and Modigliani describe a "perfect market" for financial assets in the following terms: In general, a perfect market results when the number of buyers and sellers is sufficiently large and all participants are small enough relative to the market that no individual market agent can influence the commodity's price. Consequently, all buyers and sellers are price takers, and the market price is determined where there is equality of supply and demand. This condition is more likely to be satisfied if the commodity traded is basically homogeneous (1996, 146).

However, the emission trading programs based on ERCs did not allow for the consolidation of a continuous market structure. The rules of the program impeded sufficient participation among the potential universe of participants (i.e., air pollution emitters) to create a fluid market.[13] Among the main reasons for such weak performance was the initial conceptualization of the controlled trading system being based on project-specific credit trades.

Firms were unclear about just what the local authority would count as netting or require in the way of offsets. Brian McLean, who at the time headed the Clean Air Markets Division (CAMD) at the EPA, recalled some of the main weaknesses of the early emissions trading program based on his experience as a local air quality management administrator in Philadelphia during the 1970s, saying: "This program was never designed to have trading." At the most it had become a bartering system in which local environmental regulators had to decide on a case-by-case basis what would constitute netting or offsetting (McLean 2000).

The high transaction costs associated with external trading under the first-generation program induced firms to eschew this option in favor of internal trading or no trading at all (Hahn 1989, 101). Moreover, the lack of adequate information systems providing timely information about the ERCs market (e.g., price signals and trading parties), as well as about the environmental regulatory aspects of the emissions trading system (e.g., accurate emissions inventories), encumbered the system with high transaction costs and gave regulators the dual role of environmental policy enforcers and market operators.

Also, limited institutional capacity to develop and manage emissions data to maintain the environmental integrity of the trading mechanism was pervasive. Therefore, given the structure of the first-generation emissions trading programs, the information flows necessary for an active emissions market to emerge as a cost-effective environmental management tool were absent.

More importantly, the failure of the federal government to signal a credible commitment to the emissions trading policies introduced uncertainty and distrust among potential participants. The following are examples of particular aspects in which early emissions trading programs failed to introduce the conditions necessary for a competitive environmental commodities market to emerge.

4.2.3 (A) Condition one: an adequate number of buyers and sellers

Thin Markets: The credit and permitting requirements of the early emissions trading programs constituted a set of demand suppressant rules that led to "thin" markets. John Dwyer, who did a study of the implementation of the first emissions trading programs in California, concurs with McLean's characterization of flawed policy design and has stated that the offset program was "virtually designed to suppress demand" (1993, 109). Dwyer also reports that most firms in the Bay Area Air Quality Management District (AQMD) were not able to buy offsets; only new firms or existing firms undergoing major modifications were permitted to buy credits. Moreover, those firms that were able to participate in the program had to first install specific pollution controls regardless of the availability of less expensive offset means.

4.2.3 (B) Condition two: sufficient incentives to buy and sell credits

Credible Commitment: In the early development of emissions trading in the US, legislators and regulators were reluctant to provide clear support and direction to the offset program. This attitude contributed greatly to the failure of the program. One of the reasons for the lack of political support was that Congress had to face objections by some environmental groups that creating pollution property rights was morally wrong, especially where the air quality did not meet federal standards. Furthermore, the political institutions and private actors that created and supported the policy and procedures of the status quo (i.e., command-and-control) inevitably resisted regulatory reform (Dwyer 1993, 111). Moreover, scepticism over an untested market-based regulatory scheme that could be difficult to administer and enforce lessened momentum in Congress, the EPA, and state legislatures to take an active role in the offset program.

Lack of Clearly Defined Property Rights or Entitlements: The political resistance to change the regulatory framework of air quality management during the first developmental stages of the emissions trading program resulted in regulators' opposition to the creation of too concrete a property right for the emissions credit system, one that would require that a company be compensated if the value of its ERCs were reduced and consider such action a regulatory taking.[14] Incomplete markets for environmental assets can result from the failure of institutions to establish well-defined property rights. In the case of air pollution, the lack of clear and well-defined property rights for clean air makes it difficult for a market to exist. For instance, without clear definition of property rights (and responsibilities) over an environmental commodity such as sulfur dioxide emissions, people who live downwind from a coal-fired power plant will find it almost impossible to halt the harm the plant causes and will be unsuccessful in demanding a fee from the management of the upwind facility for the costs they bear.

Uncertain Emissions Targets: When there is no certainty about the environmental goal to be achieved under a market-based approach, regulation becomes a "moving target." As a result of regulatory ambiguity, credit holders are induced to save their permits or entitlements in case regulation becomes more stringent. Thus, incentives to trade environmental entitlements are reduced by the lack of a predefined pollution reduction goal, such as a total emissions cap. The possibility of future commitments by elected officials with environmentalist groups, for instance, on higher standards for pollution control in exchange for political support in an election, is a reality that a firm must take into account for strategic business planning. Unless clear rules for changing the emissions limits are legislated, given scientific uncertainty about environmental phenomena and advances in the development of clean technologies, political factors may induce stricter regulatory measures without a warranted technical argument.

Therefore, ad hoc policy fixes, such as adjusting emission caps, along with the possibility of the elimination or devaluation of the ERCs circulating in the system negatively affected the credibility and certainty of the emerging markets for air pollution. A common strategy followed by air quality districts was to confiscate a percentage of banked reductions under the excuse of funding a community bank (i.e., an ERC reserve), which would become a de facto policy threshold adjustment (i.e., a more stringent emissions limit) to achieve local or federal air quality standards. For instance, regulators in California implementing market-based air quality management policies were accused of using unpublished policies and on-the-spot policy interpretations as well as placing unreasonably high hurdles before emission credit creators, buyers, and sellers (Dwyer 1993, 110–111). In June 1990, (as reviewed in Chapter 6) the SCAQMD in California discounted most bank credits by 80 percent (SCAQMD 1990), "thereby confirming industry's fears about regulators' confiscatory tendencies" (Dwyer 1993, 110). This type of regulatory behavior reduces the incentives for industry to participate in emissions trading. Such regulatory practices can severely impair, if not halt entirely, an emerging market.

Regulatory Discretion: Formal rules aside, agency practices and policies can reduce the security of offset rights and create strong disincentives to trade. Unless firms are confident that regulators will not confiscate their reductions, they will be reluctant to bank ERCs, invest in additional controls, make process changes (to create reduction credits), or even make trades (Hahn and Noll 1993, 132–133). Dwyer (1993) reminds us that this concern is acute where the air quality does not meet federal and state air quality standards and, consequently, regulators are under continuous political and legal pressure to reduce emissions further.

Regulators must have the flexibility to respond to new information, such as information on the quantitative relationship between emissions and environmental quality. The risk, however, is that flexibility will become an excuse for regulatory caprice. This may be inevitable when regulators accustomed to command-and-control techniques are made responsible for creating stable market conditions. The temptation to seize the market surplus to achieve other regulatory goals may be greater than the regulators can withstand (Dwyer 1993). As a result, in the face of such potential behavior by regulators, industry tended to withhold ERCs from the market.

Hoarding: Credit hoarding occurs because plant managers believe that they will need additional credits—either because the AQMD will demand new emissions reduction or because the firm will want to expand its operations in the future—and that the market will be unable to supply the credits at acceptable prices. Firms also fear, with some justification, that if they reduce emissions, the AQMD will lower their emissions limits and place a cap on future increases. Similarly, the use of innovative technologies in some cases has become the basis for new mandatory controls at the firms' other plants. For these reasons, past experience shows that the majority of external trades under ERCs programs were with firms that had ceased operations (i.e., shutdown credits), having little reason to withhold their credits from the market (Dwyer 1993).

4.2.3 (C) Condition three: moderate transaction costs

Excessive Trading Rules: Each of the program elements of the first generation of emissions trading mechanisms contained "rigid procedural requirements for reporting and approval by governmental authorities, in some programs multiple approvals, essentially making trades into rulemaking events. Consequently, these programs have suffered from high uncertainty, transaction costs, and regulatory risk" (Tietenberg et al. 1998, 19). These conditions make external trading difficult and costly.

Program Administrative Costs: Joe Kruger, the EPA's Market Policy Chief at the CAMD at the time, stated that "because of the diversity in the type of industries and pollutants controlled under the credit trading system, high levels of government oversight was [sic] required" to ensure the environmental integrity of a credit trading system (Kruger 2000). Such an "ad-hoc regulatory approach" entailed high administrative and information costs to environmental administrators as well as to potential market participants. In other words, undertaking appropriate engineering studies to quantify the emission reductions, negotiating a price, and securing regulatory approval were added frictions[15] to the process of running a smooth and efficient emissions trading program under the ERC system (Hahn and Hester 1989, 377–379).

4.2.3 (D) Information flows: key to making markets emerge

Limited Information Availability: The lack of high-quality emissions inventories makes reliable assessments of baselines and achieved emissions reductions troublesome. Because the SIPs contained inventories of industries' emissions and the emissions reduction strategies targeted at them, these documents were, in a sense, accounting mechanisms. Accounting accuracy is essential to the smooth operation of both the existing command-and-control system and emissions trading.

However, as mentioned earlier, the poor quality of many inventories and the questionable validity of many planning assumptions led to heated disputes over whether emissions trading should be permitted in many areas. Both proponents and critics of emissions trading agree that problems in inventories and assumptions make the command-and-control system flawed, but they disagree on the role emissions trading should play in remedying the defects (Liroff 1986, 10–11).

In order to create an efficient environmental commodities market, the total allowable emissions limit has to be determined. However, early experience shows that information asymmetry between regulator and regulated parties, as well as the staggering information demanded to certify permit reductions, did not allow for inventory improvements.

Using data provided by existing monitors of ambient conditions, state agencies often estimated the percentage reduction in emissions needed to achieve a national ambient standard. This method is known as the rollback technique. Then, reviewing their inventory of existing emissions, they developed combinations of technology-based requirements for reductions of emissions from existing sources. Moreover, with a limited capability to model the impact of sources' emissions on ambient air quality, and with only rough indications of existing air quality from monitoring stations of uncertain reliability, states had to employ crude, simplifying assumptions as they established the limits on emissions and devised plans to achieve the NAAQS (Liroff 1986, 23).

Poor Information Management: Perhaps the most important reason why mutually beneficial transactions may be limited, creating thin markets, relates to the level of search and information costs as well as bureaucratic transaction hurdles. Properly functioning markets reduce transaction costs. As described in Fabozzi and Modigliani:

Search costs represent explicit costs, such as the money spent to advertise the sale or purchase of a financial asset, and implicit costs, such as the value of time spent in locating a counterpart. The presence of some form of organized financial market reduces search costs. Information costs are those entailed with assessing the investment merits of a financial asset, that is the amount and likelihood of the cash flow expected to be generated. In an efficient market, prices reflect the aggregate information collected by all market participants.

(1996, 11)

Foster and Hahn (1994) show, in an analysis of offset exchanges that identifying a suitable trading partner (i.e., entailing search costs) could take anywhere from a day to a year and a half, causing great uncertainty in transactions. Implementation experiences in California demonstrate that half of all proposed trades under the early ETS fell through during the negotiation process. Under emissions trading, the problem of identifying a trading partner is compounded by the large number of potential traders relative to the number of actual trades taking place each year, and by the wide range of industries involved (Foster and Hahn 1994, 21).

Price signals are essential to jump-start nascent markets, and ERC prices in this program were not public, which had the effect of discouraging trades. Moreover, early emissions trading programs resulted in a fragmented market burdened by frictions in the form of restrictions to trade imposed by an unclear regulatory process. For instance, once a suitable trading partner was identified, the bureaucratic approval became a hurdle, taking between five and twelve months. Thus, this stage in the process may also entail significant financial costs. As mentioned earlier, the administrative process introduces a further element of uncertainty into the transaction given the potential effects of administrative discretionary measures (Hahn 1989, 101).

In summary, the basic conditions required for a competitive environmental commodities market to emerge in the US were not met during the implementation of the first generation of air pollution trading systems. The early emissions trading program in general performed poorly due to high transaction costs and the uncertainty and risk involved in obtaining the needed government approvals for ERC trades.

4.2.4 Policy analysis: failure to meet the predetermined policy goals

It should not be surprising, given the failure to meet the three necessary conditions for a properly functioning environmental commodities market, that early emissions trading programs did not meet their policy goals. One caveat is that comprehensive data on the effects of various transferable entitlement programs do not exist, because the relevant information has yet to be collected in a systematic way.

In retrospect, experimenting with environmental market-based mechanisms in the US provided valuable opportunities for policymakers and stakeholders to learn about this environmental regulatory alternative. Below is a review of the lessons learned.

4.2.4 (A) Political feasibility

The lack of credible commitment from the federal government to the emissions trading program resulted in regulatory uncertainty about the program. Institutional and political limits imposed on the new policy approach produced a mixed bag of performance achievements. The institutional uncertainty surrounding the early structure of the first emissions trading programs further reduced the possibility of achieving the original policy goals.

4.2.4 (B) Exchange efficiency

The policy failed to fully develop active external markets (between distinct economic entities). This situation reduced the program's potential to achieve substantial efficiency gains from emissions trading. The degree of gains from trade fell short of minimizing total emissions control costs at the expected targets. In fact, internal trading was the preferred strategy followed by plant managers (McLean 2000).

4.2.4 (C) Dynamic efficiency

Although one of the main goals of the 1970 CAA was to spur technological change to reduce emissions, this behavioral change in industry did not occur under controlled trading. Even worse, as suggested in Hahn and Hester, industry preferred "to keep old facilities on-line rather than modernize facilities under a trading system that includes substantial limitations on trades, thereby producing larger emissions" (1989, 109).

4.2.4 (D) Certainty of satisficing

As reported in Hahn and Hester (1989), the overall impact of early emissions trading on air quality was probably neutral. In theory, the offset ratio of greater than one-to-one ensures some reduction in pollution (US EPA 1992, 14–15). However, netting may allow small increases in pollution.[16] Tietenberg describes some of the issues associated with potential environmental risks of the trading program as follows:

> Since each credit trade is unique, they have uncertain environmental impacts, especially for shutdown credits which are allowed for offsets, as they may increase total net emissions. The uncertain environmental impact of these credit trading policies has led to criticism by the environmental community, and ultimately led to the increasingly stringent rules this review entails.
>
> (Tietenberg et al. 1998, 20)

The EPA's emissions trading programs may have saved between $5 billion and $12 billion since the program's inception in the early 1970s through 1989. Still, the economic impact of emissions trading during almost two decades was "weak" relative to its theoretical potential gains. Table 4.2 summarizes the EPA's assessment of early emissions trading programs:

Table 4.2 US EPA performance assessment of early ETS mechanisms

	Estimated number of internal transactions	*Estimated number of external transactions*	*Estimated cost savings ($ million)*	*Environmental quality impact*
Netting	5000–12,000	None	25–300 in permitting costs; 500–12, 000 in emissions control costs	Insignificant in individual cases; probably insignificant in aggregate
Offsets	1800	200	"Not easily estimated … probably hundreds of millions of dollars"	Probably insignificant
Bubbles (federally approved)	40	2	300	Insignificant
Bubbles (state-approved)	89	0	135	Insignificant
Banking	Under 100	Under 20	Small	Insignificant

Source: Hahn and Hester (1989)

The narrow scope of the policy goal to avoid facing growth bans instead of achieving environmental progress in a more economic fashion crippled the development of market-based environmental policy in its initial stages. Even fine-tuning during this period was limited. For example, Hahn and Hester describe the offset program as a "conservative, cautious approach to the reform of emissions trading. Its emphasis is on preventing transaction problems rather than on increasing the level of trading" (1989, 148).

4.2.4 (E) Policy dynamics

With respect to the policy aspects of introducing a market-based regulatory framework to improve air quality in the US, a key lesson is that industry did not warm to the offset program and to market-based pollution control strategies in general, because it was not clear whether federal and state laws would require significant additional reductions in air emissions in the future. At the end of the 1980s, support finally emerged due to the realization that federal legislators would not relax, but instead strengthen their commitment to achieving clean air through trading mechanisms and stricter standards (Dwyer 1993, 111–112).

4.2.4 (F) Legal feasibility

An additional issue is legal feasibility. This policy aspect seems to have also been critical in the development of emissions trading in the US. The regulatory history of air pollution control includes several lawsuits during the implementation phase of early market-based policies. The historical lesson as presented in Liroff shows that:

> EPA [regulators in general] must constantly bear in mind how courts might view any rule it makes for trading. In drafting the Clean Air Act, Congress did not used such terms as *source*, *plant*, and *facility* clearly or consistently in telling EPA which points should have controls applied to them. As a result, environmentalists, industry, and EPA litigators have tangled many times over just what those terms mean.
>
> (1986, 13)

At first, federal appellate judges made Herculean but largely unpersuasive efforts to reconcile appeals court opinions that sometimes have approved trading and other times have not. The result was greater uncertainty over the legality of trading policies. A key first step in providing legal grounds for the trading mechanisms was that in the 1977 CAA amendments, Congress specifically authorized the offset program. However, it was not until June 1984 that the US Supreme Court declared that, since Congress was ambiguous in drafting the CAA, the EPA should have substantial administrative discretion to decide which points to regulate. This decision, in fact, lifted much of the pall that the appeals courts had cast over emissions trading. However, it opened a Pandora's box of administrative discretion. Nevertheless, as Liroff then warned: "If EPA continues to attempt novel applications of emissions trading, legal battles surely will follow" (1986, 13).

4.3 Summary of policy lessons

Heated debates within various social interest groups, as well as expensive legal conflicts over the new regulatory framework that introduced market-based mechanisms for air pollution control, were part of the policy and implementation experience of the first generation of emissions trading programs in the US.

Institutional and political limits reduced the returns on these early programs to some limited, low-performance achievements. The main lesson derived with respect to political feasibility has been that consensus building among the social and economic interests affected by policy changes is needed to generate collaborative participation of all parties involved in the design of cost-effective air pollution policies.

In retrospect, it is clear that there were technological limits to the regulators' ability to obtain the information necessary to maintain the environmental integrity of early trading mechanisms by precisely monitoring emissions. Therefore, the degree of government oversight of the system of ERCs in order to assure the satisficing capacity of the policy instrument tended to be highly intrusive and costly.

The lack of information about trading opportunities and price signals, in addition to excessive trading rules, hindered the development of an environmental commodities market. Finally, the quality of information available to the environmental regulators on emissions levels is crucial to making a decentralized regulatory program that produces the promised regulatory relief while effectively controlling pollution emissions.

The following facts summarize the lessons that can be learned from a review of the early environmental commodity trading mechanisms in the US:

- Industry has had to comply with a long history of environmental regulation, particularly in the area of air pollution control.
- ETS of various types have existed for more than three decades. A process of learning by doing began with the first market-like programs, consisting of offsets, bubbles, netting, and banking.
- Experience in the design and implementation of emissions trading mechanisms based on trial and error became the technical foundation for the institutional development of the next generation of environmental markets.
- Political processes that determine environmental policy action at all levels of government clearly influence the choice of instrument, the ultimate design, and even the performance of market-based environmental regulation.
- The ideological debate over the use of markets to solve environmental problems also affects the political feasibility of the use of market-based mechanisms for pollution control.
- Diverse economic, political, and environmental interest groups must be given a seat at the table in democratic forums for public consultation (i.e., stakeholder dialogues) to reduce the political limitations of the implementation of market-based policies.
- The basic conditions required for a competitive environmental commodities market to emerge were not met during the implementation of the first generation of air pollution trading systems. The early emissions trading program performed poorly due to high transaction costs and the uncertainty and risk involved in obtaining the needed government approvals for ERC trades. Firms were unclear about what local authorities would count as netting or require in the way of offsets.
- Finally, poor information systems, with limited technology, were a barrier in creating a flexible and decentralized air quality program.

The next chapter will analyze how these policy and implementation lessons informed a new era of market-based environmental programs, becoming "usable knowledge" as defined by Lindblom and Cohen (1979).

Chapter 5

State-of-the-art market-based environmental policy

The United States (US) was the first country to develop a national emissions trading system (ETS). Designed to address the issue of acid rain, the goal of the program is to control emissions of pollutants that cause acid rain while minimizing implementation costs to society. In 1990, Title IV of the Clean Air Act (CAA) Amendments introduced a federal ETS for sulfur dioxide (SO_2) allowances, also known as the Acid Rain Program (ARP). This state-of-the-art regulatory approach set a politically predetermined universal cap on SO_2 emissions from the electric power sector and allowed trading of entitlements among emitters to meet its phased-in emission limits in a cost-effective manner. This market-based policy design is known as cap-and-trade.

After its implementation in 1995, the ARP "quickly evolved into a well-functioning market with low transaction costs, price transparency, and extensive trading activity" (Ellerman et al. 1997). In 1997, the Organisation for Economic Co-operation and Development (OECD) reported that the ARP ETS was "the most significant and far-reaching of its kind" (OECD 1997, 57). There were several subsequent modifications to this path-breaking application of the ETS concept, but the form and function remain intact. On the whole, the implementation of the cap-and-trade flexibility mechanism as part of the ARP is considered a success, as it has achieved its stated emission targets in a more cost-effective manner than conventional regulation.

In 1996, ARP phased in regulatory controls on nitrogen oxides (NOx) to a subset of major coal-fired power generators, where emission reductions occur through a more traditional policy design akin to rate-based regulation. NO_x are not controlled under the federal ETS but through local and regional ETS collaborative efforts. For instance, in 1998 the Environmental Protection Agency (EPA) promulgated the NO_x State Implementation Plan (NO_x SIP Call), a federal program that created a federal and regional regulatory collaborative effort known as the NO_x Budget Trading Program (NBP). The NBP was a cap-and-trade program that was based on the ARP ETS design and implemented during the months of May through September each year to reduce the regional emissions of NO_x from power plants and other sources, primarily boilers and turbines, located in the Eastern US. In 2009, this program became the Clean Air Interstate Rule (CAIR). Unfortunately CAIR, and its court-mandated replacement program, the 2011 Cross-State Air

Pollution Rule (CSAPR) have been marred by legal contention and regulatory uncertainty. Local and regional ETS developments to control NO_x will be discussed in chapters 6 and 7.

On November 15, 1999 the Acid Rain Program Division under the Office of Air and Radiation EPA was renamed the Clean Air Markets Division (CAMD). This organizational change signaled EPA's strategic decision to support and expand the use of market-based environmental policy design in federal air quality management.

In 2005, EPA promulgated several rules increasing its reliance on the cap-and-trade ETS policy design for air pollution control. As mentioned above, these initiatives have been confronted by strong legal challenges, mainly from upwind states, at the US Court of Appeals for the D.C. Circuit. The first one was the Clean Air Mercury Rule (CAMR), a new cap-and-trade system to control mercury. CAMR was never implemented as it was vacated by the Court in 2008 in *New Jersey v. EPA*. It was replaced by the Mercury and Air Toxics Standards (MATS) in 2011. A set of technology-based emissions limitation standards for mercury and other toxic air pollutants, MATS reflects levels achieved by the best-performing sources currently in operation. These new standards have effectively accelerated the retirement of coal-fired power plants in the US with the consequent elimination of their air pollution emissions but without taking advantage of potential compliance cost-minimization opportunities that the CAMR cap-and-trade market-based approach would have provided.

Another was CAIR, which affects twenty-five Eastern states and the District of Columbia and was introduced to achieve further emission reductions beyond both ARP and NBP in order to reduce fine particulate matter and ground-level ozone pollution (US EPA 2005). CAIR created three separate compliance programs: 1) phasing in a declining annual cap for NO_x emissions; 2) expanding the regional scope of the seasonal NO_x program to control ozone by replacing NBP with the larger CAIR region; and 3) making the ARP SO_2 emissions targets more stringent in this region.

The universal cap on SO_2 emissions, a fundamental policy design parameter of the cap-and-trade ETS, which had been politically negotiated and was legislated in Title IV of the 1990 CAA Amendments, was perceived for many years by the electricity sector as set in stone. This provided a long view for managing risk by this capital-intensive industry in the newly created US environmental commodities market. However, the new regulatory context proposed by EPA prompted legal battles during 2008, resulting in the suspension of the CAIR rule by the US Circuit Court of Appeals of the District of Columbia in *North Carolina v. EPA*.

Later in 2008, the court ordered EPA to revise the rule while keeping the compliance programs in place until the new one addressed the court's concerns. The CSAPR was finalized on July 2011 and was intended to replace CAIR. However, on December 30, 2011, the court reinstated CAIR pending the resolution of legal challenges against the new rule. On August 21, 2012 the court rejected CSAPR in *EME HOMER CITY GENERATION, L.P., vs. EPA* for violation of federal law. These developments have caused unprecedented regulatory uncertainty for market participants within the ARP, resulting in strong downward pressure on SO_2 allowance prices. They have also prompted concern from some analysts about the future of the US emissions trading program in general, particularly in the context of emerging climate legislation and other cyclical and structural factors.

External conditions will always change and will impact commodity prices accordingly. While ARP has been successful in providing certainty about environmental goals, unexpected program adjustments and the lack of predictable (i.e., legislated) paths for changes in policy have caused environmental markets in the US to get the jitters. Some have even predicted that the market for SO_2 allowances might never recover, as it is perceived as irrelevant by some observers.

Environmental commodities traders have pointed to a number of factors that contributed to the 2009 drop in allowance prices (Bravender 2009). For instance, the pervasive global economic downturn, which began stressing companies' finances in 2007–2008, is limiting investment decisions and economic growth. Natural gas prices are also impacting the power industry in the US, and in 2012 they hit historic lows due to abundant production arising from shale gas (i.e., by unconventional industrial processes) in North America (IER 2012). Natural gas-fired boilers have low SO_2 emissions (and half the CO_2 content) compared with coal-fired plants.

By 2012, the combined effects of the drop in natural gas prices, the reduction in electricity demand caused by the recession, and the closure of coal-fired generators due to the MATS program had resulted in a significant decline in emissions from power plants, which in turn lessened the demand for environmental commodities. As a result, the allowance market became oversupplied. More importantly, legal and regulatory uncertainties currently are the main reasons for the downtrend in allowance prices. The patchwork of rules resulting from EPA rule adjustments and legal challenges to them has impacted the market negatively. The value of the allowances has been put into question as new rules deem these entitlements unusable for compliance, rendering participation in the market as worthless. For instance, "companies' willingness to make early reduction emissions now and bank them forward" was undermined by the impasse created by the legal challenges to CAIR (Bravender 2009). As stated by an environmental commodities broker's explanation of the record low allowance prices in 2012: "other commodities markets are run by pure economics, fundamentals will win over time, but regulatory markets like these ones have made evident the threat of rule changes, and markets do not like that."

Ultimately, this market behavior can be seen as a reflection of expectations and adjustments to change by market participants, particularly in how they perceive the evolutionary nature of ETS. But again, conditions change. If there is a credible commitment by regulators to the permanence of the ETS approach, for instance, with clear and predictable paths for regulatory adjustments, this long-term commitment will be conducive to proper market functioning and the continued evolution

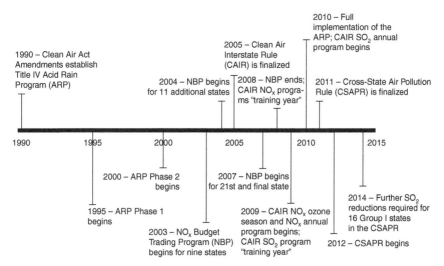

Figure 5.1 History of CAIR, ARP, CSAPR, and Former NBP
Source: EPA, 2011

of the use of environmental commodities markets as a means to limit air pollution emissions and minimize the cost of achieving a cleaner environment.

On August 22, 2012, the D.C. Circuit Court once again vacated the transport rule (i.e., CSAPR) and ordered EPA to draft new rules. In the interim, EPA must continue implementing CAIR. This decision cancels the implementation of further SO_2 emissions reductions in 16 states in the region starting January 1, 2014, as planned under CSAPR. Figure 5.1 provides a summary of the history of institutional developments in market-based policymaking at the federal level in the US.

Today, many consider the ARP as a major innovation and success story in market-based environmental policy.[1] The final 2010 limit on SO_2 emissions sets a permanent cap at 8.95 million tons per year nationwide, which is about one half the emissions from electric power plants in 1980. While there is room for improvement in cost savings and environmental restoration, this precedent-setting cap-and-trade air pollution control policy design has delivered on the promise of producing environmental and human health benefits at lower-than-expected compliance costs, as well as inducing technological change and process innovation to achieve emission reductions, demonstrating that the cap-and-trade policy approach works.

This chapter identifies the specific market design features that made the SO_2 allowance cap-and-trade policy feasible. It also explores how social and institutional dimensions reduced the efficiency (i.e., cost-saving potential) of the ARP but enhanced the political feasibility of the program. In order to understand why emissions trading became part of the CAA amendments of 1990, it is also necessary to review the political and institutional environment of air quality management in the US at the end of the 1980s.

5.1 The political economy of acid rain policy action

In 1990, a shift in the policy dynamics of clean air politics made for a favorable climate for the emergence of the first large-scale emissions trading program to control air pollution. The primary factors at work were increased societal awareness, American presidential leadership, Canadian diplomatic pressure, and a renewed spirit of international co-operation.[2] Other positive factors included increased scientific evidence of acid rain's negative impacts and the experience gained by EPA during previous attempts to implement air pollution trading systems and the Lead Phasedown Program. The ARP's cap-and-trade policy design represented a new way of doing business in environmental regulation. It shifted the traditional adversarial relationship between industry and environmental administrators to one of co-operation and partnership.

5.1.1 Political factors that supported SO₂ cap-and-trade

After the failed attempt by President Ronald Reagan and industry to weaken the CAA in 1981, Congress focused on strengthening the programs directed at acid rain and toxic air pollution reduction (Waxman 1991). The resistance of interest groups representing coal-mining states, the electric utility industry,[3] and the Reagan administration blocked progress, but loud calls for action emerged in Congress and elsewhere at the end of the decade.

In 1988, Project 88, an influential report was commissioned by Senators Timothy E. Wirth and John Heinz recommending the use of emissions trading. The study, led by Harvard Professor Robert N. Stavins, provided legislators with economic and policy analyses in support of the idea of "harnessing market forces to protect the environment." The study also argued that it would be helpful to address the acid rain issue by extending the emissions trading initiatives already in place at the time with a system of "marketable emissions permits" (Wirth and Heinz 1988).

Following campaign promises, President George Bush Sr. declared himself an "environmental president" in 1989, sparking renewed interest in air quality management. He had good political reasons for focusing his attention there. First, by 1989 the public viewed acid rain as one of the most serious environmental problems the country faced, which lent political support for strong acid rain legislation. Second, it was compatible with the new president's interest in foreign policy. In fact, acid rain was a central topic of the agenda during his first trip to Canada, as acid rain had become a transboundary issue. As the impact of acid rain became more evident to society and emerged as a source of diplomatic tensions with Canada, it became a policy priority in environmental protection policy.

By then the Environmental Defense Fund (EDF), a leading environmental advocacy organization, was energetically promoting the idea of implementing ETS as an alternative approach for air pollution control. According to Bryner (1995, 116), EDF's support was "critical in gaining congressional acceptance." EDF reports its past policy advocacy efforts as follows:

In 1989 and 1990, EDF was widely credited for advancing the "cap-and-trade" proposal to reduce acid rain emissions embraced by the Bush administration and then enacted by Congress as part of the Clean Air Act Amendments of 1990.
(Environmental Defense 2000)

Acknowledgment by a highly respected environmental group that a balance could be struck between the dual goals of economic development and environmental protection by implementing the emissions trading concept was politically valuable. The EPA took EDF's policy proposal and made it operational. President George Bush Sr. announced his decision to use markets to address the acid rain problem on June 12, 1989:

We seek reforms that make major pollution reductions where we most need them. First, our approach has reasonable deadlines for those who must comply. It has compelling sanctions for those who don't. It accounts for continued economic growth and expansion; offers incentives, choice, and flexibility for industry to find the best solutions; and taps the power of the market-place and local initiative better than any previous piece of environmental legislation.

(1989)

In 1990, EPA had announced that "the US GNP percentage devoted to environmental protection was to grow from 1.9 percent in 1990 to about 2.7 percent by the year 2000" (US EPA 1990). It forewarned that most of these costs were going to be borne by the private sector, causing concern about possible damage to US industry competitiveness.[4] This forecast gave support to the idea of implementing more cost-effective environmental protection programs such as an ETS. The 1990 CAA Amendments ultimately "expanded the regulatory control requirements of previous clean air regulation" (GAO 1993). Hailed as an innovative approach to pollution control, Title IV of the act established a new market-based regulatory program for controlling SO_2 emissions to address both dry and wet sulfate deposition, the latter being the main precursor of what is commonly known as acid rain. The cap-and-trade mechanism promised to bring about significant, cost-effective reductions in SO_2 emissions from the electric power sector.

EPA also decided to take advantage of advanced information management systems and accurate emissions monitoring devices as the program was implemented. This had several benefits. It resulted in reduced information costs to the regulator in verifying emission reductions, and it increased transparency by making data available through the Internet. The electronic monitoring, verification, and reporting of emissions also enhanced the integrity of the new system, as it ensured that the mandated predetermined emissions limit would be met. These electronic communication systems allowed for the implementation of automatic, strong sanctions against non-compliant emitters, enhancing the program's credibility among the environmental community.

In addition to improved program design and smart management, the implementation of the new ETS for SO_2 emissions necessitated advances in co-operation between state and industry to induce change in technology and processes to achieve its environmental goals. As President Bush Sr. stated: "Our challenge is to develop an emissions trading plan; their challenge is to meet the standards" (Bush 1989). William K. Reilly, EPA Administrator under the first Bush administration, wrote:

> I find the market-incentive approach especially appealing for two reasons: it makes the private sector a partner, rather than an adversary, in controlling pollution and reducing environmental risk; and it leverages the government's limited resources by exploiting market forces to achieve environmental goals.
>
> (1989)

The new ARP addressed the concerns of those opposed to costly regulation by being decentralized, flexible, and efficient. The revamped ETS for SO_2 emissions made it an environmental initiative (perhaps the only one) that industry-oriented and conservative members of Congress could accept (Bryner 1995, 115–116).

5.1.2 Evidence-based decision making: precedents and cost–benefit analysis

In the 1970s, a temporary program to phase lead out of gasoline in a more flexible manner was able to save over $200 million a year in compliance costs to refiners (Nussbaum 1992). This incentive-based program confirmed that savings could be achieved through a flexible mechanism. This policy experience and the accumulated research on potential cost savings gave support to the idea of deploying a full-fledged ETS to supplement conventional air pollution control regulation to address the acid rain problem.

Lead Phasedown Program: In 1973, EPA created the Lead Phasedown Program to set limits on the total amount of lead allowed in gasoline. At the time, the toxic effects of lead, particularly on children, became highly publicized and led to support for regulatory action. Ten years later, EPA estimated $36 billion (in 1983 US dollars) in benefits from reduced adverse health effects, versus $2.6 billion in cost to the refining industry if a more stringent control of 0.10 grams per leaded gallon standard were to be established. The advantage in terms of costs versus benefits for conventional regulation was clear. EPA introduced economic incentives as an innovative means to accelerate compliance while capping the toxic substance.

A fixed amount of lead rights (to be used during the transition to capping lead in gasoline) was distributed to participating refiners. If refiners were able to comply early by meeting the new fuel standard, they were allowed to sell their rights to other refiners. This regulatory design, based on the trading and banking concepts, created the incentives to phase out lead early and gain from the rights by selling them to other program participants. In turn, refiners with higher compliance cost (commonly small refineries) were better able to manage the transition.

This program actually resulted in earlier compliance because of the flexibility derived from inter-refinery trades. In other words, a politically negotiated deadline that would have been technically feasible for all refiners might have delayed compliance among those who had the capacity to do so earlier. The lead trading mechanism ran from 1982 to 1986 and the banking feature from 1985 to 1987. The success of this program helped to gain support for the next generation of ETS.

Potential Cost Savings and Environmental Impact: Ex ante assessments found that air emissions trading should reduce air pollution compliance costs from 50 to 95 percent (OECD 1997, 59). In 1992, EPA analyzed reports supporting this conclusion. Table 5.1 summarizes these reports.

The right-hand column gives EPA's estimates of the ratio of command-and-control cost to the lowest cost of meeting the same objective using economic incentives. All of the estimates exceed 1.0, indicating a potential cost savings over command-and-control.

Prior to these developments, in 1980 Congress authorized an inter-agency research effort regarding acid rain, The National Acid Precipitation Assessment Program (NAPAP), to study and report ten years later (in 1990) on the causes and effects of acid rain. The $570 million research program focused on assessing the risks to the environment and humans versus the cleanup costs.[5] A key concern about implementing an ETS at the time was the possibility of creating localized and temporal environmental problems or hot spots. NAPAP indicated there was a low risk of such events happening.

By the end of the 1980s, policy innovators at EPA had realized that a combination of political, economic, and technical elements should be aligned in order to introduce more cost-effective alternative policy mechanisms, such as emissions trading, to address air pollution. As seen in Chapter 4, high transaction costs and low credibility were the main flaws of the first-generation trading systems (i.e., the offset and bubble programs), and the political climate combined with the lack of understanding about the ETS concept produced barriers to the establishment of a properly functioning emissions market.

The emergence of the ARP SO_2 ETS represented a breakthrough in the evolution of market-based air quality regulation. The conventional regulatory approach relied on specific technical (e.g., scrubbers) or operational (e.g., performance standards) requirements, usually resulting in a restriction on the rate of emissions discharge but not on total discharges. As long as air pollution sources met these requirements, they were not held liable if the projected levels of reductions were not achieved (Environmental Defense 2000, 4).

Table 5.1 The EPA survey on emission trading program cost-effectiveness

Pollutants controlled	Study, year, and source	Geographic area	Command-and-control	Ratio of CAC cost to least cost
AIR—criteria pollutants				
Hydrocarbons	Maloney and Yandle (1984) T	Domestic Dupont Plants	Uniform percentage reduction	4.15[a]
Lead in gasoline	US EPA (1985) A	United States	Uniform standards for lead gasoline	See footnote for savings[b]
Nitrogen dioxide (NO_2)	Sesking et al. (1983) T	Chicago	Proposed RACT regulations	14.4
NO_2	Krupnick (1986)	Baltimore	Proposed RACT regulations	5.96
Particulates (TSP)	Atkinson and Lewis (1974) T	St. Louis	SIP regulations	6.0[c]
TSP	McGartland (1984)	Baltimore	SIP regulations	4.18
TSP	Spofford (1984) T	Lower Delaware Valley	Uniform percentage reduction	22.0
TSP	Oates et al. (1989) O	Baltimore	Equal proportional treatment	4.0 at 90 $\mu g/m^3$
Reactive organic gases/NO_2	SCAQMD (Spring 1992) O	Southern California	Best available technology	1.5 in 1994
Sulfur dioxide	Roach et al. (1981) T	Four Corners Area	SIP regulation	4.25
Sulfur dioxide	Atkinson (1983)	Cleveland		1.5
Sulfur dioxide	Spofford (1984) T	Lower Delaware Valley	Uniform percentage reduction	1.78
Sulfur dioxide	ICF Resources (1989) O	United States	Uniform emissions limit	5.0
Sulfates	Hahn and Noll (1982) T	Los Angeles	California emissions standards	1.07[d]
Six-air criteria	Kohn (1978) A	St. Louis		
Other				
Chloro-fluorocarbons	Palmer et al. (1980);Shapiro and Warhit (1983) T	United States	Proposed emissions standards	1.96
Airport noise	Harrison (1983) T	United States	Mandatory retrofit	1.72[e]

Source: EPA 1992; A—Anderson et al. (1989); O—original reference; T—Tietenberg (1985), Table 5. See also OECD (1997).

Notes:

a   Based on 85 percent reduction of emissions from all sources.

b   The trading of lead credits reduced the cost to refiners of the lead phase by about $225 million.

c   Ratio based on 40 $\mu g/m^3$ at worst receptor, as given in Tietenberg (1985), Table 4.

d   Ratio based on a short-term one-hour average of 250 $\mu g/m^3$.

e   Because it is a benefit–cost study instead of a cost-effectiveness study, the Harrison comparison of the CAC approach with the least-cost allocation involves different benefit levels. Specifically, the benefit levels associated with the least-cost allocation are only 82 percent of those associated with the CAC allocation. To produce cost estimates based on more comparable benefits, as a first approximation the least-cost allocation was divided by 0.82 and the resulting number compared with the CAC cost.

Acronyms Used: CAC—command-and-control, the conventional regulatory approach. RACT—reasonably available control technologies. SIP—state implementation plan.

While some progress had been made toward introducing flexibility to reduce regulatory compliance costs through the use of performance standards and experimentation with limited trading programs, until 1990 the US air quality management regulatory system overall remained mostly based on the effective, but relatively costly, command-and-control approach.

5.1.3 The Acid Rain Program cap-and-trade policy design

Although a minor part of the overall air quality management plan mandated in the 1990 CAA Amendments, Title IV became the center of attention for stakeholders in environmental policymaking by introducing a new version of the emissions trading concept that covered a large percentage of US SO_2 emissions—the cap-and-trade approach. Title IV provided for the creation of the world's first large-scale environmental commodities market to reduce cumulative pollution *and* reduce compliance costs for the electric generation industry.

The ARP policy design is simple, predictable, and transparent. It sets a permanent cap on the total amount of SO_2 that may be emitted by electric utilities nationwide at about one half of the amount emitted in 1980 by this sector.[6] However, it allows individual utilities to select their method of compliance; individual control requirements are not specified for sources. The only requirements are that sources (1) completely and accurately measure and report all emissions and (2) hold the same number of allowances as reported emissions in each compliance period.

Electric generation plants in the US account for more than 70 percent of total SO_2 emissions through combustion of fossil fuels. Metal smelting, other industrial processes, and transportation produce the remaining 30 percent. The ARP goal is to cap annual SO_2 emissions from electricity generators at 8.95 million tons per year starting in 2010. Program participants can trade allowances or bank them for future use. There are few restrictions for trading allowances, but strict and transparent monitoring, verification, and reporting protocols ensure the environmental performance of the ARP ETS.

The ARP also imposes an emissions limit of 5.6 million tons for other industrial sources (e.g., stationary fossil fuel-fired combustion devices) (1990 CAA § 406b). If this cap is exceeded, EPA can issue regulations to reduce emissions in these sectors. However, commercial, institutional, and residential sources were excluded from the ARP.[7] Only electric utilities (or "affected sources") take part in the trading component of the ARP.[8] Units within affected sources are subject to the emissions reduction requirements under Title IV.[9] The program was implemented in two phases. Table 5.2 shows key dates and stages for the implementation of Title IV.

Within individual power plants, there are often multiple, separate power generation units. For Phase I, Congress selected 263 utility electric generation units in 110 power plants—the highest-emitting and largest units. These units emitted 57 percent of all utility emissions in 1985 and produced only about 17 percent of total electric generation capacity.[10] These units are often called "Table 1 units" because they are officially listed (1990 CAA 40 CFR 73.10) in Table 1 of the allowance allocation regulation (US EPA 1998).

Table 5.2 Title IV implementation history—schedule of the SO_2 allowance trading program

1980	(Actual level)
	SO_2 emissions: 17.5 million tons
1990	Clean Air Act Amendments
1995	Phase I
	Cap-and-trade begins
	Units listed in Table 1 and advanced participation from Phase II units (i.e., opt-in feature)
2000	Phase II
	All sources with an output capacity of greater than 25 megawatts
2010	(Required level)
	SO_2 emissions: 8.95 million tons

Beginning at the onset of Phase II in 2000, the volume of emissions allowances allocated annually to Phase I units was reduced, and the requirement to hold allowances was extended to smaller, cleaner plants. By 2009, the ARP affected approximately 3100 electric utilities. Nationwide, the cap for all utilities with an output capacity of greater than 25 megawatts is an aggregate annual emission limit of 9.48 million allowances from 2000 through 2009.[11] For 2010, the annual cap was reduced further to 8.95 million allowances, a level below one half the amount of industry-wide emissions in 1980.

To strengthen the environmental integrity of early emissions trading mechanisms, the CAA mandated the installation of electronic monitoring systems to measure flue gas emissions continuously at the dirtiest coal-fired electric utilities (i.e., Table 1 units) (US Code 1990). Initially, precision measurement of emissions proved more elusive than expected. Ultimately, however, advances in information technologies, the decision by policy designers to take advantage of new digital data management, and the deployed electronic monitoring systems allowed the SO_2 allowance trading system to become operational, transparent, and credible (Pérez Henríquez 2004).

To correct the measurement problem, the 1990 CAA amendments expanded the Continuous Emissions Monitoring Systems (CEMS) mandate to all Phase I and Phase II units and introduced protocols and evaluation procedures to ensure accurate emissions data. The emissions readings of these devices and the electronic transmissions of this information to regulators now offer "sufficient confidence in the accuracy of emissions accounting to dispense with ancillary review and approval of emission reductions" (Ellerman et al. 1997, 46–47).

Finally, the creation of a market for SO_2 allowances was designed to supplement, not replace, the conventional regulatory framework. If the trading system failed, conventional regulatory mechanisms remained in effect.

5.1.4. Reactions by industry to the costs of alternative acid rain regulation

Electric utilities, their fuel suppliers, and, ultimately, electricity consumers are affected by the costs of alternative acid rain regulation, projections on electricity demand, and cost of fuels (e.g., coal, gas, and oil). Prior to 2011, more than half of the electricity consumed in the US was generated using coal (US DOE 2000). Coal mined in the Eastern US has a high sulfur content, while that from the West has less. Because coal-burning power plants use primarily locally mined coal, SO_2 emissions vary based on the location of the electricity generation plant.

Under a flexible policy approach where emitters have choice, emissions reductions would be achieved through a mix of switching to lower-sulfur fuels and installing flue-gas desulfurization units (i.e., scrubbers). Companies could choose between these solutions based on costs or, if applicable, legal requirements. Both options have politically undesirable consequences for elected officials: fuel switching causes electricity producers to substitute toward Western, low-sulfur coal, affecting local economies in the East. Scrubbing allows the continued use of high-sulfur coal but imposes high capital costs on the electric utility industry (US Congress 1985, 140).

Throughout the 1980s, legislation introduced in Congress for SO_2 reductions reflected competing regional interests. In 1985, the different legislative proposals to control acid rain pollution were estimated to cost between $3 and $6 billion per year by the Office of Technology Assessment, with a possible increase of environmental regulatory costs from 5 to 10 percent and electricity cost increases ranging from 10 to 15 percent as well as indirect costs for local economies (US Congress 1985, 3).

Pro-scrubber standards were introduced to protect Eastern coal producers. "The fight over universal scrubbing was among the most intense inter-industry conflicts that Congress confronted" during the authorization of the 1977 CAA. Moreover, "what was most important in tipping the balance of influence in Congress was that Eastern coal producers enjoyed the support of two powerful non-industry constituencies: the environmental lobby, and organized labor, particularly the United Mine Workers" (US Congress 1985, 378). The environmental movement was seeking stricter performance standards for industry, and the coal unions aimed to protect high-sulfur coal demand through scrubbing.

Observers criticized this political alliance as well as the resulting policy. The so-called "new source bias" was described as inefficient (Ackerman and Hassler 1981). The 1977 amendments to the CAA assumed that new and cleaner plants would eventually replace old facilities, leading to capital stock turnover. Therefore, most of the pollution control requirements were targeted at new plants. However, the problems were centered on older plants (Baylor 1990, 48). In 1990, plants constructed before 1970 emitted two-thirds of the acid rain precursors. The pro-scrubber faction continued to gain influence, despite opposition from those supporting Western coal interests (US Senate 1993, 69). Title IV explicitly encourages the use of scrubbers through special bonus-allowance provisions to existing sources, though observers regarded this as a potentially inefficient feature of the program (Ellerman et al. 1997, 48).

Perverse incentives in the new source bias rules can lead to a situation where older, dirtier plants work at full capacity or for longer than is economically efficient, while cleaner plants operate below capacity. Moreover, because of special provisions and laxer standards for existing sources, new and cleaner plants are not even built. In other words, a "differential system" with "stricter standards for new and substantially modified plants make building a new plant or substantially modifying an old plant more expensive propositions than they otherwise would be" (Nash and Revesz 2007, p. 1708).

Recent analyses show that utilities ultimately invested heavily in post-combustion scrubbing technologies, expecting high prices in the future for the newly created SO_2 allowances (Palmer and Evans 2009; Burtraw and Szembelan, 2009). ARP changed the incentive structure in the electric power generation industry by making it attractive to invest in scrubbing technology, given that units would get to keep or surrender the new financial asset that the SO_2 allowance represents depending on their level of emissions. This made it particularly appealing for Midwestern Phase I units to minimize emissions, because sulfur can be removed from their coal-burning facilities relatively easily. Ironically, deregulation in another sector of the economy, the US railroad system, reduced the cost of transporting Western low-sulfur coal, thus increasing its market share while easing compliance for Midwest utilities (Ellerman et al. 2000, 104).

Historically, the lion's share of SO_2 emission reductions, approximately 70–90 percent, comes from switching to other cleaner and cheaper fuels, such as low-sulfur coal, natural gas, and low-sulfur petroleum. The use of costly scrubbers as an emission reduction strategy has actually declined with time (Ellerman 2003; Burtraw and Szembelan, 2009). While emissions have been sharply reduced, electricity generation from fossil fuel-fired electric plants has increased. Moreover, the average retail price of electricity (in real terms) is currently less than it was in 1990 when Title IV was made into law (Keohane 2008). Estimates of the cost of compliance from a fully implemented Phase II are projected to be in the $1–1.5 billion range, depending on fuel prices, technological change, and the use of the ARP ETS (Ellerman 2003). In contrast, the NAPAP study had projected in 1990 that ARP's total cost would be approximately $6 billion.

5.2 Creating a market for SO_2 allowances

The following is a list of key market-creation parameters included in the ARP. These are the policy design elements in the ARP ETS that allowed for the implementation of a workable trading mechanism to complement air pollution control regulation.

5.2.1 Implementing market-creation parameters for SO_2 allowance trading

5.2.1 (A) Environmental commodities: defining the acid rain allowance entitlements

Select the Emission to Control: Title IV of the 1990 CAA Amendments affects both SO_2 and NO_x emissions.[12] However, the major part of the program concerns SO_2 emissions reduction through a system of fully tradable allowances applicable to electricity generation utilities.

In setting the National Ambient Air Quality Standards (NAAQS) for sulfur oxides (SO_x), the CAA first focused on the health effects of SO_2 alone and in combination with other pollutants such as NO_x.[13] A secondary standard protects aspects of human welfare other than health, such as aesthetics (e.g., visibility), damage to man-made structures (e.g., buildings and monuments), and the biosphere.[14] The CAA requires that the EPA administrator publish a list of pollutants having adverse effects on public health or welfare that are emitted from stationary or mobile sources (1990 CAA, 42 US C. 7473, § 108a1). For each pollutant, the administrator must compile and publish a criteria document.[15] The criteria documents are scientific compendia of the studies documenting adverse effects of specific pollutants at various concentrations in the ambient air (US EPA 2000).

Given that 70 percent of total SO_2 emissions are generated by fossil fuel-fired units in electric generation utilities, and recognizing the economic importance of this sector for the rest of the US economy, it was important to reduce the cost of compliance to meet the emissions reduction goal. The context of implementation within a relatively homogeneous and highly regulated and monitored industry sector such as electric generation offered a unique opportunity to experiment with controlling SO_2 emissions using an ETS. The remaining 30 percent of SO_2 emissions generated by non-utility combustion devices such as industrial and manufacturing processes, as well as transportation sources, was controlled by more conventional regulatory approaches.

Local emission ceilings imposed by NAAQS are still in place to address public concerns about possible harmful concentrations of pollutants or "hot spots," while allowing the ARP to operate at the national level. This policy approach is known as "regulatory tiering," which is the application of several regulatory regimes at the same time (Tietenberg 1995, 89). The right to exceed these standards to protect public health and welfare is reserved by the states and localities. The ARP cannot undercut local and regional air quality management programs.

Therefore, the 1990 CAA NAAQS enabled the ARP ETS to not be limited by spatial considerations, allowing for national trading. The ARP could then drive down local levels of pollution beyond these emissions standards. This policy design feature was tested in 2005 when CAIR effectively reduced the cap under Title IV and began treating facilities differently based on location. This spatial adjustment to the controlled pollutant was introduced to reduce SO_2 emissions in upwind states. Plants in the affected states that were causing more damage because of their location had to surrender more allowances than previously determined under ARP. As mentioned previously, these compliance programs were legally contested. In July 2008, the D.C. Circuit Court of Appeals partially vacated CAIR for not being able to assure the protection of downwind states' ambient quality standards. However, in December 2008, the court allowed EPA to maintain CAIR operational for two years while developing an alternate program (i.e., CSAPR) with CSAPR rejected, CAIR remains in place temporarily.

Though a contributor to acidification, NO_X was never made nationally tradable. The principal reason why it was not regulated was to avoid the added complexity in the cap-and-trade design that would come from combining regulated air pollutants in the then-new ARP ETS. However, NOx is a regionally traded pollutant, and new approaches to control for it have emerged, which are reviewed later in this book (i.e., 2003 NBP, 2005 CAIR, and the 2011 CSAPR).

Define the Extent of the Entitlement: Title IV authorized EPA to issue known and credible allowance rights that could be bought, sold, or banked.

The term "allowance" means an authorization allocated to an affected unit by EPA under Title IV to emit one ton of sulfur dioxide (1990 CAA, 42 US C. 7651a, § 402). This term was preferred over "permits" because the latter conveys the idea of a document issued after specific requirements have been fulfilled. In contrast, "allowance" is closer to the concept of a "right" or "entitlement" that could become a tradable commodity—a fungible good. In addition to the possibility of transactions among initial allowance holders, these entitlements may also be traded, bought, or sold by other market participants such as brokers.[16] To provide industry with greater flexibility, EPA has attempted to define a set of quasi-property rights that places few restrictions on their use. However, at the same time, EPA has to avoid giving firms a property right to their existing level of pollution, which would not reduce emissions.[17]

The SO_2 allowance is, therefore, an authorization to emit, rather than a property right on pollution. Under US law, this subtle distinction in the definition of the allowance entitlement means that the US government can take away some allowances if needed to improve the performance of air pollution control policies. By not calling them property rights, the government eliminated the need to compensate holders for the lost rights if the standard had to be more stringent, which otherwise would have been considered as a taking.[18]

Title IV explicitly preserved the existing CAA authority of Congress and EPA to impose additional restrictions on SO_2 if necessary. As suggested in Hahn and Noll (1982, 119–146), future allowances are expected to be reduced only in "extreme circumstances." However, if allowance budgets of emission sources are reduced after initial allocation, regulators should be careful to minimize uncertainty about the availability of future streams of allowances. Currently, the emissions limit is firmly established in legislation and difficult to change, making it unlikely that the government would take away any allocated allowance (OECD 1998, 11). This in turn gives certainty to market participants, which is a key feature of a properly functioning emissions market.[19]

Such careful policy crafting provided the SO_2 ETS with a clear and certain institutional environment that reduces the risk of participating in the allowance trading market. Friedman suggests that the success of the ARP was initially contingent on the extent to which the allowance system was credible over the long term:

> In order to create a new market in pollution allowances, it was critical that the government would issue known and credible allowance rights that apply over a

long period. The ability to sell these streams is crucial in order to get the utilities to invest in expensive but cleaner generating plants for the future. Based on the early success of this policy, the government's commitment clearly has been taken to be credible.

(1999, 217)

Appropriate risk management and the regulatory certainty that allows for long-range planning are important for the smooth functioning of an emerging environmental commodities market. However, regulatory changes such as the introduction of the 2005 CAIR rule, while environmentally and economically sound, can indeed change the perception of permanence in the allowance entitlement system and affect market participants' behavior. The implementation of the CAIR compliance programs in 2005, combined with other events, such as the impact on natural gas prices of hurricanes Rita and Katrina, and guidance from the environmental finance industry on SO_2 allowance price forecasts during that period, resulted in a drastic increase in allowance prices.

Prices reached $1600 per ton at the end of 2005, from a range of $150–200 since the inception of the ARP (Burtraw and Szambelan, 2009, 9). In 2008, when CAIR was suspended by the court, regulatory uncertainty caused inter-firm SO_2 allowances trading to decline from a historical high of almost 12.7 million allowances in 2000 (Chicago Climate Futures Exchange 2004), to less than one million that year. EPA is working to address the court's concerns, and Congress is considering passing legislation on this rule to enhance regulatory certainty.

Create a Homogeneous Unit: An SO_2 allowance is a limited authorization for a fuel-fired combustion unit within an electric utility to emit one ton of SO_2.

The unit of trade is defined as an SO_2 allowance—the entitlement to emit one ton of SO_2. With limited exceptions, the program is defined solely in terms of emissions tonnage rather than as a technological standard (which often is expressed in terms of an emissions rate or specified technology) (US EPA 1994, 73). However, this definition faced stiff opposition from most of the utility industries. First, the overall goal proposed by EPA in its 1991 initial implementation rules was more stringent than expected.[20] Secondly, a tonnage system represented a shift from the conventional emissions rate system that was well understood by utilities and regulators. The nature of electric utilities as regulated monopolies allows them to transfer to consumers some necessary expenses, such as the environmental compliance costs derived from centralized commands. Under the ARP, there is no room for negotiations about regulation by state public utilities commissions.

Despite the resistance, the tonnage system was favored because it is clear and transparent. Under Title IV, each utility has to meet emissions allowance limits by specific deadlines. No other negotiations would occur under the program, except those that occurred in the marketplace to trade SO_2 emissions allowances for environmental compliance. As Kette states, "The politics of jobs and utility rates were considered too strong to leave to the states to resist." To sidestep this problem, the federal law directly imposes emissions limits (or annual emissions budgets) to specific affected power plants in two compliance phases, taking into account size and historical emission levels. As a political matter, these emissions limits should not be negotiable (Kette 1993, 172).

As suggested by Salzman and Ruhl (2000), a new tradable commodity must assume fungibility. In other words, the tradable units must be sufficiently similar in ways important to the goals of environmental protection and resource allocation efficiency. So far, electric utilities consistently have achieved almost full compliance throughout the first two phases of the ARP. Moreover, a historical review of the ARP ETS performance shows thickening of the market for SO_2, confirming that buyers and sellers recognize SO_2 allowances as fungible homogeneous units of trade.

Establish Exchange Ratios: Title IV provides for allowances to be traded nationally, implicitly giving them equal environmental value across different air basins and regions.

Because the region for an acid rain problem is smaller than the whole nation and no review or prior approval of trades is required, emissions trading could lead to regional hot spots.[21] This result depends on the configuration and location of sources. As mentioned previously, "regulatory tiering" is used to solve this problem. In 2005, EDF reported that the coal-fired electric utilities based in the Ohio Valley were "responsible for two-thirds of the nation's sulfur dioxide and one-fifth of nitrogen oxide pollution" (Environmental Defense 2005, 1). Taking into consideration demands by environmentalists for stricter smog standards and the State of North Carolina's invocation of the Clean Air Act's "good neighbor provisions" that require states to eliminate emissions that substantially contribute to dirty air in downwind states (which in 2008 became a lawsuit), EPA issued the CAIR rule to supplement the ETS approach.

In this new regulatory context, exchange rates had to be established. Sources in the CAIR region are required to surrender for compliance two ARP allowances for every ton of emissions from 2010 to 2014 (one allowance for ARP and one allowance for CAIR), and 2.86 allowances for every ton as a permanent cap (one allowance for ARP and 1.86 for CAIR). Once an ARP allowance has been used for compliance with the CAIR SO_2 cap-and-trade program, it cannot be used again under either program. Several states and utilities demanded a judicial review of the statutory authority of EPA in issuing the CAIR rule, so the permanence of this feature for satisfying compliance in both CAIR and the ARP was in question. It was dependent on the court accepting EPA's revised rule (i.e., CSAPR), introduced in 2011 but rejected in 2012, or on legislative action from Congress to make it a statutory mandate.

Establish Duration: Each allowance permits the emission of one ton of SO_2 during or after a specified calendar year. For firms to trust that allowances will hold their value and continue to be issued in future years, it is important that regulators manifest a credible commitment to the program and establish how long permits will be valid. Currently, allowances are issued and transactions are monitored by EPA through the electronic tools provided by the Clean Air Markets Division Business System (CBS) on a vintage-year basis from 2000 to 2030 (and beyond), setting an indefinite time horizon for the program.

(1) *Allowance duration*: Under Title IV, the duration of an allowance is indefinite. Each allowance has a serial number and date (indicating the first year in which it can be used) entitling the holder to emit one ton of SO_2. For each ton of SO_2 emitted in a given year, one allowance is required after which it cannot be used again. Due to the banking provisions of the program, unused allowances may be held indefinitely for future use. The fixed emissions ceiling of a tradable allowance program minimizes potential environmental harm from opportunistic behavior from regulated parties or other unexpected sources.

(2) *Program duration:* A remaining concern about the SO_2 allowance system is the possibility of revocation or cessation of the quasi-property rights issued through the SO_2 allowance system in the future. To date, the SO_2 allowances trading program has been considered a permanent component of EPA's Clean Air Markets Program. Its permanent cap has been fully implemented since 2010, and the program is expected to continue indefinitely—and participants perceive that it will. In the face of new scientific knowledge about air pollution effects, however, adaptive environmental management strategies (or political demand) may require the reduction of the legislated universal emissions cap.[22] CAIR has brought this issue to the fore of the ARP ETS operation and tested the flexibility of its programmatic design. In the process, it has exposed to judicial challenge the legal authority of EPA to incorporate these developments through administrative measures. While the new rule attempts to preserve the value of banked emissions, the changes were perceived as a risk to the continued operation of the ARP ETS. A clear path for policy adjustments affecting these entitlements (as described in Chapter 8, Australia's carbon pricing law) should be considered in the US emissions trading regulatory frameworks in order to enhance certainty and predictability for market participants.

Set a Baseline: Setting emissions baselines for each affected source is essential for determining the initial allocation.

The broad approach for setting emissions baselines has been a fundamental reason for the success of the ARP. Underlying all compliance aspects of the program is the baseline determining the allowance budget for each affected source. The baseline to establish the aggregate cap of the SO_2 allowances trading program was politically determined based on the availability and quality of emissions inventories. However, determining each participating source's baseline was technically complex. There were, and are, only two complete sources of past SO_2 emissions estimates: the NAPAP inventory and the EPA Trends Report.[23] Since these established emission levels determine the initial allocation of allowances, the process of setting baselines was expected to be contentious. However, EPA had learned from previous experience that the baseline needed to be unambiguous in the law to ensure compliance. As Kete reported:

> EPA knew that it was important to set the baseline at a recent historical level. It had to be historical for the obvious reason that baselines set on future operations would invite utilities to behave strategically to run up a higher baseline. The baseline had to be recent to be fair and to minimize the amount of data correction needed to take account of recent changes. Most importantly, the baseline had to be set on a consistent, generic basis as opposed to an ad hoc, case-by-case basis.
>
> (1993, 239)

A three-year (1985–1987) fuel data average was then chosen to dampen out impacts of natural year-to-year variability in emissions rates at utility units. However, problems with the data emerged. Suddenly, firms realized that data reported in Form 767[24] would impact their initial SO_2 allocation. EPA therefore allowed supplemental data to correct factual errors. A special fuel intensity formula was created to avoid penalizing those affected emitters that had undertaken significant control efforts in compliance with past regulatory requirements (heat input during the historical base period of 1985–1987, multiplied by an emissions rate calculated such that aggregate emissions equal the ARP emissions cap). Ultimately, the 1980 baseline emission aggregate rate was established at 17.4 million tons of SO_2 on the basis of these estimates.

5.2.1 (B) Emissions trading system development

Emission Targets: The permanent SO_2 emissions cap for the electricity production sector is 8.95 million tons per year beginning in 2010.

Title IV established a limit on the total amount of pollution that can be emitted by all regulated sources (e.g., power plants); this cap is set lower than historical emissions.[25]

In contrast with past emissions trading programs that lacked abatement targets, the SO_2 allowance trading mechanism established a schedule of predetermined pollution abatement goals. A fixed limit of the total emissions allowances to be circulated per year is a critical feature of the ARP. The cap guarantees a predetermined emission target that was agreed upon during the policy formulation process. At the same time, the ARP ETS grants industry and plant managers the flexibility to find least-cost methods to achieve emissions reductions, thereby incentivizing technical and managerial ingenuity.

Initial Allocation: The initial allocation of ARP allowances was based on historical utilization and emissions rates, a practice commonly known as "grandfathering." The new environmental commodity, which is a financial asset, was granted free of charge to gain political support for the ETS component of the program.[26]

Sulfur dioxide allowances for each of the major power plants in the US are listed in Title IV (i.e., Table I). Emissions allowances for individual units in the power plants were computed according to detailed formulas that are provided in the law (Bryner 1995, 149). Trading is needed to realize the potential savings in compliance costs, but the optimal amount of trading depends on how the government initially allocates permits. The more the initial allocation departs from a distribution where the marginal cost of compliance at all units is equal, the greater the cost savings possible by emissions trading (Ellerman et al. 2000, 31–48).

When the program started, EPA gave every major coal-fired power plant an allowance for each ton of emission then allowed. Congress had decided that the dirtiest and largest power plants would be in Phase I.[27] This decision seemed to follow the longtime observation by Downs about what now is commonly referred as the sectoral approach:

> If a few leaders of the nation's top automobile manufacturing firms, power generating firms, and fuel supply firms could be persuaded to change their behaviour significantly, a drastic improvement in the level of air pollution could be achieved in a relatively short time.
>
> (1972, 27)

However, successful lobbying from the coal-mining industry made it possible for certain Midwestern utilities to receive additional allowances that they could sell to help finance cleanup efforts.[28] EPA was also required by Congress to set aside an additional pool of allowances (approximately 1 percent of the total allocation) to permit construction of new sources of emissions or expansion of existing ones to become a seller-of-last resource as a contingency.[29]

During Phase I (1995–1999), intermediate emission allocations of SO_2 emissions were made to 263 utilities listed in Table I of the CAA in the implementing regulation (1990 CAA, § 404a1). Under Title IV, Table I facilities generally received only about half the allowances needed to cover their baseline emissions; they needed either to reduce emissions or to acquire allowances from someone else to make up the difference.

New power plants—those that began operation after the enactment of Title IV— did not receive initial allocation allowances except under specific circumstances. New units had to obtain allowances from existing units already allocated allowances (US EPA 1994, 70). As of the year 2000, Phase II requires that all existing utility units be subject to the SO_2 requirements and be allocated allowances based on a more stringent emissions rate.[30]

Equity observations regarding the SO_2 allowance allocation method have been made as the ARP ETS program design is reviewed for possible adjustments in case of future applications to control other pollutants such as greenhouse gases. As pointed out in 1997 by Burtraw in congressional testimony, the lack of allocation to new sources has been characterized as "unfair" by some but has also contributed to the overall transparency and effectiveness of the program. Moreover, Congress granted free allocation of the new ARP entitlements in Title IV of the CAA to ensure politically feasibility.

The utilities were regulated at the time under the principle of "cost of service regulation," which ensured that customers did not pay for something utilities received for free. However, an equity concern in the long run is that SO_2 allowances are granted free of charge indefinitely under the ARP. As the current allocation design feature stands, affected units will receive free allowances "after the year 2040 based on their economic activity 60 years previous in the 1985–1987 base years." With the benefit of hindsight, and disregarding the issue of political feasibility, a phased-in auction approach (towards full auction) could have provided a more efficient and equitable allocation outcome (Burtraw 2007).

Determine Program Participants: The ARP applies to new and existing electric utility units.[31] A utility unit is a generator that produces electricity for sale, or one that did so in 1985, and also includes certain cogeneration units.[32]

Congress made a political decision to determine who was required to participate in the program. ARP focused only on the biggest category of emitters: fossil fuel-fired electric utilities (McLean, 2000). As mentioned earlier, Phase I participation in the program was mandatory for the 263 largest and dirtiest utilities listed in Table 1. Certain other units had the opportunity to volunteer to participate in Phase I of the program, most of these plants being located in the Eastern US. Given the opt-in feature,[33] 150 units that would have eventually become part of the system volunteered to participate in advance.[34]

This opt-in feature results in lower allowance prices because only those firms that expect to be able to sell allowances will elect this option. This is fine if the opt-in firms really do have a low marginal cost of reductions. However, as Ellerman et al. (2000) argue, much of the opting-in from electric utilities has been due to adverse selection—initial allocations to some participating units were too high because of imperfect government information. Thus, emitters with a large stock of allowances opted-in to be able to sell their excess allowances in the newly created market.

Starting in the year 2000, as Phase II of the program was implemented, the ARP covered virtually all fossil fuel-fired generating units.

Trading Rules: Allowances may be banked or traded to anyone for future use or sale provided EPA receives proper documentation of the trade.

According to Rose-Ackerman (1995, 9), the role of the trading rules in the allowance trading system "is to provide a predictable structure within which exchange activity might occur and flourish." As Ellerman et al. (1997, 24) point out, "Fortunately, the policy design laid out in Title IV embraces the emissions trading concept with remarkably few restrictions."

(1) *Trading*: The purchase and holding of allowances is not restricted to the utilities for which these permits become a necessary input for the generation of electricity from oil or coal. All sources receiving allowance allocations, as well as

third parties, such as brokers and individuals, are free to buy or sell allowances with any other party. Neither the frequency nor the mechanisms for trading allowances are limited. Section 403(b) of Title IV provides that allowances may be freely transferred among designated representatives of affected units or any holder of allowances. Transfers become effective after EPA receives and records the written certification of the transfer. In 2000, EPA introduced electronic submission protocols to make this process more efficient and has continuously improved the online tools available to manage ETS activity. Allowances may be transferred before they are issued (since utilities know with relative certainty how many allowances they will be allocated each year) but may not be used before the year for which they are allocated.

(2) *Banking*: Banking and multi-year compliance periods are effective tools for smoothing out price fluctuations. Title IV allows inter-temporal trading, allowing participating units to save their allowances for use in the future (1990 CAA, § 40 CFR 73.36). However, utilities are not allowed to borrow against allocations for future years. At the end of each year, each participating utility must have enough allowances in its own account to cover its emissions for that year. The allowances are deducted from the unit's account based on annual emissions data collected by electronic devices at the source.

Therefore, electric generating units face an inter-temporal optimization problem. In each period of time, utilities have to decide by how much they want to reduce SO_2 emissions, considering the current and future costs of abatement relative to expected future allowance prices. Furthermore, participants have to account for the tons of SO_2 allowances taken from their available allowance budgets, as opposed to saving them for future use (Schennach 1998). Market participants may use saved allowances to offset future emissions (i.e., banked forward) when stricter emission limits come into force or sell them when the allowance price is more favorable. The ability to bank allowances forward also provides a way to smooth the impact of transitory price shocks, as extra emissions can be covered from the bank.

Murray, Newell, and Pizer (2008, 5) note that "there can be an incentive to reduce emissions early—particularly during a gradual phasedown of emissions targets—and it is not necessary for the market to meet the target exactly each year." Regarding air quality management results, the ability to bank allowances did indeed accelerate emission reductions under the ARP. However, the authors also suggest "that requiring emissions to match the number of allowances exactly [each year] would result in either too few allowances—causing the price to skyrocket—or too many allowances—causing the price to plummet."

(3) *Annual revenue-neutral auctions and spot sale of allowances*: Title IV of the Clean Air Act provides for EPA to hold sales and auctions of allowances.[35] In order to jump-start the market as suggested in Hausker (1992), a small fraction of the allowances (2.8 percent) are withheld and sold at an annual, revenue-neutral auction administered by EPA.

These auctions were designed to signal price information to the market, particularly during the early stages of the program. Direct sales help ensure that new units have a public source of allowances beyond those allocated initially to existing units, with the aim to protect them from "hoarding" by incumbent units and to preempt a possible failure of the secondary market to achieve liquidity. The goal was to ease financing for new, independent power producers, assuring them priority in purchasing allowances (Martineau and Novello 1997, 375). The ARP direct sales provision was never used and was later abolished by EPA because the SO_2 allowance market has been relatively fluid from the start. However, this design feature was politically important in passing the ARP through Congress because it addressed allowance redistribution concerns.

(a) *Direct Sales*: Beginning in 1993, the EPA administrator was required to offer 25,000 allowances for sale, for use beginning in the year 2000, at $1500 each. The advanced sales continued through 1999. Beginning in 2000, the administrator began to hold both spot and advance sales, with 25,000 allowances offered in each. No sales at this price were actually made, given the availability of allowances at a much lower price through market trading. As an equity principle, the provision mandated that independent power producers that are unable to purchase allowances from utilities or at the auctions are entitled to purchase their allowances first. If fewer than 20 percent of the allowances offered for sale were actually sold in any two consecutive years, EPA would be required to terminate the sales and transfer the allowances in the sales sub-account to the auction sub-account (Martineau and Novello 1997, 375–376; 1990 CAA 416c7). As pointed out in Tietenberg (1996, 158), the set-aside design feature reassured potential critics of the program about the availability of allowances to new entrants in the electric power industry. This minimized political opposition at a low cost to the program.

(b) *Revenue-Neutral Auctions*: First proposed by Hahn and Noll (1982, 141), revenue-neutral auctions are a means of deriving the benefits of an auction without extracting large payments from sources.

Auctions began in 1993 and are held annually, usually on the last Monday of March. If EPA determines that fewer than 20 percent of the allowances available at auction are purchased in any three consecutive years after 2002, the administrator may terminate the auctions (1990 CAA. § 416f). The administrator may also reduce the number of allowances withheld and sold under the auction and sale provisions (1990 CAA 416e).

Two types of allowances are available at auction: (1) spot allowances, which can be used in that same year for compliance purposes, and (2) advance allowances, which will become usable for compliance seven years after the transaction date. Unsold allowances from the sale are transferred to the auction account, and leftover allowances from the auction are returned, again on a *pro rata* basis, to the units from which they were withheld (Martineau and Novello 1997, 375–376). Proceeds from both the sale and the auction are returned on a *pro rata* basis to the units from which the allowances were withheld. No proceeds from these auctions can be treated as revenue by the US government (1990 CAA. § 416c6 and 416d3). The ARP auction price and the spot market price turned out to track each other closely, contributing to price discovery for the new ETS.

5.2.1 (C) Market governance infrastructure

The ability to trade emissions allowances with virtually no restrictions is at the core of the ARP. Simplicity was the guiding principle in designing the ARP ETS. EPA had learned that case-by-case certification of tradable pollution permits in past ETS was costly and did not encourage market activity. The creation of a clearly defined and readily tradable environmental commodity made possible the quick development of the SO_2 allowance market.

To facilitate exchange activity, EPA delegated the majority of the development of the market governance infrastructure to the private sector. The market's central organizational functions such as the establishment of broker listings, the posting of current allowance prices, and the matching of buyers and sellers have all been created by the private sector (US EPA 1995, 4). Only the policy features deemed necessary to jump-start the market were managed by EPA (i.e., the revenue-neutral auction).

Organized Exchanges: From 1993 to 2005, EPA delegated the administration of the auctions to the Chicago Board of Trade (CBOT).[36] However, starting in 2006, EPA began administering these functions directly, along with direct sales.

Among the most important criteria used to select CBOT was its experience in handling and processing financial instruments and using transactional information systems.[37] CBOT states that its mission is to provide contract markets for its members and customers and to oversee the integrity and cultivation of those markets.[38] The market at CBOT provided prices that resulted from trading in open auction or via electronic platforms. The marketplace assimilated new information throughout the trading day and translated this information into benchmark prices agreed upon by buyers and sellers. Speculative allowance trading at CBOT began in 1992, and EPA's auctions and sales were launched in 1993. CBOT's trading infrastructure helped demonstrate that cap-and-trade could enable the creation of an environmental commodities market.

More recently, with the expansion of the environmental finance sector, new market platforms have developed and environmental commodities market integration is constant. For instance, in 2008 the New York Mercantile Exchange, Inc. (NYMEX) began listing emission allowance futures and options contracts as part of their Green Exchange initiative to trade new and existing environmental products.[39]

Information Services: Several information services have been developed by the private sector to support the trading of SO_2 allowances in commodities markets.

The emergence of information services such as electronic bulletin boards and trade publications serves to provide information on traded quantities, prices, and SO_2 allowance market trends. This is a standard feature of many markets and also helps price convergence. Brokers themselves offer price information to the public and their clients. Cantor Fitzgerald, Evolution Markets, and Natsource are among the companies that offer these market information services.

Brokerage Activities and Standardized Procedures: Recently, various private financial institutions and brokers have been developing standardized transaction procedures for environmental commodities markets. The development of standardized legal agreements to sell SO_2 allowances was extremely important to facilitate transactions and to enhance the efficient implementation of the ARP ETS. Online trading has further reduced transaction costs.[40] By stepping out of the way, EPA lets the market perform.

Futures and Options: Futures markets allow both buyers and sellers to establish a price for a commodity several months or even years before the actual transaction will occur, thus lessening the risk of price fluctuations. As mentioned above, there is constant evolution and integration in the environmental commodities markets.

In 1997, CBOT first proposed the establishment of a futures market for SO_2 allowances (Sandor 2012). Environmental commodities markets provide opportunities for risk management in the form of hedging. Hedging is the practice of offsetting the price risk inherent in any cash market position by taking an equal but opposite position in the futures market. Hedgers use futures markets to protect their businesses from adverse price changes.

In 2007, the CBOT merged with the Chicago Mercantile Exchange to form the CME Group. By June 2009, the CME Group, the parent company of NYMEX and the world's largest and most diverse derivatives exchange, announced the launch of its new futures and options contracts for SO_2 allowances. The futures contracts are available for clearing through CME ClearPort®, a set of environmental finance services "open to over the counter (OTC) market participants to substantially mitigate counterparty risk and provide capital efficiencies across asset classes," and they are sold in bundles of 25. Trading of SO_2 allowance futures in this exchange began in July 2009 (Reuters 2009) and has grown rapidly. In April 2012, for example, CME acquired GreenX to conduct trading of environmental derivatives including the US emissions allowances (SO_2 and NO_x), as well as the more recent European Union Allowances, UN-certified Certified Emissions Reductions, European Union Aviation Allowances, Emission Reduction Units, US Regional Greenhouse Gas Initiative carbon allowances, and California's Carbon Allowances.

Market Oversight: EPA is responsible for administering all the aspects of the ARP ETS and monitoring the performance of the market. The Commodity Futures Trading Commission and the Federal Energy Regulatory Commission (FERC) also play an important role in market oversight.

In addition to the tracking of the trading, banking, and auctioning activities of the ARP ETS, EPA also monitors the environmental commodities market to avoid manipulation. For instance, by analyzing holdings or parent company aggregate allowance holdings, EPA controls for market power. Oversight responsibility includes review of transactions by non-regulated entities such as environmental finance service providers, brokerages firms, and hedge funds.

Over-the-counter agreements, on the other hand, are not observable because of their private nature. However, some transactions prices and information on tradable prices is disseminated electronically and through brokerages. Trading and position data in the OTC markets is not tracked in a centralized way, making this market activity less transparent (Pirrong 2009, 6). However, market indexes maintained by financial institutions trading environmental commodities are tracked by EPA's CAMD. While the Allowance Tracking System (ATS) does not require the disclosure of prices, it does require that the transfer of allowance is conducted only among authorized users.

Financial market regulation by the Commodities Exchange Act provides a framework for conducting transactions based on derivatives from environmental commodities prices. Activity at NYMEX and the CBOT, such as environmental exchange platforms for SO_2 allowance trading, is overseen by the Commodities Futures Trading Commission, as directed by the Commodity Exchange Act. The Commission intervenes in the OTC market or spot market if they detect market manipulation. Finally, as part of its mandate to regulate all inputs and services involved in the generation of electricity, the FERC provides oversight to the electricity market and related input markets such as that for SO_2 emission allowances.

5.2.1 (D) Program implementation aspect

Monitoring, Reporting, and Verification: Monitoring, reporting, and verification provisions in Title IV ensure that actual emissions are tracked and accurate. This maintains the environmental integrity of the program. Real-time information and accuracy on compliance also confirms the value of the intangible asset (i.e., the actual right to emit or allowance) that the environmental commodity, in this case the SO_2 allowance, holds in the market.

The consolidation of the SO_2 allowance ETS as a fully operational environmental commodities market to supplement air pollution control regulation has been supported by the development of sophisticated electronic information tools that report and track emissions and allowances in real time by both the industry and regulators (US EPA 1996). The simple principle for regulatory compliance is to submit as many allowances as emitted tons of SO_2 to the central electronic allowance registry. Trading is left to the market, making it a very consistent regulatory mechanism to validate the environmental integrity of the ETS.

(1) *Continuous Emissions Monitoring Systems*: Each emissions unit must install continuous monitoring equipment and report its emissions regularly (1990 CAA, 42 US C. § 7651k). According to EPA, the CEMS data supply "the gold standard to back up the paper currency of emissions allowances."

However, gas-fired plants are allowed to use alternate monitoring methods based on fuel analysis.

(2) *Reporting mechanisms*: The data systems that track emissions and allowances, and that help process these sources of data, form the backbone of the ARP (Kruger, McLean, and Chen 2000).

(3) *The Allowance Tracking System*: This became operational in March 1994. ATS is a method to investigate allowance transactions within the EPA emissions trading program. It provides a framework for categorizing transactions of SO_2 within the ARP. More recently, all data submissions for all the EPA ETS programs have been conducted through the CBS an online application.

(4) *Emissions inventories*: Pursuant to Section 406 of the CAA Amendments, EPA will be conducting an inventory of all industrial emissions. Under this provision, if the inventory indicates that SO_2 emissions from electric utilities are likely to exceed annual emissions budgets, EPA is required to take action to control those emissions so that the cap is not exceeded. Since 1990, SO_2 emissions data have been tracked in the National Emissions Inventory (NEI). The NEI is a composite of data from many different sources that use different data collection methods, and many of the emissions data are based on estimates rather than actual measurements. However, for ARP-affected electricity generating units, most data come from CEMs that measure actual emissions (US EPA 2008).

(5) *Transparency*: For dissemination of emissions and allowance information, "the Internet has become critical over the past several years" (Kruger, McLean, and Chen 2000, 3). In recent years, EPA has significantly upgraded its electronic tools to ensure the fluid performance of the environmental commodities market, as the flexibility mechanism (i.e., ETS) interfaces with the regulatory aspects of the ARP. EPA tracks and reports emissions online, ensuring that a ton from one source is equal to a ton from any other source. This information management approach has allowed EPA to maintain the integrity of the ARP ETS cap. Regulators make sure participating sources fully account for each ton of emissions according to stringent protocols. EPA characterizes the resulting compliance information as unprecedented in its accuracy and comprehensiveness, offering "complete transparency" as all data are publicly available in user-friendly formats online.[41]

(6) *Certification*: In the context of the ARP, certification focuses on the CEMS monitoring capabilities through the Environmental Technology Verification Program. CEMS monitor SO_2 emissions in pounds per hour and must use both a pollutant concentration monitor and a volumetric flow monitor. EPA must certify each CEMS before it can be used in the ARP. To obtain certification, the owner or operator of a unit must conduct several certification tests and submit the results to EPA and the appropriate state agency. If the proposed system is not approved, the owner or operator must revise the equipment, procedures, or methods as necessary and resubmit a request for certification.[42]

Political Jurisdiction: The ARP is a federal regulatory framework for air pollution control supported by an ETS.

Congress decided that a national program was the best regulatory approach to addressing the problem of acid rain because no single state would have been able to successfully control pollutants that travel across jurisdictional boundaries. The electricity industry is regulated by a complex network of institutions at the federal (e.g., The Federal Power Act and FERC), state, and local (e.g. PUC) levels. To bypass the potential influence of local politics, the federal tonnage-based system established by the ARP ETS was able to introduce clear federal limits on SO_2 emissions that had to be met within a determined schedule.

Federal law establishes the authority of state public utility commissions and FERC over utilities to regulate utility rates and charges (42 USCA § 7651bf). However, all commissions are expected to "pressure utilities to maximize the economic benefit of allowance sales" (Congressional Record 1989). Nothing in the federal law precludes "a state or state regulatory authority from providing additional incentives to utilities to encourage investment in any conservation measures or renewable energy generation (40 CFR 73.86)," but the predetermined ARP emission target sets a baseline.

Enforcement: Compliance is determined through a direct comparison of total annual SO_2 emissions reported by CEMS with the number of allowances held by the unit.

(1)   *Account reconciliation*: Thirty days after the end of the year, each unit must have a number of allowances equal to the tonnage actually emitted during the previous year. Compliance with SO_2 emission standards is independent from the cost-economizing features of the ARP's trading mechanism.

(2)   *Sanctions*: Title IV provides that if an affected unit does not have sufficient allowances to cover its emissions, it is subject to an excess emissions penalty (1990 CAA 42 USCA § 7651ja). Automatic fines for excess emissions are due and payable to the EPA without demand. The penalties are adjusted each year for inflation. In 2009, fines reached $3517 per excess ton of SO_2 (US EPA 2009a). This amount is far above the cost of compliance. In addition to their penalty payment, a utility that exceeds its permitted emissions is required to reduce emissions the following year by an additional ton of pollution for each ton of excess pollutant emitted (Schwarze and Zapfel 2000, 288). This system protects the environmental integrity of the program and provides a financial disincentive for noncompliance. The transparent management of the ARP program also provides for the use of reputation as an additional disincentive to electric utilities by facilitating the public awareness of noncompliance.

This assessment of each of the key market parameters included in the SO_2 allowance trading program illustrates that the ARP implemented most of the policy design elements that are necessary for an emissions trading program to become a successful, market-based air quality management mechanism.

5.2.2 Fostering a market for SO₂ allowances

It is important to highlight the fact that the first operational ETS was designed for participants from a monopolistic industry, such as electric power generation. These highly regulated companies did not have a clear incentive to minimize production costs, since by virtue of the structure of the industry they could just pass along their costs to consumers. Launching the first environmental market trading SO_2 allowances in the context of a non-competitive industry presented an even greater challenge than doing so in a competitive market setting. This section reviews how the market-creation parameters included in the ARP helped consolidate the three basic market development requirements of its allowance trading mechanism.

5.2.2 (A) Condition one: adequate number of buyers and sellers

Increased Market Participation: An initial assessment of the market for SO_2 showed significant allowance trading activity (Joskow, Shmalensee, and Bailey 1996). As pointed out by Kruger and Dean (1997, 2): When looking at the number of allowances traded in transactions between economically distinct entities, the overwhelming impression is one of growth. The number of allowance transfers between unrelated parties has increased steadily since the start of the program.

Ellerman et al. (1997) conclude, "By around the middle of 1994, an efficient market for allowances had emerged." The large volume of trade indicates utilities' recognition that trading SO_2 allowances is an efficient mechanism for abatement cost minimization. In 2000, 4690 transfers involving 25 million (mostly future) allowances were reported to the ATS. Approximately 50 percent of these allowances (12.7 million) were transferred between economically unrelated parties. EPA characterizes transfers between different entities as those "which represent 'true' market activity to most observers of the program."[43] These transactions are referred to as "significant transfers" and have ranged from 0.9 million in 1994 to a high of 12.7 million in 2000. In 2005, around 70 percent of this type of trading activity was conducted by large electric utilities and financial agents. In the year 2008, 5.9 million allowances out of 13.9 million reported were significant transfers. Since the inception of the program, 379 million allowances have been transferred, and about 68 percent were traded in private transactions (US EPA 2009b, 2).

5.2.2 (B) Condition two: sufficient incentives to buy and sell credits

Incentives to Trade: Market mechanisms generally emerge when activities appear to be profitable both for intermediaries and participants in a trading system. As suggested by Ellerman et al.:

> One way to assess market development is by observing prices and trading volume. When transactions are few and information poor, prices show considerable dispersion, whereas, in a reasonably competitive market with good information, transactions are sufficient in number and frequency for a readily

recognizable "market price" to become established, around which bids and offers cluster.

(Ellerman et al. 1997, 25)

Prices quoted by brokerage firms and other environmental finance service providers involved in the SO_2 emissions market have become increasingly aligned not only with each other but also with the market-clearing price in the annual EPA auction as well as private spot market transactions.[44] Incentives to trade in the SO_2 allowance market will exist as long as certainty over the value and entitlements of allowances remains. In addition to the ARP regulatory commitment, which provides for long-term planning, the prices of SO_2 allowances reflect the marginal cost of abatement for electric utilities. These prices are also influenced by inputs such as the cost of fuels to operate their generators and abatement technologies such as scrubbers.

The history of SO_2 allowance prices shows the impact of these exogenous factors. SO_2 allowances traded at around $150 per ton in 1995. After dipping to around $68 per ton of SO_2 in 1996, erratic prices in 1999, ranging from $100 to $200, reflected jitters over possible regulatory change. In 2000 SO_2 prices went above $200 per ton as the result of the implementation of Phase II of the ARP combined with antici-pated new regulations. In 2000, the Clinton administration had expressed intentions to strengthen particulate matter ambient standards (of which SO_2 is a precursor) and was planning for a "new clean air strategy" to "significantly reduce emissions from US power plants that contribute to global warming" (Clinton 2000).

Prices were then stable for approximately three years, but in 2004 they rose as a result of high natural gas prices and an increase in electricity demand, which was met by coal-based electricity generation. The second Bush administration's opposition to the regulation of greenhouse gas emissions, which was highlighted by the rejection of the KP, allowed an increase in coal-fired generation. Increased demand sent prices to $700 per SO_2 allowance.

In 2005 hurricanes Katrina and Rita caused disruptions in the natural gas supply that led to soaring gas prices. Higher estimates on future costs of SO_2 emerged, as electric utilities prepared for anticipated regulatory changes due to the CAIR rule, which was then being developed. The CAIR rule was introduced that year, chan-ging the ARP caps for the Eastern US. The SO_2 allowance prices reflected the electric utilities' expected compliance effort, and by the end of 2005 prices reached their highest level in the history of the ARP: $1600 per ton of SO_2.

In 2006 the price of natural gas retreated. Electric utilities preparing for the new compliance targets under CAIR realized that they could be met with cleaning technology and with the SO_2 allowance supply available in this market. Prices of allowances fell back to around $300 per ton. However, the price of natural gas kept dropping for the next couple of years, eventually reaching historic lows. Cheap natural gas, combined with the D.C. Court's action vacating CAIR in July of 2008 caused the price of allowances to fall to $115 per ton on the day the decision was announced.

At the end of the year the court remanded the program, but the depressed SO_2 allowance market reached levels only seen at the onset of the program, around $65 per ton. Utilities reassessed their compliance strategies in the face of the court's revision of EPA authority. The electricity industry had already made some capital investments to meet the CAIR rules. When the court intervened with a possible elimination of the program, the industry had to consider the possibility of having to comply under a more expensive conventional regulatory program. Plant managers put some projects on hold and almost immediately had to reevaluate these decisions at a high cost to the electricity industry when the CAIR was remanded.

Therefore, affected units in the ARP ETS change their views and behavior about trading environmental commodities in the face of major regulatory change (and litigation), as this sends conflicting signals to the market. The decision of when and how to conduct fine-tuning of the emissions target or cap needs to be clearly defined and legislated during the policy formulation process. Environmental, market-based regulation requires a transparent and clear path on how to make these adjustments. This in turn enhances the predictability of the regulatory aspects of an ETS to affected entities and participants in the market. Unanticipated changes can jeopardize market incentives and consequently the trading functions of this flexible mechanism and lead to a loss of faith in the regulatory framework.

5.2.2 (C) Condition three: moderate transaction costs

Transaction Costs Reduction: In an environmental commodities market, brokers can reduce transaction costs by helping buyers and sellers come together (Stavins 1995). Thus, the commission paid for SO_2 allowance trading becomes a proxy of the transaction costs involved in participating in open exchanges. Actual brokerage fees charged for trading in SO_2 permits have been declining over time. This suggests a gradual reduction in transaction costs, such as identifying potential partners, and therefore an improvement in the efficiency of the market.

Commissions per allowance per trade averaged $3.50 in mid-1994 and $2.00 in late 1995, the first years the trading mechanism operated. By September 1996, the commission averaged $1.50, or about 2 percent of the prevailing allowance price. This rate of commission has converged with those charged on regular stock market transactions (Joskow et al. 1998). *Ex ante* estimates of transaction commissions predicted them to fall further to a level of around 1.5 percent of the prevailing allowance price. However, it is noted that transaction costs will depend on several variables such as the number of participants in the market, the volume of sales, the number of transactions, and the competitiveness of brokers and the service they provide (Parker and Kiefer 1993). In 2009, commissions charged for SO_2 allowances in CME futures market launched that year were $0.25 per ton ($25 per contract of 100 tons, the trading unit) (NYMEX 2009).

The implementation of Phase II of the ARP in 2000 brought more potential trading partners into the system. Increased participation means more transactions, generating more information and thereby reducing market uncertainty. The number of intermediaries who only match buyers and sellers will diminish as

Internet trading increases, which further reduces transaction costs (Tapscott, Ticoll, and Lowy 2000, 46–47). Janice K. Wagner, then-head of the Market Operations Branch of EPA CAMD, foresaw in 2001 that participants in clean air markets would eventually trade allowances and other environmental entitlements online with the regulatory assurance of the full environmental integrity of market transactions (Wagner 2001). More recently, in order to reduce transaction costs in the financial industry, many commodity exchanges including CBOT and NYMEX have become electronic.

5.2.2 (D) Condition four: good information for trading and its regulation

Transparency: Emissions trading mechanisms must provide good information in order to foster market efficiency and maintain environmental integrity (Stavins 1995). While designing the ARP ETS, EPA administrators eliminated past regulatory practices such as certification or permitting processes, which had increased transaction costs and discouraged trading. Since these mechanisms were the primary methods used to ensure compliance with environmental standards in the past, new mechanisms had to be designed to replace them. The implementation challenge was to maintain the environmental credibility of the program while the number of program participants gradually expanded (either by opt-in measures, new facilities, or by inclusion during Phase II) and demand increased for market exchanges.

Therefore, the ARP required information management systems to support careful tracking of allowance transactions and close monitoring of actual emissions. After implementing Phase I of the ARP, EPA administrators acknowledged that their main administrative task was collecting and disseminating large quantities of information. They also reported increasing efficiencies: "To the extent that electronic reporting, verification, and processing of emissions data becomes more prevalent, a larger universe of sources can be included in a program for a given amount of administrative resources" (Kruger, McLean, and Chen 2000, 10). As stated by Kruger et al.:

> In its role as the emissions and allowance "accountant," EPA must handle vast amounts of information. In addition to processing the information for compliance purposes, EPA must make emissions and allowance information accessible to facilitate an efficient allowance market and to build public credibility in the emissions trading approach. Without recent advances in information technologies, these activities would be considerably more difficult if not impossible.
>
> (2000, 1)

There are three key program elements based on information technologies that have enabled the SO_2 allowance trading system to become operational:

(1) *Allowance Management System*: The ATS was developed as the central registry of allowances used for compliance with the ARP. ATS was created as the

backbone of the ARP, relying on data systems that track all allowances transferred since 1994. The CBS is EPA's most modern electronic platform for recording information submitted by regulated entities and other program participants, including the electronic transfer of allowances between accounts. Figure 5.2 shows an online reporting form.

ATS is an electronic system that enables allowance transactions to be investigated more efficiently. Kruger and Dean (1997, 2) state that ATS was designed as "an information system for tracking compliance rather than for analyzing market activity." In other words, ATS only reports the quantity of emissions, not market prices for SO_2 allowances. ATS has been making transaction-recording processes incrementally more efficient since the program began. For instance, when the program was first implemented in 1995, records were processed in five days. This processing time has been reduced to nearly real time by new communication technologies.

Because of the expansion in the use of markets, electronic inventories, and emissions tracking for air quality management by the CAMD, the ATS has now become the Allowance Management System (AMS) of the CBS. That change is the result of the ARP phasing in NO_X, the implementation of new applications of the cap-and-trade mechanism to other air pollutants (i.e., mercury (Hg) and mercuric chloride ($HgCl_2$)), and the development of national carbon dioxide emissions (CO_2) inventories. The AMS is responsible for recording the transfer of allowances among various entities under the CAA and collects all emissions data submitted under the various clean air market programs developed by the CAMD.

The AMS's Quarterly Report Review Process uses final data from each affected source for allowance reconciliation and compliance determination and is made available to the public on the Internet. All quarterly reports submitted to EPA are entered into the AMS, which performs automated data processing. EPA checks the quarterly reports by utilities on transactions and emissions for errors and contacts the utilities to resolve data problems. The AMS database records account balances and transaction records. The system is very transparent: it allows public access to the trading history of each allowance until its retirement. No price information is provided. This function is provided by environmental finance service providers. Market participants (e.g., brokers, environmental groups, and individuals) can maintain accounts in AMS to publicize their market data.

The AMS records support compliance assessment by consolidating utilities allowance records with actual emissions records. At the end of each calendar year, EPA compares the number of tons emitted with the allowance holdings of each utility unit to ensure that it is in compliance. If the utility unit is not in compliance, it is penalized in accordance with the rules for the program.

The CBS, where AMS is housed, now serves as a repository for SO_2, NO_X, CO_2, and mercury emissions data by source from the utility industry. The SO_2 and NO_X emissions data may also help states design programs for compliance with the NAAQS provisions of the CAA for SO_2, ozone, and particulate matter. In 2009, two

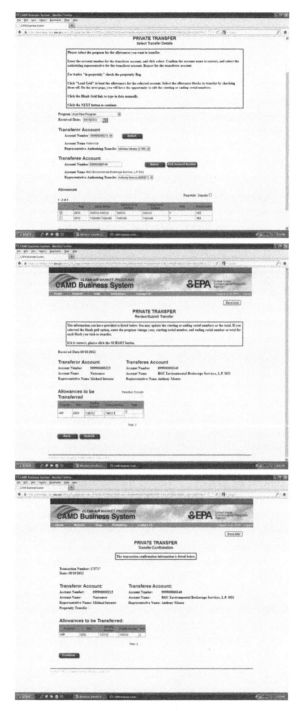

Figure 5.2 CAMD Business System: online allowance transfer report
Source: EPA 2012

interim EPA traceability protocols have been prepared that establish procedures for the qualification and certification of elemental and oxidized mercury gas generators tracked by CEMS. Finally, the CO_2 data currently being collected by ETS will provide a valuable emissions inventory database for assessing US progress toward the goal of stabilizing greenhouse gas emissions.

(2) *Continuous Emissions Monitoring Systems*: CEMS are mechanical devices used to sample, analyze, measure, and record emissions and flow on continuous basis.[45] This type of information technology monitoring device has provided both environmental credibility and facilitated the emergence of a relatively efficient market for SO_2 allowances (Ellerman et al. 1997). The earliest CEMS data were submitted by phone, then fax, then modem, and now online. The advancement in technology has made the use of CEMS much easier and faster.

Emissions are continuously monitored from affected units. In 1998, an average annual cost of about $124,000 per CEM (including operating and annualized capital costs) was estimated (Schmalensee et al. 1998). Continuous emissions monitoring, therefore, remains relatively expensive and hence limited in its applicability. However, technological advances and mainstreaming of the use of electronic monitoring, reporting, and verification systems will make this policy design feature more affordable. As mentioned earlier, gas-fired plants are allowed to use alternate monitoring methods based on fuel analysis. Units have the option to use CEMS or to measure fuel flow hourly and estimate SO_2, CO_2, and heat input based on fuel sampling. Alternative methods are also being tested and introduced, including predictive emissions modeling systems, which use mathematical models to estimate emissions based on each unit's operating parameters and the pollutants analyzed (Schakenbach 2001, 301).

The requirement to have a CEMS on the stack of every affected unit accounts for a noticeable percentage of observed compliance costs. According to Ellerman et al. (1997), capital and operating costs of CEMS amounted to 7 percent of total observed compliance costs in 1995. If these costs are assumed to be "representative of the whole, the additional cost of monitoring for Title IV in 1995 amounted to $48–54 million" (Ellerman et al. 1997, 46). An estimate of incremental annualized costs for the period 1993 to 2010 in millions of 1990 dollars shows expenditures in the amount of $203.5 million for CEMS monitoring (Parker and Kiefer 1993).

In the words of former CAMD director Brian McLean, "The significant efforts by industry installing, testing and operating continuous emissions monitors are paying off with high quality data and documentations of early environmental benefits from industry actions to reduce emissions" (US EPA 1995, 2). For an ETS to function, it is crucial to accurately measure the pollution commodity being traded. The CEMS requirements, therefore, instill confidence in the market-based approach by verifying the existence and value of the traded allowance.

(3) *Information management and organizational innovation*: In 2000, CAMD transferred all of its current collection processes, data, systems, databases, and organizations to a new, centralized server. This information system compiles data including quarterly reports, annual allowance reconciliation, initial emissions allocation, and annual auction transactions.

The CAMD has evolved into a regulator *infomediary*.[46] An infomediary is defined as "an entity that captures trusted information from customers and manages it on their behalf for potential use [...] in this case for regulatory compliance" (Tapscott et al. 2000, 160). As opposed to an infomediary in the business sector, EPA's CAMD does not benefit economically from distributing information to those who need it for commercial purposes, but this function provides certainty about the environmental integrity of clean air markets operations.

As mentioned earlier, EPA's most recent version of an information management platform is the CBS. CBS is an interactive application that allows sources to perform various tasks online. This system also allows the general public and commercial businesses to set up general allowance accounts and conduct investigations.[47]

Information technologies are continuously increasing their capabilities, presenting EPA with the ongoing opportunity to improve its information management systems. Therefore, CAMD continuously re-engineers the process and data systems associated with emissions, monitoring, and certification data. CAMD also reviews the tools available for checking and submitting data on a quarterly and ozone season basis. In the first quarter of 2009, the Emissions Collection and Monitoring Plan System was implemented to submit data to EPA for the Acid Rain and CAIR programs.

In short, information technology has become an important tool that helps regulators overcome the asymmetry of incentives between themselves and industry: firms have no incentive to provide information to the regulator about the industrial processes being regulated. Digital processing changed EPA's role from inspecting compliance choices to measuring results and tracking emissions and allowances—a less costly duty that depends on credible and precise information flows about both pollution emissions and allowance transfers (Pérez Henríquez 2004, 12).

5.2.3 Policy analysis of the Acid Rain Program

Using traditional policy analysis criteria, we now systematically examine the policy design aspects and achievements of ETS.

Exchange Efficiency: Estimate of the potential gains in resource allocation from implementing ETS over command-and-control regulation.

A key goal of the ARP was to achieve exchange efficiency. Sources are each given a certain number of allowances (referred to as the initial distribution). Because initially sources have unequal costs of reducing, some find it in their interests to buy and some to sell, and both parties to the exchange are reducing their costs of staying within their allowed amounts. Exchange efficiency means that at the final, after-trading allowance holdings, no source is willing to pay enough for an additional allowance to induce another source to sell one. This occurs when each source has the same value for an additional allowance, and this also implies that the reductions have been achieved at the least possible total cost.

As reviewed in Chapter 2, when properly designed and implemented, incentive-based mechanisms can lead to the attainment of selected environmental standards and, in appropriate circumstances, can also do so at or near the minimum cost to society (Montgomery 1972; Baumol and Oates 1988; Tietenberg 1995). Despite the monopolistic structure of the electric industry in the US, the ARP developed into a well-functioning market for emissions allowances. The first large-scale ETS allowed for low transaction costs and price transparency while fostering extensive trading activity from the start. As suggested by Ellerman et al. (1997, 32), "The development of an effective private market for allowances can also be seen in the dispersion of bid and offer prices in EPA auctions[48] since 1993." By 1997, the dispersion became very narrow, with few allowances traded at prices much above the market-clearing price. The lack of dispersion means that marginal costs are mostly the same for all sources, support-ing the argument that social costs are approximating the minimum. This suggests the emergence of a relatively efficient market for allowances (Joskow et al. 1998).

There has been considerable heterogeneity in the magnitude and form of responses to the ARP cap-and-trade system. Schmalensee et al. (1998) estimate that 45 percent of emissions reductions were due to the installation of scrubbers, with the remaining 55 percent the result of switching to lower-sulfur coal. Their analysis found that utilities took advantage of the flexibility provided by Title IV to employ alternative compliance strategies, something not possible under traditional command-and-control regimes. These authors concluded that "the heterogeneity of unit-specific response strategies … indicates that Title IV was an economically significant departure, as well as a conceptually significant departure, from the tradi-tional 'one size fits all' conventional approach of setting unit-level emissions rate standards" (Ellerman 1997, 32).

Since its implementation, the ARP has achieved an almost perfect compliance rate on emissions limits for less than a third of the originally estimated costs. The overall compliance cost of the ARP is estimated to be $3 billion annually. As mentioned earlier, EPA's NAPAP reported to Congress an *ex ante* estimate of $6 billion in implementation costs. It should also be noted that while allowance prices have reflected changing expectations from industry and market participants to factors exogenous to the ARP ETS, they have been considerably below the theoretical projections made before the program started. In the early 1990s, analysts predicted allowance prices of about $291–760 per ton (based on estimates of marginal costs of abatement).[49]

As reviewed earlier, allowance prices fell to the $68–150 range once the system was underway. This was in part because the early allowance prices represented only the variable costs of units that had previously been required to install scrubbers. But some of the lower-than-expected cost is also attributed to the downward pressure caused by rail deregulation on the cost of delivering lower-sulfur coal from the Western states. During the first years, ARP allowance prices were stable. Low actual costs suggested that tradable allowances provided at least some economic motivation to achieve emissions reductions at a lower cost than had previously been considered possible.

Several reasons explain why estimates of the annual and marginal costs of compliance had declined:

- Trading triggered a search for ways to reduce emissions at lower cost (Burtraw 1996).
- Advantageous trends in fuel markets contributed to the decline in emission rates, making it easier for utilities to attain emissions limits, thereby reducing program costs (Ellerman and Montero 1998; Burtraw 1996).
- The structure of industries offering compliance services to utilities has dramatically changed under the ARP ETS. As the program introduced choice and flexibility to reduce the cost of compliance, previously independent markets supplying services to utilities (coal mining, rail transport, and scrubber manufacturing) were forced into competition with each other (Burtraw 1998).

When the CAIR Interstate Rule was proposed in 2003, the price of allowance began an upward trend. More stringent caps and changes in compliance deadlines introduced uncertainty into the market. In 2005, when the rule was finalized, the prices reached a historic high of $1600 during the month of December. Concerns about CAIR's implementation overtook the market. At those, prices, the electric industry began to install equipment to control emissions as the most cost-effective strategy. After the Court's decision to first vacate and then reinstate CAIR temporarily, prices adjusted downward throughout 2008 from $509 per ton in January to $179 by the end of the year. By March 2009, the price of an allowance for SO_2 was $62 (Reuters 2009a). EPA suggested then that policy analysts and market observers "should not confuse temporary high prices in the market response to major regulatory changes (more or less regulation), where buyers and sellers are searching for a new equilibrium based on available information they have from consultant and various services, with price volatility" (US EPA 2009b).

But as discussed earlier in this chapter, regulatory uncertainty over EPA's attempts to modify CAIR with more stringent regulations under the CSAPR and the subsequent court battles over these changes has resulted in allowance prices reflecting the lowest clearing price yet for SO_2 allowances in the history of US emissions markets (Evolutions Markets 2012). This situation, described by traders as "regulatory limbo," was evident in March 29, 2012, as the SO_2 allowance spot price cleared at $0.56 and Vintage 2019 cleared at $0.12 at the annual EPA auction.

Dynamic Efficiency: Degree to which market incentives of ETS induce technological progress toward reducing pollution emissions.

In theory, choice regarding compliance strategies should produce an incentive for sources to seek cheaper ways of complying in the long run. Additionally, an incentive-based system that charges based on the discharge remaining after control procedures creates a greater incentive for emissions reduction than a regulation specifying that same level of discharge (Bohm and Russell 1985; Wenders 1975).

Aside from electricity demand-side reductions, the two main techniques for reducing SO_2 emissions are fuel switching and scrubbing. Fuel switching involves minimal capital cost. In 1989, scrubbing involved investments of about $125 million on average for 500-megawatt generating units (Schmalensee et al. 1998, 458). EPA administrators believe the SO_2 emissions market has indeed provided a strong incentive for cleaner, more efficient technologies.

It could be argued that some of the advances in scrubbing technology may have been spurred by the special incentives included in the law that subsidized the use of scrubbers as a concession to high-sulfur coal producers. Also, over-investment in scrubbing may have induced technological change in this industry, given the high demand for this control technology caused by the high expected values of allowances when the program was launched. Popp (2004) analyzes patent data to show that the "removal efficiency of scrubbers" improved with the implementation of Title IV.

From an econometric perspective, the magnitude of innovation caused by the program is difficult to assess because these motivations are not easily separable from other forces that affect the cost of compliance. However, Burtraw (2000) suggests that the current total cost of the program is 40–140 percent lower than projections (depending on the timing of those projections and the counterfactual baseline considered). He further explains:

> Innovation accounts for a large portion of these cost savings, but not as typically formulated in economic models of research and development (R&D) efforts to obtain patent discoveries. Innovation under the SO_2 allowance trading program involves organizational innovation at the firm, market and regulatory level and process innovation by electricity generators and upstream fuel suppliers. An important portion of the cost reductions that are evident was already in the works prior to and independent of the program. Nonetheless, the allowance trading program deserves significant credit for providing the incentive and flexibility to accelerate and to fully realize exogenous technical changes that were occurring in the industry.
>
> (Burtraw 2000, ii)

More recently, Keohane (2008) reported to Congress that perhaps the "most important and unexpected innovation" came as a shift in the conventional wisdom among power plant engineers occurred. With the implementation of ARP, engineers figured out how to adapt boilers designed to burn high-sulfur Eastern coal to instead burn low-sulfur Wyoming coal, something previously believed to be technically infeasible. Wyoming coal was abundant and became cost-effective once the new total costs were calculated (2008, 26).

Market Transaction Efficiency: Degree to which ETS reduces those costs not included in price incentives.

Because of market fragmentation, transaction costs are ubiquitous in market economies. They can arise from the transfer of any property right because trading partners must find one another, communicate, and agree to the terms of any transaction (Stavins 1995, 136) In the ARP ETS, the expected bias toward internal trading within firms, as opposed to external trading among different economic entities, was demonstrated during Phase I.

Over the life of ARP ETS, a reduction in transaction costs has resulted in an increasing volume of trading between distinct economic entities. Costs have been reduced because information-sharing technologies have improved and because brokers provide standardized economic transactions mechanisms. Allowance traders use third-party brokers because it is cheaper than conducting transactions without them. A growing proportion of brokered trades, as well as lower brokerage fees, indicate that transaction costs are decreasing. As mentioned earlier, of the nearly 379 million allowances transferred since 1994, about 68 percent were traded in private transactions. In 2009 EPA emphasized that "private transactions are indicative of both market interest and use of allowances as a compliance strategy" (EPA 2009a).

Equity: Distributive effects of implementing the ARP ETS.

Any policy choice inevitably leads to different impacts on different groups. As with all policies that improve overall welfare at a cost to a few, those who are adversely affected may take measures—political or otherwise—to block implementation. Thus, it is important to consider the distributive impacts of economic instruments as well as overall gains (OECD 1994). The creation of the emissions allowance required policymakers to decide how to distribute this economic rent.

(1) *Grandfathering*: Since the ARP represented the creation of a relatively untested market-based program for controlling SO_2 emissions, there was no serious attempt by the government to keep the economic rents formed by creating a new environmental asset. Instead, SO_2 allowances were intentionally granted free of charge to the regulated parties. Allocations were based on historical patterns of fuel use (MMBtu) and on input-based emissions performance standards using the period 1985–1987 as a baseline (to avoid political opposition to the implementation of Title IV). However, this initial allocation approach

had an impact on the overall cost-effectiveness of the program relative to other design features such as the use of auctioned permits (through a full or partial approach). Studies of "double dividends" observe that a tax on an environmental externality creates incentives for emissions reductions (first dividend) while also providing revenue to minimize distortions of the tax system, thereby providing greater efficiency gains (second dividend) (Goulder 1995).

(2) *Impact to local economies*: It may have been less obvious that the allowance mechanism would also affect other product prices, including the possibility of transition costs to workers who lose their jobs as a result of the market adjustment. As mentioned previously, the ARP affects the electric-generation sector directly as well as related industries such as coal production. The program provides a limited training fund for displaced workers who lose their jobs because of Title IV but does little else to mitigate coal-mining dislocation impacts. Greenstreet (1999) provides an illustration of how the economic impacts of Phase II of the ARP were expected to affect a local economy at the time. West Virginia, a coal state affected by Title IV, was expected to be impacted in the following ways:

- *Capital expenditures on scrubbers*: Mount Storm electric generating plant decided to invest in a new scrubber at a cost of $166 million.
- *Reduction in West Virginia coal sales*: The broader and more stringent SO_2 emissions standards in Phase II may further change the balance between low-sulfur and high-sulfur coals in West Virginia and national markets. The impact is estimated at a 5 percent reduction in West Virginia coal orders.
- *Price of SO_2 emissions allowances*: Taking Phase I allowance prices at $90 per ton, in 1999 estimates of the future cost of allowances were $303 per ton in 2010 and $240 in 2020.
- *Increase in the price of electricity compared with baseline prices*: Electricity price increases to local consumers are estimated to be 0.8–2.9 mills/kWh.

Table 5.3 summarizes the results from the West Virginia study.

Table 5.3 Economic impacts of Phase II SO_2 limits in West Virginia

	2000	2005	2010	2020
Output (millions of 1992 $)	−260	−341	−415	−464
GSP (millions of 1992 $)	−170	−225	−273	−305
Employment	−2,200	−2,700	−3,000	−2,800
Annual wage rate ($)	−28	−30	−18	−8
Wages and salaries (millions $)	−70	−94	−109	−122
Per Capita income (1992 $)	−38	−18	−11	−7
Population	−1,100	−4,300	−6,000	−6,600

Source: Greenstreet (1999).

There was little uncertainty about whether Phase II of the ARP would be implemented by the year 2000, since the law clearly mandated an implementation timeline. However, uncertainty remains about future changes in environmental policy and their interaction with Title IV, the future prices of SO_2 allowances, and the market for West Virginia coal. Other impacts not taken into account in the West Virginia study (because they were considered negligible or difficult to quantify) include (1) lime purchases for scrubber operation; (2) shifts in the mix of sources to generate electricity (renewables, hydro-power, etc.); (3) utility windfalls from distributions of emissions allowances; (4) reductions in national electricity consumption due to higher prices; (5) labor productivity gains brought about by improved health; and (6) improvements in agricultural and forestry yield (Greenstreet 1999).

The West Virginia case illustrates that dislocation and other economic impacts to localities from the implementation of the ARP can be significant. If negative local impacts were pervasive in a large group of states, this condition could threaten the sustainability of the emissions trading program.

Political Feasibility: Degree to which the different design features of the ARP ETS lessened the political pressures that were likely to arise in the process of gaining legislative approval.

Several policy features included in the original design enhanced the political feasibility of the ARP.

(1) *Cap-and-trade system*: The key to political feasibility for the implementation of a sulfur dioxide emissions allowance trading system in the US was to implement a strict overall emissions cap. This design feature provided a strong signal of commitment to the environmental movement. As mentioned previously, the acid rain plan proposed by the Bush administration in 1989 obtained the endorsement of the EDF.

Bryner (1995) suggests, "There was more agreement in Congress about the basic approach to controlling acid rain in Title IV than about any other main provision" of the 1990 CAA Amendments. It helped that the Bush administration's proposals were as stringent as the ones suggested in many of the bills previously supported by environmentalists (1995, 166–167).

As pointed out by Environmental Defense (2000, 1), "At the time, a pollution control program that made polluters explicitly liable as a matter of law for limiting their total emissions to a specified level while permitting them to use emissions trading was simply unprecedented." Confidence in the environmental benefits of ETS was crucial to ensuring broad support of this market-based regulatory approach.

(2) *Grandfathering and initial allocation*: The initial allocation is the number of allowances granted to the affected units (or electric generating units) based on their historical utilization and emission rates specified in Title IV. The strategy of

distributing allowances based on a historical emissions rate has a great deal of political appeal for existing firms, thus increasing political feasibility (Leman 1980). The underlying idea behind this policy feature is that "those who have been gaining from current policy should or, for political reasons, must be cushioned from the elimination of the inefficient current policy" (Weimer 1989, 20). Ultimately, three types of allowances allocations were made: (1) "Initial Allocations" were granted to electric-generating units affected by the program based on the product of their historical utilization and emission rates specified by Title IV; (2) "Allowance Auctions" (250,000) were set aside in a Special Allowance Reserve at the start of the original ARP allocation; and (3) "Opt-in Allowances" were allocated to units entering the program voluntarily.

The government did not keep the economic rents created by the allowance assets—they were distributed to the regulated parties. As pointed out by Zeckhauser (1981, 146), the distribution of gains and losses arising from a policy is likely to have greater effects on whether that policy is adopted in a democratic society than the magnitude or even the sign of net benefits. Allowances were given to utilities rather than sold because there was no way that a sales-based program (e.g., allowance auctioning) could have passed Congress. Indeed, the only politically feasible alternative to a simple grant of allowances was to impose an electricity tax that would have forced the customers of "clean" utilities to help pay the cleanup costs of "dirty" utilities (Schmalensee et al. 1998, 458). As stated by Stavins (1995, 146), "For any tradable permit system, political feasibility can be established or destroyed over this single aspect of design."

(3) *Gradualism*: The implementation of a two-phase program effectively diffused potential opposition at the time of the passage of the new regulatory framework. It separated regulated groups between the phases by size of generators and type of industry, avoiding antagonistic coalitions from the private sector.

(4) *Certain regulatory framework*: In order to increase certainty about the air quality management program, the 1990 CAA amendments reduced the regulator's discretion. As Senator Waxman recalls:

> To an extent unprecedented in prior environmental statutes, the pollution control program of the 1990 Amendments includes very detailed mandatory directives to EPA, rather than more general mandates or broad grants of authority that would allow for wide latitude in EPA's implementation of the CAA's program.
>
> (Waxman 1991, 1742)

In addition, a series of deadlines and rule-making actions were mandated for the Amendment's implementation. One result of the implementation rules for the CAA is that it takes time to make any amendments, which enhances ARP regulatory predictability, increasing the long-term certainty for businesses about the permanence of the program. However, the CAIR Interstate Rule is an example of how administrative regulatory actions affecting emission caps can take a toll on the performance of an ETS. When CAIR imposed new rules in order to meet air quality standards for fine particles in non-attainment areas in the Eastern US, reducing the ARP cap by 60–70 percent, it tested the ability of the ARP to fine-tune its emission targets according to regional and seasonal ambient standards needs.

(5) *Special allocation of allowances (i.e., subsidies)*: Title IV initially "gained the support of all in Congress but the most stubborn defenders of Midwestern electric utilities and high-sulfur coal miners" (Bryner 1995, 165). In order to gain the support of these interest groups, some states with high-polluting plants were given extra allowances that could be sold to help generate revenues to offset cleanup costs. For instance, power plants in Illinois, Indiana, and Ohio were given 200,000 additional allowances during each year of Phase I. Plants that were part of a utility system that reduced its use of coal by at least 20 percent between 1980 and 1985, and that relied on coal for less than 50 percent of the total electricity generated could also receive extra allowances. Clean states were given additional allowances to facilitate economic growth (Bryner 1995, 166).

Some 3100 utilities are now required to reduce their emissions further to ensure that no more than 8.9 million tons of SO_2 will be emitted per year in Phase II of Title IV, which began on January 1, 2000. Phase II gives companies a number of additional special allowances to help them raise money for cleanup efforts (1990 CAA § 404). However, as pointed out in Ellerman et al., these features reduced, in part, some of the economizing aspects of the SO_2 allowances trading program:

> The gap between allowance prices and average abatement costs is that some utilities were forced by political pressures, reinforced by the utilities' status as geographic monopolies subject to cost-plus regulation, to invest in high-cost abatement technologies—in particular, scrubbers—which facilitated their continued use of local high-sulfur coal deposits, thereby helping protect local business and jobs. Indeed, Title IV explicitly encourages the use of scrubbers through special bonus-allowance provisions.
>
> (1997, 48)

(6) *Access to new electricity generators*: Through direct sales, 25,000 allowances are offered each year at a price of $1,500 each (adjusted for inflation). This policy provides a source of SO_2 allowances for new industry entrants, in case no allowances are available through private transactions. The proceeds from the sales (as well as any unsold allowances) are to be returned to the utilities providing the allowances (1990 CAA, § 405; Bryner 1995, 166). As mentioned earlier, while this design feature was not being used, at minimal cost to the program, direct sales reduced potential opposition of industrial sectors interested in participating in electric generation in the future.

(7) *Social participation:* Although the impacts are small, some observers believe that there is symbolic importance in allowing environmental advocates to participate actively in reducing SO_2 emissions by acquiring allowances to take them out of the market. As EPA reports:

> A small but growing number of environmental, non-profit, and student organizations have purchased allowances with the goal of retiring them and reducing pollution. Retiring an allowance ensures the emission of one less ton of pollution into the air in a given year, since the total number of allowances is fixed under the acid rain emissions cap.
>
> (EPA 1996, 12)

It is thus suggested by EPA that the option to retire allowances "democratizes pollution abatement by empowering individuals and non-governmental organizations to take direct action to reduce pollution" (EPA May 1996, 12). EPA's CAMD website currently reports that the Clean Air Conservancy Trust actively purchases allowances and then provides donors with a "Clean Air Certificate" documenting the amount of pollution their donations or gifts have prevented. Other environmental groups currently listed as interested in allowance retirement are: The Acid Rain Retirement Fund, the Adirondack Council, and the Environmental Resources Trust.[50]

Certainty of Satisficing: Degree of assurance that ETS achieves predetermined environmental and economic policy objectives within a given regulatory regime.

The ARP's politically negotiated goal to reduce annual SO_2 emissions by 10 million metric tons per year from the 1980 baseline has been achieved. EPA's own assessment of the initial phase of implementation was that the ARP was "proving to be extremely effective" in reducing pollution emissions and in providing "multiple environmental and health benefits in a cost-effective manner" (US EPA 1999). By allowing the trading of SO_2 allowances and permitting the holders of these entitlements to transfer them among one another or to bank them for later use, ARP promoted overall cost-effectiveness.

In 2009 EPA reported that the program was at 100 percent compliance, and substantial additional emissions allowances have been banked for future use (US EPA 2009c). The 2011 NAPAP Report states that ARP has

> successfully reduced emissions of SO2 and NOX from power generation (i.e., the sources covered by the ARP). SO2 emissions were down to 5.7 million tons in 2009, 64 percent lower than 1990 emissions and below the 2010 statutory cap of 8.95 million tons. NOX emissions were reduced to 2 million tons in 2009, 67 percent lower than 1995 emissions and substantially exceeding the Title IV goal.
>
> (NAPAP 2011, p. 3)

At the end of Phase I of the ARP (1999), EPA claimed that acid rain-affected environments seemed to be "on the path to recovery" (US EPA 1999). However, critics questioned environmental gains, as in the case of the acidification of lakes and streams in the Adirondacks (Dao 2000). EPA acknowledges that "the relationship of emission reductions to ecological and air quality improvements is complex and not entirely commensurate with the level of ARP emission reductions" based on accumulated data and analyses of the problem (US EPA 2009d). More recent studies indicate that some environmental problems remain, including slower than expected ecosystem recovery in some areas.

At the onset of the ARP, some economists claimed that limited participation in the current programs impeded further efficiency gains. By December 1994, a few months before the initial phase of the ARP was to be fully implemented, the Government Accountability Office released an analysis projecting that an allowance trading system could save as much as $3 billion per year, over 50 percent compared with conventional policy approaches. Four years later, Title IV enabled emissions reductions to be achieved at a cost 25–34 percent lower than a command-and-control regime (Schmalensee et al. 1998). This is a considerable efficiency gain ($225 to $375 million annually) but fell short of most savings estimates in the literature comparing actual command-and-control policies with ideal tradable permit systems.

The lion's share of economically quantifiable emissions control benefits result from the reduced risk of premature mortality, especially through reduced exposure to sulfates. These expected benefits measure several times the expected costs of the program. Significant benefits are also estimated for improvements in morbidity, recreational visibility, and residential visibility. These areas, especially human health and visibility, were not the focus of acid rain research in the 1980s, and new information suggests these benefits are greater than were previously anticipated (Burtraw 1996).

It was reported by EPA that more complete analyses of the benefits of ARP show a 40/1 benefit/cost ratio. In particular, Chestnut and Mills (2005) predicted that annual health benefits in 2010 of the ARP reductions of fine particulate matter and ozone would be valued at $119 billion, with an additional $2.6 billion in benefits for improvements in visibility and natural resources (Chestnut and Mills 2005). Burtraw and Szambelan point out that "there remains a large difference between the marginal benefits and the marginal costs of emissions abatement, indicating that emissions levels under the program remain too high to reap substantial economic benefits" (2009, 7). The 2011 NAPAP Report also estimates the benefits of implementing Title IV. Human health benefits from improved air quality due to ARP are estimated to be in the range of $170–430 billion in 2010 alone, on top of the additional benefits resulting from improved visibility and improved ecological conditions.

The use of a cap-and-trade mechanism, which now applies to fully 96 percent of the nation's total electricity generation from fossil fuel, significantly lowered compliance costs by giving utilities flexibility in achieving SO_2 emissions reductions. There is no doubt that the ARP ETS has met its predetermined emission target and cleared the path for other applications of the cap-and-trade policy. In addition, it is now clear that adjusting its caps for increased stringency is possible, but it needs to be done in a manner that maintains the long view and predictability of the program.

Legal Feasibility: Degree to which ETS encountered resistance within the existing legal framework.

The ARP encountered few legal challenges. When President Bush Sr. decided to seek congressional support for the passage of the 1990 CAA, he emphasized that the program "must be capable of being administered in a straightforward and sensible manner, one that minimizes the kind of time-consuming litigation that could prevent the law from being implemented on schedule (1990)." Ten years later, Ellerman et al. (2000) confirmed the achievement of this policy goal in an assessment of the ARP by stating that the Title IV was implemented "on time, without extensive litigation, and at costs lower than predicted."

Administrative Efficiency: Degree to which ETS improved the bureaucracy.

From the perspective of its administrators, the implementation of the ARP has been a total success and has come at a low cost to taxpayers. In addition to the compliance cost savings for regulated entities from trading, this management approach has low administrative costs. In 1997 it was estimated that the ARP's administrative costs of approximately $10–12 million per year would translate into 1.5–1.0 percent per ton of pollution reduced (Kruger and Dean 1997). Of the estimated $3.5 billion in total air pollution control efforts in the US, the SO_2 allowance trading program budget only represents $50–60 million. In other words, the ARP is achieving "40 percent of the emissions reductions mandated under the 1990 CAA with only about 2 percent of the staff and other resources" of national air quality management efforts (McLean 1996). Even with the expansion of ETS, CAMD's operational budget for fiscal year 2011 was only $20.7 million, and has remained at this level for several years now.

As summarized by Kruger and Dean, the design that ultimately resulted from the policy process of developing the 1990 ARP incorporated key components necessary to make it workable and credible:

> A large part of the program's success is attributable to the design of Title IV. Features included for environmental reasons, such as the emissions cap and stringent monitoring, also helped facilitate an emissions trading market and lower administrative and transaction costs. These same features led to greater acceptance by environmental groups and the public, because they provide environmental results. A fundamental "deal" struck in Title IV—large reductions of emissions with a cap, stringent monitoring and automatic enforcement provisions in return for flexibility and trading—was one of the best environmental bargains ever cut by Congress, industry, environmental groups and other stakeholders.
>
> (1997)

5.3 Summary of policy lessons

The ARP ETS experience has been successful in that the predetermined emission reduction targets have been met at costs lower than those of a traditional regulatory program. The framework of the environmental market and careful attention to politics and program design were critical to the success of this first national application of an ETS.

In hindsight, we may conclude that there is room for improvement regarding potential cost saving to be realized by the current policy design, and that ARP's environmental benefits can be enhanced by tightening its emissions targets. From an institutional evolutionary perspective, the ARP ETS experience served to demonstrate that market-based mechanisms for environmental control can work at a large scale to manage air quality in a cost-effective manner.

Much success has been achieved in air pollution control through conventional regulation. One-size-fits-all environmental standards are particularly effective when technologies and processes to reduce emissions are known or readily available and costs are reasonable. But when the regulated industry is complex, a more decentralized approach can be more cost-effective.

The monopolistic, capital-intensive, and highly regulated electric power industry provided a good context to experiment with the implementation of a full-fledged ETS to harness market incentives for cost-effective air pollution control. In the electric-generation industry, with operating equipment that varies in age and uses different fuel-fired-generation technologies, corporate executives and plant managers confront complicated and expensive investment decisions contingent on the regulatory environment and world energy markets. Therefore, developing and implementing a program prescribing *what*, *when*, and *how* to comply with air quality standards can be a cumbersome and costly experience. The ARP ETS contributed to the advancement of market-based environmental policy by successfully implementing the cap-and-trade design, a simple, predictable, and transparent alternative regulatory approach.

The EPA's introduction of new rules of the game with CAIR in 2005, its legal battles, the 2011 Court decision to put the replacement program CSAPR on hold, and CSAPR's rejection in 2012 have resulted in crippling regulatory uncertainty. This situation, along with other exogenous factors, continues to negatively impact this phase in the evolution of US emissions markets. External factors and conditions will change with time, but developing predictable legislated paths for changes in program rules can be an enhancement to minimize regulatory uncertainty in the future.

The following policy features and implementation practices were necessary to make this application of the cap-and-trade system feasible and provide a cost-effective mechanism to address the acid rain problem in the US:

Cap: The ARP's cap set a maximum emissions level for the US power sector. A strict overall emissions cap was crucial to gain support from key politicians and members of the environmental movement. The emissions cap was negotiated and accepted by most stakeholders during the policy formulation process. In contrast to early air pollution ETS developments and the Lead Phasedown Program that allowed permit exchanges on emission differences from some preexisting or external standard, a predetermined emissions cap is a simple and transparent expression of the overall environmental goal.

ETS: Simplicity guided the design of the ARP ETS, with respect to units to be traded, approval of trades, monitoring, reporting, and review. The ARP market component introduced the flexibility necessary for regulated emitters to decide *how*, *where*, and *when* to comply with this predetermined emissions reduction limit, enhancing the flexibility and thus the cost-effectiveness of the program. Reframing the relationship between regulator and industry as a cooperative partnership to control pollution and reduce environmental risk using a market-based mechanism was important to gain support from more conservative stakeholders.

Environmental commodity: It was critical to the ARP that allowance entitlements were known, credible, and applicable over a long period. Incentives to trade in the SO_2 allowance market exist as long as certainty over the value and entitlements of allowances remains. Regulatory uncertainty or opaque paths for adjustment or change have a negative impact on environmental commodities markets.

Allocation: The government decided not to keep the economic rents formed by creating a new environmental asset (i.e., emission allowance) under the ARP in order to increase the political feasibility of this innovative program and minimize the financial burden to the electricity industry and consumers. The initial allocation was based on historic use and was given free of charge instead of using alternative allocation features such an auctioned permit system that would have forced electric utilities to pay full market price for the allowances.

Auction: The so-called zero revenue auction implemented by EPA, which allocated only 3 percent of the allowances, served to jump-start the market as allowances were sold to the highest bidders, and their payments were considered an approximation of the emerging ETS market-clearing price. Revenues from the sales are refunded to the electric utilities from which the allowances were retained on a proportional basis.

Trading rules: ARP rules are clear and unambiguous. Allowances may be traded or banked to anyone for future use or sale provided EPA receives proper documentation of the trade. Flexible timing and inter-temporal trading of allowances under the banking rules have been key design elements. The banking provision became an effective design feature for encouraging early emissions reductions.

Institutional learning and capacity building: Policy designers avoided the bad practices of the first-generation market-like mechanisms. For instance, by not incorporating too many sources and diverse polluting substances (e.g., steel smelters, asphalt plants, etc.), and focusing on the highly regulated and well-monitored electric power generation industry, EPA has been able to experiment and develop the institutional capacity and technical capabilities to implement emissions markets successfully.

Moreover, administrators reduced regulatory uncertainty by eliminating past certification or permitting processes that increased transaction costs and discouraged trading.

Cost savings: While much of the cost saving actually came from an exogenous regulatory reform—the deregulation of the railroad industry—which enhanced the ability of utilities to switch to low-sulfur coal from the West, the decentralized nature of the ARP provided the flexibility to managers to actually take advantage of these events. A more prescriptive approach would have limited managers' capacity to realize this cost-savings opportunity.

Innovation: The ARP has induced some innovation and technological change in scrubbing removal efficiency, as demonstrated by using conventional methods of analysis such as patents. However, the most significant advances came from unexpected changes in non-patentable process adjustments and creative solutions to minimize pollution emissions at the plant level.

Credible commitment and regulatory consistency: For industry, emission targets set in advance allow long-term planning, as the cap is important for market price forecasting and the incorporation of emission costs into capital project planning. A predictable regulatory mechanism allows for long-term view. Certainty in emissions targets and the indefinite nature of the program's time horizon supported the emergence of a well-functioning SO_2 allowance market. The phased-in implementation approach also made ARP predictable, transparent, and consistent as the legislation clearly specified the cap of allowable tons in the system from 1995 to 1999, 2000, and 2010–beyond.

Efficient implementation and smart management practices: The decision to take advantage of advanced information management systems and accurate emissions monitoring devices resulted in reduced information costs to the regulator in verifying emissions reductions and increased transparency by making data available through the Internet. These tools simplified the ARP operation, allowing for a minimal role for regulators, and making the administration of the program relatively more efficient.

Environmental integrity, credibility, and automated control: The electronic monitoring, verification, and reporting of emissions enhanced the environmental integrity of the new air pollution control system, as it ensured that the mandated predetermined emissions limit or cap would be met. These electronic tools allowed for the implementation of automatic, strong sanctions against non-compliant emitters, thereby enhancing the program's credibility among the environmental community.

Fine-tuning: While the ARP includes design features that allow for adjustments, given new scientific information on the environmental problem (or because of other external factors such as technological advances), the legislated cap in Title IV of the 1990 CAA had been perceived by regulated parties and market participants as difficult to change. Recent changes to the program (i.e., CSAPR and CAIR Rules) confirmed that changes to such informal understandings have an impact on price volatility as predictability and perception of the permanence of the ETS program is negatively affected.

Supplementary nature: The ARP ETS is a flexibility mechanism devised to reduce the cost of complying with environmental regulation by complementing the law. The market does not substitute for regulation. If the market-based mechanism fails, local and federal environmental quality standards prevail.

Ultimately, the proposal to develop a regulatory program to address the issue of acid rain based on the theoretical concept of an ETS for air pollution control had to be scrutinized, as with any other policy initiative, by the diverse social forces at play within the US institutional environment. Therefore, negotiated agreements among regulators, state public utilities commissions, industry, and third parties for allowing the passage and implementation of the ARP did reduce the cost-effectiveness attributes of the cap-and-trade system. Incentives to minimize compliance costs may be reduced by complementary regulation of a particular industry, and/or political decisions to compensate affected and related industries, thereby reducing the potential gains from an emissions allowance market. A prime example is the subsidization of scrubbers. The trade-off between efficiency and political feasibility is evident in the historical review of the institutional development of first national ETS.

The CAIR interstate compliance programs introduced the first administrative change to the ARP emission goal. Environmental regulation tends to evolve slowly because of the adversarial nature of the US legal system. Legal battles, judicial involvement, and slow development of the replacement program as requested by the court introduced regulatory uncertainty to the ARP ETS, causing some erratic behavior in the allowance market. These events highlight the importance of incorporating more clarity on how to manage program adjustments, particularly on the emissions targets, while maintaining the incentives to participate in the ETS component of a market-based environmental program.

In summary, the development of the federal ARP was able to provide a predictable structure in the form of the cap-and-trade ETS within which exchange activity developed rapidly. Title IV embraces the emissions trading concept with remarkably few restrictions and avoids the mistakes of the past such as requiring prior approval of individual trades. The purchase and holding of allowances is not restricted to the utilities. All sources receiving allowance allocations, as well as third parties, such as brokers and individuals, are free to buy or sell allowances with any other party. Individuals or interested groups may buy allowances to retire them from the market and consequently eliminate such emissions from the environment. Neither the frequency nor the mechanisms for trading allowances are limited.

To support the exchange activity, EPA delegated the majority of the development of the market governance infrastructure to the private sector, while important policy features to jump-start the market were implemented by EPA. Therefore, the central market organizational functions such as the establishment of broker listings, the posting of current allowance prices, and matching buyers and sellers focusing on the allowance market have all been created by the private sector. Co-operation between the private sector and interest groups in the design and implementation of the ARP achieved the development of a viable environmental market that enhances the cost-effectiveness of this US EPA air quality management program.

The following two chapters will focus on the policy lessons and know-how developed during the process of adapting the ETS approach to different institutional contexts of implementation and environmental problems within the US. Chapter 6 analyzes the use of ETS at the local level in Southern California to address urban ozone issues under the Regional Clean Air Incentives Markets program, and Chapter 7 reviews the implementation process for the regional air pollution trading programs mentioned in this chapter (i.e., NBP, CAIR, and CSAPR).

Chapter 6

Local market-based environmental policy

California's South Coast Air Quality Management District (SCAQMD or AQMD) is a pioneer in the use of emission trading systems (ETS) at the local level. In 1994, amidst poor economic conditions, SCAQMD implemented the Regional Clean Air Incentives Markets (RECLAIM) in the Los Angeles air basin; it was the first cap-and-trade system to address the pervasive problem of ground ozone (i.e., smog). The program affects four counties (Los Angeles, Riverside, San Bernardino, and Orange), and their jurisdictions include 161 cities. In its design, administrators made a point of incorporating local community and businesses interests by considering impacts to the economy, environmental justice aspects, and cost-effectiveness. RECLAIM's emission caps decline over time to ensure that the environmental goal established through the policy formulation process will be met. Emission credits under this program are valid for one year only, and they may not be saved for use in future compliance years. The program also introduces incentives to encourage business to utilize advanced emissions control technologies to further reduce emissions.

From an institutional development perspective, addressing the worst case of urban smog in the nation using a trading mechanism has been a testing experience. Several innovative features first introduced by RECLAIM (multi-industry application, taking into account macroeconomic conditions, cost management features, seasonal and geographical considerations, inter-jurisdictional coordination, strong community involvement, and an "offset" feature) offer important policy lessons. Program adjustments were necessary in order to respond to challenges posed to RECLAIM's environmental and economic performance during the California power crisis in 2000 and 2001. These events made salient several program vulnerabilities. RECLAIM was amended in 2005 to address these issues.

6.1 Developing the RECLAIM ETS

6.1.1 Background

Historically, air pollution in Los Angeles has been among the worst in the United States (US). Significant sulfur dioxide (SO_2) emissions and chemical reactions of nitrogen oxides (NO_x) with volatile organic compounds (VOCs, also referred to as reactive organic compounds) create high concentrations of ozone (O_3), a key element of smog,[1] which concentrates in part because of the region's unique climatic and geographic features (Klier, Matoon, and Praeger 1997, 753). The Environmental Protection Agency (EPA) has identified these air pollutants as endangering public health and welfare. As indicated in earlier chapters, EPA establishes and enforces health-based air quality standards, the National Ambient Air Quality Standards (NAAQS), that all states must achieve under the federal Clean Air Act (CAA).

A strict regulatory framework was developed in the 1970s to support the Los Angeles air quality program in complying with state and federal environmental protection laws. However, these conventional regulatory approaches had not proven effective in bringing the region into compliance with the national NAAQS and had become very costly (SCAQMD 1995). The state responded in 1988 with the California CAA, mandating a 5 percent per year reduction of NO_x, SO_2, and VOC emissions in air quality districts that were not meeting federal standards. By the late 1980s, the public and private sectors both supported investigating the use of market-based incentives to attain clean air in the Los Angeles air basin (SCAQMD 1993, EX-5).

The 1990 CAA amendments identified the Los Angeles area as an "extreme" non-attainment zone, in fact the worst in the nation. Ultimately, the 1990 CAA amendments mandated that the Air Quality Management Plan (AQMP) of the local air district had to achieve NAAQS for ozone by the year 2010. Also, since compliance with the new requirements in Title I of the CAA represented significant control efforts, it also authorized the use of economic incentives to achieve those goals in a more cost-effective manner (Thompson 2000, 653). The AQMP was submitted in 1991 to the federal EPA, specifying how SCAQMD would achieve the overall targets. After broad multi-stakeholder consultations and with technical assistance from the federal EPA—which conveyed the accumulated know-how from developing first-generation federal trading mechanisms and the design experience of the then-new Acid Rain Program (ARP)—SCAQMD decided to implement a cap-and-trade system: RECLAIM ETS. By capping facility mass emissions for the first time, the AQMP introduced more certainty in overall emission reductions. As in ARP, the introduction of continuous emission monitoring systems (CEMS) allowed regulators to obtain in real time electronic measurements of controlled emissions which are expressed in lb/h (i.e., mass emissions) to establish flows during 15-minute, hourly, and daily periods. RECLAIM is designed to achieve the environmental goals of the AQMP at a lesser cost than under command-and-control rules through added compliance flexibility and by providing additional incentives to industry to reduce emissions and improve control technologies.

At the state level, the California Air Resources Board (a semi-independent body under the State of California's EPA) had oversight of the plan. The SCAQMD steering and advisory committees offered local, inclusive, and diverse perspectives on how to design and implement RECLAIM to minimize the health risks and economic impact to their communities. In total, their work included six months of concept development, a 12-month feasibility study, and 18 months of rule language development (SCAQMD 1993, EX-5). This constituted a short development period in comparison with the ARP ETS. Every three years, SCAQMD presents a new, or updated, plan to be included in California's state implementation plan (SIP). Each version of the AQMP has a 20-year horizon.

RECLAIM was adopted by the SCAQMD on October 15, 1993. Implementation began in January 1994 (some facilities participate based on the calendar year, January 1 through December 31, while others are based on the fiscal year, July 1 through June 30). RECLAIM's cap-and-trade system went into effect a year earlier than Phase I of the federal ARP ETS, making it the first operational ETS in the nation.

6.1.2 Adapting the cap-and-trade model to meet the needs of SCAQMD

6.1.2 (A) Environmental commodities: defining the RECLAIM entitlements

Select the Emitted Substance(s) to Control: After holding lengthy public hearings and conducting a feasibility study that evaluated numerous design alternatives, the District Governing Board ordered the development of the rules and technical papers necessary to implement the RECLAIM program for NO_x, sulfur oxide (SO_x), and VOC emissions from large facilities. However, pressure from environmental groups as well as technical and other policy considerations caused them to cancel the commoditization of VOCs.[2]

The first notable feature of the RECLAIM program is that it creates a multi-source, multi-industry air quality management program to cut NO_x and SO_2 emissions in the Los Angeles metropolitan area region. Including both emissions in a single program was ambitious and unprecedented.

Define the Extent of the Entitlement: The NO_x and SO_x allowances are expressed as RECLAIM Trading Credits (RTC), where one unit of RTC is valid for one pound of emissions for a specific compliance year. RECLAIM requires facility owners to ensure that their facility-wide NO_x and/or SO_x emissions do not exceed the amount of RTCs available in their allocation account for any year.

Create a Homogeneous Unit: Due to concerns about the distribution of the pollutants in the airshed and the particular geography of the region, additional constraints were placed upon NO_x emissions trading in the South Coast air basin area (Stavins 1995, 145).

Los Angeles is in a basin with a mountain range to the east and the industrial area in the coastal zone to the west. In the morning, the wind blows from the ocean in the west toward the mountains to the east. By midday, the mountains block continued airflow, trapping collected pollutants. In the evening, the wind blows east to west, giving natural pollution relief (Evolution Markets 2002). The difference in the impact of emissions based on their location led to the decision to create two zones of RTCs: inland and coastal.

In this design, known as a two-cycle system, not all NO_x RTCs are equivalent. Although permits may be traded across zones, coastal facilities are not allowed to use inland zone credits for compliance. Facilities inland have no such restrictions (Evolution Markets 2002). The rationale behind this constraint is that reductions in the coastal zone are particularly critical to meeting the environmental goals of the program (Klier, Matoon, and Praeger 1997, 755).

Set a Baseline: The baseline allocations were based on actual facility annual emissions between 1987 and 1992. Facilities were able to select the year in that period that best reflected, in their own opinion, a reasonable production year.

The baseline establishment system was one of the most contentious design features of RECLAIM, since the baseline affects the initial allocation of permits.[3] The allocations allowed estimates adjusting for recession periods for each participating facility, if necessary. As stated in Thompson (2000), the business community favored this approach to determine initial RTC allocations because it enabled them to use activity levels from non-recessionary years (pre-1990) to determine starting allocations. They also agreed with the emissions reduction factors used to calculate future allocations. Environmental and public health groups did not like this proposal because initial allocations were much higher than recent actual emissions. Nevertheless, because the program met the objectives of the AQMP and the affected businesses supported it, the board of the District approved this proposal in October 1993 (Thompson 2000, 656).

6.1.2 (B) Emissions trading system development

Emissions Targets: Initially, RECLAIM required major facilities in the region to reduce their NO_x emissions by about 70 percent from business-as-usual over a ten-year period from 1994 through 2003 (Thompson 2000, 2).

The program established a declining cap for ozone compounds emissions for each year from 1994 to 2003, with a stable cap afterwards. The total cap was to be 23,435 tons of NO_x and 6435 tons of SO_2 per year in 2003. The SO_2 component was also implemented in preparation for compliance with Phase II of the federal ARP, as the implementation schedule of Title IV expanded its SO_2 allowance trading mechanism nationwide in 2000 (SCAQMD 1993, EX-29). However, in 2005, RECLAIM was amended to require an additional 22.5 percent reduction in NO_x allocations by 2011, taking into account advances in emission control technology while also correcting for initial design flaws. The reduction in RTC holdings is known as the "NO_x RTC shave," and was fully implemented by January 2011. These additional reductions in NO_x allocations were phased in as well. Four tons per day were reduced in 2007. During the period 2008–2011 most participants had their

RTCs reduced further and have had to account for a cumulative reduction by 2011 of 7.7 tons of NO_x per day. No further reductions are planned starting with the compliance year 2012. This process was partially the result of new evaluation assessments based on best available retrofit control technology.

Since SO_2 emissions contribute to the formation of ozone and fine particulate matter, RECLAIM supports California's goal to achieve the $PM_{2.5}$ (fine particulate matter with an aerodynamic diameter of up to 2.5 μm) federal 24-hour average ambient air quality standards by 2015, and a more stringent 8-hour level by 2024, through trading and by accelerating the adoption of existing commercially viable control technologies. Significant reductions are needed from all sources, but controlling emission from mobile sources is essential for achieving attainment "since the bulk of the remaining air quality problems stems from Mobile Source emissions." Supplementary measures such as introducing ultra-low emission standards for both new and existing equipment in the transport sectors, as well as acceleration of fleet turnover are expected (SCAQMD 2007).

Exemptions from additional allowance reductions may be requested of SCAQMD based on adoption of advanced emissions control technologies, but those investments must be additional and verifiable to avoid exceeding the program's cap. On November 5, 2010, SCAQMD adopted amendments that will result in cumulative reductions of 5.7 tons per day, or more than a 51 percent reduction, of sulfur oxides from all RECLAIM facilities by 2019 (i.e., SO_x RTC shave). The changes are to be implemented in phases: three tons per day in 2013, four tons per day in each year from 2014 through 2016, five tons per day in 2017 and 2018, and 5.7 tons per day in 2019 and beyond.

Initial Allocation: Using the grandfathering allocation method, each participating facility was allocated a declining number of RTCs based on historic emissions for free. Initial allocations of RTCs were made at the facility level rather than at the corporation level.

Incumbents (i.e., RECLAIM facilities that at the time of adoption were emitting more than four tons of any of the controlled substances per year) were granted a base number of RTCs for free each year. As discussed above, RECLAIM's initial design allowed participating facilities to choose which year to use for the basis of 1994 and 2000 allocations. This period reflects a period of economic growth, therefore presenting a high baseline of reference to measure emissions.

Ex post analyses show that the consequence of selecting maximum emissions over a historic baseline period of four years resulted in an over-allocation of RTCs in the initial years of the program (Schwarze and Zapfel 2000, 287). In the first year of the program, 37 percent of credits went unused. On average, 20 percent of annual RTC allocations went unused (SCAQMD 2007, I-4-2). Then as the declining cap tightened the RTC market, meaningful trades began to register in 2000. However, due to the different factors that caused the power crisis in 2000 and 2001, demand for allowances from the electric sector outpaced market supply, and the

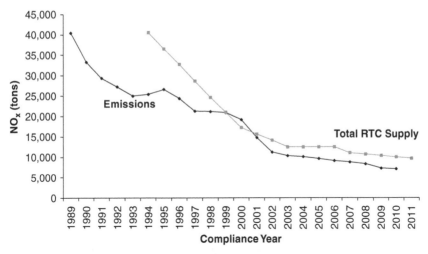

Figure 6.1 RECLAIM NO$_x$ Emission Trends and ETS Implementation
Source: SCAQMD

program's cross-over point between actual emissions and the overall emission limits was surpassed. Electricity generators during this period emitted 24 percent over their total allowance holdings, breaching the RECLAIM emissions cap. Figure 6.1 shows the trends of actual NO$_x$ emissions and RECLAIM ETS allocations.

The initial permit allocations were set based on a percentage reduction from baseline NO$_x$ and SO$_2$ emissions from each regulated facility.[4] The allocation (i.e., Total RTC Supply) used a straight-line depreciation method with a beginning point in 1994, a midpoint in 2000, and an endpoint in 2003. The 2000 midpoint was based on SIP retrofit requirements. The 2003 endpoint was based on SIP inventory requirements. Allocations after 2003 use the corresponding year as their endpoint (Evolution Markets 2002). In addition to being able to pick maximum production levels for the basis of their allocation, participating facilities were allowed to "amend prior emissions reports," mostly to increase their emissions permits. Facilities were also able to convert conventional ERCs held by them before the adoption of RECLAIM into the new RTCs during the first six months of the program (RECLAIM 2007).[5] ERCs that resulted from real, permanent, and quantifiable emission reductions and external offsets that were provided for New Source Review (NSR) purposes were added to each facility's allocation.

As reviewed in chapters 4 and 5, NSR is a preconstruction review required under both federal and California statutes for new and modified sources located in "non-attainment" areas such as the SCAQMD. It requires facilities to install pollution control equipment before they are built or modified. Facilities with a net increase in emissions are required to offset the emission increase by use of ERCs.

Each RECLAIM facility for its initial allocation receives non-tradable emissions credits equal to the difference between the highest year's emissions between 1987 and 1991, and the allocation. The non-tradable credits are devalued by one-third each year for three years. The non-tradable credit may be used only for increased hours of operation. However, to utilize the non-tradable credit, the facility must pay an impact mitigation fee of $5000 per ton. In the event a facility sells any tradable RTCs, the non-tradable credits become invalid and are no longer available to the facility. Conversion rules added 1183 tons to the RECLAIM allocations from 1994 to 2000. This allocation source gradually declined to 850 tons in 2003.[6]

In order to attain the ambient air quality standards set in the AQMP, the overall program emissions reductions were set at 8.3 percent per year for NO_x and 6.5 percent per year for SO_2 (under conventional regulation, VOC emissions are to be reduced by approximately 7 percent per year). Refineries and electric utilities were given NO_x allowances totaling 23,289 tons, while other industries received 18,139 tons. The amount initially allocated to utilities and refineries represented more than 56 percent of overall RECLAIM NO_x allocations.

As mentioned above, allocations were made at the facility level and not to parent or holding companies. However, companies are able to transfer RTCs among facilities, and SCAQMD records these transactions as "trades for no price" (Klier, Matoon, and Praeger 1997, 757–758). Under the original rules, the RECLAIM ETS reached a level of 34.2 tons per day of NO_x RTC in the market. After the 2005 policy refinements were introduced (i.e., the NO_x RTC shave), an exchange ratio was introduced by multiplying the amount of an affected source's current RTC holdings by specific adjustment factors, depending on each compliance year.

Determine Program Participants: RECLAIM covers a mix of stationary sources located in the SCAQMD region. As discussed earlier, sources with NO_x or SO_2 emissions greater than four tons per year are required to participate in the RECLAIM program (and like the ARP, some are exempt—schools, firefighting facilities, restaurants, hospitals, public transit agencies, equipment rental facilities, and essential public services). The initial universe of participants emitted approximately 65 percent of total allowable stationary NO_x emissions in the SCAQMD air basin. By 1995, 37 of the original 390 permitted facilities had exited the program, as some sources were found to have emissions lower than four tons per year or to have met the criteria for exemption.

As in the case of ARP, RECLAIM allows facilities to enter the program voluntarily. Once facilities opt into the program, they are not able to return to the traditional command-and-control regulations (SCAQMD 1993, EX-16). By 2000, the number of facilities participating in RECLAIM had grown slightly, to 364, through the opt-in option (SCAQMD 2001, ES-1). However, due to facility shutdowns the total number of participating facilities was down to 281 as of June 30, 2011 (SCAQMD 2012).

Regulated SO_2 sources are exclusively 33 electric utilities. However, for NO_x emissions, the RECLAIM program design expands the range of participants beyond just electric utilities, oil refineries, and petrochemical plants to include industries such as the aerospace industry, foundries, glass processors, breweries, cement manufacturers, dry cleaners, and even theme parks such as Disneyland (Evolution Markets 2002). Despite the breadth of participants, nearly 85 percent of the NO_x emissions initial baseline came from just 14 facilities in the following industries:

* oil and gas extraction;
* stone, clay, and glass industry;
* petroleum and coal products; and
* electricity, gas, and sanitary services.

As mentioned above, the largest source of NO_x emissions is actually motor vehicles.[7] An interesting novelty of the RECLAIM program is the development of project-based offsets from mobile sources. For instance, Rule 1610 allows certain mobile source emission reductions to attain RTCs. Conversions of emission reduction credits owned by RECLAIM and non-RECLAIM facilities, and conversion of ERCs from mobile and area sources are included in the RECLAIM program's RTC supply.[8] For example, a facility could earn RTCs by scrapping high-emissions vehicles. However, the EPA did not approve the SCAQMD's early mobile source credit rules. Therefore, in order to avoid lawsuits under federal regulations, facilities did not use this feature. Rule 1612.1 allows facilities to generate mobile-source RTCs by replacing heavy-duty diesel trucks, warehouse yard hostlers, or refuse trucks with clean-fueled, lower-emission models. The goal is to reduce toxic diesel emissions in the neighborhoods where they are used.

In 2001, SCAQMD and EPA developed pilot credit rules for mobile sources sanctioned under federal law, hoping to ease RTC market demand during the electricity crisis. Also, these rules aimed at additional air quality improvements, since 9 percent of the credits generated are to be retired and thus will not be eligible for use in the RECLAIM ETS (SCAQMD 2001). As the RECLAIM program continues to expand its scope of participants, mobile sources are expected to become a more significant source of RTCs. For example, pending mobile source credit generation programs expected to be implemented by SCAQMD are: (1) fuel cells to power ships in port; (2) electrification of truck and trailer refrigeration units; and (3) the replacement of diesel-fueled agricultural pumps. The inclusion of project-based credits did not have a significant effect on the market during the electricity crisis since there were not enough of them to buffer price volatility due to a surge in demand for RTCs at that time.

Trading Rules: Credits are assigned each year. They can be bought or sold for use within that year, but because of the nature of the environmental problem (i.e., non-uniformly mixed substances forming ozone), no banking is allowed. The staggered trading allows for partial banking activities (i.e., borrowing and saving) during a period of six months under RECLAIM's two-cycle design.

As in the case of the ARP, the SCAQMD placed minimal restrictions on how RTCs can be traded. Facilities must hold credits equal to their actual emissions. They can sell excess credits to firms that do not meet their limits. Organizations and individuals who are not RECLAIM facilities are free to participate in the market (Klier, Matoon, and

Praeger 1997, 753). The SCAQMD maintains a list of all parties holding credits. No matter who buys or sells, regulators require that total emissions be reduced each year. SCAQMD does not need to approve trades, nor does it operate a formal auction or clearinghouse for RTCs. The lack of a full banking provision caused significant problems during the 2000–2001 period when RTC price volatility was exacerbated by the electric crisis and the government decided to intervene in the market.

As electric utilities scrambled to meet a surge in demand during the power crisis in 2000 and 2001, old, high-emitting facilities were brought back online, causing companies to quickly use up their allowance budgets and to buy more than the usual number of additional RTCs from the RECLAIM ETS. This external event caused a scarcity of the environmental commodity and consequently a spike in the price per ton of NO_x.

SCAQMD amended the rules during this time, and temporarily removed the electric power sector from the RECLAIM RTC market, allowing some flexibility on compliance methods by presenting action plans. For instance, electric utilities were able to mitigate excess emissions by paying mitigation fees that were then used by SCAQMD to reduce emissions from other sources, such as mobile sources and agricultural equipment. Also, electric utilities were required to install additional emissions controls, overlaying a more conventional approach on top of the RECLAIM ETS to address financial and environmental issues caused by the electricity crisis (RECLAIM 2007, I-3–8). Burtraw et al. (2005) suggested that a preannounced fee on emissions excesses could have been a more efficient solution.

The following are two innovative rules introduced by the RECLAIM program:

(1) *Staggered trading*: A unique feature of the RECLAIM program is that the annual budget of emissions credits that each facility receives is established in staggered trading cycles. Facilities are assigned to one of two cycles, their annual RTC budget being valid from either January 1 to December 31 (Cycle 1) or July 1 to June 30 (Cycle 2). Figure 6.2 illustrates how a Cycle 1 facility can purchase NO_x RTCs from a Cycle 2 facility to offset emissions during the first six months of year 2.

   The goal of staggered trading cycles is to smooth trading behavior. Approximately half of the facilities are assigned to each cycle. However, facilities are free to purchase RTCs in the other cycle (SCAQMD 2001, 2–3). Consequently, two types of credits are available within a compliance year, each of which expires at a different time. Partial flexibility is granted by RECLAIM as sources are able to trade between sources during the overlap period. However, experience shows that this short-term flexibility was not enough to address the spike in RECLAIM ETS prices during the 2001 power crisis.

(2) *Price cap or safety valve*: As a cost management feature, the SCAQMD Governing Board adopted a maximum average price of RTCs. The Governing Board may reevaluate the program if the price of RTCs exceeds a predetermined level of $25,000 per ton of NO_x. Although this feature may increase the political feasibility of the program, it may also interfere with the efficiency aspects of the policy design (SCAQMD 1993, EX-13).

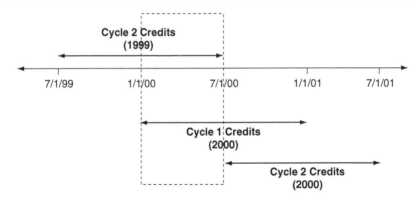

Figure 6.2 RECLAIM Trading Cycles
Source: SCAQMD (2001)

In 2000, Governor Davis invoked this feature because of the electricity crisis in the state. RECLAIM experienced a sharp and sudden increase in RTC prices, limiting the capacity of electric power generators to participate in the market. By the end of 2000, RTC prices went as high as $50,000 per ton of NO_x as the power sector scrambled to buy allowances to cover for emissions from the now-active older and dirtier facilities.

In 2005, a new rule to address price volatility (i.e., safety valve) was added with a price and temporal trigger. If prices go above $7.50 per pound for a three-month period, SCAQMD can request the Governing Board to increase annual allocations up to peak levels of 2004 (i.e., non-tradable RTC) for the following year, and launch a review of the program. If the rolling average price exceeds $15,000 per ton, then the SCAQMD Governing Board may direct RECLAIM administrators to trigger the safety valve. This action reinstates RTC holdings that had been deemed not-tradable/non-usable by the program refinements (i.e., NO_x RTC shave) for the next compliance Cycle 1 period after the finding. In another 2005 rule change, electric power sector facilities that were removed from the market during the energy crisis were reinstated to participate in the RECLAIM ETS. Their participation was limited initially to avoid excess supply in the market. These facilities could only sell their allowance holding to new generators (i.e., on-line in 2004) and for compliance years 2005 and 2006. On January 1, 2007 large producers regained full trading authority (Evolution Markets 2012).

6.1.2 (C) Market governance infrastructure

Environmental Financial Services, Exchanges, and Auctions: The SCAQMD does not operate as a formal clearinghouse. Firms are free to enter into private negotiations directly with other firms (Klier, Matoon, and Praeger 1997, 757).

While the ARP auctions are held based upon a legal mandate, RECLAIM auctions are organized by the private sector. They take place semi-annually (Schwarze and

Zapfel 2000, 290). RECLAIM and the ARP also differ in the type of auction used: all RECLAIM RTCs are traded at one market-clearing price, whereas in the ARP, each successful bidder pays the price of their successful bid (Schwarze and Zapfel 2000, 289). In the RECLAIM auctions, RTCs for several years can be traded, but each can only be used in its designated year. The SCAQMD keeps track of each transfer of RTCs between facilities and brokers, or other non-RECLAIM entities, and between separate facilities of a firm. However, it does not record intra-trading (Klier, Matoon, and Praeger 1997, 757).

The private sector participates in the RECLAIM market as intermediaries and by standardizing exchange activities. However, the Automated Credit Exchange, a key online brokerage system launched by EonXchange at the onset of the program in 1995, went bankrupt in 2004 after the founder was arrested on multiple felony counts of fraud, and was convicted in 2008. The RECLAIM auctions are completely dependent on the secondary market (i.e., offers submitted by RTCs holders). Auctions allow prospective buyers and sellers to submit offers to buy or sell RTCs. Cantor Fitzgerald (now BGC Environmental Brokerage Services), a firm that played an active role in the development of the SO_2 allowance market, runs the Clean Air Auction Market, one of the private trading systems currently conducting RECLAIM brokerage services. Cantor Fitzgerald holds semi-annual auctions. Another major player is Evolution Markets, which offers a similar trading platform and brokerage services.

Because the SCAQMD needs to know who holds RTCs at any given time, it requires that facilities transfer RTCs to the broker's account before selling them. Once a buyer is found, the RTCs are transferred again, this time from the broker to the buyer. Accordingly, the SCAQMD records a successful sale through a broker as two transactions: one from the seller to the broker (usually recorded for no price). If the broker is unable to find a buyer for the RTCs it holds, the seller may take the RTCs back for no price, or may allow the broker to continue to hold the RTCs for future sale (Klier, Matoon, and Praeger 1997, 758). Finally, SCAQMD requires the reporting of the price for which the RTCs traded.

Information Management Services: The SCAQMD operates a publicly accessible, computerized bulletin board system posted on the Internet (SCAQMD 2011).

The bulletin board contains two types of accounts: compliance accounts and general accounts. Allowances are identified by zone and cycle. However, NO_x allowances do not have serial numbers as in the ARP. Transactions are recorded by the date on which the paperwork is received at SCAQMD (Evolution Markets 2012). The SCAQMD publishes an annual report (Klier, Matoon, and Praeger 1997, 758), and the private sector also provides information on the RECLAIM market.[9]

6.1.2 (D) Program implementation parameters

Monitoring, Reporting, and Verification: RECLAIM requires submission of periodic emissions reports and certified quarterly compliance statements. RECLAIM has three levels of emission reporting requirements depending on the type and size of sources: major sources, emitting over ten tons per year, report on a daily basis by electronic means; large sources report on a monthly basis; and minor sources report on a quarterly basis.

Industry initially opposed the RECLAIM project because of the potentially high costs of its monitoring requirements.[10] However, the argument that these costs would be balanced by lower overall compliance costs for each facility prevailed. As reported in SCAQMD (2007, I-6–1), the data pathway from CEMS to Remote Terminal Units to SCAQMD's central station for electronic reporting, known as the Emissions Reporting System, was established very early in the design and has "remained relatively unchanged." The following are the most important features developed to support the monitoring and reporting activities.

Continuous Emissions Monitoring Systems: CEMS, such as the ones required for all sources under the ARP, are mandated for two-thirds of RECLAIM affected facilities. Major sources (i.e., electric power utilities) report daily, using ARP-type CEMS. Less accurate and cheaper technologies are allowed for non-major sources (Schwarze and Zapfel 2000, 288).

During the initial years of the program when CEMS were being installed and certified, many facilities had substantial periods of missing data. To provide incentives for emitters to use accurate CEMS, a procedure by which emissions data were replaced with substitute data was implemented. The Missing Data Procedures (MDP) helped SCAQMD to determine emissions when actual emission data were not obtained by a CEMS or other allowed methods. MDP is based on very stringent, conservative, emission substitution protocols, thus creating an incentive to correct problems quickly (SCAQMD 2007).

This was important, since initially RECLAIM participants had to pay fees based on the amount of RTCs they held, regardless of whether the RTCs were being used for compliance. This rule required retirement of a substantial number of RTCs to cover the worst-case emissions scenarios resulting from the MDP. The SCAQMD later changed this requirement so facilities only pay fees based on actual emissions but, as in the SO_2 program, emissions estimates for non-monitored periods were doubled progressively (Margolis and Langdon 1995). Also, to improve monitoring, a transportable CEMS unit allows testing of alternative monitoring systems by positioning the equipped vehicle "side-by-side with traditional CEMS for 30 days to establish system validity" (SCAQMD, March 1999).

Emissions Management System: EMS provide market information support and oversight capacity. SCAQMD requires traders to report all trades, including how the RTCs are going to be used. As in the ARP's EMS, SCAQMD records this information to facilitate its monitoring and recording procedures, not for market evaluation purposes (Klier, Matoon, and Praeger 1997, 765). Market analysis is conducted by the private sector. Because of RECLAIM's market volatility during the energy crisis of 2000–2001, amendments to the RECLAIM program were introduced to increase the information regarding RTC trades.

As in the case of the ARP, technological progress in the area of information management allows RECLAIM reporting to be automated. An internal data entry system was developed to collect submitted data, provide facility quality control review of submittals, and track the processing of submittals. Moreover, the data entry software allows entry of data reported automatically from RECLAIM facilities and performs calculations for comparing this information with the data submission reports. The RECLAIM tracking system and database follow each submittal and potential data discrepancies (i.e., MDP), and prioritize the processing order of submittals (SCAQMD & Ecoteck 2001, 1). As described earlier, RECLAIM's emissions monitoring, reporting, and recordkeeping include extensive and detailed protocols that cover CEMS, periodic reporting for large sources, source testing requirements, electronic reporting, and reference methods. Accuracy in measurement is a program design priority and is based on redundancy systems such as the MDP, data bias tests, equipment tune-ups, and CEMS data quality and performance audits (SCAQMD 2007).

Emissions Inventories: The Annual Emission Reports filed by over 3000 medium-to-large stationary source facilities provided the basis for the SCAQMD's emissions inventory. The accuracy of the inventory has significant implications, since it is used for planning, rule development, and emissions fee calculation purposes, as well as for determining the applicability of federal, state, or local programs (SCAQMD & Ecoteck 2001, 1). Given the demand for this type of sophisticated information management system, a market niche for environmental consultants emerged. The private sector now provides software services to assist companies in conducting emissions inventories of their operations in order to quantify emissions released by each piece of equipment and by the facility as a whole.[11]

Transparency: As mentioned earlier, SCAQMD hosts an electronic bulletin board, making information about RECLAIM facilities and their available RTCs and about RTC transactions available to the public. The bulletin board allows access to information for independent analyses of program performance. However, limited information is publicly available on factors motivating firm trading behavior.

Certification: RECLAIM includes annual and three-year audits to ensure that program goals are being achieved and that air quality control technology is being improved. The RECLAIM Governing Board submits these reports to the California State Legislature. The reported data are also audited by SCAQMD to ensure compliance with district rules, policies, and emissions calculation guidelines (SCAQMD & Ecoteck 2001, 1).

RECLAIM Fees: SCAQMD rules require all sources to pay emissions fees on NO_x and SO_2 pollutants above four tons. In addition, a unique feature, and an important source of revenue to help fund the administration of RECLAIM, is the processing fees that apply to different operational elements of the program such as monitoring, certification, permit renewals, reporting errors, and technical assessments under Rule 301–Permitting and Associated Fees (SCAQMD 2002). For example, facilities entering the program after its initial implementation in 1994 will pay 10 percent of the sum of the permit fees from the Summary Permit Fee Rates tables for each piece of equipment added to the RECLAIM facility's permit. Facilities opting in with new equipment will pay a Facility Permit Fee equal to the sum total of permit processing fees from the fees schedule for each piece of equipment merged into the facility permit.[12]

Overall, SCAQMD collects approximately $20 million (almost 15 percent of its budget) annually in fees. Along with annual operating permit renewal fees, emissions fees are intended to recover the costs of SCAQMD's compliance, planning, rule making, monitoring, testing, source education, civil litigation cases, and stationary and area source research projects (SCAQMD 2009, 95).

Political Jurisdiction: RECLAIM was designed to meet the requirements of the federal and state CAAs for all sources. RECLAIM ensures compliance with other state and federal requirements, such as using the local Best Available Control Technology. Moreover, SCAQMD conducts emissions modeling to ensure that facilities operating under RECLAIM do not hinder the attainment of the NAAQS.

Enforcement: Variation from RECLAIM emissions caps is prohibited. Exceedances are established during annual reconciliation periods. Facilities exceeding their emissions cap face penalties and abatement orders that require them to install control equipment and mitigate excess emissions (SCAQMD August 2000). Larger facilities must submit compliance plans.

Sanctions: RECLAIM sanctions are less strict (i.e., up to $500 per violation) but more burdensome to regulators than those of the ARP. While the emission of one ton of excess SO_2 triggers an automatic penalty under ARP, RECLAIM requires SCAQMD to file suit against each delinquent participant, and each suit may or may not result in sanctions. These procedures add transaction costs to the program in the form of legal fees and time-consuming litigation. However, as in the case of the ARP, RECLAIM automatically offsets uncovered emissions by an equivalent reduction to the allowance budget for the subsequent compliance period. In addition, new disclosure rules were introduced on March 31, 2001. Since then, hefty sanctions are levied for not complying with reporting requirements. SCAQMD established that failure to comply with this reporting order is "subject to civil or criminal penalty of up to $10,000 per day for each day between the report's deadline and its actual submittal."[13]

Program Noncompliance and Community Action: If RECLAIM does not meet its emissions targets, environmental and civil society groups may file suit against

SCAQMD for violating federal and state law. If the SCAQMD is found to be in violation of the federal and state CAAs, several sanctions could be imposed, most importantly the elimination of new source-permitting authority.[14] Without new source permitting, no construction of new facilities emitting NO_x and SO_2 could take place, with implications for the local economy (Thompson 2001, 670).

6.1.3. RECLAIM's implementation record

6.1.3 (A) Environmental progress

SCAQMD (1995) reported that in 1977 the area experienced 121 cases of Stage 1 episodes, or what is considered very unhealthy air quality. In 1989, the area experienced only 54 such episodes, and by 1995, the number was down to 14. However, SCAQMD (1996) recognized that 14 percent of RECLAIM facilities failed to comply with RECLAIM emissions budgets by emitting more NO_x than permitted. Some analysts believe that this was the result of a lack of understanding of the program rules (SCAQMD 1996). Then, during the first five years of RECLAIM implementation (1994–1998), excess RTCs were available in the market due to facility shutdowns, relocations outside the SCAQMD jurisdiction, and improved process efficiency. These RTCs were available at a much lower cost than the installation cost of control equipment (SCAQMD 2001).

Nevertheless, in 1999, SCAQMD announced the first year without a single Stage 1 episode in 50 years (SCAQMD October 1999). In 2000, SCAQMD reported that, for the second year in a row, the South Coast air basin was no longer the worst ozone pollution area in the nation (SCAQMD October 2000). By 2007, SCAQMD administrators stated that RECLAIM "has proven to be a valuable tool in reducing air pollution in the South Coast region" of California (SCAQMD 2007). Figure 6.3 shows smog levels over time.

6.1.3 (B) Market performance

RECLAIM was implemented in January 1994, but trading was slow at first. Unlike the 1990 ARP, the traders in RECLAIM initially had to find trading partners without the help of centralized auction mechanisms. Emitters are heterogeneous and often do not participate in similar input or output markets, so searching the RTC markets was time consuming and costly for RECLAIM facilities. Also, analysts were surprised by the fact that RECLAIM ETS participants were not behaving according to predictions based on rational behavior. Regulators observed that firms were not selling their excess RTCs despite implementing emission reduction strategies that would have allowed them to do so.

Trading picked up as new facilities were added in 1995, and the market is now relatively active (SCAQMD March 1998). Private sector brokers played a key role as market makers by providing information and exchange services. RECLAIM

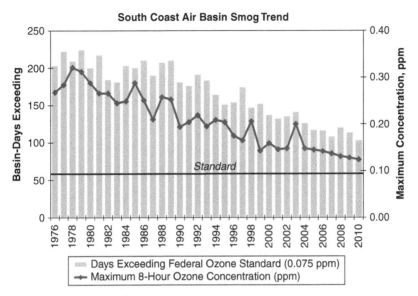

Figure 6.3 South Coast Air Basin Smog Trend
Source: http://www.aqmd.gov/smog/historicaldata.htm

participants are now using the RTC market as a means to comply with their allocations. As described by SCAQMD (2001, 4):

> Since the adoption of RECLAIM, an active trading market has developed for both NO_x and SO_x RTCs. During the early years of the RECLAIM program, RTCs could be obtained at a very low price. Therefore, many RECLAIM operators relied on purchasing credits rather than making investments in air pollution control equipment. The average price per ton of SO_x RTCs from 1996 to 2000 remained relatively stable, ranging from $1,500 to $3,000. However, the price of NO_x RTCs increased dramatically in 2000.

SCAQMD observed increased emissions during 2000. This was mainly due to the increase in generation rates at local power plants in response to the deregulated market. SCAQMD's year 2000 market assessment describes these market pressures:

> Beginning June 2000, RECLAIM program participants experienced a sharp and sudden increase in NO_x RTC prices for both 1999 and 2000 compliance years. The average price of 1999 NO_x RTCs traded in 2000 was $15,377 per ton, which was almost ten times higher than the average price of $1,827 per ton of NO_x RTCs traded in 1999 for the same compliance year. More significantly, the average price of NO_x RTCs for compliance year 2000, traded in the year

2000 increased sharply to over $45,000 per ton compared to the average price of $4,284 per ton traded in 1999.

(SCAQMD 2001, ES-2)

Figure 6.4 shows the RTC prices for NO_x (the diamond pattern) traded in 2000 relative to earlier years in RECLAIM. The increase in RTC price for NO_x corresponds quite closely to the reaching of the cross-over point where emissions equal allocations, as shown in Figure 6.1.

In May of 2001, the SCAQMD Board approved amendments to RECLAIM to help lower and stabilize RTC prices and alleviate some of the burden caused by California's energy crisis. The amendments separated large power plants from the rest of the market and required best available retrofit technology on power plants. The board also embarked on the development of further refinements to RECLAIM (South Coast Air Quality Management Nov. 2001).

Despite the high costs in 2000–2001, a congressional study anticipated that RECLAIM would be successful in reducing both emissions and compliance costs. The success of the RECLAIM program can be measured by a two-thirds reduction in total emissions, a reduction in emissions beyond allocated levels, a decrease in the market cost of emissions allowances below national averages, and a reduction in job loss to 4 percent of levels anticipated under command-and-control (United States 1997). Reviews after more than a decade of implementation experience were mixed. Green et al. (2007) concluded that "RECLAIM never came close to operating as predicted ...," while Stavins (2007) stated that "despite problems, RECLAIM has generated environmental benefits, with NO_x emissions in the regulated area falling by 60 percent and SO_2 emissions by 50 percent." With regard to trading, SCAQMD

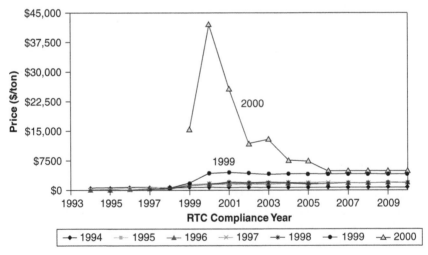

Figure 6.4 RTC Prices for NO_x for the Period 1994–2010
Source: SCAQMD (2001)

(March 2008) reports that market activity in calendar year 2007 included 622 registered RTC transactions with a total volume of 17,359 tons and a total value of just over $74 million.[15] Total RTC trade value in 2010 and 2011 was $47.6 million and $12.9 million, respectively. Since the inception of the RECLAIM program in 1994, more than $1 billion in RTCs have been traded SCAQMD (April 2012, p. 3).

6.2 Policy analysis considerations and implementation lessons

6.2.1 Using previous policy experience in RECLAIM

SCAQMD used technical assistance from the federal EPA in the development of the RECLAIM program and in making adjustments throughout the years. The following are four of the most effective elements of the RECLAIM development and implementation experience:

6.2.1 (A) Democratic forums for implementation discussions

At the RECLAIM program's outset in 1990, developers held public workshops to obtain input from interested parties. The result was a draft concept paper prepared by SCAQMD that reflected a collaborative, multi-stakeholder effort (SCAQMD 1993, EX-14). This exercise improved the political feasibility of the program and its refinements and fostered further stakeholder collaboration.

6.2.1 (B) Ex ante assessments of RECLAIM's distributive costs

The State Legislature required RECLAIM to be assessed for socioeconomic impacts.[16] The Draft Environmental Assessment conducted for RECLAIM indicated that no significant negative impacts to the local economy were expected, compared with the traditional command-and-control rules for the same sources. This measure helped gain support for RECLAIM from industries and communities that might otherwise have believed the environmental regulatory measures would hurt the local economies.

6.2.1 (C) Information management systems and technological progress in emissions monitoring

RECLAIM program management and market functions are strongly supported by information management systems and online communications. As in the case of the EPA's Clean Air Markets Division, software has helped the SCAQMD improve data quality and program efficiency and has made the reporting process significantly easier and more efficient for the program participants. The private sector has strongly supported this area by providing customized software services to regulators and by assisting RECLAIM facilities in developing systems to collect, store, process, and report emissions data to submit to SCAQMD.[17]

The "SCAQMD 2007" report describes the challenge to "balance automation needs with cost, complexity and time constraints." It also claims that prerequisites to support an efficient ETS are simplicity, accessibility, and enforceability, all characteristics that depend on an "information dissemination system" that makes important market information readily available to all market participants. Moreover, RECLAIM information management systems ensure that RTC transfers are "certifiable and official ownership is recorded" (I-6–2).

6.2.1 (D) Incorporating new emitters into the program

As in the case of the ARP, RECLAIM grants free permits to existing emitters. In order to reduce barriers to entry for new firms or facilities, and to enhance political feasibility, RECLAIM provides special access features for new emitters, providing RTCs to companies that are clean and create jobs (i.e., high employment/low emissions—HILO designation). Starting in 2007, RECLAIM provides a bank of 91 tons per year of each RECLAIM pollutant that can be issued to new facilities. However, private brokerage firms provide the bulk of RTCs to new emitters.

6.2.2 The policy implementation experience

RECLAIM has encountered strong technical, political, and economic obstacles during implementation. This implementation experience and its policy results now offer several key policy lessons for future market-based policy design and implementation.

6.2.2 (A) Policy results

At the outset of the program, the SCAQMD projected compliance-cost savings relative to command-and-control regulations averaging $56 million annually (a 42 percent saving). Despite the price hikes of the 2001 California energy crisis, the RECLAIM program has achieved a two-thirds reduction in total emissions and a reduction in the cost of emissions allowances. Actual job loss stemming from the emissions controls has been a fraction of the expected levels. The overall volume of trading has been high and expanding every year as the market includes transactions for future vintage years. Projections estimated that the RECLAIM allowances would trade at around $25,000 per ton, however, RECLAIM market prices for allowances so far have ranged between $200 and $10,000 per ton (SCAQMD 2012). For the compliance year 2012, trades before July of that year occurred at a range of $1880–6500 per ton. Notwithstanding the economic gains to sources, health benefits from reduced smog levels are also significant, as SCAQMD points out, if we account for fewer lost days of school or work in the population due to respiratory illnesses.

Studies comparing affected facilities under conventional regulation in other non-attainment areas with RECLAIM facilities show that their compliance costs under the SCAQMD ETS program were an average of 24 percent lower than those not participating in the program (Burtraw and Szambelan 2009, 20). Moreover, SCAQMD reports that "No RECLAIM facility attributed any job losses to RECLAIM in calendar year 2011 and one RECLAIM facility attributed two job gains to RECLAIM during the calendar year 2011. There was an overall gain in employment at RECLAIM facilities of 1.06 percent during calendar year 2011" (March 2012).

6.2.2 (B) Technical considerations and policy dynamics

RECLAIM demonstrates that the cap-and-trade mechanism can be implemented for a wide variety of sources, not just electric generation plants. RECLAIM also demonstrates that it is possible to incorporate spatial and inter-temporal restrictions on trading, which were used because of the geographical and physical characteristics of downwind pollution in the Los Angeles air basin. However, the failure to include VOC is a reminder of the pervasive technical difficulties in creating environmental commodities from certain polluting substances when faced with effective political lobbying to avoid or delay controls.

6.2.2 (C) Political feasibility

Some features of any ETS are set to satisfy politicians or constituent groups who would otherwise block passage of the program. However, concessions derived from the "political market" may increase transaction costs, reducing the program's overall cost-effectiveness. Well-organized interest groups, such as consumers and industrial organizations, can influence the design and performance of a cap-and-trade program. For instance, their lobbying helped avoid the implementation of the VOC component of the RECLAIM program, and over-allocation of RTCs occurred at the onset of the program because of the flexible system of choosing baseline years and conversion of conventional ERCs into RTCs. In order to increase the political feasibility of RECLAIM, in particular to gain the support of existing facilities, initial permits were allocated for free to those facilities. This grandfathering was more politically acceptable than the more efficient method of an initial auction, which would take advantage of locating the permits from the start with those who valued them the most. The grandfathering allocation approach needs to be balanced by special program features that ensure access to new sources within the geographic scope of the program. The existence of privately run auctions democratizes access to the environmental entitlement and also allows individuals or groups to retire RTCs without using them.

RECLAIM was the first cap-and-trade program to confront environmental justice concerns. For instance, in 1997, Communities for a Better Environment (CBE), a California-based environmental group, argued that RECLAIM's market for pollution and the mobile source rule would lead to the concentration of air pollutants in the region's least affluent neighborhoods, in particular the Latino communities within the SCAQMD's jurisdiction (Drury et al. 1999). While the federal lawsuit by CBE was dismissed, the group succeeded in raising awareness on this issue. SCAQMD has since focused on monitoring the hot spot issue and worked closely with community leaders to address their concerns.

6.2.2 (D) Administrative efficiency

The RECLAIM ETS replaced multiple conventional regulations and standards that required expensive monitoring and inspection duties by SCAQMD. By using a decentralized regulatory approach and allowing firm flexibility on making emissions control investment decisions, RECLAIM minimizes the regulator's enforcement costs.

Most of the development costs for the regulatory agency are incurred during the initial steps of implementing a trading mechanism. Capital investments in electronic data management systems and monitoring technology are upfront expenses. However, once these systems are in place, the role of the regulator becomes that of a bookkeeper and overseer to assure the environmental integrity of the program, leaving the market to offer cost-saving opportunities to program participants. This case study reflects how the private sector plays a key role in market creation, providing the necessary infrastructure, services, and information systems to facilitate trading among participants and interested parties in the RECLAIM program. During the development phase of the program, RECLAIM planners were able to negotiate for the ability to impose fees on some more conventional aspects of the program to sustain its modest administration costs and even to contribute to the overall SCAQMD budget.

6.2.2 (E) Legality

Market oversight is a requirement, since fraud and abuse can occur as in any other commodity trading market.

6.3 Summary of policy lessons

In using RECLAIM as a case study, there are four key components of interest: the environmental market creation parameters, the use of previous policy know-how, the actual implementation record, and policy analysis considerations. Perhaps the single most important lesson that emerges from the analysis of the institutional development history of RECLAIM is that regulators should strive to create confidence and trust in environmental commodities markets. In particular, regulators should ensure that information flows smoothly between the trading and the regulatory aspects of the program. In other words, adequate regulatory oversight over the environmental integrity and market functions of the program, ample communication with regulated facilities, and coordination with other regulatory authorities and processes are all essential to enhance certainty, transparency, and performance. Simplicity, flexibility, and gradualism also remain as basic considerations for the successful implementation of a well-functioning ETS.

The review of RECLAIM's market creation parameters demonstrates both similarities and differences with the ARP ETS implemented under Title IV of the 1990 CAA Amendments. Among others, the following policy lessons emerged from this analysis.

The nature of the controlled substance has an impact on program design: ARP addresses acidification under a national plan. In the ARP ETS, allowances are treated as a uniform polluting substance, disregarding the potential issue of "hot spots." The backstop provision that allows such treatment of sulfur dioxide emissions under the ARP is that the program supplements the existing regulatory framework, and if the emissions trading system fails to control emissions in accordance to NAAQS, conventional regulation is reinstated. ARP grants equivalence to the traded environmental commodity at all times across the entire country. RECLAIM, on the other hand, addresses NO_x—a non-uniformly mixed pollutant, in a geographic region determined by the jurisdictional scope of the SCAQMD. Monitoring NO_x emissions is technically more complex, and the trading of NO_x RTCs is constrained by spatial and inter-temporal restrictions.

Trading rules and flexibility: A key vulnerability in RECLAIM is the lack of a full banking provision, which would give industry more flexibility to manage market risk. As reviewed in Chapter 5, banking allows ARP ETS participants to smooth the impact of transitory price shocks, as extra emissions needs can be covered using banked allowances. However, California regulators were concerned about over-allocation in the early years of RECLAIM, given the peak production year baseline approach. Both regulators and community leaders lobbied hard for decisive action to reduce pollution emissions in order to address the pervasive and negative health impacts of air quality in the Los Angeles basin. These concerns weighed against the implementation of a full banking rule during the policy formulation process. As with ARP, this RECLAIM case study demonstrates that social, economic, and political forces influence the ultimate design of market-based policies, and that there is a tradeoff between political feasibility and cost-effectiveness.

Allocation method, economic considerations, and political feasibility: As with ARP, grand-fathering RTCs enhanced the political feasibility of RECLAIM. Given the general economic environment in which the program was being developed, protecting existing industry garnered support from business and community groups worried about the job market. However, SCAQMD regulators later concluded that basing the initial allocation on average prior activity levels would have been more appropriate than peak activity levels. They also concluded that baseline allowance determinations should incorporate all upcoming reductions required to comply with local, state, and federal regulatory requirements; planned energy savings requirements; or other industrial evolutionary trends that would lead to emission reductions even in the absence of the ETS.

Information, transparency, and credible commitment: As noted above, another lesson from the implementation of the RECLAIM program is that exogenous factors (i.e., regulatory change in related economic sectors, price fluctuations in energy markets, and extreme weather conditions) may necessitate adaptation and refinement strategies, but these adjustments should not compromise the government's credible commitment to the ETS component of an air quality management program. Predictability is essential for long-term planning by affected industries. SCAQMD did not communicate sufficiently that the cross-over point was approaching at the time of the electricity crisis in 2001 when demand for RTC depleted the market. Brokers and environmental financial services providers did not provide enough, or in some cases credible, information about the market situation. SCAQMD reduced the maximum emissions of NO_x in July 2000, just when demand for RTCs began to increase. This reduction in the allowed NO_x levels pushed up the variable operating costs of electric generators, which in some cases fell into noncompliance. According to Burtraw and Szambelan (2009, 19), this is the only case in which "an emissions cap within a cap-and-trade program has been breached." After the 2001–2002 crisis, enhanced information dissemination and accessibility was necessary to encourage more efficient operation of the market.

Energy sector and environmental policy coordination: The cost of energy is a politically contentious topic in the United States. While the price signal reflected in the environmental commodity can change the behavior of polluters and force them to reduce energy production and therefore emissions, dealing with angry consumers is something politicians want to avoid. In particular, they are sensitive to threats from local businesses to close or move on account of high local energy prices. ETS for air quality management must be designed to react quickly and effectively to unforeseen external factors. For instance, the 2000–2001 electricity crisis required the revision of the program's implementation because the pre-established price threshold ($15,000 per ton of NO_x) was reached, which triggered RECLAIM's backstop under Rule 2015. Regulatory relief had to be provided. These circumstances emphasized the importance of coordinating environmental policy action to control air pollution with other regulatory processes, in this case the deregulation of California's electricity market.

Cost control and market intervention: Once a program is up and running, major regulatory changes are disruptive. Statutory procedures are to be followed in case of extremely volatile trading conditions that trigger cost management measures or backstop features. However, policymakers need to be aware that market intervention in an ETS can provide immediate relief during a volatile period, but it will hinder the long-term credibility of the market component of this regulatory approach. Any actions taken to change or stabilize the market should thus be incremental and market-based rather than programmatic.

Fine-tuning and adequately informed regulation: Regulators need to have a strong understanding of the regulated facilities and the factors impacting their decision-making, which is more challenging in a situation like RECLAIM's, where there is a heterogeneous mix of sources. A key design feature to ensure the performance of an ETS is the accurate monitoring and reporting of emissions. Regulators may require an upfront, one-time investment in CEMS technology from all sources. However, for a smaller RECLAIM facility emitting ten tons per year to spend $125,000 on a CEMS is a disproportionately expensive proposition, as compared with requiring the same thing of a much larger facility. After amending RECLAIM, the SCAQMD concluded that periodic evaluations, revisiting of program design assumptions, and contingency strategies are crucial to keeping programs on track.

Environmental justice considerations: Given the region's diverse population and its geographical distribution within the Los Angeles metropolitan area, regulators implementing RECLAIM were the first to have to address the issue of environmental justice in the context of creating environmental markets. Community leaders voiced their concerns and sued SCAQMD as a tactic to raise awareness about the issue. These activists were troubled by the potential "hot spot" effects on minorities and also pointed to claims that reduced emissions benefited only affluent areas while oil refineries, for instance, were located in Latino communities. This issue became a policy priority within SCAQMD as part of their implementation plan, which resulted in collaborative work with the community, pertinent additional research on emissions impacts on human health, and close monitoring of RECLAIM performance, emission reduction trends, and geographical concentrations.

The following chapter reviews the program design and implementation cases of inter-state emissions trading programs. These efforts are positive examples of collaborative regional, multi-stake, and inter-agency market-based air quality management.

Chapter 7

Interstate market-based environmental policy

Continuing the review of emissions trading policy diffusion across different institutional environments within the United States (US) this chapter examines the development of interstate cap-and-trade systems. The efforts in the Northeast and New England region to address the transport of air pollutants across state boundaries through trading mechanisms represent more than 15 years of an evolutionary institutional process. A complex web of local action, multi-state voluntary agreements, state-federal coordination, direct federal intervention, and inter-jurisdictional and inter-agency collaborative efforts supported the emergence of the interstate emissions trading system (ETS) as a more flexible and cost-effective regional air quality management policy tool.

As pointed out in earlier chapters, Title I of the 1990 US Clean Air Act (CAA) Amendments includes provisions designed to address the fact that the National Ambient Air Quality Standards (NAAQS) for ground-level ozone were continually exceeded, a problem states and regions had been fighting for several decades. Based on this legal authority, the Environmental Protection Agency (EPA) requires the submission for approval of State Implementation Plans (SIPs), in which states outline the actions and programs to be conducted in order to attain the NAAQS. While EPA mandates non-attainment areas to meet the NAAQS, states maintain the authority to decide on how to best comply. Historically, compliance involved regulatory programs for multiple types of sources (e.g., electric, industrial, kilns, waste incinerators, turbines, etc.) under command-and-control regulatory approaches. By 1994, US total nitrogen oxides (NO_x) emissions had stabilized at around 24.7 million tons.

As mentioned in Chapter 5, the Acid Rain Program (ARP) also included controls for NO_x emissions based on relatively more flexible conventional regulatory approaches such as performance standards. These provisions apply boiler-specific emissions limits in pounds per million British thermal units (lb/MMBtu) on certain coal-fired boilers in the electric sector, but do not establish a limit or universal cap on emissions. In 1996 NO_x limits were applied to large boilers in the power sector. Ultimately, affected coal-fired steam electricity-generating facilities were required to decrease emissions by 2 million tons by 2000. Despite these efforts and the resulting progress, EPA still had to address the issues of long-range transport ozone and temporal regional concentrations of ground-level ozone.

The 1990 CAA also includes a set of so-called "good neighbor provisions" to address the transport of air pollutants across state boundaries, enabling downwind states to petition for stricter controls on upwind states that contribute to their NAAQS non-attainment status (US CAA 1990, Section 126). As several Northeastern states began to realize that they would not be able to meet the NAAQS because of out-of-state emissions, EPA began to explore new mechanisms to manage regional air quality in the Northeast and New England region in a more integrated and coordinated manner. Through the SIP's federal-state coordination process, EPA emphasized the need for these plans to include provisions to control for statewide emissions that "contribute significantly to the non-attainment in, or interfere with the maintenance by, any other State ..." (US CAA 1990, Section 110).

EPA also acknowledged that: "Since air pollutants do not recognize political boundaries, states and communities cannot independently solve all of their air pollution problems" (US EPA 2002, 3). Because of the magnitude of the emission reduction effort required to meet NAAQS in this region, EPA decided to enhance the cost-effectiveness of state and regional efforts to reduce emissions of NO_x while fostering interstate co-operation. EPA gradually encouraged the use of market-based air quality management programs in the region that would target large stationary sources. A progression of overlapping rules, initiatives, and programs that built incrementally on a template cap-and-trade policy design first introduced in 1999 in a small subset of states and affecting most fossil-fuel electric power plants in the region (mainly old coal-fired plants), has gradually moved towards the creation of a much larger, harmonized, and well-functioning regional interstate NO_x ETS system.

The regional interstate ETS experience—the development, harmonization, and integration—offers lessons on both inter-agency and multi-jurisdictional coordination, in particular between economic and environmental regulators. Also, it illustrates the complexities of joint implementation of air quality management programs between state and federal authorities (i.e., conjoint jurisdiction) that not only involved EPA from the executive branch but also interventions by the courts. The policy dynamics of program development and implementation of these multi- and interstate programs have been shaped by this political relationship. For instance, this experience shows the gradual transition from a small, voluntary, multi-state trading program towards a large-scale, federally administered, harmonized region-wide ETS. This process reflects the leadership, coordination, and commitment of a heterogeneous and continuously expanding group of independent political jurisdictions (i.e., states) to reduce NO_x emissions using environmental markets. The learning process of the lead ETS states was supported by EPA through coordination and technical assistance. Eventually, the federal agency implemented a higher degree of control and oversight into the system as the demand for further pollution control action became urgent.

The coordination and integration role played by EPA has been useful in maintaining the overall credibility, environmental integrity, equity, and cost-effectiveness of an evolving regional system based on strong, local ETS programs. Initially, EPA only provided technical assistance to states to develop their own emissions trading infrastructure. Given this technical support, an active environmental commodities market emerged and has been operating through private firms. EPA developed a key design feature in the harmonization of measurement, reporting, and verification (MRV) systems to effectively administer a seamless oversight mechanism supported by information technologies.

From the environmental performance standpoint, by 2005 when the Clean Air Interstate Rule (CAIR) was introduced, the sum of all US emissions trading programs (i.e., ARP and the NO_x Budget Trading Program or NBP), including the interstate NO_x ETS programs, had stabilized emissions at around 19 million tons total. By 2011, EPA reports that reductions in the emission of precursors to fine particulate matter ($PM_{2.5}$) and ozone formation (sulfur dioxide (SO_2) and NO_x), have benefited human health and welfare by decreasing ambient sulfate concentrations in air quality problem regions across the US (by 51 percent in the Mid-Atlantic, 52 percent in the Midwest, 57 percent in the Northeast, and 48 percent in the Southwest). Acid deposition, an effect of acid rain, has decreased by an average of 51 percent across the Eastern US, and surface water chemistry indicators show that lakes and streams near the Adirondack Mountains and the Northern Appalachian Plateau are on their way to recovery (US EPA 2011). The cap-and-trade approach has no doubt contributed to advancing the solution to the ground ozone and acid rain issues in a cost-effective manner.

Moreover, by 2005, US coal-fired power plants decreased emissions by 3.4 million tons from 1990 levels. New supplementary and more conventional regulation, such as the 2011 Mercury and Air Toxics Standards (MATS) are accelerating this process, as discussed in Chapter 5. In addition, according to data from the US Department of Energy, natural gas is fast becoming the new fuel of choice for the US power sector. Between 2011 and 2012, coal-fired power generation dropped by 19 percent while gas generation increased by 38 percent. The expectation of future climate legislation may be a factor in the decision-making by executives in the power industry to switch to a cleaner fuel, as a gas-fired plant produces half the CO_2 emissions of a coal-fired one (Chazan 2012). As confirmed by the International Energy Agency in its World Energy Outlook 2011, "primarily due to ongoing switching from coal to natural gas in power generation and an exceptionally mild winter, which reduced the demand for space heating" emissions in the US "have now fallen by 430 Mt (7.7 percent) since 2006, the largest reduction of all countries or regions" surveyed.

As discussed in Chapter 5, EPA introduced a new rule on July 6, 2011, in response to legal challenges to the CAIR. In the opinion of the court, "EPA's approach—regionwide caps with no state-specific quantitative contribution determinations or emissions requirements—is fundamentally flawed," therefore requesting EPA to "redo its analysis from the ground up" to replace CAIR.

The 2011 Cross-State Air Pollution Rule (CSAPR) as established by EPA requires 27 states in the Eastern half of the US to significantly improve air quality by reducing power plant SO_2 and NO_x emissions that cross state lines and contribute to ground-level ozone and fine particle pollution in other states. In addition, a supplemental proposal requires six states—Iowa, Kansas, Michigan, Missouri, Oklahoma, and Wisconsin—to make summertime NO_x reductions under the new control program. Five of those states were already covered in the final rule for interstate fine particle pollution ($PM_{2.5}$). Finalizing this supplemental proposal would bring the total number of covered states under the CSAPR to 28. Market observers believe this new rule could have resulted in market fragmentation, as state-specific caps are allowed and were to be enforced by 2014. By the end of 2011, the implementation of the new EPA rules, along with remaining uncertainties of the regulatory process, produced an oversupplied market, which made it very difficult for the power sector to plan how to meet future emissions requirements. EPA's rulemaking activity beyond the caps legislated in the 1990 CAA Amendments, and other supplementary regulations for air pollution in general, affected the credibility of the US emissions trading program because of unanticipated changes and effective elimination of sources. On August 21, 2102, the D.C. Circuit Court for the second time sent the EPA back to the drawing board in what some legal experts, like Dan Farber at Berkeley Law, see as an "activist ruling" coming "close to writing the rule itself" in the decision. As a consequence, the CAIR program introduced by President George W. Bush in 2005 remains in place despite the court's objections over to its "flawed" emissions trading approach. Two negative court decisions in less than four years represent major setbacks in EPA's effort to introduce equity, flexibility, and cost-effectiveness to air pollution control in the region. The evolution of this multi-state regional environmental market has exemplified interstate and state–federal co-operation, but has also been plagued by regulatory uncertainty given constant litigation over new rules, court decisions, and the limited authority available to deal with cross-border issues under the good neighbor provisions.

The following sections describe the historical institutional path followed towards the implementation of an integrated interstate NO_x ETS in the Eastern US, a process that despite complexities has contributed to substantial air quality improvements.

7.1 The Ozone Transport Commission (OTC): the NO_x budget program

Under Section 184 of the 1990 Clean Air Amendments, Congress established the Ozone Transport Commission (OTC), a multi-state organization[1] responsible for advising the EPA on transport issues and for developing and implementing regional solutions to the ground-level ozone problem in the Northeast and Mid-Atlantic states during summertime. At the time of its creation, this collaboration represented the first multi-state cooperative partnership to address a regional air quality problem using a market-based approach.

On September 27, 1994, a Memorandum of Understanding (MOU) for large stationary source NO_x controls was approved by all OTC states except Virginia.[2] The goal was to reduce region-wide NO_x emissions by 75 percent as part of each state's plan to attain ground-level ozone NAAQS through the establishment of an interstate cap-and-trade program. The effort would require harmonization of each participating OTC state's program rules and provisions. The CAA did not explicitly authorize the EPA to intervene and implement cap-and-trade systems in each state, but EPA provided guidance and helped create uniformity among OTC states regarding critical market design parameters, such as monitoring and reporting provisions, compliance determination, and penalties.

The adoption of model rules in 1996 also helped created uniformity, given that OTC states independently controlled their own air quality management systems (Carlson 1996). Northeast States for Coordinated Air Use Management and the Mid-Atlantic Regional Air Management Association jointly developed the model rules as a template for each state's regulations to ensure that all participating states' needs were met. Among the policy design elements to be harmonized under these model rules are: program applicability, control period, NO_x emissions limits, emissions monitoring, record keeping of emissions and allowances, and electronic reporting requirements. Still, some states departed from the template to acco- mmodate local environmental, economic, and political interests. A photograph of the state of affairs at the time is reported in Farrell and Morgan (2000, 11–12):

> The states at the extreme upwind and downwind have tended not to participate. Vermont and Maine (two of the most downwind states) decided to operate traditional permit-based programs, because the small number of sources involved (less than three in each state) and their regulatory status did not justify the administrative burden of developing an emissions trading program. At the upwind end, Virginia did not join the NO_x Budget but it has not taken any other action to regulate the sources that would have been part of the program. In fact Virginia has been an uncooperative participant in the OTC negotiations all along, being the only state that did not sign the original MOU in 1994, and obstructing and ignoring many other OTC activities.

Ultimately, it was the responsibility of each state to go through its own regulatory process to develop and adopt state rules that were consistent with the model rule. Moreover, Maine and Vermont were in attainment of the ozone NAAQS and were not required to adopt the program rules.

According to some observers, at the onset of the program there was some level of confusion and delay in state government action despite the guidance provided by the model rules. For instance, Farrell, Raufer, and Carter (1998) point to "regulatory uncertainties" that induced the implementation of "expensive but ineffectual" program design restrictions that impeded an operational ETS in the first years of the OTC process. In fact, NO_x emissions in the OTC states continued to be regulated until 1998 under a command-and-control framework, and it was not until 1999 that the implementation of the more flexible NO_x Budget Program that emissions trading began in the OTC region.

Moreover, affected sources required time to adapt to the new approach in what seemed to be the start of a much more complex regulatory environment. For instance, the NO_x Budget Program was separate from and additional to all federal

NO$_x$ reduction requirements. Ultimately, affected sources were responsible for demonstrating compliance with an array of federal and state NO$_x$ emission limits already in place (e.g., New Source Performance Standards, ARP NO$_x$ limits, Title V permit requirements, Title I requirements for NO$_x$ Reasonably Available Control Requirements (RACT), and specific standards for coal-fired units).

The OTC's new ETS rules were, therefore, gradually phased in to enhance political feasibility and to allow states and industry to adapt to the new approach. When Phase I of the program began in 1994, participating states implemented modest emissions limits based on RACT on major stationary sources of NO$_x$. In Phase II, OTC states gradually added controls for power plants and other large fuel combustion sources as mandated in the ARP NO$_x$ controls. The higher cost of compliance imposed by these new requirements accelerated the need to implement a market-based solution for the region. The more flexible OTC NO$_x$ Budget Program was introduced in 1999 as an optional cap-and-trade program for large point sources of NO$_x$ from the electricity generation industry based in OTC states, and represented EPA's preferred method of achieving NAAQS attainment.

In Phase III, the 1999 NO$_x$ Budget Program introduced the basic cap-and-trade institutional architecture that has served as the foundation for the development of an operational regional environmental commodities market as described below. A two-phase approach of declining emissions caps was implemented. In May 1999, a cap on regional summertime (May–September) NO$_x$ emissions was first set at 219,000 tons. OTC states agreed to set the permanent regional cap at 143,000 tons—less than half the baseline emission level of 490,000 tons—by 2003. To meet the program's regional cap, participating units (i.e., budget sources) were required to reduce emissions significantly below 1990 baseline levels and, as previously pointed out, had the option to use emissions trading to achieve the most cost-effective reductions possible. Eight states and the District of Columbia chose to join the original system. However, as discussed in the next section, Phase III was replaced by the NO$_x$ SIP Call Federal Budget Trading Program (NBP ETS) that was created as a response to EPA's call for revisions to the SIPs in 1998 to better control the transport of ozone over a wider geographic region than OTC.

7.1.1 Implementing market creation parameters for the NO$_x$ budget program

Environmental Commodities: A defined and homogenous tradable instrument, the NO$_x$ Emission Allowance was created for vintage years from 1999 through 2002 for the OTC region. For 2003 and after, the allowances were issued to participants in the successor programs, NBP ETS, and CAIR. The unit established by the NO$_x$ Budget Program is the "NO$_x$ Allowance," an environmental commodity that permits its holder to emit one ton of NO$_x$ during the "Ozone Season" (May 1 to September 30) for a given vintage year. For each ton of NO$_x$ discharged in a season, one allowance was retired from use. For instance, a 2002 allowance could have been used for compliance with the 2002 season or in the future, but not for the 2001 season.

Seasonal Cap: Initially, imposing a cap on NO_x emissions over a specific period of time was controversial because of the episodic nature of the ground-ozone problem. Smog is a phenomenon that is influenced by variations in intensity due to changing rates of precursor substances, which are in turn affected by differences in emissions rates and temperature.

The NO_x Budget Program implemented a seasonal cap based on regional budget zones. A budget represented the limit of total tons of NO_x allowed in the atmosphere by the affected sources within a determined geographical area as described in the next section. This was a summer program only—there was no winter NO_x program. A few states in the region were beginning to develop and implement wintertime NO_x controls at levels commensurate with the regional program. However, any allowance issued under the winter programs could not be used for compliance. Thus, any NO_x emissions reduction made during the winter does not count toward compliance under the regional summer season system. The sum of NO_x emissions from all sources in participating states was not to exceed the number of allowances allocated to individual states within a budgets zone during the control period (May 1 to September 30).

Budget Zones: The program created three geographic areas called budget zones, imposing geographical limits to allowance trading as in the case of the Regional Clean Air Incentives Market (RECLAIM) in California. Sources located in each zone faced different emission reduction targets or performance standards as agreed in the OTC MOU. For instance, for Phase I (1999–2003), the Inner Zone, which was composed of coastal Atlantic states, Virginia to New Hampshire and inland— the area most prone to hotspots and unhealthy pollution levels during the ozone season—faced a 35 percent reduction from 1990 levels. The Outer Zone, adjacent to the Inner Zone from Western Maryland to part of New York to the north was required to reduce emissions by 35 percent from 1990 levels. And the Northern Zone, which includes the northernmost sections of New York and New Hampshire, including Vermont and Maine, faced no requirement in Phase I. For Phase II, which began in 2003, the Inner and Outer Zone budgets were established with a 25 percent reduction in emissions compared with 1990 levels, as well as a 45 percent reduction in the Northern Zone. Alternatively, companies also had the option of complying through performance standards which represented a reduction requirement of 0.20lb/MMBtu for both Inner and Outer Zones for Phase II, and 0.15 lb/MMBtu for both areas in Phase II. During this phase, the Northern Zone would face a 0.20 lb/MMBtu performance standard.

Program Participants: The OTC states allocated their NO_x allowances to specific units called budget sources. Budget sources included all electric utilities with power generators greater than 15MW and all industrial boilers with steam generating capacity greater than 250 MMBtu/hour. State governments are ultimately responsible for attaining the ozone NAAQS. Those that elected to take part in the voluntary, regional ETS were responsible for enacting regulations consistent with the 1996 model rules in order to achieve region-wide NO_x reductions in a consistent and enforceable manner. Participation in the NO_x allowance market was not limited to polluters. Similar to the ARP ETS, any individual or entity could open a general account through the EPA and acquire allowances for trading and/or to retire them. Unlike the SO_2 program, new sources received allowances and had to open a compliance account for each unit (they were also able to open an overdraft account for entities with more than one unit for internal trading), but they had to hold enough allowances to cover their emissions in their compliance account (i.e., general account).

Initial Allocation: The NO_x Budget was established by applying the OTC's 1994 MOU emission reduction targets to each budget source contributing to the state-wide 1990 baseline for NO_x emissions. The EPA allocated a proportion of the region-wide seasonal cap of 219,055 tons for Phase I (and a planned permanent cap of 142,874 tons for Phase II in 2003 and beyond) to each participating state. Allocations were based either on a percentage of total emissions or as a performance standard equivalent as discussed in the budget zone section. Budget sources were given allowances by their respective state governments and had the option to choose the standard most appropriate to each one of them. There was no large-scale interstate trading in 2000 and 2001: most activity was at the intra-state level. Initially, some observers had expressed concerns about the differences in allocation methods among participating states adding a layer of administrative complexity to the overall program. Uncertainties also emerged from differences in budget updating cycles and other special provisions, as described below in the trading rules section (Farrell et al. 1998).

However, according to Kathryn Petrillo, Senior Policy Analyst at the EPA's Clean Air Markets Division at the time, after a few years of program activity, administrators in her division indicated that, from their perspective, these complexities tended not to affect NO_x regional trading activity:

> In the OTC, EPA was not really involved in how the state chose to allocate their allowances. Under the OTC program states are allocating in a variety of ways—some based on heat input, some on output, some are updating them yearly, some every few years and some are not updating. Some states are allocating some years in advance of the relevant ozone season and some are not allocating until immediately before the relevant ozone season. Theoretically, you'd expect sources in states where there is less lead-time between receiving allowances and needing them for compliance (i.e., in a state were the allocations are updated yearly) to be at a competitive disadvantage in the market. Anecdotally though, from what we've seen most sources

have been able to adjust—if they are feeling disadvantaged in the market it is not visible to us.

(Petrillo 2002)

Trading Rules: While the program was implemented on a state-by-state basis, the regulations governing the NO_x ETS were fairly consistent from one state to another, and there were no restrictions placed on the transfer and use of credit throughout the region. As reported by the environmental brokerage firm Evolution Markets, by 2002 the NO_x program had become "a fairly liquid environmental market and routinely trades on a daily basis" (Evolution Markets 2009).

(1) *Banking*: The allowances were fashioned to be standardized, tradable, and bankable. Unused allowances of a given vintage year may also be banked for future use but under certain control rules as described below. Borrowing was allowed.

(2) *Progressive Flow Control*: As in the case of RECLAIM, special banking provisions were introduced to address the particular temporal and spatial concerns of ozone formation (i.e., hotspots). The Progressive Flow Control (PFC) was an innovative design feature introduced to provide sources with a financial incentive to avoid using a high volume of banked allowances. While allowing unlimited banking by sources, the PFC established a discount rate on the use of banked allowances over a certain level. Specifically, a two-for-one discount rate is applied to the use of allowances whenever the total number of banked allowances in the program exceeds 10 percent of the allowable NO_x emissions for all emitters covered in a season. The PFC discount factor is cumulative and non-linear. According to a joint OTC and EPA progress report published in 2002, "The use of banking (in combination with PFC) did not result in any single season peaks above budget levels" (US EPA and OTC 2002). PFC does not give individual sources any reason not to save below the 10 percent threshold because individual decisions have trivial effects on the aggregate savings rate. Furthermore, it creates incentives to save further into the future when above the threshold level (not use allowances in the current year).

Brokers, Derivatives, and Futures Markets: As suggested in Krowlewski and Mingst (2001), at the time there were indications that sources within the OTC were "increasingly using derivative instruments to manage the substantial risks associated with the volatile allowance prices and stiff noncompliance penalties." The use of these instruments by certain emitters and brokerages suggests a "higher level of market sophistication" in this regional environmental commodities market (Energy Information Administration 2002, 32).

Enforcement Regime: For compliance, budget sources in participating states have to turn in an allowance for every ton of NO_x emitted during the ozone season. Affected emitters with a shortfall of allowances may buy them from those whom have reduced emissions below their allocated level. Should an emitter not obtain sufficient allowances to offset emissions, penalty provisions apply automatically. Failure to meet compliance requirements occurs when the emissions from a budget source exceed allowances held in the budget source's compliance account for the control period as of December 31 of the subject year. The penalty would be to deduct allowances from the budget source's compliance account for the next control period at a rate of three allowances for every one ton of excess emissions. The total number of allowances deducted in 2001 was 188,116 (183,283 to cover emissions with an additional 4833 banked allowances that were taken at two-for-one under the PFC requirements). This represents approximately 91 percent of all 2001 allowances issued and about 68 percent of all allowances available, which included 60,514 banked allowances for the years 1999 and 2000. Five sources had a total of 57 allowances deducted for the year 2002 because they did not hold enough allowances in their compliance accounts to cover their emission for the 2001 ozone emission season (US EPA & OTC 2002).

On an annual basis, for each ton emitted during the ozone season, one ton is retired in the program's Nitrogen Allowance Tracking System (NATS) (see Allowance and Emissions Tracking section, below). This reconciliation process is implemented by freezing the regulated unit's account for that year's allowances at the end of the year. After the states have reviewed all documentation to justify the actual emissions levels for the specific ozone season, the corresponding number of allowances is deducted from the unit accounts and the accounts are unfrozen (usually within 90 days).

Information Services: Private sector environmental finance service providers such as BGC Environmental Brokerage Services, Evolution Markets, and Natsource LLC, among others, began, and continue, to provide information on trade volume and prices for NO_x allowances transactions during the different regional interstate NO_x ETS development stages.

Allowance and Emissions Tracking: Sources of emissions are required to monitor and report NO_x emissions during each control period. The NO_x Budget Program, as in the case of the ARP ETS, requires the use of continuous emission monitors (CEMs). EPA administers the information management systems to conduct MRV for the accurate monitoring and enforcement of the regional cap-and-trade program. The NATS and a NO_x Emissions Tracking System were developed as a modification of the federal allowance tracking system (ATS) infrastructure developed for tracking SO_2 allowances in the ARP ETS. The fact that the monitoring system was integrated and required uniform data collection technologies and reporting protocols enhanced the environmental integrity of the trading component of the program. This key policy design parameter has provided a solid foundation for a harmonized MRV system for the ozone region's ETS and its constantly evolving regulatory framework and expanding geographic scope.

Political Jurisdiction: As pointed out earlier, the creation of OTC represents the recognition that independent actions by states would not be sufficient for the region as a whole to attain the NAAQS for ozone. In effect, the OTC NO_x Budget Program is a state-level, market-based compliance measure to address this issue as mandated by Congress in Title I of the 1990 CAA Amendments. Farrell and Morgan (2000) describe the institutional framework supporting this arrangement:

> Title I creates a governance structure called "conjoint federalism," under which the Federal Government (specifically the Environmental Protection Agency, or EPA) is responsible for setting air quality standards, creating and enforcing some emission standards for new sources, while the states' environmental agencies are responsible for controlling emissions from existing sources and operational controls such as automobile inspections.

As reviewed in Chapter 4, states are required to develop SIPs detailing the steps they will take (in addition to federal control measures) to attain the NAAQS. The EPA has oversight authority over the states and must approve their SIPs. States have to prove that the NAAQS will be attained with technical studies. EPA can force action if necessary through federal intervention under certain conditions.

Under Title I, EPA's limited implementation authority gave OTC states the ability to establish their own rules in accordance with the local political climate. Title I was originally drafted in 1970 when urban ozone was considered only a local occurrence. Nevertheless, the EPA was able to act as a coordinating agent and a source of policy experience for the development of the program. A particularly smart move was achieving direct oversight on monitoring and reporting aspects of the program by building on the ARP ETS experience in the use of CEMs and other information technologies. As emphasized throughout this book, these are key environmental commodities market creation parameters. By implementing MRV features supported by state-of-the-art information technologies uniformly across all OTC states, the institutional design and credibility of this regional interstate cap-and-trade program was and continues to be strengthened.

Changes in the CAA of 1977 and 1990 added provisions that allowed states to use legal means to force other states to control emitters believed to be increasing the levels of pollution in their air mantle. These measures are known as Section 126 Petitions. Historically, this rule has been difficult to implement, mainly because of legal challenges between upwind and downwind states involved in such actions. Therefore, states are virtually independent as to how they regulate ozone sources as long as they can prove that their emissions do not affect downwind states (those located on the Eastern seashore).

Finally, when the evidence warrants, the EPA can issue a SIP Call, which contains new regulatory requirements for states that contribute significantly to smog or ozone pollution in other states. (See Section 7.2) SIP Calls are the legal instruments used by EPA to define the total emission reductions a state must make under the interstate

ETS initiatives. However, as pointed out earlier, EPA cannot create specific requirements for any of the source categories over which the states have authority, so each
state had to choose a compliance regime.

7.1.2 Using previous policy experience in developing a multi-state NO_x ETS program

The NO_x Budget Program represents a clear example of the diffusion of knowledge
accumulated in the policy design and implementation of the ARP ETS. During a
congressional hearing on the lessons derived from the Acid Deposition Control Act
in 1998, Brian McLean, then EPA's Director of Acid Rain Division (now Clean Air
Markets Division[3]), cited the OTC NO_x Budget Program as an example of how the
ARP's successful policy design features were adapted to other mechanisms to address
air pollution. He identified the use of an overall limit (i.e., the cap) to be achieved
through a trading system as "the most relevant institutional lesson derived from the
Acid Rain Program that was implemented in the OTC NO_x Budget Program" (US
Senate 1998).

The OTC states requested that the EPA assist in developing and managing a
regional emissions trading program modeled on the SO_2 program. Partly as a result,
the OTC's NO_x Budget Program rules are similar to those of the ARP ETS (US
Senate 1998). As noted above, another practical lesson transferred to the OTC was
the use of information technology systems, which greatly expanded the EPA's
emissions tracking capabilities with only a small increase in staff (Kruger, McLean,
and Chen 2000, 10).

The following examples show how exogenous factors, such as advances in
information technologies and their use in policy design, enhanced the interstate
NO_x ETS programs' monitoring capabilities, and thus their overall environmental
integrity.

7.1.2 (A) Nitrogen oxides allowance tracking system

NATS, the EPA's record-keeping system, was first developed to track the allowances
that emitters held. NATS maintains information on:

- the issuance of all allowances;
- the holding of allowances in accounts;
- the deduction of allowances for compliance purposes; and
- the transfer of allowances between accounts.

EPA's NATS was modeled after ATS (i.e., the ARP's allowance tracking mechanism), so when the program was launched, web administrators structured query/
reports similarly. Currently, EPA centralizes all of its information systems for ETS
programs under the allowance management system, harmonizing data collection and
search aspects.

7.1.2 (B) Clean air mapping and analysis program (C-MAP)

Emerging information technologies at that time such as Geographic Information Systems (GIS) also allowed environmental administrators to begin mapping emissions over geography.[4] Since environmental protection is inherently geographic by nature, when this technology became readily available the Clean Air Markets Division at EPA used GIS data to assess the environmental effectiveness of its programs, including the ARP ETS. This technology also helped assess progress in the reduction of NO_x emissions in the Northeast. According to EPA (2001), the use of these new technologies enhanced their air quality management and environmental protection capacity:

> With additional NO_x reductions expected in the Northeast under the NO_x Budget Program, the ability to describe the ecological response to these reductions becomes increasingly important in determining whether current control levels provide adequate protection to human health and the environment. C-MAP helps administrators determine if further pollution control steps are necessary.

7.1.3 Implementation record

This section reviews the environmental progress in the region under the OTC NO_x Budget Program. Also, it analyzes the early performance of its multi-state NO_x allowance trading mechanism that serves as the institutional foundation for advancing the regional interstate ETS market concept.

7.1.3 (A) Environmental progress

While the OTC's multi-state approach to NO_x reductions provided some flexibility for participating states, the uniformity of certain program elements ensured that the region-wide reductions occurred in a consistent, enforceable manner. However, actual reductions during the 1999 season represented reductions from the initial eight OTC states only. The maps in Figure 7.1 illustrate the geographic and temporal trends in state-level utility NO_x emissions before and during implementation of Phase I (1996–1999) of the ARP, including the first year of the OTC NO_x Budget Program (1999). Sources affected by both programs were responsible for demonstrating compliance with the requirements of each of these distinct programs.

Total utility NO_x emissions (Phase I and II sources) were reduced by an average of 23 percent nationally between 1990 and 1999. In 1990, the highest NO_x emissions occurred in the Midwestern, Mid-Atlantic, and Southern regions of the US. In 1999, the highest NO_x emissions came from a small number of Midwestern states, as well as Florida and Texas. Improvements were observed in many states including Pennsylvania, West Virginia, Massachusetts, New York, and New Jersey.

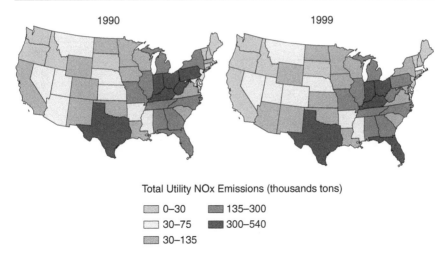

1990   1999

Total Utility NOx Emissions (thousands tons)

☐ 0–30   ▨ 135–300
☐ 30–75   ■ 300–540
▨ 30–135

Figure 7.1 Interstate air transport emissions OTC region
Source: EPA C-MAP

By the end of 1999, between 350,000 and 400,000 tons of annual NO_x emissions had been reduced under Phase I of the ARP, and approximately 209,000 tons of annual NO_x emissions had been reduced by the eight states participating in the OTC NO_x Budget Program (Krowlewski and Mingst 2000, 3).

Beginning in 2000, Phase II of the ARP aimed at reductions of over 2 million tons of NO_x annually, relative to what emissions were predicted to be in the absence of Title IV. On April 4, 2002, the OTC and EPA reported that participating air pollution emission sources emitted NO_x at approximately 12 percent below the NO_x Budget Program limit during the ozone season of May through September 2001. The total NO_x emission for the affected sources in the participating states represents reductions of over 60 percent from their 1990 levels (US EPA & OTC 2002).

7.1.3 (B) Performance of the NO_x budget program allowance trading

The OTC NO_x Budget Program market began to develop steadily in its first season. Trading began in the summer of 1999, and according to one estimate, over 35,000 tons were traded before the season began. The fact that the market reflected early emerging spreads between the 1999 vintage year and those of future years was evidence of some maturity in environmental commodities markets development, as in the case of the the ARP's SO_2 allowances futures markets (Emissions Trading Education Initiative 1999, 45). However, unanticipated behavior by program participants seems to have had an impact on price fluctuations. For instance, Farrell (2000) points to the fact that Maryland, an expected net buyer of allowances, did not participate in the program's first season.

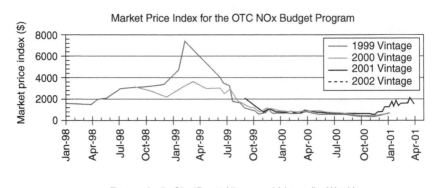

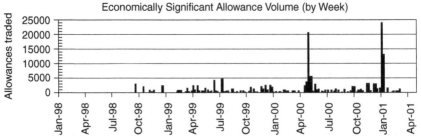

Figure 7.2 NO$_x$ budget program market performance
Source: Krowlewski and Mingst (2000)

The first market performance information available came from brokerage firms. Starting in August 1998, 1371 private transactions, equivalent to 138,790 NO$_x$ allowances, were transferred in the initial ozone control season. Approximately 40 percent of these NO$_x$ allowances (53,563) were transferred between distinct economic entities (as opposed to within a single operating company or holding company). This reflects an important volume of allowance market activity in the OTC NO$_x$ Budget Program between economically distinct entities (Krowlewski and Mingst 2000, 8). Figure 7.2 presents data on the NO$_x$ Budget Program market. The top graph displays the market price index for four vintages (1999–2002) traded under the OTC Budget Program, while the lower graph reflects economically significant allowance exchanges by week. NO$_x$ markets initially were quite volatile, as reported by Chartier (2000, 23):

> In 1998, trades were stable in the $3000 per ton price range. Then as the first NO$_x$ season approached, prices rose to over $7,000 per ton based on market fears of a shortage of allowances. However, as operating data became available during the ozone season, dispelling those fears and pointing to a year-end surplus, prices have declined steadily. Current prices were at $710 per ton in December.

Krowlewski and Mingst (2000, 9) provide an explanation for the volatility in 1999:

For example, the finalization of several rules less than a year before implementation—rather than the timely promulgation of these regulations—likely caused uncertainty about the proposed program elements. The ambiguity reduced the lead-time during which firms could test compliance strategies against the allowance market. For this and other reasons, sources may have turned to last minute allowance purchasing as an alternative to more preemptive compliance strategies.

Nonetheless, the NO_x Budget Program's flexibility on compliance strategies worked better than expected. As in the case of the ARP ETS, adjustments through managerial and technical ingenuity were made at the plant level. For instance, to reduce emissions from combustion sources, fuel-switching capabilities were enhanced in boilers. Utilities also introduced load-shifting electrical demand management programs in order to shift energy use from on-peak to off-peak periods. These strategies were so successful that they put downward pressure on the NO_x allowance market and triggered the use of PFC as the excess supply of the environmental commodity increased by the end of 1999.

Of the significant volume of trading in 1999, two-thirds of all allowances were purchased by sources of NO_x emissions (utilities, non-utility generators, industrial boilers, fuel suppliers, and cogeneration facilities), and nearly three-quarters of all allowances were sold by sources of NO_x. Figure 7.3 shows the percentage of allowances transferred among distinct economic entities under the OTC NO_x Budget Program.

Brokerages and power marketers bought or sold the balance of allowances. Of the ten largest emitters (as defined by total sales), two installed the most efficient emissions reduction technology—selective catalytic reduction systems—a couple of months before the program began.[5] Together, these two facilities sold nearly 20 percent of all allowances (Krowlewski and Mingst 2000, 8). While transfers among utility plants comprised the majority of the NO_x allowance transactions,

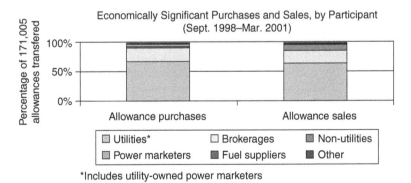

*Includes utility-owned power marketers

Figure 7.3 OTC trading activity by participant (Sept. 1998–Mar. 2001)
Source: EPA (June 2001)

there were also interactions between other affected and non-affected participants that account for 13.3 and 21.7 percent of total volume, respectively. In general the level of OTC allowance transfers was substantial despite the early price volatility. This implies that high transaction costs did not inhibit efficient allowance movement between firms. More importantly, it suggests that sources effectively used allowance trading to meet the emission reductions (Krowlewski and Mingst 2000, 10). The economics of the OTC allowance market were noticeably different from other cap-and-trade programs such as the ARP ETS. The allowance market in the OTC initially featured very high prices and some volatility. However, the market developed rapidly, and a brisk business in derivative products quickly materialized, providing risk management tools for participants that allowed for market price stabilization.

As opposed to the market intervention actions taken on RECLAIM during the electricity crisis in California, OTC states and EPA regulators decided not to intervene during high volatility periods by imposing cost management features such as a price cap. This nascent NO_x ETS market and its participants were able to weather these price fluctuations without affecting the credibility of the program. Emissions never exceeded the OTC budget despite the fact that more than 90,000 allowances were banked thanks to the PFC provisions.

The OTC NO_x Budget Program also appears to have had significant and unique impacts on the technologies used in power plants in the Northeastern US and on how these plants are operated (Farrell April 2000). Seventy percent of the budget sources participated in significant market transactions, and the program showed a near-perfect record of compliance. Finally, a potential problem that can occur when independent political jurisdictions choose to participate in an ETS regime while others do not, known as "leakage," did not materialize. In other words, emissions and/or economic activity from the OTC region were not transferred to other states or regions outside the NO_x Budget Program's regulatory regime.

7.2 The NO_x SIP Call: the NO_x budget trading program

Despite the initial success of the OTC efforts, non-attainment problems persisted in the Eastern US. Further NO_x emission reductions were required to effectively address summertime ozone transport in this region. In 1998 EPA issued a rule known as the "NO_x SIP Call" that required 22 states and the District of Columbia to revise their SIPs in order to achieve further emissions reductions in the region through local NO_x budgets. These more stringent NO_x emission standards were to be achieved gradually, over the course of three compliance deadlines (i.e., May 2003, May 2004, and May 2007) for a total reduction of more than one million tons, an emissions budget 70 percent below 1990 levels. In addition, through federal regulatory intervention, EPA expanded the scope of the OTC multi-state ETS approach used in the NO_x Budget Program, both geographically and in coverage. As part of a state-by-state emissions budget implementation strategy, the new program included industrial sources in addition to electric-generation units. This complex system of federal and local programs had to be integrated and harmonized in a federal–state coordination effort to create a more cost-effective, workable, and credible NO_x interstate ETS. As mentioned earlier, EPA used its SIP Call authority granted by the 1990 CAA to create a de facto federally controlled interstate cap-and-trade system for the region. The NO_x SIP Call effectively replaced the OTC NO_x Budget Program before the implementation of its second emissions cap by instituting, on May 1, 2003, the NBP ETS.

The federal fine-tuning of the NO_x multi-state trading approach did not occur in a vacuum. For instance, the Ozone Transport Assessment Group (OTAG), an overlapping collaborative effort to the OTC process based on a larger group of stakeholders and a wider geographical scope, was very active in deliberations and offered useful guidance on policy design refinements to EPA. Most importantly, OTAG was able to provide technical evidence to support a more active federal role in managing, through a regional ETS, the then little understood environmental problem of summer ozone transport. Also, the deregulation of the electric power sector was being debated at the national level. A review of the policy formulation process at the time reflects opposition by some stakeholders, in particular the power sector lobby, warning of a potentially significant increase in the cost of electricity generation due to more stringent environmental controls on power generators in upwind states. Ultimately, this debate made evident the lack of coordination between energy and environmental regulators.

Federal intervention was triggered by formal petitions from downwind states under Section 126 of the 1990 CAA. Following its assessment, EPA made technical findings of a significant contribution to ground-level ozone from upwind states in the petitioning states. In September 1998, EPA issued the "NO_x SIP Call" mentioned above. Instead of mandating reduction from specific sources (i.e., Emissions Unit Groups), as in the case of the NO_x Budget Program, EPA required affected states to meet their own emissions state budgets while providing flexibility on compliance methods to meet the regional cap.

The EPA threatened to develop Federal Implementation Plans (FIPs), along with fines and other potential sanctions, to be imposed on states that failed to revise their SIP in compliance with the final NO_x SIP call. However, Court decisions vacated part of the 1998 rule. On March 3, 2000, the D.C. Circuit upheld the rule for 19 states and the District of Columbia but vacated it for Wisconsin, Georgia, and Missouri, sending the portions of the rule focusing on those states back to EPA for further rule making. The Court also found that the record supported the inclusion of only a portion of the states of Georgia and Missouri. As a result of the court's decision, EPA divided the emissions reductions of the NO_x SIP Call into two phases (Phase I and Phase II). Phase I addressed those portions of the rule that the court had upheld affecting 19 states. Because of some litigation, the third and final phase was published in the *Federal Register* in April 2004. The following section describes in more detail some of the historical and institutional developments that shaped program design refinements for the region that led to the implementation of the federal NBP ETS.

7.2.1 External political factors and policy dynamics

7.2.1 (A) The ozone transport assessment group: mainstreaming measures

On May, 18, 1995, OTAG—a collaborative partnership between the EPA; the Environmental Council of the States, comprised of the 37 easternmost states; and various industry and environmental groups—was established to assess the progress achieved by existing policies in the Northeastern US and to reach a consensus agreement on how to expand participation and to accelerate reductions in ground-level ozone and the pollutants that cause ground-level ozone in this region. A major research effort led mostly by local environmental agencies and research institutions was launched to better understand the different technical aspects of the problem.

While this process failed to expand the NO_x ETS to all 37 participating states, it did inform the policy formulation process and enhance the application of this approach in the region. In particular, the OTAG assessment provided analyses on scientific and technical aspects of shared environmental problems. The social dynamics of this collaborative exercise helped improve the level of understanding of the concept of ozone transport and its environmental impacts while mainstreaming possible solutions. In fact, at the closing of this process, two years later, the concept of ozone transport was no longer debated among stakeholders. What to do about it became a priority. Some of the key recommendations that emerged from OTAG in relation to air quality market-based policy design were:

- Implement an allowanced-based interstate cap-and-trade system.
- Use a state tonnage-based limit or cap and not allow rate-based programs for participating states as a compliance mechanism for large combustion sources.
- Require certain elements of the individual state programs to be consistent or harmonized in order to be part of the interstate trading component.

Ultimately, a modest consensus was reached on the need to reduce emissions in the region. Initially, some observers in the downstream states, those most impacted by ozone transport, questioned the OTAG collaborative, characterizing it as a delay tactic. In contrast, some stakeholders in upwind states saw this process as a means to transfer compliance costs to them. Despite the initial tensions, the collaborative assessment process tempered the adversarial nature of environmental policy formulation. This process traditionally involves expensive litigation that in some cases only delays the implementation of needed environmental protection policies and measures.

As mentioned earlier, OTAG also provided federal policymakers with evidence to support a more forceful call for region-wide policy action to address ozone formation and transport episodes during the summer. More importantly, this process jump-started work on a key element for effective air quality management and market-based policy design: the development of accurate emission inventories for NO_x

emissions at the state level. In short, OTAG generated a collaborative political environment, along with the technical foundations that led to the creation of a more advanced version of the interstate regional NO_x ETS.

7.2.1 (B) Electricity sector deregulation and environmental policy: regulatory disconnect

During 1996 the deregulation of the electric power industry brought national attention to the environmental and economic implications of the implementation of further NO_x controls by EPA in the context of the debate over open access to electricity transmission and distribution systems (i.e., the Open Access policy).[6] By the late 1990s, the electric power generation sector accounted for about one-third of US NO_x emissions and about 4 percent of gross domestic product, giving it enormous power to influence political decision making, particularly at the federal level. The electric industry lobbied in support of electricity markets deregulation while opposing additional air pollution controls using the threat of higher rates to consumers if such regulatory actions were carried out.

In contrast, environmental groups saw deregulation of the power sector as a negative outcome because the Open Access policy would diminish the leverage of both advocates and government to influence electric company decision making as monopolies through the processes of public utility commissions. They were also concerned, as were Northeastern environmental regulators, about more coal-fired power production in the Midwest and thus more barriers to entry for cleaner renewable energy (Keating and Farrell 1999, 109). Moreover, under the Open Access policy rules greater inter-utility trading of power was expected to result in increased emissions from older, dirtier, and lower-cost electric-generating units (EGUs) from the Midwest. Older plants were exempt by law from new source performance standards and were not subject to the more stringent controls placed on units adjacent to urban areas that were non-compliant under NAAQS in downwind states. Moreover, changes in prices and the price structure of electricity have an impact on managerial decisions about the mix of generation technologies and levels of electricity supply, which in turns affects the level of air pollution emissions linked with power generation (Burtraw et al. 1998).

The Federal Energy Regulatory Commission (FERC) acknowledged overlooking the issue of future emissions reduction requirements when introducing Open Access and Stranded Cost Recovery (FERC 1995). The later policy, as defined in Title 18 of the Code of Federal Regulations allows for "legitimate, prudent and verifiable cost incurred by a public utility or a transmitting utility to provide service," in this case, as a result of the restructuring of the electric industry. Thus, FERC missed "the opportunity to evaluate the interaction between environmental and economic regulation of the electric industry fully" (Keating and Farrell 1999, 110). This situation created some tension between the EPA and FERC at the time. While recognizing the economic benefits of deregulation, the EPA expressed concerns about the long-term consequences of Open Access, in particular about NO_x and carbon dioxide emissions (Browner 1996).

Given this situation, EPA, as authorized by the CAA and the National Environmental Protection Act (NEPA), referred the Open Access rule to the Council on Environmental Quality (CEQ) at the White House to resolve this inter-agency conflict.[7] However, FERC ultimately concluded that the "NO_x regulatory program could best be developed and administered under the CAA, in co-operation with interested states, and offers to lend Commission support to that effort should it become necessary" FERC (1996).

In 1996, it became clear to the EPA that a federal market-based control strategy should be implemented, given the OTC's trailblazing efforts and as a result of the recommendations derived from the larger OTAG stakeholders' negotiation process. EPA favored a region-wide cap-and-trade program for NO_x emissions enhancing state accountability on this issue. Carol Browner, the EPA Administrator, was ready to use her authority under Title I of the CAA to advance this approach. Browner (1996) stated that EPA was "prepared to establish a NO_x cap-and-trade program for the OTAG region through 'Federal Implementation Plans' (FIPs) if some states are unable or unwilling to act in a timely manner." On June 14, 1996, the CEQ stated:

> CEQ believes that the economically efficiently way to address NO_x air pollution is through a regional cap-and-trade system that covers all sources of pollutants. Such a market-oriented approach recognizes that the problem is regional rather than site-specific, and permits the flexibility to comply with a regional pollution cap in the most cost-effective way. CEQ therefore applauds the efforts of the EPA and the 37 states of OTAG to consider such a system to reduce emissions of NO_x from all sources.
>
> (McGinty 1996)

Finally, in March 1998, the Comprehensive Electric Competition Plan outlined (but never implemented) by the Clinton Administration recommended that the EPA be given explicit authority to oversee the development of the new federal interstate NO_x emissions trading program. The next section will describe the policy actions followed by EPA to integrate NO_x emissions control policies and rules throughout the region as the agency developed the new federally controlled institutional arrangement.

7.2.2 Federal–state coordination: calls for action, harmonization, and integration

7.2.2 (A) Section 126: request for action from downstream states

In general, during the ozone transport summer episodes, downstream states are interested in further controlling pollution, while upstream states dislike the idea of paying for the additional environmental controls required as these costs bring no apparent local benefits. In accordance with Section 126 of the 1990 CAA, the EPA

Table 7.1 Section 126 Region

Delaware	New York
District of Columbia	North Carolina
Indiana	Ohio
Kentucky	Pennsylvania
Maryland	Virginia
Michigan	West Virginia
New Jersey	

responded to petitions filed in 1998 by eight Northeastern states (Connecticut, Maine, Massachusetts, New Hampshire, New York, Rhode Island, Pennsylvania, and Vermont), asking EPA to make a "finding" that NO_x emissions from certain major stationary sources in upwind states significantly contributed to ozone non-attainment of the one-hour federal NAAQS in the petitioning states because of the ozone transport issue. Section 126 actions affected 12 Northeastern states and D.C., as listed in Table 7.1.

7.2.2 (B) NO_x SIP Call Program: harmonizing regional ozone transport action

To reduce long-range transport ozone in the OTAG region, a new rule on this issue was promulgated in October 1998.[8] EPA, using its authority to review SIPs (i.e., SIP Call), required the 22 easternmost states and the District of Columbia to include provisions for addressing ozone transport in their plans (US EPA Oct. 1998).[9] After some litigation, the final rule published by EPA in 1999 ultimately required upwind states (i.e., NO_x SIP Call States) to reduce their NO_x emissions.[10] As seen in Table 7.2, not all OTAG states were included in the SIP Call:

Table 7.2 SIP Call and OTC states

Alabama	Illinois	Michigan	Ohio	Virginia
Connecticut	Indiana	Missouri	Pennsylvania	Wisconsin
District of Columbia	Kentucky	North Carolina	Rhode Island	West Virginia
Delaware	Massachusetts	New Jersey	South Carolina	
Georgia	Maryland	New York	Tennessee	
OTAG States not subject to the NO_x SIP Call action (*OTC states)				
Arkansas	Kansas	Minnesota	Nebraska	South Dakota
Florida	Louisiana	Mississippi	New Hampshire*	Texas
Iowa	Maine*	North Dakota	Oklahoma	Vermont*

Source: EPA

7.2.2 (C) NBP ETS: integrating a federally controlled regional interstate ETS

The EPA began the difficult process of integrating and coordinating ongoing and new regulatory actions (on the one- and eight-hour ozone standards and on the SIP

Call and the Section 126 findings) with state governments in the region, with the goal of implementing the federal NBP ETS. Reaching that goal required swift and determined action by EPA to move the process along and transition to a more integrated system. In 1998, EPA also reframed the approach, stating that "the overall purpose of the ozone transport rule is to reduce regional transport of NO_x that contributes to ozone non-attainment in multiple Eastern states, not to reduce emissions from a specific source in a particular state" (Parker and Blodgett 2002, 4).

The new NBP ETS was conceived using the same emissions rate formulas as the NO_x SIP Call Program. The EPA integrated the NO_x SIP Call Program into the federal program to expand cost-saving opportunities. The environmental goal of the new emissions trading program was to reduce summer-season NO_x emissions from participating states collectively by 510,000 tons per from 2007 levels. EPA imposed a complicated trigger mechanism to implement a federal cap-and-trade Program for NO_x sources in areas that failed to submit and/or implement the prescribed SIPs.

The Section 126 action required the same level of emissions reduction as the SIP Call Program and from the same set of sources. EPA established that, as soon as each state under the Section 126 action submitted an approvable and complete SIP including ozone transport provision, EPA removed the Section 126 findings for sources in that state. In other words, EPA no longer required compliance with this program if a state met the full requirements of the SIP Call. However, this EPA rule states that if a Section 126 state does not meet the full requirements of the SIP Call Program, then SIP reviews will take place on a state-by-state basis to determine whether the reductions they would achieve under their SIP will be adequate to remove the 126 findings, making the state responsible for the overall emissions budget.

Upwind state governments and power companies filed numerous lawsuits against these programs, and other legal disputes were emerging separately over the ozone standard itself. These legal actions delayed the implementation of both the SIP Call and the Section 126 policy actions. Courts vacated the eight-hour ozone NAAQS promulgated in 1998 as the basis for Section 126 findings, and it was returned to be listed as the previous, less stringent one-hour ozone NAAQS. Ultimately, this program became more stringent as a result of the January 18, 2000, final rule taking a number of important actions on the transported NO_x matter.[11] First and foremost, the agency reiterated its finding that NO_x emissions from sources in 12 states and the District of Columbia are contributing to downwind ozone formation and that those sources must therefore reduce NO_x emissions. It also promulgated a final federal cap-and-trade program for NO_x that took effect on February 17, 2000.

As stated by Kathryn Petrillo (2002), the goal was "to have one single trading program requirement for each source—not to have a source covered by a multitude of programs." However, EPA administrators and observers also acknowledged that significant differences in the way each of these programs impact controlled sources in participating states remained at the outset of the integration process. Table 7.3 illustrates the differences, similarities, and integration processes between interstate regional NO_x programs in the Northeastern US.

Table 7.3 Ozone Region Programs Integration

	Ozone Transport Commission (OTC) NO_x Budget Program	Section 126 Federal NO_x Budget Trading Program	NO_x State Implementation Plan (SIP) Call
States covered	CT, DC., DE, MA, MD, ME, NH, NJ, NY, PA, RI, VT	DC., DE, IN, KY, MD, MI, NC, NJ, NY, OH, PA, VA, WV	AL, CT, DC., DE, IL, IN, KY, MA, MD, MI, NC, NJ, NY, OH, PA, RI, SC, TN, VA, WV
Compliance periods	May 1–September 30 of each year	May 1–September 30 of each year	May 1–September 30 of each year
Initial compliance year	Phase I (NO_x RACT): May 31, 1995. Phase II: May 1, 1999 Phase III: May 1, 2003	2003	2004 (Phase I), State NO_x Budget Programs (and NO_x reductions) must be met by May 31, 2004; budgets should have been achieved by 2007
Emissions cap	219,000 tons in 1999; 143,000 tons in 2003	289,983 tons	
Baseline year	1990	1995	1995
Baseline emissions	490,000 tons		4,526,538 tons
Projected emission reductions and target year	320,000 tons/yr (2003)	510,000 tons per ozone season (2007)[1]	880,000 tons per ozone season (2007)[2]
Program Administrator	OTC; Allowances set by OTC states and the program is administered by EPA	EPA	States and EPA; States have the option of participating in the trading program and establishing unit allocations, program administered by EPA

Source: EPA

Note:
1 Reductions under the Section 126 action are required to have begun on May 1, 2003. States may chose to regulate some or all of the same sources that EPA is regulating under Section 126 under the NO_x SIP Call starting in 2004. For 2004 and beyond, therefore, emission reductions from the SIP Call Program and Section 126 action should not be considered additive.
2 As originally finalized, the NO_x SIP Call under Section 110 covered 22 states and the District of Columbia and required 1.1 million tons of NO_x reductions. Based on a March 3, 2000, D.C. Circuit Court Decision, the geographic scope of the SIP Call and the overall reductions were slightly reduced to nineteen states and the District of Columbia. Some additional reductions were required upon finalization of rules developed to address issues remanded to EPA.

In terms of the scope of the program, the SIP Call (Section 110) and the FIP (Section 126) cover the same core sources of pollution—EGUs with greater than 25 MW of generation power and non-electric-generating units (non-EGUs) with a nameplate capacity of more than 250 MMBtu/hour. The key difference is that under the SIP Call states were allowed to expand coverage to include other EGUs and non-EGUs. For instance, many of the OTC states include EGUs as small as 15 MW, while others only regulate 25 MW EGUs. These states are listed in the third column to the right in Table 7.3.

Another difference between these programs is in the emissions baseline year. The OTC program baseline is derived from 1990 emissions data, whereas the SIP Call and the Section 126 action state budgets are based on 1995 or 1996 emissions, whichever is higher, on a state-by-state basis. In 2003 the OTC NO_X Budget Program and the NO_X SIP Call Program were essentially merged by EPA. The only exception to this integration process was New Hampshire: it is the only state in the OTC program that is not required to comply with the SIP Call.[12] As mentioned earlier, as soon as a state submits an approvable and complete SIP, the EPA will remove the Section 126 findings for emission sources in that state.

The case of Massachusetts illustrates how these different programs affected a particular state, as well as how they eventually decided to integrate into one regional NO_X cap-and-trade mechanism. In the OTC NO_X Budget Program, Massachusetts committed to meeting Phase III in 2003. At the same time the state was required to meet the SIP Call in 2004. Since Phase III of the OTC program and the SIP Call Program both required NO_X emissions reduction of the same order of magnitude, Massachusetts (as well as the other states covered under both programs) chose to meet their Phase III commitment by complying with the NO_X SIP Call Program, which is also the reason why the OTC states choose to stay with the 2003 compliance date even though the court moved it to 2004. In other words, they implemented their SIP Call by meeting both the SIP Call Program and the OTC NO_X Budget Program commitments.[13]

The NO_X SIP Call was proposed after the NO_X Budget Program had begun to take shape but before the cap-and-trade system was actually implemented. The SIP Call expanded coverage to include all relevant sources (the power generation sector is just a component of this program). The program design closely followed the recommendations of the OTAG process (US EPA 1998, 45). Both the SIP Call and the Section 126 policy action require NO_X emission reductions. However, the SIP Call allows a larger number of states to choose how to make these reductions. Under Section 126, EPA directly regulates emitters (Petrillo 2002).

The EPA has worked for almost a decade towards the harmonization of all key market design parameters, as well as a coordinated integration of emissions trading programs, to consolidate a cost-effective and workable regional interstate seasonal NO_X ETS. The following are three key design considerations of the NBP ETS.

State Allowance Budget System: EPA's focus since the 1990 CAA Amendments had been on controlling emissions from electric utilities as the most cost-effective source of NO_X reductions. Under the NBP ETS, each state's NO_X budget was developed based on the application of an average, population-wide NO_X emission rate of 0.15lb/MMBtu (about an 85 percent decrease from 1990 levels) for large EGUs. However, in contrast to the OTC NO_X Budget Program, it also aimed for a 70 percent reduction of uncontrolled emissions from large industrial sources. In short, the state allowance budgets under NBP ETS represented every sector within the state; the power generation sector is just one component of a state's SIP Call budget. Along with these controls and other necessary measures including mobile source controls, states were expected to meet their overall regional NO_X emission reductions (US EPA 1998, 3).

Early Reduction Credits: To minimize risks to electricity reliability, EPA established a compliance supplement pool of 200,000 tons of NO_X to be allocated to participating states in proportion to the size of the reduction they must achieve. States could use these additional allowances to allocate emission tons to sources that reduce emissions prior to May 2003 in an early reduction credit feature. Also, these allowances could be used to provide relief to electric utilities having trouble meeting the compliance deadline. For this latter allocation, sources requesting such treatment would be required to demonstrate that the compliance deadline creates undue risk for the source, in particular for the electric generation industry. The EPA planned to retire any tons from this pool of additional allowable emissions if they were not allocated by May 2001 (Committee for the National Institute for the Environment).

Political Jurisdiction: Another key difference from the OTC NO_X Budget Program is that the SIP Call Program was to be implemented at the state level but enforced federally by EPA. The rule does not prescribe how states should reduce emissions to meet their budget. Instead it allows states the flexibility to develop customized plans that will most effectively help them meet their reduction goals.

7.2.3. NBP ETS performance

The NBP ETS provided a flexible compliance mechanism to further control emissions from EGUs and large industrial combustion sources. More than 2600 affected units were part of the program by 2008. Eighty-eight percent of units were EGUs. In 2004, 11 non-OTC states were formally integrated into the new program as they took part in that year's reconciliation process for compliance. The new participating states were Alabama, Illinois, Indiana, Kentucky, Michigan, North Carolina, Ohio, South Carolina, Tennessee, Virginia, and West Virginia. In 2007, Missouri was integrated into the NBP ETS.

Ultimately, the NBP ETS allowed states to meet their emissions budgets during the ozone season between 2003 and 2008 through participation in an expanded region-wide cap-and-trade interstate program. Participating states shared responsibility with EPA in how allowances were allocated, in inspecting and monitoring sources, and in enforcing compliance. States had flexibility in implementing a compliance regime for their own affected sources either under a local budget

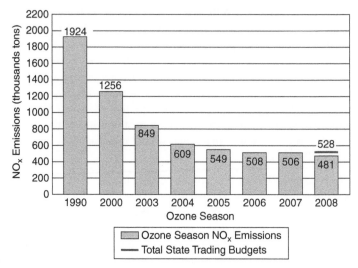

Figure 7.4 NBP ETS Ozone pollution trends 1990–2008
Source: EPA (2009)

approach or through the NPB ETS. However, EPA imposed automatic penalties if affected sources did not cover actual emissions with allowance holdings during the annual reconciliation period. The sanction was to surrender the following year's allocation at a three-to-one ratio.

The NBP ETS significantly improved regional air quality. EPA 2009 reports that by 2008 the ozone season NO_X emissions were 9 percent below the 2008 NBP ETS cap, 62 percent lower than in 2000 before the program's implementation, and 75 percent lower than in 1990, before the implementation of the CAA (US EPA Oct. 2009). Figure 7.4 reflects the progress in ozone season emissions reductions over time.

7.3 The Clean Air Interstate Rule NO_X ozone season ETS

As first introduced in Chapter 5, in 2005 EPA issued the CAIR with the goal of achieving, in a cost-effective manner, further NO_X (as well as $PM_{2.5}$, mercury, and SO_2) emission reductions from EGUs located in the summer ozone transport region. CAIR also relies on the cap-and-trade approach, the agency's preferred compliance strategy for participating states. Eastern and Mid-Atlantic states are familiar with and experienced in using market-based policies and have developed the institutional capacity to effectively participate in the region-wide ETS programs administered by EPA.

Based on the finding that "28 States and the District of Columbia contribute significantly to nonattainment of the national ambient air quality standards (NAAQS) for fine particles ($PM_{2.5}$) and/or 8-hour ozone in downwind States," EPA issued a rule to further reduce these substances. The initial CAIR rule, issued on March 10, 2005, required upwind states to revise their SIPs in order to include control measures to reduce emissions of SO_2 and/or NO_x. Sulfur dioxide is a precursor to $PM_{2.5}$ formation (as discussed in Chapter 5), and NO_x is a precursor to both ozone and $PM_{2.5}$ formation. The aim of CAIR was to build on the emissions reductions under the NBP ETS and the ARP ETS. CAIR was also intended to improve visibility in areas such as national parks, monuments, and wilderness.

Three distinct compliance programs were also created by CAIR: an annual NO_x program, an ozone season NO_x program, and an annual SO_2 program. Each of the three programs uses a two-phased approach, with declining emission caps in each phase. The first phase began in 2009 for the NO_x annual and NO_x ozone season programs, and in 2010 for the SO_2 annual program. The rule also establishes a second phase for all three programs beginning in 2015. Similar to the NO_x SIP Call and the NBP ETS, CAIR gave affected states NO_x emissions budgets and the flexibility in their state implementation plans to reduce emissions using a strategy that best suited their circumstances. Monitoring and reporting according to EPA's stringent regulations for the NO_x programs began in 2008; monitoring and reporting for SO_2 began in 2009.

The 28 affected states and the District of Columbia chose to be part of the EPA-administered regional CAIR NO_X ETS program. However, on July 11, 2008, the US Court of Appeals for the D.C. Circuit issued a ruling vacating CAIR in its entirety in *North Carolina v. Environmental Protection Agency*, 531 F.3d 896 (D.C. Cir. 2008) after legal challenges from some states and industries. For instance, industry groups contested that the EPA does not have the right to change the 1990 CAA passed by Congress and focused in particular on the number of allowances to be allocated under the CAIR NO_X rules and on how many should be surrendered per ton of pollutant in the case of SO_2 compliance rules. The court decided that EPA's approach of "implementing region-wide caps with no state-specific quantitative contribution determinations or emissions requirement—was fundamentally flawed."

The EPA had the support of environmental groups and other parties and requested a rehearing on September 26, 2008, arguing that (1) the court had imposed a remedy unsought by the petitioners (i.e., vacating the rule in its entirety); (2) CAIR was similar to other rules affirmed by the court, in particular EPA's NOX SIP Call, which was challenged in *Michigan v. Environmental Protection Agency*, 213 F.3d 663 (D.C. Cir. 2000); and (3) the CAA allows further regulation of SO_2 pursuant other titles of the Act. EPA also argued that the court erred by rejecting its approach to allocating NO_X allowances. On December 23, 2008, the Court revised its decision and remanded CAIR to EPA without *vacatur*. This ruling left CAIR and the CAIR FIPs—including the CAIR trading programs—in place until EPA issued new rules (US EPA October 2009).

After the 2008 D.C. Circuit Court decisions discussed earlier—first to vacate the CAIR in its entirety and then temporally reinstating the rule and its federal trading programs—in May 2009, the NBP ETS was replaced by the CAIR NO_X ozone season trading programs. EPA specified that the emissions reductions in all of the CAIR programs were to be implemented in two phases. The first phase of NO_X

reductions began in 2009 (covering 2009–2014), and the first phase of SO_2 reductions started in 2010 (covering 2010–2014). The second phase of reductions for both NO_X and SO_2 starts in 2015 (covering 2015 and thereafter).

In first announcing it final rule in 2005, EPA pointed to the policy criteria of fairness and cost-effectiveness stating: "attainment will be achieved in a more equitable, cost-effective manner than if each nonattainment area attempted to achieve attainment by implementing local emissions reductions alone" (US EPA 2005). By reducing upwind ozone precursor emissions EPA CAIR trading programs were expected to assist the downwind $PM_{2.5}$ and eight-hour ozone non-attainment areas in achieving the NAAQS.

The CAIR's three federal compliance programs are directed to control fine particles, ozone, and both substances. The program expanded the geographical scope of the NBP ETS as all participating states, except Rhode Island, are included in the CAIR's NO_X ozone season program along with six additional states: Florida, Iowa, Louisiana, Mississippi, Arkansas, and Wisconsin. Rhode Island must continue to meet its NO_x SIP Call reduction requirements.

All CAIR federal rules apply to Alabama, Missouri, and Michigan. The 2009 CAIR NO_x ozone season cap was 580,000 tons. The integration process required some transitional design features. For instance, flow controls no longer apply under CAIR, so transferred NBP allowances may be used under CAIR on a straight one-to-one basis with no restrictions or time limits. Furthermore, sources outside the NBP region can buy and use pre-2009 NBP allowances in the CAIR NOx ozone season trading program (Figure 7.5).

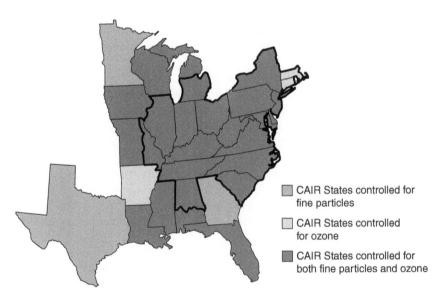

Figure 7.5 Geographical integration of the NBP
Source: EPA (2009)

7.4 New rules of the game, new court rejection: a setback to ETS in the US or another step in the evolutionary path of this policy approach?

On July 6, 2011, EPA announced the CSAPR, formerly known as the Clean Air Transport Rule, in response to the Court's remand of CAIR. EPA issued the new rules seeking to introduce tighter controls on ozone. With CSAPR and other local and federal actions, EPA aims to reduce power plant SO_2 emissions by 73 percent over 2005 levels and NO_x emissions by 54 percent by 2014. The new program sets a pollution limit for each of the 27 states covered. EPA also proposed rules that would require six states—Iowa, Kansas, Michigan, Missouri, Oklahoma, and Wisconsin—to make summertime NOX reductions under the CSAPR ozone-season control program. Five of those states are already covered in the final rule for interstate fine particle pollution ($PM_{2.5}$). Finalizing this supplemental proposal would bring the total number of covered states under the CSAPR to 28 (US EPA August 2011).

The program allows for limited interstate trading among power plants to address reliability issues as long as states can make assurances that they will meet pollution reduction requirements. EPA estimates that annual direct costs to the power sector for complying with CSAPR and supplementary proposed rules will be $800 million by 2014, along with the roughly $1.6 billion per year in capital investments already under way as a result of CAIR. Benefits derived from improving air quality in the region will result in $120–280 billion in annual benefits, including the value of avoiding 13,000–34,000 premature deaths each year (US EPA August 2011).

Financial analysts responded negatively to the new rule when it was first proposed in July 2010. As reported by Environmental Finance (July 8, 2010), the proposed rule makes the regional cap tighter than the ARP ETS (Title IV, 1990 CAA) and creates a new set of SO_2 allowances under the new regulation. These potential actions placed immediate downward pressure on SO_2 allowance prices. Before the 2008 decision, SO_2 allowance prices were above $300. Due to the Court's intervention and continued regulatory uncertainty, allowances were selling at around $15 in June 2010. After the new rule was announced in July, allowance prices went down further; vintages 2008 and earlier were traded at $5.50, and the 2010 allowances slid to $3. Analysts believe these regulatory actions may bring ARP ETS allowance prices to zero, as stated by a market analyst for this report: "It's almost a reversion to the old command-and-control regimes of the 1980s" (Environmental Finance 2009). Moreover, market brokers have pointed out that under the proposed rule at the time, "restrictions designed to ensure that each state is able to meet the NAAQS could severely curtail trading opportunities" (Tesoriero and Watson 2010). Under the new rule, states would be allowed to develop a state plan to achieve the required reductions, replacing its federally coordinated plan, and may choose which types of sources to control by 2014. As the final 2011 CSAPR was unveiled, questions about its legality remained and observers worried about possibility of ending up with a fragmented market (Carlson, August 2011).

On September 2, 2011, President Obama released a statement requesting EPA to withdraw its proposed ozone NAAQS (of 60–70 parts per billion when averaged over an eight-hour period), arguing for "the importance of reducing regulatory burdens and regulatory uncertainty," particularly when the economy is faltering. Obama also objected to "asking state and local governments to begin implementing a new standard that will soon be reconsidered" in 2013 (White House, September 2011). EPA plans to enforce the ozone standard of 75 parts per billion, adopted by the EPA in 2008 under President Bush Jr., which tightened the ozone limits from 84 parts per billion. Scientists had advised EPA to introduce standards within the range of 60–70 parts per million to minimize human health impacts. The debate around this decision is illustrative of the impact of political cycles and the economic context in environmental policy formulation.

Constant changes and regulatory uncertainty have caused downward pressure on this environmental commodities market. Utilities have already "overbuilt" NO_X control devices to comply with CAIR rules which remain in place. In 2010, seasonal NO_x allowances traded at $40 after the announcement of the new rule, while annual NO_x allowances traded at $365, showing little variation from previous levels.[14] EPA estimated annual NO_x allowances would cost $500 and seasonal NO_x allowances $1300 in 2012. However, reports over the first "brokered 100 tons of vintage 2012 allowances for both seasonal and annual NO_x," show prices at $3750 per ton. According to market analysts, these prices "reflect concerns that regulated entities will bank allowances in anticipation of their emissions budgets shrinking in 2014, which risks creating a liquidity issue, and the possibility of exceeding budgets, which could lead to substantial penalties" (Environmental Finance, September 5, 2011).[15]

The August 21, 2012 court decision to reject CSAPR, because "EPA's Transport Rule exceeds the agency's statutory authority" just adds to the environment of regulatory uncertainty and constant changes to the rules of the game that hamper, and may paralyze, emerging environmental markets in this region. Several factors have already undermined the necessary credible commitment from government to ETS that make the rules of the game stable and nurture nascent environmental commodities markets: (1) court intervention limiting EPA's regulatory authority to implement ETS in the region; (2) a lack of potential legislative action to "fix the problem"; (3) strong lobbying against costly environmental regulation during difficult financial times; and (4) a highly politicized environment in Washington, D.C. against the cap-and-trade concept as a climate policy of choice. While EPA stayed within the limits of the law in pushing for the expansion, the perception is that cap-and-trade is losing its institutional foundations in the US. Clear, predictable, and transparent rules are necessary. Even more importantly, as in the case of the 1990 CAA Amendments and the ARP ETS, the commitment to a market-based policy program needs to be made as permanent as possible by legislative action to provide the necessary flexibility, investment incentives, and emissions reductions.

7.5 Summary of policy lessons

Despite recent political uncertainty over cap-and-trade's credibility at the federal level in the US, the institutional history of an integrated regional interstate NO_X ETS in the Eastern US demonstrates that this policy approach is appropriate for complex, multi-jurisdictional contexts of decision making and implementation. It also demonstrates the viability of stringent emissions limits or caps introduced gradually as part of a flexible mechanism, such as an ETS and the cost-effectiveness of methods to regulate industries beyond the electric power sector. Experience shows that the implementation of multilateral interstate ETS is effective and feasible from the economic, environmental, and administrative perspectives.

From the policy design perspective, a key lesson to consider is the process of integration and harmonization of multiple and independent programs based on the standardization of critical ETS design components such as MRV to ensure the compliance of all participants and enhance the environmental integrity and cost-effectiveness of these programs. Trading rules governing the interstate NO_X ETS program were fairly consistent from one state to another; no restrictions had been placed on the transfer and use of credit throughout the region. Private sector environmental brokers reported that this approach provided the appropriate regulatory framework for the rapid emergence of a liquid environmental market. Moreover, collaborative efforts to develop model trading rules enabled convergence towards transparency, simplicity, and integration, which eventually allowed for the emergence of the streamlined, federally administered, regional NBP ETS. Further integration by EPA, through federally coordinated programs and supplementary conventional rules (i.e., MATS) is expected to result in more emission reductions, but cost-effectiveness is at risk. The more stringent mercury and air toxics rules will be in place by 2015 and are expected to force the decommissioning of old, coal-fired plants.The good news is that air quality and other environmental conditions are improving in these regions. However, impacted downwind states will remain vulnerable to winds bringing NO_X emissions that lead to ground-level ozone and its health effects. New regulatory frameworks are getting quite complicated, and they lack predictability for businesses to plan and take advantage of the existing US emissions trading programs. The EPA regulatory fixes in recent years in fact diminished trading opportunities.

While the ARP ETS and RECLAIM ETS experiences provided EPA with the credible policy design elements necessary to support interstate collaborative efforts towards an integrated NO_X ETS in this region, "critical to this development was the leadership and innovation by the states, which provided valuable information, data, and a set of committed stakeholders" (Aulisi et al. 2005, 1). Fostering co-operation among independent political jurisdictions that face differing costs and benefits from environmental control, as well as different technical capabilities and interests (e.g., internal political cycles or economic competitiveness), is difficult at best. Collaborative efforts such as OTC and OTAG allowed politicians, industry, environmentalists, regulators, scientists, federal authorities, and other interested stakeholders to better understand the issues at stake and led them to favor the flexibility offered by the market-based approach.

The following chapter examines the prospects for the transferability of the ETS concept to a global scale. It suggests a model for an evolving system that relies on strong national and regional (i.e., multi-state and/or sub-national) emissions trading programs and mirrors the process of model rules and common policy design features development implemented in the Northeastern US. It proposes a multilateral governance regime that sets institutional thresholds (or accession protocols) for nations to participate in an international emissions market mechanism.

As in the case of the OTC and preceding versions of a multi-state ETS, nations and sub-national jurisdictions willing to participate in international emissions trading must meet certain predetermined performance standards and ETS design protocols mutually recognized under international treaties. These "model rules" and practices must be previously agreed to by all participants and sanctioned by a central international authority (such as the United Nations Framework Convention on Climate Change Secretariat) based on the accumulated policy experience of good practices from existing programs. A set of multilaterally agreed upon protocols for design and performance standards can ultimately foster certainty and credibility in the implementation of workable and cost-effective global environmental commodities markets. The framework of environmental market creation parameters, as applied in the previous case studies, underscores the key policy design features that can facilitate the development of future market-based international environmental governance structures.

Chapter 8

International market-based environmental policy

Several decades of policy experimentation show that a properly designed emissions trading system (ETS) can deliver cost-effective emissions reductions swiftly and provide certainty in accomplishing an environmental goal. While not a "silver bullet," ETS is a key policy tool within a multifaceted policy strategy to address the risks and dangers of climate change.

Greenhouse gas (GHG) emission sources are diverse and heterogeneous. The complex nature of the climate policy challenge makes it critical to focus on controlling GHG emissions in a timely manner. Customized complementary measures and incentives for different sectors of the economy such as energy, transport, and the built environment, among others, are necessary elements of an integrated approach to enable the transition to a low-carbon future. However, a high degree of institutional coordination is required in the design and implementation of regulatory instruments to achieve the diverse set of policy objectives that a systems approach to climate problem solving demands.

With climate change, we face a stock problem: the capacity of the atmosphere to store carbon is not limitless and timely action matters. By using prices and market-based regulatory approaches we can cost-effectively manage atmospheric carbon storage while at the same time fostering smart, clean economic growth. From an economics perspective, a carbon tax may theoretically remain more appealing to control GHG emissions (Pizer 1999; Nordhaus 2005). However, experience shows that implementing a cap-and-trade ETS gradually (starting with grandfathering or free allocation followed by clearly determined and predictable implementation phases) may be a more politically feasible and cost-effective strategy to address climate change. The focus is on the emissions cap that sets a legal limit on pollution; the trading component provides flexibility to meet it.

This flexibility facilitates the potential for key stakeholders to reach a political agreement to start taking action towards an emissions reduction goal and allows them to adjust using environmental markets. From the industry's perspective an ETS with free allowances during the initial phase of implementation can make it more affordable to meet the emissions targets set by the policy process. For environmental groups, potentially weaker or uncertain emissions reductions under a carbon tax represent a risk not worth taking.

Introducing a cap-and-trade ETS with a full auction allocation mechanism (that raises revenue for the government) may prove to be a more equitable and desirable approach, but it is more politically contentious as the environmental goal gets intertwined with fiscal policy. Again, a gradual implementation approach, along with predictable legislated paths to possible future program revisions or adjustments, is recommended for economy-wide systems.

From an institutional comparative perspective, a key theoretical advantage of an ETS over a carbon tax system is that the regulator needs less information to achieve the environmental goal at minimum cost. Once the cap is set, the market provides the cost-effective allocation through trading. The ETS utilizes the superior information that sources have about their control options (compared to the regulator) in a way that a carbon tax cannot. As established earlier in Chapter 2, the regulator has to find the right charge level; with ETS the market sets it while providing a clear, transparent, and more permanent environmental goal.

However, when there is free allowance allocation, good information *ex ante* is also required to avoid competitive distortion among market participants. Gradual implementation allows ETS regulators to improve the quality of information provided by the market and regulated parties, to assess the level of assistance needed by industry at competitive risk, and to plan for measures to minimize carbon leakage caused by increasing GHG emissions outside the climate policy jurisdiction or by companies moving outside the jurisdiction. Moreover, phases in the development of an ETS should allow for the incorporation of new scientific evidence on environmental risks in order to sustain a meaningful emissions cap.

The better the initial information, the less need for government intervention to fine-tune the ETS. Moreover, as past experience shows in the United States (US), a long view in environmental markets is important. Too much unplanned regulatory intervention can dampen ETS market signals. Ideally, predictable policy adjustment paths should be outlined as much as possible from the onset. A credible commitment to the ETS cap-and-trade policy approach from governments and multilateral organizations, regardless of the necessary adjustments from learning-by-doing provides a signal of permanence. As a senior executive from a global energy company recently told me: "We need to be reassured constantly by governments that the carbon market is here to stay." A sense of permanence is an essential condition for environmental commodities markets to perform their functions, particularly if we want to create a global carbon market to meet national and international carbon emissions caps at the lowest possible cost.

The emerging carbon market can also become an important source of needed investment capital for climate finance projects. Major investments will be necessary in the industrialized world as nations reconvert their current fossil fuel-based energy and production systems to cleaner processes. Significant financial and technological resources will be necessary to enable low-carbon economic growth paths for the developing world. By putting a price on carbon, attitudes towards energy consumption change, fostering energy efficiency and the development of alternative industrial processes and clean technologies to enable low-carbon economic growth.

Moreover, the carbon market engages the private financial sector's capacity to identify and to develop climate investment opportunities and risk management strategies within the ETS frameworks both at the compliance and the voluntary action levels. In short, innovative climate finance solutions are essential to shore up the transformational effort of creating a global clean economy.

According to scientists, global warming is unavoidable at this point, and we will have to adapt to some degree. Depending on our choices and timely actions, potentially damaging impacts to humans and to biodiversity can be mitigated. National governments need to fully commit to reduce the current trends of accumulation of global GHG emissions by 50–80 percent before the end of this next century to avoid catastrophic climate change impacts. Estimates based on a portfolio of technologically viable solutions as suggested by Pacala and Socolow (2004) project that we have the capability to stabilize emission at current levels for the next 50 years. Carbon sequestration through forestry, land-use change, and geo-engineering programs, while presenting their own policy implementation challenges, can also assist in climate problem solving.[1]

Despite these necessities, regulatory uncertainty for real climate action continues at the international level, as key nations hamper the prospects for the emergence of a truly global carbon market. Conventional international processes to create climate-related governance structures have proven to be time-consuming and convoluted; after decades of negotiation rounds under the United Nations Framework Convention on Climate Change (UNFCCC) process, little progress has been made to stabilize GHGs.

Despite the unprecedented number of heads of state and government in attendance, the 2009 UNFCCC Conference of Parties (COP15) summit in Copenhagen epitomized the lack of incentives and commitment to move toward significant climate action and binding commitments. Some observers believe that the culprits for lack of action at the international level are the UNFCCC's top-down approach based on an all-or-nothing vision and "a-wait-and-see-what-others-do" attitude among countries reluctant to compromise the competitiveness of their national economies.

A key challenge is to solve the energy transformation challenge cost-effectively through reforms of fossil fuel pricing. International agencies such as the Organisation for Economic Co-operation and Development (OECD) and the International Energy Agency (IEA) help articulate policy recommendations and provide guidance to their members by recommending, for example, the phasing out of subsidies to fossil fuels. The IEA argues that "well-executed reform on energy pricing can generate important economic, energy security, and environmental benefits."[2] Well-designed GHG ETS can assist in this process.

The current uncertain policy landscape on global carbon governance is not conducive to fostering energy transformation and technological innovation to reduce GHG emissions. It does not provide a sense of clear direction and consistency on the future climate policy paths that are necessary to enhance confidence for those seeking business opportunities in following a green growth economic development path.

In theory, trading a ton of carbon emitted in the US with a ton of carbon from China should be a seamless transaction conducted in a well-functioning and harmonized global environmental commodities market. However, integrated global environmental commodities markets will not emerge in the near future unless a set of minimum policy design criteria, standards, and good practices are put in place based on technical considerations for commodity trading. Validation by a credible commitment from an expanded group of key governments around the world—either through the UNFCCC institutional process or, in the interim, through more national, multinational, and regional climate legislation and co-operation arrangements—is important to underpinning environmental integrity throughout the evolution of the institutions supporting the creation of the global carbon market.

International collective action for climate change supported by environmental commodities markets is already taking place. Climate-related ETSs are now being implemented in a diverse set of institutional contexts including multinational, national, and sub-national political jurisdictions. In the international context, market-based policy design was introduced to enhance the cost-effectiveness of the first global environmental agreement as part of the 1987 Montreal Protocol (MP). Its goal was to reduce ozone-depleting substances (ODS) in the form of a limited trading program known as Industrial Rationalization (IR). At the country level, in 2002 the UK experimented with a voluntary carbon ETS, and in 2008 it enacted the first national Climate Change Act in the world. In 2003 legislation was passed to create the European Union Emissions Trading Scheme (EU ETS), and in 2005 the largest ETS to date was launched as part of a regional multinational climate strategy to comply with the UNFCCC's Kyoto Protocol (KP) carbon dioxide (CO_2) emissions reduction commitments of its Member States.

In North America, the US, though party to the UNFCCC, has never ratified the KP and has been unable to pass climate legislation in part because of political polarization in the energy and environment debate. Moreover, there is no tradition of developing an integrated, national US climate or energy plan. Several legislative initiatives have been introduced there, but did not survive the policy process. However, GHG emissions reductions in the US for 2011 have been significant, mostly because of conventional regulation accelerating the closure of coal fueled power generators and fuel-switching to natural gas for electric generation as reviewed in chapters 5 and 7. Canada, in the aftermath of its most recent electoral cycle, reduced its level of ambition on climate policy. In addition, in December 2011, the newly elected conservative government officially withdrew from the KP. Finally, Canada's sector-by-sector climate policy approach is not on track to meet its stated commitment to reduce GHG emissions by 17 percent below 2005 levels by 2020.[3] In contrast, on April 19, 2012, Mexico committed to national, legally binding emissions goals to combat climate change, making it one of only two countries in the world to do so, the other being the UK. Mexico passed its climate change bill with a vote of 128 for and 10 against in the Chamber of Deputies. The Senate passed the legislation unanimously.

Canada, Mexico, and the US are all signatories to the North American Free Trade Agreement, and their economies are closely interrelated. As political and policy positions evolve with time, as well as macroeconomic conditions, perhaps in the future North America will eventually see the emergence of the largest regional ETS in the world (NA ETS), a building block that could catalyze the establishment of a truly global carbon market. Sub-national climate action in North America does reflect institutional developments in that direction.

Sub-national governments (i.e., states and groups of states or provinces) around the world are actively developing regional climate action plans and programs, including ETSs, as a GHG mitigation and economic transformational strategy. Given the lack of federal policy in the US, sub-national climate action is of special relevance in North America. In 2003 the Regional Greenhouse Gas Initiative (RGGI) in the Northeastern US was created, providing a potential model for a national or North American GHG trading system. The program went into effect on January 1, 2009. In 2006, the State of California passed Assembly Bill 32 (AB 32), and in August 2010 the state introduced a cap-and-trade system to be implemented in 2013. California also leads an effort for regional multinational action in the Western US, Canada, and Mexico as part of the Western Climate Initiative (WCI) established in 2007. Canadian provinces are introducing diverse carbon pricing approaches. For instance, Quebec has launched its own ETS, which will begin in January 2013. A WCI partner, the province is working with California on linking systems. In 2008 British Columbia, also a WCI partner, introduced a revenue-neutral carbon tax. Moreover, collaborative approaches such as North America 2050—which is open to all US states, Canadian provinces, and Mexican states and is "committed to policies that move their jurisdictions toward a low-carbon economy"—demonstrate the interest by regulators to create policy exchange forums to learn from regional implementation experiences and leadership in climate action. Multijurisdictional international organizations such as the R20 Regions of Climate Action, the Governors' Climate and Forest Task Force, and Local Governments for Sustainability are among the plethora of collaborative sub-national climate action groups emerging internationally, and California plays a leading role in this context.

Policy innovation for market-based climate solutions continues to emerge at the national level as well. Australia, for instance, has demonstrated that smart policies, supported by political leadership and a credible commitment by government to climate action, eventually can circumvent politics and electoral cycles. In 2011, after a period of strong political opposition to cap-and-trade, a carbon pricing policy was passed into law as part of the Clean Energy Legislative package and entered into force in 2012. The new national, market-based mechanism implemented has established an interim fixed price (through the issuance of fixed price units with an ETS) as a first step toward converting to a full-fledged flexible cap-and-trade ETS in 2015. Clear, legislated paths for revision and adjustment have been included in the law to enhance predictability and market certainty.

Regional carbon markets integration has begun in that region of the world. New Zealand has had an ETS in operation since 2010, and began a process to assess its performance and how to best coordinate action with trading partners the following year. Links with other emerging ETSs in the Asia-Pacific region may occur sooner than expected. South Korea passed a law in May 2012 establishing its own ETS, and immediately New Zealand announced a joint study to analyze the prospects of linking their respective ETSs.[4] Before that, the Australia-New Zealand Carbon Pricing Officials group conducted a similar study. Both of these governments expect that linking could commence in 2015—at the start of the flexible pricing period of Australia's carbon pricing mechanism.[5]

The lack of participation of major emerging economies, in particular China and India, in a global binding agreement to control GHG emissions has been a major hurdle in the US Congress to pass any meaningful climate legislation. However, this does not mean that these nations are not taking action on energy and climate-related issues. China is strategically positioning itself to become a clean tech powerhouse by leveraging the business transformation opportunities of green economic growth while also actively experimenting with seven pilot ETSs at the city level to serve as the basis for a national carbon market to be implemented in 2015. In 2010, India introduced a carbon tax on coal and decontrolled its markets for gas, diesel, and cooking gas fuels in a move towards market-based energy pricing.[6]

Acknowledging the slow pace of the UNFCCC institutional build-up for real global climate action, some developed nations see value in supporting the efforts of emerging economies to strengthen their capacities to achieve their voluntary pledges made at the UNFCCC 2010 Cancun climate summit (COP16) to "reduce emissions in the years before any new agreement entered into force."[7] The World Bank is supporting "market readiness" by providing funds to build capacity and support the development of ETS programs in middle-income countries. The goal is to scale up the carbon market potential, while focusing on providing technical assistance on a key design aspect of the carbon market: measurement, verification, and reporting (MRV).

In 2010, at Cancun, Mexico (COP16), both developing and developed countries made official pledges to take action to reduce GHG emissions. These included the introduction of the concept of "new market mechanisms" to enhance emissions reduction capacity by scaling up efforts under the flexible mechanisms of the UNFCCC compliance system. All of the countries party to the UNFCCC, except Bolivia, reached consensus in support of global climate action.

In 2011, at Durban (COP17), parties agreed to adopt the Durban Platform—a roadmap to a global legal agreement applicable to all parties. This decision again emphasized the central role of international law and multilateral institutions in addressing climate change over national, voluntary action within the UN process. The intention is to incorporate binding emissions targets for all countries, except the poorest and least developed. A Green Climate Fund was formally established to support the poorest countries in tackling and responding to climate change. Parties also agreed to a second commitment period for the KP beginning in 2013, despite some dissenting opinions from countries like Japan and Russia.

The challenge for the future of the UNFCCC process is to deliver on its promise to stabilize GHG emissions by setting a legally binding global cap. Scientific evidence on climate change and its potentially negative effects on humanity keep mounting with higher degrees of confidence. Impacts on communities and ecosystems are expected to be significant and are likely to trigger civil unrest and conflict.[8] Scientific warnings should be taken seriously in the policy process as we lack a "workable alternative" to obtain evidence for decision making.[9] Politicians have the responsibility to assess risks to society and take action to mitigate the impacts of climate change. However, climate risk remains a diffuse concept to societies, and communicating the right message on this issue to trigger climate action is still a challenge in many parts of the world.

Enabling a functional and agile international carbon governance architecture that provides both environmental integrity and regulatory certainty through its policy mechanisms is becoming paramount. The transformational effort to implement a green growth strategy, along with maximization of the business opportunities that energy reconversion and sustainable production efforts offer, requires a clear signal of permanence for international market-based policy solutions to operate cost-effectively.

This chapter will review some of the key policy design parameters introduced by a sample of international jurisdictions as part of the evolutionary process towards developing a global environmental commodities market, in particular the carbon market. Finally it will offer some concluding remarks about the state of the international ETS policy development experience based on learning-by-doing.

8.1 Introduction to international market-based solutions: the Montreal Protocol

8.1.1 Background on the Montreal Protocol

Derived from the 1985 Vienna Convention on the Protection of the Ozone Layer, the MP on Substances that Deplete the Ozone Layer entered into force on September 16, 1987. It was the first multilateral treaty to take on a global ecological problem. The MP grants national governments and industry compliance flexibility in order to allow for cost-effective implementation. However, experience shows that environmental policymaking at the multilateral level multiplies the complexity for problem solving (Benedict 1998).

Ozone occurs naturally in the stratosphere and is produced and destroyed at a constant rate. It can be good or bad for the ecosystem depending on its location in the atmosphere. As reviewed in chapters 6 and 7, ground-level ozone located in the troposphere, the layer surrounding the earth's surface, is a key ingredient of urban smog. In contrast, ozone that lies in the stratosphere, which extends upward from about 10 to 30 miles above the earth, helps protect life on earth from the sun's harmful ultraviolet rays (UV-b). Good ozone has been gradually destroyed by man-made chemicals including chlorofluorocarbons (CFCs), halons,[10] and other

ODS. The MP sets a timetable for the gradual elimination of the production and consumption of certain ODS. To introduce cost effectiveness into the system, the MP includes market-like provisions, known as IR, for ODS production and consumption rights in the transition to a complete phase-out of these substances (OECD 1998).

8.1.2 Policy design parameters

Trading Mechanism: The IR system concept is defined in Article 1.8 of the MP as the transfer of all or a portion of the calculated level of production of one party to another, for the purpose of achieving economic efficiencies or responding to anticipated short-falls in supply as a result of plant closures. Industrial Rationalization in the MP allows the production quota from a country where production becomes uneconomic to be used by a company in another country where it is cost-effective to increase production. Trade in ODS rights is limited to the transfer of rights from one large (industrial) ODS producer to another (OECD 2008, 25).

Exchange Ratios: The MP takes into consideration the fact that different types of CFCs are likely to have different effects on ozone depletion. The treaty assigns weights to each CFC on the basis of its depletion potential, which determines the number of allowances required to emit a particular type of CFC.

Trading Rules: The market mechanism is devised as bilateral contracts between large companies to implement IR trades. Governments have the option of allowing trading of ODS across governmental boundaries and must formally allow companies within their jurisdiction to trade. The IR system rules for transferring production quotas between signatory parties of the MP include the following:

- The total combined levels of production of the parties concerned are not allowed to exceed the agreed-upon production limits.
- The United Nations Environment Program (UNEP) Ozone Secretariat (Nairobi) must be notified of transfers no later than at the time of the transfer.
- Initially the transfers were not allowed to increase the individual production levels of countries by more than 10 percent over the base year (1986) level, except for parties with very low levels of production. However, the London amendments of 1990 to the MP removed this restriction.

Market Performance: Unfortunately, information to analyze the efficiency of the market is limited. Trading activity under this program is opaque because of commercial confidentiality concerns, in particular from the chemical industry. However, some observers suggest that transaction costs for IR are low. Because a small number of firms produce ODS, trading takes place between well-known, large firms, and pre-approval of trades requires little administration, making the system relatively cost-effective (Hammitt 2009).

A regulatory impact analysis report conducted by the Environmental Protection Agency (EPA) in 1988 concluded that the marketable permit system for US producers and importers of CFCs resulted in a number of savings relative to a program that directly controlled end uses. EPA needed just four staffers to oversee the program, rather than the 33 staffers and $23 million in administrative costs it anticipated would be required to regulate end uses. Industry estimated that a command-and-control approach to end users would cost more than $300 million for recordkeeping and reporting, versus only $2.4 million for the allowance trading approach (US EPA 1988).

8.1.3 Summary of policy lessons

Despite its restrictive nature, the MP is regarded in environmental diplomatic circles as a successful implementation experience. It also introduced the concept of working cooperatively with a specific sector or group of industries (i.e., sectoral approach) to achieve significant environmental gains at the global level. In 1997 a group of experts gathered in Canada to commemorate and assess the first decade of the implementation of the MP and expressed the opinion that, "We have learned that international environmental agreements can work and are workable" (Centre for Global Studies 1997). This group also reflect that the MP has demonstrated that global environmental challenges reflect the interdependence of nations and that these issues cannot be resolved without the active participation of all pollution-emitting nations and other interested parties, including industry. The following are some of the main policy lessons from the implementation of the MP:

Scientific Information: The science underlying the Protocol provided the catalyst to actively pursue the elimination of the most dangerous ODS around the world. Environmental science and knowledge are essential investments for informed decision-making; acknowledgment of the environmental threat by government and societies is a necessary step to purposeful international action. Once the risks are assessed and potential costs are well understood, citizens, nations, and industry are willing to pay for pertinent policies and measures to minimize risks and prohibitive economic impacts.

Technological Innovation: Industry demonstrated ingenuity in finding alternative ways to deliver solutions to this ODS problem while creating gains from the reconversion process. The MP has effectively stimulated the development of technological alternatives to ozone-depleting chemicals used in refrigeration, foams, solvents, metal cleaning, dry cleaning, fire protection, and aerosols. Despite the high initial cost estimates for developing substitutes, the creativity and ingenuity of engineers and businesspeople flourished under a system that sets clear environmental goals and includes flexible compliance mechanisms.

Realistic Approach: The MP has served as a model for other international environmental agreements due to the realistic way it addressed the issue, and the cooperative spirit it engendered (Benedick 1998). It's targeted, non-punitive, apolitical, and science-based approach in working with the biggest consumers of ozone-depleting substances (i.e., industrialized countries) led to consensus building and common action. However, it also includes key policy features such as trade provisions that preclude Parties from trading in ODS with non-Parties. These, and related institutional design aspects, have encouraged ratification and helped the Protocol to achieve universal participation.

Fairness: The MP established a partnership based on the principle of common but differentiated responsibility, recognizing that the circumstances of the low-consumption countries (i.e., developing countries) are different from those of the developed world. Moreover, since the problem originated in the industrialized world, it was there that action was initially taken, giving developing countries a grace period. Further, differentiation in implementation was made for countries with economies in transition (EITs) from Eastern Europe. Most important to developing countries and EITs was the notion that costs should be borne principally by the developed countries that had caused most of the problem. As shown below, MP institutional design elements reflect consideration of equity issues.

Finance Support: In the 1990 London Amendment to the Protocol, a Multilateral Fund (MLF) was established. A balanced membership of developed and developing countries on the governance of the fund signaled a shift from the historic donor-driven nature of funding entities and carried forward the Protocol's spirit of equality. The MLF has evolved into a key driver of success. Its Executive Committee—made up of 14 Parties, seven from developed countries and seven from developing countries—allocated vast sums to ensure compliance and ease the transition for developing countries (UNEP 2007). All parties are required to submit annual reports on their production, import, and export of the chemicals to be phased out. An implementation committee of ten Parties, countries from different geographical regions, reviews the reports to assess compliance.

Flexible Design: A key feature of the Protocol was the innovative, dynamic, and flexible arrangement that it put in place. Under a global governance framework, in 2009, the MP became the first treaty in history to achieve universal ratification with 196 party governments. This represents the first time that the global community has legally committed itself to meeting specific time-bound targets for the virtual phase-out of nearly 100 chemicals that have ozone-depleting properties. The crafters of the new ozone environmental regime designed it to facilitate the integration of science into policy, thereby allowing for the adjustment of phase-out schedules and the control of all ODS, not just those initially identified in the Protocol. However, it also relied on a balanced approach, recognizing that certain products, such as the metered dose inhaler used to treat asthma, should be designated an essential use exemption and not banned until appropriate alternatives are found.

Adaptive Management: The Protocol relies heavily on scientific, environmental, technical, and economic assessments for its cost-effective implementation but allows for periodic assessments of the ozone regime knowledge base. At least every four years, studies are conducted to assess the ozone regime knowledge base. They are conducted in a way that puts them at arm's length from political considerations, thus providing a basis for further pertinent decisions on ODS management and multilateral environmental policy action. An impartial peer-reviewed approach oversees the provision of new technical data and knowledge on the ozone layer depletion issue. The MP successfully used the consensus arrived at on science and technology through the assessment process as a powerful driver to update the Protocol and its implementation.

Cost-Effective: The inclusion of market-like principles in its IR mechanisms minimized compliance costs. Although the MP operates under the principle of a targeted, non-punitive approach, the institutional design includes the following key features: (1) the possibility of trade sanctions to stimulate action and avoid ODS smuggling; (2) the inclusion of an "escape clause" as a cost-management design parameter that goes into effect when controlling emissions become too costly to participating countries (Victor 2001); and (3) the inclusion of an "adjustment provision" that enables the Parties to use new science to adjust controls on previously agreed upon ozone-depleting substances without waiting for a multi-year, national ratification process (UNEP 2007, 21).

In preparation for the twentieth anniversary of the MP, Kofi Annan, the UN Secretary-General, described it as "perhaps the most successful international agreement to date." Momentum towards achieving a total phase-out was accelerated in Montreal on September 16, 2007 during this event. At the gathering it was announced that developing countries had agreed to a more aggressive phase-down of ODS by freezing the production and consumption levels of hydrochlorofluorocarbons (HCFCs) in 2013 rather than 2016. Developing nations are expected to totally phase out production by 2030. Developed countries are committed to reducing HCFC consumption by 75 percent in 2010 and to completely phase out consumption and production by 2020. As stated by Annan's successor, UN Secretary-General Ban Ki-moon (Zerefos et al. 2009), "The success of the Montreal Protocol shows us that there are global instruments that can help curb the impact of human activities on the global environment. We should draw lessons from this experience, and strive to replicate it."

In reality, the scale and scope of the trading mechanism developed for the MP is small relative to the challenge that the overall climate change issue poses. Nevertheless, sound information, effective institutional design, a spirit of co-operation, and inspired individuals helped to bridge political differences in favor of the pursuit of the common good as the first international agreement to address a global environmental challenge became a cost-effective and equitable arrangement for all parties.

8.2 Creating global environmental commodities markets under the United Nations Framework Convention on Climate Change

8.2.1 Background on the KP

In contrast to the MP, creating an international GHG emissions trading mechanism faces significant political, technical, and institutional obstacles. It is a much more complex policy design and implementation challenge in comparison with all past ETS experiences. To effectively control carbon emissions, every sector of the economy needs to be included since practically every economic activity produces GHG emissions. It is an intergenerational sustainability challenge of global scale and impacts, and nations have diverse financial, technical, and human capabilities to mitigate, adapt, and transform their economic systems toward low-carbon development paths.

Conventional multilateral processes to create international global governance structures to address climate change have proven to be time-consuming and complex. A complicating factor is that at international negotiations, delegates come from almost 200 countries. Each represents his or her own national interest, and each is subject to internal political pressures. For most countries, delegates represent multiple agencies within their governments. While the global community signaled its willingness to take collective action to deal with climate change at COP 16 in Cancun, the challenge of designing functional and cost-effective frameworks to address climate change and limit global warming remains.

The UNFCCC entered into force on March 21, 1994, to set an overall framework for intergovernmental efforts to tackle the challenge posed by climate change. It enjoys near universal membership, with 194 countries and one regional economic integration organization (i.e., the EU) having ratified it to date. The Berlin Mandate of 1995, agreed to by all major parties, stipulated that developed nations should have "quantified emission limitation and reduction objectives" while developing nations should not. This policy position has evolved: by 2011 at Durban (COP 17) all developed country governments and 48 developing countries affirmed their emission reduction pledges up to 2020. However, it took almost two decades under the UNFCCC process to reach "a path to negotiate a new legal and universal emission reduction agreement by 2015, to be adopted by 2020," marking a historic shift towards real global climate action. However, as pointed out by the UNFCCC Secretariat "the emissions gap" is still 40 percent away from safety. The sum total of official emission reduction pledges from all countries so far amounts to only around 60 percent of what is needed to limit the temperature increase to 2° Celsius above pre-industrial levels, the environmental goal agreed on at Cancun.[11]

The KP was created in 1997 at COP3, held in Kyoto, Japan, in recognition of the need to address scientific recommendations, accelerate the curbing of future GHG emissions, and stabilize the accumulated stock of these gases in the atmosphere. Originally 37 nations (Annex B, known as Annex I Parties), mostly from the industrialized world, agreed to mandatory emissions reductions under this multilateral instrument. To make the instrument legally binding, the treaty required ratification by at least 55 countries. Some major economies, namely the US and Australia, rejected the treaty. The Russian Federation was the 55th country to ratify the KP. More than seven years after adoption, it finally entered into force on February 16, 2005. With that event, a new era in international environmental policymaking was launched. The KP's initial target is an average emissions reduction of 5.2 percent from the 1990 base level by parties to the treaty. This was to be achieved during its first commitment period from 2008 to 2012. All signatory parties to the convention have committed to supporting voluntary action to address the dangers of climate change. There are 192 Parties (191 states and one regional economic integration organization) under the protocol to date. Annex I Parties' emissions represent 63.7 percent of global GHG. As mentioned above, Canada officially withdrew from the KP effective December 15, 2012.

In summary, the 2011 Durban Platform establishes a roadmap to a global legal agreement applicable to all parties to be advanced at Doha 2012 (COP18) and beyond. If the UNFCCC process is successful, binding emissions targets for all countries, except the poorest and least developed, will be set in place. The KP's second commitment period will be in place starting 2013, despite some dissenting opinions by countries like Japan and Russia.

8.2.2 Policy strategies and instruments

Mitigation: Under Article 4.1(b) of the UNFCCC, all Parties are required to undertake efforts to mitigate climate change. The ultimate objective of the UNFCCC is to stabilize greenhouse gas concentrations in the atmosphere at a level that prevents dangerous anthropogenic (i.e., human) interference with the climate system.

Controlled Pollutants: In 2011 at COP17, the list of GHGs under the KP was amended to include the following gases: CO_2, methane (CH_4), nitrous oxide (N_2O), hydro-fluorocarbons (HFCs), perfluorocarbons (PFCs), sulfur hexafluoride (SF_6), and nitrogen trifluoride (NF_3). Moreover, a decision was made regarding the second commitment period of the KP, in which actual emissions of the HFCs and PFCs listed in the Fourth Assessment Report of the Intergovernmental Panel on Climate Change (IPCC), and of SF_6 and NF_3, should be estimated, reported, and included in the coverage of the quantified emissions limitation and reduction commitments for that period. The UNFCCC process also acknowledges that there are other new GHGs with high global warming potential, also reported by the IPCC, that are not yet produced in significant quantities but which should be further monitored to identify whether it is necessary to address them as part of mitigation commitments.

Adaptation: The Convention refers to adaptation in Article 2, stating that the objective of stabilizing GHG emissions in "a time-frame sufficient to allow ecosystems to adapt naturally to climate change [is] to ensure that food production is not threatened and to enable economic development to proceed in a sustainable manner." Moreover, in Article 4 (4.1(b, e, f), 4.8, and 4.9) signatory nations accept that climate change will happen to some extent, as the convention states the need for nations to adjust to the climatic changes and outlines commitments for specific actions to address adverse effects.

In 2007 international negotiators identified the need for enhanced action on adaptation by Parties to the Convention. There are many options and opportunities for countries to adapt, with adjustments and changes required at every level: community, national, and international. According to the UNFCCC Secretariat, appropriate adaptation strategies involve a synergy of the correct assessment of current vulnerabilities to climate change impacts; use of appropriate technologies; and information on traditional coping practices, diversified livelihoods, and current government and local interventions.

Compliance Budgets: As established under the UNFCCC, countries with commitments under the KP to limit or reduce GHG emissions must meet their targets primarily through national measures. These targets are expressed as levels of allowed emissions, or "assigned amounts," over the 2008–2012 commitment period. The second period agreed to at Durban gives continuity and certainty regarding the direction of this policy approach. The emissions allowed are divided into "assigned amount units" (AAUs).

Flexible Mechanisms: As an additional means of meeting these targets, the KP introduced three market-based mechanisms, thereby creating what is now known as the "carbon market." As described by the UNFCCC Secretariat, emissions trading as set out in Article 17 of the KP allows countries that have spare KP AAUs—emissions permitted but not "used"—to sell this excess capacity to countries that have surpassed their targets. The other units or environmental commodities that may be transferred under the scheme, each equal to one ton of CO_2, may be in the form of:

A *removal unit (RMU)* is based on land use, land-use change, and forestry activities such as afforestation and reforestation. The rate of build-up of CO_2 in the atmosphere can be reduced by taking advantage of the fact that carbon accumulates in vegetation and soils in terrestrial ecosystems. Any process, activity, or mechanism that removes a greenhouse gas from the atmosphere is referred to as a "sink."

An *emission reduction unit* is generated through a mechanism known as "joint implementation" (JI). Defined in Article 6 of the KP, this measure allows a country with an emission reduction or limitation commitment under the KP (Annex B Party) to earn emission reduction units (ERUs) from an emission-reduction or emission-removal project in another Annex B Party, each equivalent to one ton of CO_2, which can be counted towards its Kyoto target. Crediting began in 2008. ERUs are verified and issued by the Joint Implementation Supervisory

Committee (JISC). There are two UNFCCC "tracks" based on the MRV institutional capacity to implement such projects that are sanctioned by JISC:

(1) Track 1: Assumes perfect carbon MRV policy design features at the country level. Therefore there is no need for external monitoring and verification at the project level. Compliance is then automatically accounted for through the national AAUs target system. At the moment, no one is eligible for Track 1.
(2) Track 2: Assumes that MRV capacities are still being developed and need to be enhanced. Therefore, JISC becomes the verifier and approver of projects to ensure that the ERUs being sold by Annex B countries maintain the environmental integrity of the system and are in line with predetermined, aggregate KP AAU targets.

A *certified emission reduction (CER)* is generated from a Clean Development Mechanism (CDM) project activity. As defined in Article 12 of the Protocol, CDM allows a country with an emission-reduction or emission-limitation commitment under the KP (Annex I Party) to implement an emission-reduction project in developing countries. This policy feature is designed to stimulate sustainable development and emissions reductions, while giving industrialized countries additional flexibility in how they meet their emissions reduction or limitation targets. A CDM project must provide emissions reductions that are additional to what would otherwise have occurred. The projects must qualify through a rigorous public registration and issuance process. Approval is given by the Designated National Authorities. Public funding for CDM project activities must not result in the diversion of official development assistance. The mechanism is overseen by the CDM Executive Board, which is ultimately answerable to the countries that have ratified the KP. CDM became operational in 2006. Its qualification processes have been criticized as bureaucratic, and the CDM Executive Board decisions have been characterized as highly politicized rather than based on technical considerations. Efforts to reform and streamline the qualification and approval procedures of this important source of climate finance to the developing world are underway, but alternative institutional development may be required under a more independent international carbon standard system, as suggested below.

CDM reductions need to be approved by the CDM Executive Board in order to maintain the environmental integrity of the system. For qualifying projects, certified emission reductions for CDM activities are issued. Project-based emissions reductions allow KP signatory nations—mainly those of the EU and Japan—to reduce compliance costs by providing a larger scope for cost-minimization opportunities outside UNFCCC Annex I compliance regions/countries.

Aside from pure AAUs trading, the CERs and the ERUs, a new form of AAU has emerged in the carbon market. Because of highly optimistic expectations for economic growth in Russia and the EITs at the time the KP was negotiated and the period of economic downturn that followed instead, emissions budgets in excess of their actual emissions were assigned. Russia and Ukraine account for more than

60 percent of these excess emissions commonly referred to as "hot air" and are likely to be sellers. For instance, Russia's emissions in 2007 were 37 percent below the 1990 baseline year and are expected to go beyond 40 percent below because of the 2009 global economic downturn. To avoid the environmental impact of hot air, side environmental agreements have been developed for the "greening" of AAUs trading to avoid purchases from Russia and Ukraine. However, if AAUs from these countries are considered, clauses that direct part of the proceeds to additional energy efficiency projects or mitigation efforts are included to maximize mitigation of GHGs.

Before Durban (COP17), the failure to agree to a second, post-2012 commitment period KP introduced high levels of uncertainty about the prospects of the carbon market. How to bridge this possible gap in the international climate governance system was a key decision faced by the UNFCCC Secretariat, OECD, IEA, EU leaders, and climate action national and sub-national jurisdictions, which all encouraged governments to extend the KP. The expectation in diplomatic circles and among pragmatic negotiators is that meaningful climate action will still need some additional time to be brokered among key players. But perhaps the make-no-first-move game that politicians temporarily support will eventually be overridden by business lobbies that may believe regulatory certainty on climate action is better that the current scenario. In addition, as oil reserves begin to decline and extraction becomes more risky and expensive, the expectation of a carbon-constrained world becomes more entrenched, a fact that may prompt businesses to better manage energy costs and other asset management risks. Business transformation opportunities toward clean development paths may also encourage governments to actively support this alternative engine for economic growth by properly accounting for carbon emissions.

Since the ideal integrated global carbon market is still not in place, mechanisms are needed to support and accelerate harmonization in the context of emerging heterogeneous systems. An alternative institution building process under the UNFCCC could be a process of setting standards and market system accession protocols for industrialized nations and developing countries that reward significant climate action and effective emission reduction programs at the national, multinational, and sub-national level. For instance, once countries meet these environmental design and performance standards through mutual recognition, peer review, or by complying with guidelines from an independent standard setting organization (as described below), they could be allowed to integrate their national or regional ETS into the global carbon market system currently led by the EU ETS developments. Access protocols could mirror the processes that Eastern European EITs must undergo to gain membership into the EU. In terms of specific policy design issues, the institutional development process could also be similar to those introduced by international financial market standards. For instance, in order to receive credit from international financial institutions, national governments are currently required to regularly provide transparent, credible, and verifiable information on their national accounts.

Given the UNFCCC's flexible mechanisms, there are two types of market processes underpinning the development of the global carbon market.

Transactions in the market are either the result of a specific voluntary carbon emission reduction activity (i.e., offsets) or are derived from allowances allocated to pollution sources by regulators under the cap-and-trade ETS approach as part of a compliance program such as the AAUs. In the voluntary market, there is no overall cap and participants receive credits or offsets in exchange for activities or investments that reduce GHG or carbon dioxide equivalent (CO_2e) emissions. Offsets are sold to individuals, businesses, or governments taking voluntary action to mitigate CO_2 emissions. However, voluntary actions can also be integrated into the compliance systems if the system is open to allow offsets that provide real, verifiable, and permanent GHG reductions. Moreover, well-designed, out-of-system reductions can provide an effective cost-management tool for energy-intensive industries.

The UNFCCC Secretariat, perhaps through alternative independent institutional agents, should maintain market oversight, enforcement supervision, and standard-setting authority for international GHG emissions trading to ensure the environmental integrity of the system. The UNFCCC Secretariat should uphold the international legal requirements of treaties and agreements, but it is too politicized in the area of energy and climate policy at the moment. Technical bodies are therefore required to look into the commoditization aspects of environmental markets. For example, an International Carbon Standard that certifies all aspects of carbon trading, akin to the ones validated by the International Standards Organization, could be created. Under such a system, technical aspects would rule the standard-setting process, perhaps overseen by expert committees and peer reviewers. It would prevent politics from interfering with the market development aspects in carbon trading, as currently seems to be the case in the multilateral climate organizations such as the CDM Executive Board. Like any other financial mechanism, relying on the market is preferable over a heavy regulatory hand. At the same time, the cost-minimizing aspects of a well-functioning carbon ETS, along with providing substantial financial resources for low-carbon development programs, can allow policymakers to reduce potential political opposition to climate action at the national level and increase the economic feasibility of achieving emissions reduction targets and green economic development strategies. Eventually, the evolutionary path of commodities markets will lead to more advanced, exchange-based trades of GHG allowances and other climate financial derivative products, a market beyond over-the-counter (OTC) transactions, with more fluid, lower transaction costs and standardized trading platforms. Figure 8.1 shows the current trend of a gain in market share by exchange-based trading of climate-related environmental commodities in the EU ETS vis-à-vis OTC transactions.

Technological progress over time can increase the abatement capabilities of emissions sources and provide the more accurate and seamless monitoring and compliance infrastructure required to enhance the regulatory aspects of the ETS approach. Commodities exchanges are continuously changing, including the expansion of trading through advanced IT systems and electronic platforms. Moreover, the growing use of state-of-the-art information management systems and satellite capabilities will enhance the transparency and accountability of global environmental

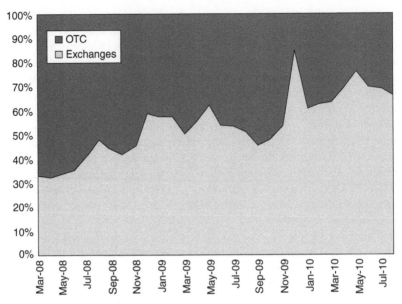

Figure 8.1 OTC vs. exchanges market share (%)
Source: Carbon Idea (2010)

markets. Already, the UNFCCC requires that all transfers and acquisitions of environmental commodities under its system be tracked and recorded through the registry systems under the KP, and the international transaction log ensures secure transfer of ERUs between countries.

Despite its promise, advanced MRV infrastructure can be costly, so technical assistance and financial support may be required for small businesses and developing nations to develop such systems and enter a truly global digital compliance network. Programs such as the World Bank's "Partnership for Market Readiness" are an important step forward in this direction. The implementing country participants in this program to date are: Brazil, Chile, China, Colombia, Costa Rica, India, Indonesia, Jordan, Mexico, Morocco, South Africa, Thailand, Turkey, Ukraine, and Vietnam. This is a clear signal of interest and commitment from major developing countries on building institutional capacity around the world for the implementation of ETSs in their countries.

8.3 Global leadership in climate action: key ETS developments

8.3.1 National climate action: the United Kingdom's Emissions Trading Scheme (UK ETS)

Let's now review an example of the institutional development of market-based climate policy at the national level. Through a series of pioneering policy actions, gradually implementing and experimenting with a set of well-integrated climate and energy regulatory measures over a decade, the UK has established itself as a global leader in climate change policymaking. In 1997 it engaged with the international community, both at the bilateral and multilateral level, to find a practical and cost-effective solution to address the issue at a global scale and ratified the KP to the UNFCCC.

UK leaders opted to take early action to enable a low-carbon economy, and in 2002 created the United Kingdom Emissions Trading Scheme (UK ETS), which represents the first voluntary, economy-wide cap-and-trade system designed to control CO_2 emissions. In November 2008, at the conclusion of a decade-long, inclusive policy formulation process, the UK Parliament passed legislation that introduced "the world's first long-term legally binding framework" for a nation to address the risks that climate change presents. The Climate Change Act of 2008 (UK Legislation 2008) requires that "net UK carbon account for the year 2050 is at least 80 percent lower than the 1990 baseline."

8.3.2 Identifying pertinent policy measures and making business a partner

In March 1998, Lord Marshall, the President of the Confederation of British Industries, a major business lobby group, was commissioned by the government "to lead a Task Force on the subject of whether and, if so, how to best use new economic instruments to improve the industrial and commercial use of energy and help reduce emissions of greenhouse gases" (Marshall 1998). Five months later the report was issued. The following are some of its key recommendations:

Emissions Trading: The report expressed support for the creation of a voluntary ETS, recommending a "dry-run pilot with interested players" with the objective of "learning lessons for the participation" of the British economy in the emerging international carbon market. A key concern among business representatives at the time was the impact on competitiveness from implementing domestic and international climate policy measures.

Green Taxes: The report also envisioned a role for taxes "if businesses of all sizes and from all sectors are to contribute to improved energy efficiency and help meet the UK's emissions targets." In 2001, the UK Government introduced a Climate Change Levy (CCL) in its annual budget, which was a somewhat controversial and unpopular measure propelling the ETS concept as a second-best but more politically feasible policy approach.

The CCL program aimed at revenue neutrality via a 0.3 percent cut in employer national insurance contributions and provided financial support for energy efficiency programs to enhance the role of renewable energy in the British economy. Since then, the CCL has remained part of the British tax system (UK HM Revenue & Customs 2001). In 2009, it was estimated that the CCL adds approximately 8–15 per cent to the energy bills of businesses (British Standard Institution 2009). It does not apply to households, charities, or energy-intensive industries.

Negotiated Agreements: Another element suggested by the report was the implementation of negotiated agreements with specific industrial sectors. In 2001, the Climate Change Agreements (CCA) program was created to assist energy-intensive industries covered by the so-called Integrated Pollution Prevention and Control regulations (IPPC), a regulatory system introduced by the European Community (EC) (2009) to ensure that industry adopts an integrated approach to pollution control in order to achieve a high level of protection for the environment and human health. CCA granted a reduction of 80 percent of the CCL in exchange for binding targets to improve energy efficiency and/or reduce CO_2 emissions. Performance assessments by an independent contractor are conducted biannually to maintain the reduced CCL-rate status. More than 6000 businesses were included in the program and 44 industry associations have adhered to the CCA measure to date.

The actual regulatory framework that emerged from the consultation process was more of a hybrid policy program than a purely voluntary approach. De Muizon and Glachant (2007) concluded that the program participants met their targets from the CCA, and that overall emissions declined by about 9 percent due to the program. Their estimates also show that emissions were likely to be 10 percent higher under the CCA compared with full implementation of the CCL. The ETS component was introduced as a flexible mechanism to bring about GHG emission reductions in a cost-effective manner. However, Martin et al. (2009) disagree on these estimates, considering that the actual emissions reduction impact of this policy was neutral at best.

8.3.3 The Carbon Trust: fostering the emergence of a low-carbon economy

To further enhance the incentives for British society to transform itself into a low-carbon economy, in 2001 the UK government incorporated The Carbon Trust (CT) as a private company.

The CT currently serves several functions. First, it serves as a consultancy to explain and analyze the risks and opportunities surrounding climate change and carbon mitigation. Second, it develops strategies for public–private partnerships that can better address these issues. Third, it aims to introduce pragmatic solutions for the business and the public sectors to assess mitigation challenges and devise mechanisms to reduce emissions in a cost-effective manner. Fourth, it provides economic incentives to promote climate action. It fosters the development of commercially viable low-carbon technologies "through partnerships, funding, expert advice and large-scale demonstrations" (HM Government 2008).

At the onset of the implementation of the UK's early climate action plan, the CT emerged as an institution that would support industry in its effort to adapt to a carbon-constrained world. The CT supported businesses' efforts to participate in the UK ETS and later to transition to the EU ETS. The UK Government gave holders of CCAs and participants in the UK ETS the opportunity to "opt out" of the first phase of the EU ETS. No opt-outs are allowed in Phase II.

8.3.4 The emergence of a voluntary UK ETS: the first carbon cap-and-trade system

The Department of Environment, Food and Rural Affairs (DEFRA), which was in charge of the issue at the time, launched a process to explore the implications of a comprehensive UK Climate Change Program. As part of this consultation effort, the Confederation of British Industries and an ad hoc organization—the Advisory Committee on Business and the Environment—formed the Emissions Trading Group (ETG) in 1999.

The ETG emerged first as an informal group of 30 founding members whose goal was to submit "outline proposals to the UK Government as the basis for the pioneering five-year voluntary UK Greenhouse Gas Emissions Trading Scheme (UK ETS)." Following the Marshall Report's advice, the UK ETS was successfully launched in April 2002, creating the world's first economy-wide greenhouse gas trading system to reduce carbon emissions. It served multiple objectives: (1) to enable businesses to gain practical experience with trading; (2) to assist in achieving the UK's ambitious climate change targets in a cost-effective manner; and (3) to position the City of London as a global center for the nascent international carbon market, in advance of the EU ETS that was due to start in 2005. ETG, now incorporated as a non-profit organization, continues to work closely with the UK Government on emissions trading implementation issues. Its current membership represents the emitters of 95 percent of UK carbon emissions covered by the regional EU ETS.

The UK ETS began with the participation of 33 organizations, known as "Direct Participants" (DPs) in the program, who voluntarily took on emission reduction targets against 1998–2000 levels. An auction held over the Internet in March 2002 set targets for each direct participant and determined the share of incentive money each receives. DPs committed to reducing their emissions by 3.96 million tons of CO_2e by the end of the pilot phase. Over the lifetime of the UK ETS, DPs achieved emissions reductions of over 7.2 million tons of CO_2e. It ended in December 2006, with final reconciliation completed in March 2007 (UK DEFRA 2010a). The program allowed non-IPPC sectors to mitigate the CCL and abatement costs through carbon trading and the ETS incentive fund. CCA participants were granted more flexibility in managing the risk of defaulting on their negotiated commitments.

There were some doubts about the compatibility of CCA with the EU ETS. Some observers characterized the program as "baroque" because of the complex interrelation of the set of climate measures implemented (Ellerman et al. 2010). DEFRA commissioned an independent contractor to review the first four years of the UK ETS program. The objectives were to determine which policy design features could be improved and/or carried over to a new system. Also, the study aimed to explore the "differences between the environment in which the UK ETS was developed" and the new context of engaging the EU regional effort and the strong support at the time from stakeholders for mandatory climate policy action among other issues (UK DEFRA 2006).

Smith and Swierzbinski (2007) assessed the UK experience and highlight that as "incompatibility" with the EU ETS became apparent to program participants, uncertainty grew regarding the value of the permits and the future of the program. In addition, the study emphasizes the "critical" role of the cap and the difficulties encountered in setting the baseline, based on the UK implementation experience. Given this nontrivial policy design challenge, it concludes that "retrospective adjustments of targets or other parameters" affect the stability and credibility of the system and can be costly to market participants. Therefore, the report concludes that "the long-term effectiveness of ETS markets will depend on achieving reasonable clarity about the future of the market and stability in the policy parameters critical to the value of allowances" (p. 155).

8.3.5 Organizational restructuring and evolving climate regulation

In September 2006, the Office of Climate Change was created as a shared resource to work across UK Government institutions to support analytical work on climate change and the development of climate change policy and strategy. A transition mechanism to integrate into the EU ETS system was also developed to move from a voluntary to a compliance system.

In May 2007, DEFRA announced its Carbon Reduction Commitment policy that resulted from a consultation and analysis process focusing on the energy performance of non-energy-intensive commercial and public sectors. The decision was to transition to a mandatory policy to reduce carbon emissions that would recognize early action, while fostering additional reductions. In October 2008, the UK Government created the Department of Energy and Climate Change (DECC), signaling the climate issue's higher degree of precedence within the British central government. Along with the impact of setting meaningful energy-efficiency targets, analysts suggest that climate change regulation creates an "awareness effect" in which cost-effective efficiency improvements are brought to the attention of industrial managers who might not have been aware of them. Industries that make these cost-saving improvements use less energy, reduce their CO_2 emissions, and improve the UK's international competitiveness all at the same time (Barker et al. 2007; Ekins and Etheridge 2006).

The Climate Change Act became law on November 26, 2008, and created the Committee on Climate Change (CCC) as an independent advisory body. Among other mandates, the CCC is in charge of recommending all carbon budgets and monitoring whether the UK is on track to meet its emission targets (or caps). The CCC prescribes when recommendations have to be made. The first three five-year budgets were recommended in December 2008 and enacted in spring 2009 for the period 2008–2022. The fourth UK carbon budget was recommended by the CCC in December 2010 and became law in June 2011. The level was set at 1950 $MtCO_2e$, in line with the CCC recommendation. Supplementary policies and proposals to meet the first three carbon budgets are being developed by the CCC. The most important contributions of the budget approach are to provide certainty and transparency on climate policy objectives as well as to establish the long-term credibility of climate policy in the UK by creating clear institutional mechanisms to review progress in achieving the medium-term (2020) and long-term (2050) GHG emission reduction caps set by CCC. Moreover, as pointed out by Bowen and Rydge (2011), predictability and permanence can be enhanced by "making public commitments, backed up by legislation, to a course of action that can be easily monitored by the electorate, creating a political cost of reneging" (p. 28).

8.4 Multinational climate action: the European Union Emissions Trading Scheme

8.4.1 Committing to global climate action and the carbon market

The EU's greenhouse gas ETS is the biggest such system in the world to date and represents the first concerted effort to develop a multinational market for carbon emissions. The EU ETS closely follows the classic cap-and-trade policy design parameters developed for the US Acid Rain Program (ARP ETS) under the Clean Air Act Amendments of 1990 as discussed in Chapter 5. It also resembles some of the collaborative and innovative federal–state decentralized coordination and harmonization aspects of multilateral trading developments in the early ETS programs developed to reduce transport ozone in the Northeastern US.

At this point in the history of the evolution of the ETS as an environmental policy tool, current and future developments in the EU will shed light on the likelihood of sustaining the emergence of a truly global environmental commodities market. If the EU policymakers get the design right, as they keep learning-by-doing, the EU ETS will continue to assist this multinational region in meeting its GHG emission cap in a cost-effective fashion, and hopefully will later integrate with similar efforts around the world.

The EU currently consists of 27 Member States that centralize functions to coordinate and harmonize regulation in their region through the EC. Despite a decentralized governance system with national and local interests, political cycles that influence willingness to act for the global common good, and differences in financial and institutional capacity that determine readiness to address the climate challenge, the EU was successful in its climate policy coordination efforts. To support national climate action, the regional program (i.e., the EU ETS) was implemented gradually using general objective and policy design guidelines under well-established EU equity criteria principles. The process was aided by not centralizing key decisions at the start, particularly in areas such as fiscal matters (i.e., raising revenue from allowance auctions). For instance, EU Directive 2003/87/EC, the internal accord that launched the EU ETS program, sets the objectives and timeline for action but leaves the implementation details to be regulated by legal instruments at Member State level.[12]

The EU ratified the KP on May 31, 2002, prompting the need for EU Member State and regional climate action coordination. Under this treaty, the EU, which then consisted of 15 Member States, committed itself to reducing greenhouse gas emissions by 8 percent below 1990 levels during the period 2008–2012. In practice, this implied an estimated reduction effort of 14 percent compared with business as usual (BAU) forecasts. The emissions reduction effort was distributed under the European Burden-Sharing Agreement (BSA) of 1998, giving less-developed countries room for economic development and time for adjustment. At the same time, it put pressure on more industrialized and wealthy economies to achieve more ambitious emissions reduction targets within the UNFCCC compliance period. Table 8.1 shows the emissions reduction efforts allocated under the EU BSA.

To achieve this environmental goal, in 2000 the EC—the executive branch of the EU—proposed that "a coherent and coordinated framework for implementing emissions trading covering all Member States would provide the best guarantee for a smooth functioning internal emissions market as compared to a set of uncoordinated national emissions trading schemes." Scale effects at the level of the EU region presented an opportunity for significant cost savings.

Initially, there was some discussion among the EU15 about whether to establish a voluntary trial period to jump-start the EU ETS. Germany and the UK were pushing for just such an approach along with other special adjustment arrangements for certain industries because of strong domestic lobbying and to maintain some of their own experimental climate policies in place. New EU Member States had fewer external political commitments and minimum internal political demand for climate action. These nations also had no influence on the design of the EU ETS launched in 2005, as the main enlargement process took place in 2004 with the

Table 8.1 European Burden-Sharing Agreement (BSA) of 1998

% changes shown are from 1990	% Target 2008–2012
Austria	−13
Belgium	−7.5
Denmark	−21
Finland	0
France	0
Germany	−21
Greece	25
Ireland	13
Italy	−6.5
Luxembourg	−28
Netherlands	−6
Portugal	27
Spain	15
Sweden	4
UK	−12.5
EU 15 Kyoto target	**−8**

inclusion of Malta, Cyprus, Slovenia, Estonia, Latvia, Lithuania, Poland, the Czech Republic, the Slovak Republic, and Hungary. In 2007, Romania and Bulgaria also joined the EU. Croatia is expected to join in 2013 once the accession process is finalized and approval from all other EU countries is secured.

New Member States accepted, with some legal changes, the rules of the EU ETS as part of their new membership status as part of the accession package. Currently, they can influence institutional design at the seat of the EU in Brussels. As full-fledged members, Eastern European Member States can now vote according to their differences in economic and institutional development conditions. For instance, Poland, where coal-fired plants provide most electricity, vetoed the EU 2050 Low-Carbon Roadmap on June 21, 2011. The roadmap proposes emissions reduction milestones in 2030 and 2040 to achieve the 80 percent reduction in GHG emissions below 1990 levels by 2050. Poland is concerned that these stated goals at the EU Council of Ministers would become legally binding targets. These dynamics showcase the balancing act that decision-makers in Brussels must maintain in order to develop a common climate policy that is cost-effective and equitable for all and that is also in line with achieving the EU regional, social, and economic development objectives for an increasingly diverse group of Member States.

In 2008, an enlarged EU of 27 members decided to set more ambitious goals for reducing GHG emissions to 20 percent below 1990 levels by 2020 in a unilateral EU common policy, known as the 20/20/20 plan because it also seeks to increase renewable energy usage by 20 percent. A 30 percent EU GHG emission reduction target was announced but is conditional upon other major economies such as the US and China joining the global effort with binding reduction commitments.

A chief stated goal of the EU ETS was to "lead to one single price" for carbon allowances traded within the system. This would avoid the emergence of an array of different, unconnected national schemes with different prices within each scheme. A multinational ETS in the EU region would establish a common regulatory arrangement that would keep administrative costs as low as possible (EU Commission 2000, 4). While some observers and analysts have characterized the performance of the initial phase of the program as a failure, proponents at the EU were clear from the start that it was experimental:

> As emissions trading is a new instrument for environmental protection within the EU, it is important to gain experience in its implementation before the international emissions trading scheme starts in 2008. There is a good case for the European Community and its Member States to prepare themselves by commencing an emission trading scheme within the Community by 2005.
>
> (EU Commission 2000)

In 2009, an amendment to the EU ETS directive (i.e., a legislative instrument from the EU Parliament and Council of Ministers) was adopted "to improve and extend the greenhouse gas emission allowance trading scheme of the Community" based on proposals accepted by all Member States in the December 2008 EU Energy and Climate 2020 Package (European Parliament 2008).

At the end of Phase II, the debate centered on the effect of multiple policy goals and the appropriateness of policy instruments to achieve them because of low carbon price expectations given unprecedented circumstances. The economic turmoil that began in 2008, the start of Phase II, depressed allowance prices to record lows in 2012, the end of this compliance period, because it resulted in a significant drop in emissions (11.6 percent compared with 2008) due to the slowdown in growth (EU 2010). Moreover, at the end of Phase II, multiple EU ETS stakeholders stressed the need to address the issue of an oversupplied carbon market. This prompted action from the EC to advance the review schedule of the program and its features to propose a solution (i.e., a set-aside or temporal removal of allowances from the auctions) for Member State decision making.

As noted by the EU regulators, however, from the perspective of the different industrial sectors included in the EU ETS, while companies continue "to build up a surplus of allowances to be traded in the third trading period starting in 2013," this "highlights the flexibility that emissions trading offers to businesses and also confirms that more can be done to reduce emissions in the next phase at a reasonable economic cost" (EU 2011).

This situation revived the debate about complementary measures and policies at the EU and national levels (e.g., UK carbon floor price) that aim at inducing investments in renewable power generation. These policies are perceived as tainting the EU ETS price signal. Some EU leaders would like to accelerate the region's decarbonization by using multiple policy mechanisms or, in line with perspectives from traders and environmentalist, argue for "fixing" the EU ETS by adjusting the cap). Market analysts believe that, to a certain degree, complementary measures are pressuring carbon market prices further down, while reducing the overall cost-effectiveness of the EU ETS. In addition, oil and gas industry analysts, for instance, argue that regulatory overlay in energy and climate policy affects "technology-neutrality," or the choice of technology and fuel, thereby limiting choice and increasing compliance costs. However, all carbon pricing policies (taxes and markets) implicitly aim to provide good incentives for low-carbon transformation independent of its form. Even a single carbon price violates technology-neutrality with regards to low-carbon technologies (Calel 2011). Moreover, taking dynamic efficiency into consideration, as suggested by Newell (2010), a "well-targeted policy" can enhance incentives for innovation in climate mitigation technology through R&D and other innovative policy mechanisms and has the potential to lower the overall cost of attaining long-term climate goals. Therefore, "incentives in the form of a market-based price on GHG emissions and directed government technology support" could provide incentives to invest in areas "unlikely to be undertaken by the private sector."

These measures introduce multiple policy goals that require careful regulatory coordination and craftsmanship to avoid unintended consequences. So far, the EU ETS has delivered in making significant GHG emission reductions affordable in the region. The price of carbon under a single GHG emissions reduction goal provided by the EU ETS should allow for long-term planning by businesses and industry.

Judging from this debate, policymakers need to maximize regulatory coordination as well as to better communicate their plans, programs, and goals as there is constant demand from the private sector for reassurance from governments about their commitment to maintain the carbon market as a permanent climate policy instrument. This is particularly important at this stage of the ETS institutional evolutionary process. Phase III, from 2013 to 2020, harmonizes key EU ETS rules, introduces longer time horizons with the aim of strengthening price signals, centralizes registry functions and allocation to minimize threats to fair competition, and induces the incremental use of allowance auctioning.

8.4.2 Emissions trading system components

The following summarizes the market design features and implementation strategies that have made the EU ETS cap-and-trade program a practical and cost-effective solution to achieve multinational climate policy goals. Table 8.2 shows key dates and stages for the implementation of EU ETS.

Gradual, Sector-Based Coverage: The EU ETS it is not an economy-wide cap-and-trade system, it is a unilateral multinational/multi-sector regional climate policy. Its implementation has been gradual, predictable, and based on pragmatism. In general, EU policies respond to national differences in economic and institutional capacities in their multinational programs. As in the ARP ETS, policymakers followed the most practicable approach by including highly regulated, energy-intensive sectors, such as electric power generators and large, stationary industrial

Table 8.2 EU ETS Implementation History

2000	ETS concept is introduced as the regional climate policy approach
2003	EU Directive mandates the creation of the EU ETS
2005	Phase I
	Cap-and-trade is implemented—learning or trial period
	– Establishment of national registries
	– Robust emissions monitoring and verification systems
	– Signs of important over-allocation
	Carbon market activity begins
	Price on carbon emissions is signaled
2008	Phase II
	Compliance period 2008–2012—aligned with Kyoto period
2012	Inclusion of the aviation sector
2013	Phase III (2013–2020)
	Implementation of EU policy goal adjustments to achieve a 20 percent reduction in GHG by 2020 compared with 1990 levels. Possible 30 percent reduction if other major emitter countries set legally binding targets
	Extended phases (i.e., beyond seven years to strengthen price signals with longer time horizons), centralized allocation, and incremental use of allowance auctioning

sources. Initially, the scheme included industries such as cement, ceramics, electric power generators, glass, iron and steel, pulp and paper, and refineries based in the EU region. It regulates downstream (i.e., point of regulation is the installation) of about 12,000 emission sources, which account for half of the EU region's emissions. It does not include transport, small businesses, or homes. However, coverage has been expanding. There are opt-in mechanisms currently in place, and new sectors have been included through EU directives. Aviation, for example, became the first transport sector to be included in the system on January 1, 2012. Under the 2013–2020 Phase III, carbon emissions from petrochemicals, ammonia, and aluminum will be covered.

Selecting the Controlled Substance: Initially, the program established a cap on annual emissions of CO_2, but the EU ETS allows for other GHGs to be included in the future. For instance, the Netherlands has already included nitrous oxides as part of their national system. The following are incorporated into Phase III of the EU ETS: CO_2 emissions arising from (1) petrochemicals, ammonia, and aluminum and (2) nitrous oxide (NO_x) emissions from the production of nitric, adipic, and glyoxylic acids, as well as petrofluorocarbons. Phase III also calls for the capture, transport, and geological storage of CO_2 emissions. Under Phase III, Member States are allowed to opt out small sources highly impacted by the implementation cost of the program.

Extent of Entitlement: Under the EU ETS, rights to emit CO_2 (or CO_2e) emissions are commoditized as tradable permits known as European Union Allowances (EUAs). The term "EUA" defines the extent of the entitlement as an authorization allocated to a covered installation to emit one ton of CO_2. As in the case of the ARP ETS (Chapter 5), the term allowance was preferred over "permits" to make it a de facto "right" or "entitlement" that could become a tradable commodity—a fungible good.

Create a Homogeneous Unit: The EUAs as a new environmental commodity quickly assumed fungibility. As stated by a carbon trader in London, compliance EUAs are equivalent to any other bonds issued by national governments, "they are like cash to us" (Goupille 2008).

In 2004, the "Linking Directive" formally opened the EU ETS design by accepting allowances, ERUs, and CERs from other systems validated under the UNFCCC protocols and institutions, linking it to the UN-coordinated global climate effort. These offsets produced by the KP flexible mechanisms (JI and CDM) have qualitative limitations as the EU ETS does not accept nuclear or forestry sinks and sets strict limits on hydropower credits. There are no freestanding EU offset institutions and rules, but joint implementation in Member States is limited to avoid double counting. Recent amendments, as part of the Climate and Energy Package 2020, to the EU ETS restrict the extensive use of international offsets unless they are from a list of "least" developed countries or can be swapped for certified emissions reductions from "least" developed countries to ensure that more emission reductions are produced within the EU region after 2013.

Gradual Integration of New Participants: The EU ETS has integrated new nations as the EU expands its union and economic links with other nations. The EU ETS was first implemented in 2005 and included the 15 original EU Member States. Since then, the EU accession process has granted membership to ten Eastern European nations plus Malta and Cyprus for a total of 27 EU Member States. Also, three countries from the European Economic Area (EEA), Iceland, Liechtenstein, and Norway joined the scheme for a total of 30 participating nations. System harmonization, greater transparency, and effective central market monitoring, surveillance, and enforcement mechanisms, will enhance market access and fair competition in the EU ETS market. Increased global environmental commodities market integration (i.e., linking with other systems) will eventually bring another set of institutional challenges, but the accumulated policy lessons in these areas will be invaluable in building the infrastructure for a global carbon market.

Compliance and Enforcement: Each covered source (or installation) has to surrender allowances corresponding to its verified emissions by April 30 annually. Compliance is determined through a direct comparison of total annual CO_2 emissions reported by covered installations and the number of EUAs that must be surrendered to be in compliance. Failure to surrender the required number of allowances leads to a financial penalty, which for Phase I was €40 and for Phase II is €100 per non-surrendered allowance, and the obligation to surrender remains. The names of delinquent sources are published widely by the EU Environment Directorate.

The EU ETS provides for allowances to be traded regionally, implicitly giving them equal environmental value across Member States' political jurisdictions. The EUA was designed to be equivalent to the KP AAU. As mentioned earlier, UNFCCC validated Certificates of ERUs and CERs from joint implementation and CDM projects respectively are accepted on a one-to-one basis within the EU ETS, making these environmental commodities fungible between systems. Linking to other regional systems not yet part of a UNFCCC system may require establishing additional exchange ratios.

Duration of Allowance: A key difference with the ETS experience in the US is the existence of multi-year compliance periods in which "allowances distributed for any given year are valid in any other year in the compliance period" (Ellerman et al. 2008, 3). Under the EU ETS, the duration of an allowance is indefinite, as the program does not contain a sunset clause. It is important to note that Phase I did not allow for banking across periods, showcasing the importance of inter-temporal flexibility for adequate asset management. By ending the life of the Phase I EUAs at the end of the learning period, their value became zero.

Emissions Cap: The EU ETS cap represents the sum of the 30 Member States caps. The EU ETS set a cap on the total amount of allowable CO_2 emissions for the electric and industrial sectors (i.e., historic emissions baseline). Initially, caps were negotiated between the EU Commission and Member States as part of a bottom-up strategy to facilitate the launching of the learning phase of the system through the more politically feasible national allocation plans (NAP) system. The cap in Phase I was set to about 2.2 billion allowances per year. As in the US Atlantic states in the early development of their regional Ozone ETS, the central government, in this case the EC, scrutinized Member States' NAPs. The decentralized approach was plagued by significant errors in the emissions data used to project BAU emissions, and gaming led to over-allocation.

In Phase II, the cap was slightly reduced to 2.08 billion allowances from the Phase I EU-wide cap, but it included two new Member States—Romania and Bulgaria. For this phase, revised monitoring and reporting rules were also introduced. At the same time, coverage was expanded by linking with other countries (i.e., Norway, Iceland, and Liechtenstein) in 2008 and adding the aviation sector in 2012. For Phase III, beginning in 2013, an EU-wide cap will be established using the average total quantity of allowances issued by Member States in Phase II as the starting point. It will then be gradually reduced by 1.74 percent annually. The cap is expected to deliver an overall reduction of 21 percent below 2005 verified emissions by 2020. The expectation is that "in due course, the declining emissions cap in Phase III (2013–2020) could drive genuine emissions cuts" in other words, in absolute terms (House of Commons 2010, 3).

Perhaps the most important change in the policy implementation approach of the EU ETS for Phase III is that the EU has started to harmonize the system by centralizing some key policy decisions and recommending some voluntary actions to its Member States to enable low-carbon growth paths. The EU-wide cap on emissions will now be centrally determined. The past practice of discretionary NAPs ended up producing 30 different allocation systems making the system politically feasible but administratively complex. This NAP structure will be replaced under Phase III with one centrally determined EU-wide cap. EU regulators acknowledge that the key policy lesson from Phase I and II, aside from the need for verified data, is that "greater harmonization" is required to ensure that emissions reductions objectives are achieved at least cost and with minimal competitive distortions. They also emphasize that the need for harmonization is "clearest with respect to how the cap on overall emission allowances is set."

Importance of Accurate Emissions Inventories and Modeling Assumptions: As mentioned above, because of unreliable emissions data-reporting systems, allowances were over-allocated in Phase I. In 2005, emission reports revealed an excess of 44 million allowances at the end of the scheme's first year (House of Commons 2007). By the end of Phase I, more than 260 million excess allowances had been allocated (Ellerman et al. 2010). The oversupply of allowances minimized the incentives for firms to reduce emissions or to invest in low-carbon technological innovations. Also, excess supply combined with some design flaws in the EU ETS led to a high degree of price volatility at the end of the period. This overshooting was caused by inaccurate baseline data for industrial emissions that were based on an optimistic, constant, industrial output growth scenario.

National Interest Gaming Strategies Weakening Regional Policy Design: Competitiveness concerns prompted a race to the bottom as some Member States, especially new ones, behaved strategically in the design process to avoid submitting their own industrial sectors to tighter caps relative to others. While the EU plays a key role in coordinating collective action among Member States, ultimately EU members are independent sovereign nations that can act in their own self-interest. In the case of the EU ETS, many states faced an incentive to free-ride on the action of others.

Inter-temporal Flexibility and Environmental Asset Management: Lack of inter-temporal flexibility to use allowances (i.e., bank) between Phases I and II complicated the asset management strategies of companies and market participants who held the newly created environmental commodity (i.e., EUA) under Phase I as the value of the allowance was fixed to each period. The price of Phase I allowances decreased to zero at the end of this stage of the program. While this bar to saving across phases has since been removed, there is very little opportunity for sources to borrow allowances, which has been criticized (Deason and Friedman 2010).

Successful Mechanism for Reaching Political Agreement on Regional Climate Action: The main success of Phase I was that the EU Commission was able to reach a political agreement to jump-start through the creation of the EU ETS, the most ambitious and largest multinational climate program to date in the world. By sharing in an equitable manner the economic and technical effort of achieving carbon emission reductions for the region, while recognizing the differences and capacities of each participating Member State, the EU was able to initiate a regional market-based policy approach that has served as a starting point for the EU's climate and energy goals.

Flexibility of Compliance: The EU ETS is a unilateral climate program. It is a compliance mechanism, legally binding and with absolute emission reduction targets set and enforced by the members of this economic and political multi-national partnership. In order to align it with the UNFCCC process, its Phase II was designed to coincide with the KP's commitment period. Once the adjustments to the learning phase were made, the program was designed to provide flexibility to Member States to comply with their national and regional emission reduction commitments under the KP. Each Member State submitted NAP for Phase I and II to the EU Commission that were in line with their individual KP targets. National governments decided how their allowance budgets were assigned to industrial sectors participating in the EU ETS. Allocation determines the amount of effort or burden and cost individual sectors have to bear. Other policies and measures have to be implemented for sectors outside the system—such as transport, small businesses, households, and agriculture—to meet national annual GHG targets. Finally, individual participants were allocated their budgets. For the most part, allowances were granted free of charge.

Emissions Measurement, Monitoring, Reporting, and Verification: During Phase I the main problem was the quality of data available at the facility level. The MRV problem, which was significant among initial EU members, was compounded by the lack of institutional preparedness to implement up-to-standard MRV technologies and processes among new Member States accessing the union. This prompted the creation of a process to improve the reliability of data on actual emissions for affected facilities and the implementation of a transition period for the less institutionally ready new Member States, as accurate emissions data are essential for a proper allowance allocation process and in setting the overall emissions cap. It is difficult to undo the transfers of wealth (i.e., the new environmental commodities) once they are made through the allocation mechanisms. Because of the large, multinational scope of the program, cost-minimization opportunities are enhanced. However, it is difficult for regulators to assess data quality and strategic behavior from ETS participants initially unless well-established processes for the collection and dissemination of data bring light and transparency to the expanding carbon market.

For Phase II, a process was implemented to verify emissions data submitted by Member States and to calibrate emissions projection models. The "real" program required the caps to be in line with national commitments under the KP's first commitment period as the EU ETS evolved into a legally binding compliance mechanism for the region. The EU Commission therefore began to centralize, setting the EU-wide cap by sanctioning with a high degree of scrutiny the maximum emissions allowed for each of the Member States' caps.

Even with greater scrutiny in the NAP process, some industries were recipients of windfall profits. As discussed below, this approach was perceived in policy and academic circles as inefficient and unfair, as well as potentially less effective in spurring innovation and the development of renewable sources for clean energy production. The world economic recession that began in 2008 has made it easier for countries and industrial sectors within the EU to meet the EU ETS emission caps. But, as anticipated in 2010 by parliamentarians in the UK assessing the performance of the EU ETS, because of a slow and faltering recovery, over-allocation has once again become an issue, as energy-intensive industries have little incentive to reconvert or enhance energy efficiency (House of Commons 2010, 20).

Program Duration: Despite the uncertainties under the UNFCCC-sponsored nego-tiation process, the EU has signaled its commitment to the global carbon market system. The program has no sunset clause, but the lack of commitment to similar efforts by other key players like the US and large developing countries such as China and India may dampen the carbon market's potential to supplement international climate policy beyond 2020.

Compliance Periods: At the start of program the cap for each period was determined separately and sequentially to jumpstart the system but with the "disadvantage of making the long-term allowance price signal that determines investment in CO_2 emission reduction projects considerably more uncertain" (Ellerman et al. 2008, 3). The revisions to the ETS directive have addressed this issue by expanding the compliance period to seven years instead of five years as contemplated by the KP.

Grandfathering: Allowances for specific industrial sectors will be allocated for free on the basis of product benchmarks on energy efficiency. Benchmarks will be based on the average of the top 10 percent of the most GHG efficient installations in the EU. Leakage is to be prevented as sectors deemed at significant risk of relocating production outside of the EU due to the carbon price (i.e. carbon leakage) will receive 100 percent of the benchmarked allocation for free. Gradual phase-out of free allocation is to be implemented. Sectors not deemed at significant risk of carbon leakage will receive 80 percent of their benchmarked allocation for free in 2013, declining to 30 percent in 2020 and zero percent in 2027.

Auctioning Allowances: The European Commission has gradually increased the amount of auctioned allowances in the system. Auctioning has emerged as a politically feasible alternative because of a perceived higher degree of fairness in the process, while at the same time the expanded use of this design feature is expected to enhance environmental effectiveness and economic efficiency. This in turn will eventually provide substantial resources to EU governments to be invested in enabling low-carbon technological and economic development paths both within the EU region and in support of the developing world. However, so far, most of the revenues raised have ended up in general budgets and have not been earmarked for such purposes. In addition, reduced access to project credits from outside the EU will be in place for Phase III, favoring only "least developed economies" and eliminating options for investment in these instruments.

In Phase I, the EU ETS allowed up to 5 percent of the allowances to be auctioned. Phase II allowed for up 10 percent auctioning, but in practice it only reached a 3 percent level. Denmark was the only country to auction allowances up to the limit. Auctioning is the preferred means of allocation for Phase III (2013–2020), although it is not obligatory. The EC expects that atleast 50 percent of the EU ETS allowances will be auctioned starting in 2013.

While in the US, free allocation of allowances greatly enhanced the political feasibility of ETS developments, in the EU free allocation has become a controversial feature of the post-Phase I EU ETS. More specifically, there were concerns based on the Phase I experience about windfall profits for power companies that received free allowances but were able to pass on the cost to consumers anyway. Industry was less of a concern since competition from abroad limited the ability to raise prices. The issue of "windfall profits" during the trial period because of over-allocation of

EUAs was widely discussed in the press and in academia (Ellerman et al. 2008; Ellerman and Joskow 2008). Also, the research community took notice of the issue and estimated these direct or indirect gains. For instance, in the UK, the power industry was estimated to have earned an additional £800 million per year during Phase I (IPA Energy Consulting, 2005). Belgian, French, German, and Dutch power companies obtained an additional €4.5–13.5 billion per year in Phase I (Sijm et al. 2006).

In Phase II, the ten largest non-energy-related industries that benefited from the over-allocation (i.e., iron, steel, and cement companies) made €4.1 billion in extra profits (Sandbag 2011). Others have offered evidence of companies subject to EU ETS regulations marking up prices to pass costs along to consumers, despite free allowances (e.g., Oberndorfer et al. 2010). Regulators expect the environmental effectiveness and economic efficiency of the EU ETS to improve with the inauguration of Phase III in 2013, when at least 50 percent of allowances will be sold at auction.

Distribution of 88 percent of allowances between Member States will be according to each country's verified emissions in 2005 or the average for the 2005–2007 period, whichever proves to be higher. Across most of the EU, 100 percent of the power sector allowances will be sold at auction. After threatening to veto the auctioning rule, new members from Eastern Europe have been granted a transition period and support. For example, 10 percent of the total allowances auctioned are to be redistributed to Member States with the lowest gross domestic products. Two percent will be distributed among Member States that in 2005 achieved emission reductions of 20 percent below KP base levels. However, all EU members, including new members, will be required to implement auctioning of emission allowances for the electric generation industry by 2020. On November 19, 2009, the UK held Europe's first carbon allowance auction in Phase II, selling four million allowances and raising £54 million. The UK plans to auction 100 percent of the allowances needed by its power sector starting in 2013 (Newnet 2008).

Global Carbon Market and Offsets: Offsets are going to be limited. Affected emissions sources under EU ETS regulations reconcile their annual carbon budgets by surrendering allowances in the amount equal to their annual CO_2 emissions, or they may also use supplementary allowances obtained for compliance purposes under the UNFCCC flexible mechanisms (e.g., JI and CDM). Therefore, the quality, availability, and price of these KP instruments do impact allowance prices in the EU carbon market. In Phase III, access to project credits under the KP from outside the EU will be limited to no more than 50 percent of the reductions required in the EU ETS—a 226 percent reduction from Phase II. While the goal is to foster emissions reductions within the EU, this change will have important implications globally since the EU ETS is the most important source of demand for international credits. Offsets were initially included as a cost-effective compliance design feature, but EU leaders believe they can also leverage the EU's market position and climate action leadership to foster international climate action while assisting developing nations in their low-carbon development efforts.

Energy Policy, Industrial Support, and Technology Subsidies: From the start, the EU ETS imposed burdens on a wide variety of emitters and consumers while promising benefits to an equally wide variety of interest groups. The EU region recognized early the advantages of transforming itself into a low-carbon economy by fostering energy efficiency and technological innovation. To meet the ambitious greenhouse gas emission reduction goals, as well as to enhance energy security, the EU is set to provide 20 percent of its energy needs by 2020 through renewable sources. *Ex ante* studies on the impact in several sectors of the economy estimated small impacts for most sectors. Industries such as cement, iron and steel, and aluminum are expected to see modest effects, with aluminum being the most impacted by higher energy costs (Baron et al. 2008; Carbon Trust 2004). These sectors will be assisted with longer transition periods and centralized allocation of free allowances.

8.4.3 Performance of the EU carbon market and effective climate action

On the environmental performance side, gains from Phase I were limited. The program resulted in a roughly 3 percent relative reduction of EU emissions from the projected estimate of BAU emissions in the absence of the EU ETS (Ellerman and Buchner 2008; Anderson et al. 2011). However, in absolute terms, GHG emissions increased in the region during the same period.

Phase I began swiftly due to trading activity from some market participants already active in the carbon market in London (thanks to the UK ETS). In its first year, 362 million allowances worth about $8 billion were traded along with environmental financial instruments such as futures and derivatives. Carbon tons reached their peak price at €30 in mid-2006, and total market value reached $24 billion. However, in May of that year analysts reported on generous NAP that would grant windfall profits and minimum incentives for emissions reduction efforts. Without scarcity, and with the upcoming bar on saving Phase I allowances into Phase II, the EU carbon market saw its prices decline steadily. By September 2007, Phase I EUAs were trading at €0.10.

As mentioned earlier, verified emissions data from 2009 show that the economic downturn produced a fall in emissions from 2008 of 11.6 percent, and market analysts estimated that, in consequence, this would result in a surplus of allowances of approximately 418 Mt for Phase II. Despite this information, the price for a ton of CO_2 remained stable at €13–14 during the first half of 2010 (Lancaster 2010, 17). The implication is that allowance surpluses make it easier for industry to meet the 20 percent emissions reduction target. Carbon allowance prices, while still seeming to provide some incentive to invest in clean technologies and promote energy efficiency practices that make economic sense and can be produced at no net cost to society, perhaps are not enough to deliver much change relative to a BAU baseline. By 2011, carbon emission fell more than 2 percent, but as carbon markets analysts reported, "an oversupply of permits key to driving greener energy use worsened." The "glut" is expected to grow to nearly 900 million allowances. More than half (i.e., 456 million) of the allowances circulating in the EU ETS came from international CERs, mostly from China and India (Reuters 2012).

A well-designed ETS should produce a price on carbon that can actually deliver the needed changes in behavior. Tightening of the emissions targets seems to be the logical next step and is needed as absolute emission reductions have yet to be achieved in the EU region and at the global level. However, too aggressive an adjustment may result in carbon leakage. Other policy mechanisms need to be implemented in tandem, including carbon taxes where appropriate (on excluded sectors) and expanding coverage of sectors. The EU Commission originally estimated revenues from auctioning could amount to around €50 billion annually by 2020, while the OECD estimates this revenue may reach almost €90 billion. This so-called ETS dividend could be used to fund additional climate change protection measures (European Parliament 2008).

However, in April 2012, the EUA prices hit a Phase II historic low of €5.99 per ton compared to a maximum of nearly €30 per ton of carbon in 2008. By May 2012 EU allowance prices had rebounded somewhat, reaching €6.60 per ton. The source of the carbon market's volatility during this period was characterized by energy and environmental commodities market analysts as follows: "The potential for regulatory intervention and the aviation dispute shifted the attention of carbon traders away from energy and macroeconomic fundamentals to the corridors of Brussels" (Bloomberg 2012).

Low prices at the end of Phase II represent significant losses in expected revenue from allowance auctions, thus underscoring for some stakeholders (e.g., politicians, environmentalists, and market traders among others) the need to adjust or "fix" the EU ETS. For the carbon trading industry there is little business to be done in a depressed, irrelevant carbon market. For UN flexible mechanisms, EU demand is critical, and there is none at the moment. The situation is particularly urgent for traditional suppliers in more "advanced developing countries," a term not formally defined under the UNFCCC process. It is not clear where these countries will find markets (i.e., EU ETS eligibility risk) for their KP carbon credits after 2013 when they may no longer be allowed in the EU system. Industry rejects regulatory overlay, increased costs, and lost focus on the EU ETS cost-effectiveness advantages. This has forced regulators at the EU level and politicians from the Member States to reassess the current program and explore how to best align political demands with fine-tuning the ETS policy design. For the carbon market, there is a trade-off, as any unscheduled intervention in the market itself sets a negative precedent. A strong argument for action is that the unprecedented economic downturn suffered during Phase II merits intervention. Experience also shows heightened uncertainty and downward price pressure during transition periods from one phase to another. On April 19, 2012, the EU Climate Commissioner, Connie Hedegaard, tried to appease carbon market stakeholders as follows:

We are now rapidly approaching the start of the third phase of the European carbon market. Major changes will apply as of next year to the regulatory underpinning of the EU ETS. 2012 marks the final preparations for the transition to the new rules. Our regulatory work over several years has aimed for a smooth transition into Phase 3. Difficult and unexpected macroeconomic circumstances arising from the economic and debt crisis complicate this aim, as they have substantially altered the supply-demand balance in the European carbon market for the early years of Phase 3. I have therefore asked DG Climate Action to bring forward the first annual report on the ETS. This report is foreseen by the ETS Directive in 2013, but I have asked for it to be prepared already now. This offers an opportunity to include a review of the auction time profile. Based on this annual report, I will consider bringing forward a proposal to the Climate Change Committee for decision this year.

It is obvious that for any major change to be made to the EU ETS, the political body of the EU would have to adjust the cap, a fundamental feature of the program. EU regulators do not have that authority to make an adjustment. Ultimately, an overlapping and hybrid policy approach may be appropriate for cost-effective and equitable climate action in the EU region, but this requires the highest level of regulatory coordination. A set of gradual, realistic, legislated measures that allow for predictable implementation paths can make more ambitious climate policies feasible. The EU ETS should remain the chief mechanism to provide cost-minimization in meeting GHG emissions reduction goals in the region, as it awaits other nations and regions to follow suit.

8.4.4 Summary of policy lessons

The EU ETS has been implemented gradually through both predictable programmatic phases and legislative refinements to the EU ETS Directive to improve the economic and environmental quality aspects of the program. The implementation of new rules for Phase III has been based on lessons learned and practical experience gained from Phases I and II.

Role for a Central Coordination Agent: The EU Commission provided a readily available institutional structure to coordinate the efforts of launching such an ambitious initiative. As a confederation of nations with weak central powers, the EU has well-developed incentive vehicles to ensure participation from unequal partners, for instance through burden-sharing mechanisms. These are characteristics not easily transferable to a UNFCCC-led regime but, as suggested above, some technical aspects may be better managed through independent standard certification agents endorsed and supported by the EU and other key players in the carbon market. However, gradual centralization of some functions and decisions is strengthening the program.

Importance of Monitoring, Reporting, and Verification Features: Accurate MRV practices have been essential to optimal ETS performance throughout the history of this policy instrument in the US and Europe. Strong carbon accounting methodologies for precise monitoring and enforcement on emissions data and budgets enhance the regulatory aspects of an ETS providing transparency, integrity, and credibility to the system. Only sectors and sources that can develop and implement such systems at a reasonable cost should be included in the carbon market. Monitoring and reporting provisions ensure that actual emissions are accurately tracked. In order to foster market efficiency and maintain the environmental integrity of the program, the EU ETS followed closely the lessons learned in the US with regard to using information technologies to monitor allowance trading for regulatory compliance. The EU ETS created the Community Independent Transaction Log (CITL), which constitutes the central registry for the EU ETS. While it indicates the registry of origin (Member State), it does not reveal the installation to which surrendered EUAs were issued. Each Member State has to develop record-keeping systems to document the issue, holding, transfer, and cancellation of allowances. It took longer for new EU Member States to implement the needed MRV infrastructure. In general, each covered source is obliged to monitor and report its annual emissions each March 31. Self-reporting is subject to third party verification or independent audits. Any affected source (i.e., participating installation) and any interested party may open a trading account in an EU registry that is linked to the CITL that monitors EU-wide activity. The EU adopted new MRV regulations for Phase III in December 2011, while also developing stand-alone legislation for the verification of emissions and the accreditation of independent verifiers. In 2012 CITL became the European Union Transaction Log (EUTL), a secure web-based system. This online, centralized registry will automatically check, record, and authorize all transactions occurring between accounts in the EU ETS registries. This verification will ensure that any transfer of allowances from one account to another is consistent with the ETS rules while also enhancing transaction and information security, a major vulnerability of the system.

Fraud and Security Issues: Implementation of the EU ETS has proven to be vulnerable to criminal activity. A few "phishing" and "hacking" attacks on the carbon market worth more than $125 billion (by 2010 estimates) demonstrated the weakness of the EU ETS's information management systems to criminal activities. Between November 2010 and January 2011, almost $70 million in EUA allowances were stolen from private sector carbon registry accounts and from Austria's national registry. These EUA allowances were sold by criminals on the spot market, prompting a possible increase in regulatory oversight of the carbon market by the EU Commission. Additionally, in 2009, value-added tax fraud occurred in a scandal known as "carousel trading." On March 16, 2010, emissions offsets from Hungary "were still circulating in the EU ETS even though they had already been used once by firms to offset their emissions." Amendments were introduced to require that CERs surrendered under the EU ETS be placed in a specific "retirement account" in each registry, out of which resale or so-called "recycling" is forbidden (Caisse dés Depôts 2011). These events forced the EU Commission to suspend carbon trading in all national registries while security of the system was enhanced. Like any other financial institution, the carbon market is vulnerable and must be protected. Therefore, ETS information management systems must be state of the art. Carbon accounting best practices must be fostered among market participants and tax policy must be followed. In short, information technology security and legality in carbon trading transactions must be maintained in order to minimize the dangers of cyber attacks and fraudulent criminal behavior.

Flexibility in Trading Rules: To provide greater flexibility to the system, the EU ETS Directive does not regulate trading. Similar to the US experience, in addition to the possibility of transactions among initial allowance holders, these entitlements may also be traded, bought, or sold by any other willing market participant who opens an electronic account in the EU ETS bank. Trading takes place between companies and is facilitated by brokers or market intermediaries through OTC transactions at organized exchanges around Europe. As of Phase II, banking of allowances in future phases is unlimited. This design feature provides a cost-management feature within the program. Also, it has helped to control cost as it serves to diminish price volatility, both to cover positions by all shorts (those with not enough EUAs to cover their emissions) and to maintain market demand for times when it is necessary to make up for borrowed allowances. In Phase I, this possibility was at the discretion of Member States and most decided not to allow banking into a future phase. The EU ETS does not allow borrowing from a future phase, and only allows a very restricted form of borrowing within a phase (new allowances are issued a few months before old allowances are due for compliance and can be used for the previous compliance period). This is an area in which improvements are possible. In fact, even this very limited "borrowing turned out to have been a particularly cost-effective means of compliance (Ellerman 2008, p. 32)."

Adjustments to New Entrants Reserve Policy: As mentioned earlier, a reserve of free allowances is set aside for new sources coming into the system in the future or for established sources that undergo significant expansions (i.e., expanding capacity by at least 10 percent or where a substantial increase is linked to capacity expansion), a feature that has reduced political opposition to the implementation of this approach. Under Phase III, the new entrants reserve contains 5 percent of the EU-wide allowances. Reserve allowances left over at the end of Phase III will be auctioned by Member States.

Managing Carbon Leakage Risk: The EU ETS includes exemptions to sectors at risk of carbon leakage. These are industrial sectors that may suffer material competitive disadvantage against competitors located outside the EU's political borders, which do not have similar GHG emission reduction commitments. Assessments of exposure of certain sectors to carbon leakage that could result in access to free allocation and other financial measures to compensate energy cost increases will be conducted every five years. Commitments to be made on the successor to the KP by other parties to the

UNFCCC, as well as unilateral actions under national and regional plans will be key in determining support for EU industries.

Emergence of the Carbon Trading Industry: Brokers have played a key role in reducing transaction costs in the EU ETS. London has established itself as the carbon trading capital of the world as the UK national climate policy intended. Brokerage activities and standardized procedures have been emerging from various private financial institutions and brokers that have been developing standardized transaction procedures and derivatives for the environmental commodities market and risk management financial tools for a carbon-constrained future. Several information services prompted by the EU ETS have been developed by the private sector to support carbon trading, among them financial and energy market information companies such as Thomson Reuters' Point carbon, Bloomberg, Argus Media, the Platts *Emissions Daily*, *Carbon Finance*, and banks and brokerage firms that produce reports for their own clients such as Barclay's carbon market reports and Caisse de Dépôts' *CDC Climat Recherche*. These climate financial information services follow closely any new developments in the area of environmental commodities markets around the world.

Market Signals, Long View, and Policy Coordination: The global financial turmoil that began in 2008 has had a significant impact on allowance prices. However, it is important for the EU to clarify the role of each policy instrument in operation to enable the EU's ambitious climate and energy 2020 agenda towards a low-carbon future. The EU ETS should remain the central climate policy instrument to offer cost-minimization in achieving GHG emission goals. Regulatory overlay with the intention to accelerate decarbonization of the EU economy presents economic trade-offs that need to be addressed through the policy process without disrupting the cost-effectiveness attributes of the EU ETS.

Strategic Positioning and Enhanced Economic Competitiveness: The EU region sees its climate and energy policy not as pure altruism for the global commons. Instead, EU leaders see the competiveness benefits that positioning the region as a first-mover in the process of developing a low-carbon economy can bring. Perhaps, just as the City of London was able to gain supremacy as the carbon trading capital of the world while experimenting with the first national voluntary carbon ETS, the EU will gain a competitive advantage by continuing to move toward a green economy as oil peaks and new clean and sustainable technological pathways are developed.

8.5 Climate action leadership in the United States

8.5.1 Regional greenhouse gas initiative

The RGGI is the first mandatory (i.e., compliance), market-based carbon dioxide downstream cap-and-trade program established in the United States. Its founding members include the following ten Northeastern and Mid-Atlantic states: Maryland, Delaware, New Jersey, New York, Connecticut, Rhode Island, Massachusetts, Vermont, New Hampshire, and Maine. However, on May 26, 2011

Republican Governor Chris Christie announced that New Jersey would withdraw from the program based on the notion that the RGGI cap-and-trade ETS is a new form of taxation for the electric sector which in turn passes additional costs on to consumers. The withdrawal could affect New Jersey's carbon allowances that are currently in circulation within the RGGI ETS, setting a negative precedent for market development purposes (Navarro, May 2011).

Emissions Cap: Analysts portray RGGI market-based environmental policy design "as a model for a national program to limit greenhouse gas emissions" (Burtraw 2007). It is a sectoral ETS as it only covers the electric power generation industry. RGGI states put a cap on the carbon dioxide emissions of fossil fuel-powered electric power generators that run at a capacity of at least 25 megawatts. This includes approximately 209 facilities in the region. The first three-year compliance period began on January 1, 2009 and concluded on December 31, 2011. From that point, the states have six years to stabilize their emissions and then are required to reduce their carbon dioxide emissions by 2.5 percent each year between 2015 and 2018, for a total of 10 percent. This effort is equivalent to emissions 13 percent below the 1990 level. The program has relatively low administrative costs of about 0.05 percent of the overall emissions allowance revenue. Table 8.3 shows some RGGI key implementation phases and features:

Table 8.3 RGGI Implementation History

2009	Start of the RGGI Program Compliance Period is three years, 2009–2011 allowance equivalent emissions —Reconciliation March 1, 2012
2009–2014	Phase I: Stabilization at initial level for regional cap: 188 million tons of CO_2
2014–2018	Phase II: 2.5 percent reduction per year for a total 10 percent reduction

There are three policy design features that deserve to be highlighted as part of the historical evolutionary process of the ETS concept now being applied for climate purposes:

Allowance Auctions: RGGI states decided to sell 87 percent of allowances. Auctions are open to any interested market participant. As in the case of the EU ETS, auctions are perceived to enhance fairness and transparency in the allocation process. Also, this approach avoids possible market distortion by awarding pollution entitlements to those who value the allowances most. The states participate in quarterly allowance auctions. The proceeds from these auctions are being reinvested in consumer benefit programs, energy efficiency improvements, and renewable energy technologies. The initial RGGI auction, held September 2008, raised $39 million for the member states. In August 2010, Potomac Economics issued a report assessing the RGGI market activity in its first year of operation. The report reviewed the six auctions that took place in 2009 in which 172 million allowances were sold for $494 million. The report concluded that the price of allowances fell considerably in 2009 as confidence in the market grew and expectations of future price volatility fell (RGGI 2010a). The first auction for RGGI's second three-year control period (2012–2015) generated $41.6 million in proceeds. Total cumulative proceeds from all auctions surpassed $1 billion in 2012 (RGGI 2012). The secondary market provides a cost-effective market mechanism to acquire allowances though brokerage services at any given time besides the regular auctions. Allowances not sold are offered for sale and use in the future. In addition, strict market oversight measures have added transparency and confidence to market transaction in the aftermath of the synthetic derivative impact on overall financial markets. Market manipulation has not been a problem in RGGI auctions, as the entire process is scrutinized by third parties who monitor the administration of the program and the behavior of participants.

Reserve Price: An innovative feature introduced by RGGI is the so-called "reserve price," which establishes a minimum price of $1.86 per ton for RGGI allowances. Establishing a floor price prevents allowance prices from dropping to zero once emission limits are met. Although the reserve price can distort the market price, it serves to maintain incentives for further energy efficiency measures and sustain a minimum level of revenues to fund clean energy programs.

Offset Standards: The RGGI ETS allows the use of offsets from projects outside the electricity sector. These emission reduction credits follow traditional criteria in so far as they are real, verifiable, permanent, enforceable, and additional to BAU. However, the innovative aspect of RGGI is that its governance system developed a standardized method to streamline the evaluation process and avoid the UNFCCC approach of case-by-case assessment to reduce transaction costs. RGGI requires demonstration that a project is unsubsidized, not legally mandated, and not a common practice in the industry. Some additional measurable or performance standards are also required. Unfortunately, this feature has not been used so far, as the cap turned out to be too loose given the economic downturn of 2009. However, it provides a model to streamline the UNFCCC CDM that has been administratively burdensome and difficult to access for less-developed countries that wish to partici-pate in the global carbon market.

The following statements summarize the two contrasting perspectives about RGGI that reflect the polarization in the climate policy formulation process in the US at the moment.

A critical statement declares that: "Bottom line, the program has raised electricity prices, created a slush fund for each of the member states, and has had virtually no impact on emissions or on global climate change" (Linowes 2010). In contrast, RGGI proponents such as the Center for American Progress, who see the program as a model for US climate legislation, declare:

> RGGI provides a working model and active case study of how reducing pollution can actually drive economic growth. By 2018 the ten RGGI states will have reduced their power sector carbon emissions by 10 percent, created

thousands of homegrown clean energy jobs, and driven billions of dollars of public and private investment into the clean energy technologies of the future. RGGI proves that a market-based price on power-sector emissions is both possible and effective in the United States, and it has big implications for federal clean energy legislation. As Congress continues considering such legislation it should take a closer look at what RGGI is doing and learn from both its strengths and weaknesses.

(Center for American Progress 2010)

Official reports showed major environmental gains ahead of schedule in 2009: Emissions had fallen 34 percent to just above 120 million tons of CO_2, beyond the initial RGGI 188 million-ton cap set for 2014 and even below the 2019 emissions reduction goal. Critics of what they describe as a "cap-tax-spend model" are quick to point out that other factors played a role in achieving these reductions. Mild weather and the economic downturn caused a significant drop in the region's electricity consumption. Lower natural gas prices caused fuel switching away from coal and toward cleaner-burning natural gas. Also, critics point to the fact that the RGGI program added about 0.9 percent to retail electricity prices in New England "with little tangible benefit for ratepayers beyond another government program" (WindAction Editorial 2010).

The use of the auction dividend has also been criticized as opaque, favoring ventures that are not necessarily successful or useful. However, RGGI reports that "each RGGI Participating State is investing its share of CO_2 allowance proceeds in programs that benefit consumers and build a clean energy economy." The program administrators also emphasize that "These investments reduce CO_2 emissions, and generate important consumer benefits, including lower energy bills, greater electric system reliability, and more jobs. Each state directs its own strategy for investing CO_2 allowance proceeds in consumer benefit programs" (RGGI 2010c). To date, in general, state governments are investing the majority of the proceeds as follows:

- *60 percent* of proceeds to improve energy efficiency;
- *10 percent* to accelerate the deployment of renewable energy technologies; and
- *10 percent* to provide energy bill payment assistance, including assistance to low-income ratepayers.

A salient issue with the RGGI dividend is that some states "given the recession, have attempted to divert their share of auction revenues away from job-creating clean energy programs in order to fill other budget gaps" (Center for American Progress 2010). Mixing fiscal policy with the ETS adds a degree of political complexity.

As in the case of other US emissions trading programs and the EU ETS, the impact of the economic downturn, combined with other external factors such as the abundance of natural gas in the United States, has impacted the effectiveness of the cap to induce change. For the first compliance period, RGGI's total cap was set at 564,230,928 short tons and an equal quantity of RGGI CO_2 allowances was issued.

Actual emissions were 384,866,265 short tons, which resulted in program compliance. Therefore, 179,364,663 surplus allowances, or nearly 32 percent of the total number created by the RGGI states, remain in the system. In 2012 RGGI began a program review that will consider how best to address this issue. Regulators control 83 percent of the surplus allowances, which gives them the option to cancel or retire them or to introduce other program adjustments (Pace Energy and Climate Center 2011).

Selling allowances at the floor price still produces revenue, but overall there is little incentive at this time for the electric power sector to transform itself toward cleaner energy sources in preparation for a low-carbon future. The auction reserve price does maintain some incentives for low-carbon transformation. However, it is external factors that have allowed for dramatic emission reductions. These exogenous circumstances will eventually change. A mature carbon market should allow long-run investment decisions to be determined not by a single year's allowance price but by the expected price path over many years.

Overall, RGGI has been a remarkable success in interstate coordination to implement a regional climate action program. Moreover, it does showcase that a GHG ETS is a practical approach for the electric sector in the US, while also providing a series of policy lessons for similar policy developments elsewhere. As with the EU ETS experience, there is room for improvement, but only learning-by-doing can make this approach a cost-effective tool for addressing climate change. Finally, increases in energy prices from climate-related programs remain unpopular in the US political context. Climate action is a highly controversial policy issue in the US, and New Jersey's decision to pull out of RGGI reminds us that political cycles can negatively impact the credible commitment to regional co-operation in this area and to the cap-and-trade policy approach more generally. These actions can affect the predictability of an ETS, diminishing the capacity of businesses to make long-term investment decisions.

8.5.2 Assembly Bill 32: California's Global Warming Solutions Act of 2006

8.5.2 (A) Background of AB 32

In the absence of federal climate action, and drawing from a longstanding tradition of innovation in the area of urban air pollution control policy design and the pioneering development of effective energy efficiency programs, on September 27, 2006, Governor Arnold Schwarzenegger signed Assembly Bill 32 (AB 32), a landmark climate change bill aimed at reducing California's greenhouse gas emissions.

The California Air Resources Board (CARB), which is part of the California Environmental Protection Agency, is charged with implementing AB 32 and determining how the state will achieve its GHG reduction goals. These strategies are outlined in the Climate Change Scoping Plan released in December 2008. The Scoping Plan uses a host of methods to fund and administer AB 32, including direct regulation of specific sectors, market-based mechanisms like cap-and-trade, voluntary early actions, and monetary and non-monetary incentives. Some of the specific provisions of the plan include: an increase in California's Renewable Portfolio Standard from 20 to 33 percent; improved building and appliance efficiency standards; city and county growth and development plans; and the Low-Carbon Fuel Standard, which is designed to reduce the carbon content in fuel by 10 percent (CARB 2010a). Earlier legislation, known as the Pavley Bill for Clean Car Standards, calls for a 30 percent reduction in vehicle GHG emissions by 2016.

With the support of national and international expert opinion, and through the use of broad, transparent, and inclusive consultation processes, CARB is finalizing the design of an economy-wide California cap-and-trade system. It will include 85 percent of the state's emissions with a broad coverage including the electricity, transportation, natural gas, and heavy industry sectors (CARB 2010a). The design of the California model is one of the most ambitious to date, as it is comprehensive in its reach and it addresses the complex nature of the GHG emissions reduction problem with an array of policy tools ranging from direct regulation to energy efficiency. Cap-and-trade is only one component of the state's climate action plan. In October 2011 CARB approved the final regulatory framework of the CA ETS. Given the litigation challenges as discussed below and the need to implement design refinements to avoid market manipulation, CARB decided to push back the start of the program. This rule enters into force on January 1, 2012, and the first compliance period using the cap-and-trade trading system begins in 2013.

California is leading the bottom-up approach wherein emerging regional blocks attempt to provide momentum toward the creation of a national GHG ETS. At the same time, California is starting to build international links with Canada and Mexico—links. On November 2011, WCI was incorporated to support these efforts that could eventually represent a major step towards a global carbon market. These actions provide an important policy laboratory for co-operation between developed countries and a major developing economy that could provide valuable lessons and demonstrate that high-quality climate action can be achieved in such a context. The eventual creation of a NA ETS would dwarf the EU ETS in size and could potentially integrate this regional market with other emerging ETS systems around the world if the top-down UNFCCC process remains stalled.

8.5.2 (B) ETS policy design parameters

Governance Structure: The California Emissions Trading System (CA ETS) will be administered by CARB. California, in conjunction with members of the Western Regional Climate Initiative, will support the development of the institutional infrastructure to support a regional market while sharing some of the administrative costs of advancing this process (discussed below). The cap-and-trade program is expected to contribute to 20 percent of the AB 32 GHG emissions reductions goals (Wed-Works 2008). CARB is working with relevant stakeholders to ensure that the program satisfies the goals of AB 32 and does not disproportionately impact low-income or other vulnerable communities. The following are the key policy design parameters.

Emissions Cap: Through a mix of market-based incentives and regulatory mechanisms, this bill requires the state to reduce its greenhouse gas emissions to 1990 levels by 2020, a 15 percent decrease from current emissions levels (CARB 2010b). Furthermore, Governor Schwarzenegger signed an executive order mandating the state to reduce GHG emissions to 80 percent of 1990 levels by the year 2050 (California Office of the Governor 2009). The program establishes a hard cap on about 85 percent of total statewide emissions. These decisions pose a challenge to the California economy to embark on a low-carbon development path. Climate action in California originally was seen as an opportunity to spur clean technological developments and to foster alternative sources of energy and savings from further efficiency improvements. Its ultimate goal is to eventually consolidate a prosperous green economy in the state.[13]

Absolute emissions reductions are legally required. Every year the cap will decline. The gradual reduction in allowances is designed to harness the economic incentives caused by scarcity in a market-based mechanism in order to promote energy efficiency and the development of low-carbon technology.

Gradual Implementation and Design Priorities: While California has tried to incorporate gradualism and predictable design features into its plans to phase sectors into the program, the state's efforts to create predictability have been somewhat undermined by implementation delays. Table 8.4 reflects the original implementation timetable and planned phase-in of sectors in the CA ETS.

The implementation delay affects the first three-year compliance period (2012–2014) by shortening it to two years. The delay does not extend the 2020 target date required by AB 32. The first of the quarterly auctions of emissions allowances that each large emitter in California must turn in for compliance was conducted on November 14, 2012. Entities that emit more than 25,000 metric tons of CO_2 per year will commence trading credits at the end of 2012 to cover emission reduction obligations for January 1, 2013, the new start of Phase I. CARB remains

Table 8.4 CA ETS Original Implementation Plan

2012 January 1, first compliance period begins (three years).

- Electricity generation, including imports into the CA electric grid.
- Large industrial sources and process at or above 25,000 MT CO_2e

2015 January 1, second compliance period begins

- Industrial fuel combustion from sources with emissions below 25,000 MT CO_2e and all commercial and residential fuel combustion of natural gas and propane
- Transportation fuels

committed to the implementation of CA ETS, sending strong signals of a credible commitment from government to this policy approach.

An internal trigger for delay, based on careful design and implementation considerations, was articulated by the Chair of CARB, Mary Nichols: "we will only launch this program in full when we are entirely confident that every piece of it is fully developed and ready to go."[14] For instance, certain covered emitters will obtain GHG allowances from CARB for free (primarily industry and utility distribution companies). However, the primary means of allocating allowances will be by auctions. To limit volatility, a CARB reserve of allowance (i.e., set-aside) reflecting 4 percent of total allowances will be available for periods of unexpected short supply in the market. Also, regulators have set a minimum (i.e., floor) price of $10 per metric ton, which after implemented will then grow at 5 percent per year in real terms. CARB will award the allowances to the highest bidders. As with any commodities market, the potential for manipulation, frauds, and deception exists. Therefore, CARB has emphasized "rigorous market oversight and strong enforcement" design features.

Trading Rules: The CA ETS plan allows for the carry-over of unused allowances or offsets from one three-year compliance period to another. Its rules limit the use of offset credits to 8 percent of the maximum compliance obligations of an entity per period. Also, borrowing is not allowed across compliance periods. Past experience shows that banking creates the incentive for sources to make early reductions under the expectation of higher allowance prices in the future, given a declining cap over time. Moreover, as suggested in Deason and Friedman (2010), borrowing constraints in cap-and-trade systems can impose substantial unnecessary costs, so inter-temporal flexibility like the three-year compliance periods is a valuable feature.

Offsets: The buying of offset credits has been a controversial issue in the design of the CA ETS. Therefore, the Scoping Plan suggested a "limited use of offsets." In addition, geographical considerations for protocol development, such as a limitation to US-only projects or to projects linked with particular programs like the WCI, are being considered. Offsets complement the flexibility provided by the trading mechanism. However, as in the case of the EU ETS, the quality of the projects is an important issue. By law, in the CA ETS offsets must demonstrate that emission reductions meet the consensus criteria of being real, permanent, verifiable, enforceable, and quantifiable. They also have to be additional efforts beyond BAU improvements or what law or regulation already requires. With substantial modifications, CARB used the Climate Action Reserve (CAR) voluntary market standards and protocols (described below) as the basis for its offset rules (CARB 2010b). The CARB compliance offset protocols as of 2012 are: live livestock digesters, ODS, urban forests, and other US forestry projects.

Linking Protocols: The CA ETS can link with other systems under special agreements provided that they follow detailed protocols of compatibility that would allow for all

MRV aspects and certification of offsets to ensure compliance with the system rules and periods.

Measuring, Reporting, and Verification: A high standard in MRV practices is perhaps the key to the future expansion and development of the carbon market in North America and at a global scale. In 2007, CARB approved California's mandatory reporting regulation and transitioned from the voluntary reporting system established through the California Climate Action Registry (CCAR). CCAR was created by the State of California in 2001 to address climate change through voluntary calculation and public reporting of emissions. This non-profit organization established protocols to guide emissions inventory reporting and served as a central database for emissions reports. Since 2009, reporting to CCAR is not a substitute for CARB reporting requirements. CA ETS facilities also comply with federal GHG reporting requirements established by the US EPA.

The registry's work expanded, and its protocols were widely accepted in the state and served as the basis to develop the mandatory reporting requirements. However, there are several standards servicing the region in MRV aspects as part of the voluntary market. Emissions inventory reporting under the state's registry protocol (i.e., California Action Registry Reporting Tool) was transitioned to a regional carbon standard to support the development of the WCI. In this institutional evolutionary process, CCAR is now part of CAR, which has emerged as a leading national offsets program working to ensure integrity, transparency, and financial value in the US carbon market. It does this by establishing regulatory-quality standards for the development, quantification, and verification of greenhouse gas emissions reduction projects in North America. CAR issues carbon offset credits known as Climate Reserve Tonnes generated from projects that meet its standards. CAR supports its members with high standards and by tracking the transaction of credits over time in a transparent, publicly accessible system. As stated by this organization, "Adherence to the Reserve's high standards ensures that emissions reductions associated with projects are real, permanent and additional, thereby instilling confidence in the environmental benefit, credibility and efficiency of the US carbon market" (Climate Action Reserve 2010). This role was validated by the carbon market information service provider Thomson Reuters' Point Carbon in 2010, which reported that, "Offsets certified to the Climate Action Reserve (CAR) standard made up the bulk of transactions, accounting for 37 percent of total volumes and 65 percent of the US offset market value in 2009" (Point Carbon 2010). The report went on to suggest in a prospective analysis that "CAR offsets are viewed as the most likely carbon credits that would be allowed in a federal cap-and-trade system" (Point Carbon 2010).

The Climate Registry is a non-profit collaboration among North American states, provinces, territories, and Native Sovereign Nations that sets consistent and transparent standards to calculate, verify, and publicly report greenhouse gas emissions into a single registry. The Climate Registry provides information management services to support its members' mandatory reporting programs with a trusted system.

This allows GHG emissions data to be reported consistently and in a streamlined manner within the region.

The American Carbon Registry (ACR) is the first private voluntary GHG registry in the US. Previously known as the GHG Registry of the Environmental Resources Trust, ACR has extensive experience in developing carbon offset standards and methodologies for producing high-quality offsets.

Finally, the Verified Carbon Standard (VCS) is a GHG accounting program used by projects around the world to verify and issue carbon credits in voluntary markets. VCS reflects state-of-the-art knowledge and global good practice.

Environmental Justice and Litigation: The creators of the CA ETS have worked to ensure that no community is affected more than others by co-pollutant emissions that create hot spots. California has placed an emphasis on this issue, which is of particular concern to lower-income communities, throughout the policy formulation process. Despite these efforts, an environmental justice association sued CARB in 2010. In *Association of Irritated Residents (AIR) v. California Air Resources Board* it was argued that the analysis of the policy alternatives conducted by CARB in 2009 was insufficient for informed decision making and public review under the California Environmental Quality Act. The suit argued that a more thorough analysis of the use of alternatives to cap-and-trade such as a carbon fee or tax should have been carried out. A final ruling by a Superior Court judge halted CARB's implementation of the cap-and-trade program but allowed progress to continue on other AB 32 provisions. California's appeal to the decision allows CARB to proceed with the development of AB 32's cap-and-trade system. *AIR v. CARB* may still jeopardize the program's start date. CARB produced a supplement to the AB 32 Scoping Plan Functional Equivalent Document (FED) "to remove any doubt about the matter ..." reassessing five policy alternatives including a carbon tax or fee (CARB 2011). Based on public consultation and internal deliberations, CARB determined on August 24, 2011 that cap-and-trade is an appropriate policy approach to achieve AB 32's climate action goals. The FED satisfied the Superior Court judge, who lifted the stay.

In March 2012, the Citizens Climate Lobby and Our Children's Earth Foundation filed another suit in the California Superior Court for the County of San Francisco. The claim is that offsets cannot meet the statutory requirements set under the state's climate change law, AB 32 (Argus 2012). American regulatory law often gives stakeholders an opportunity to challenge and shape new legal interventions. This is especially true in the field of environmental law. It is expected that CARB will continue to confront statutory and potentially constitutional challenges before the CA ETS cap-and-trade and other AB 32 rules are fully implemented.

Political Economy: Finally, California is a good example of the impact that political cycles and economic reality have on policy formulation and the implementation of new regulatory mechanisms to address climate change. As mentioned earlier, supporters of AB 32 championed this bill as the opportunity to transition California to a clean-energy economy that would create jobs, decrease oil dependence, and protect public health. CARB released a report in March 2010 projecting that AB 32 would create 10,000 new jobs in California. However, opponents argue that AB 32 will place an undue burden on state industries and will increase unemployment, particularly given the difficult economic times. Charles River Associates (2010) issued a report in March 2010 stating that AB 32 will cost the state between $28 and $97 billion in the next decade. On November 2, 2010, California voters soundly rejected the opportunity to delay implementation of AB 32 by defeating Proposition 23, which would have suspended the program until the state unemployment rate decreases to 5.5 percent or lower for at least four consecutive quarters (California Secretary of State 2010). Thus California will continue in its leadership role domestically and at the international level in developing a vanguard climate action plan.

8.6 Continuous process of policy innovation and integration in market-based environmental policymaking

New design and implementation approaches to create carbon markets are emerging around the world. As mentioned earlier in this chapter, the Australian carbon pricing policy that enters into force in 2012 implements a fixed price (through the issuance of fixed price units) before converting to a cap-and-trade ETS within a legislatively predetermined period. Australia's long-term target for the reduction of carbon emissions has been raised from 60 to 80 percent below 2000 levels by 2050. The carbon price will start at AUS$23 per ton in 2012–2013. In each of the following two years it will rise in line with inflation to AUS$24.15 in 2013–2014 and AUS$25.40 per ton in 2014–2015. Beginning July 1, 2015 the carbon price will no longer be fixed by regulators but will be set by the market.

Aside from this innovative implementation approach, Australia's key contribution to the evolution of ETS policy design is that an independent Climate Change Authority was established at the outset. It is charged with advising the Australian Government on the setting of carbon pollution caps with clearly established periodic reviews of the carbon pricing mechanism and other climate change laws. In other words, it provides a transparent legislated policy path for revisions and adjustments to the program, enhancing certainty and a sense of permanence in the emerging ETS.

Finally, on August 28, 2012, Australia and the EU announced their intention to fully link their ETSs by July 1, 2018. In the interim, the EU will enable Australian businesses "to use carbon units from the Australian emissions trading scheme or the EU Emissions Trading System (EU ETS) for compliance under either system (EU 2012)." This effort represents an important step towards adding scale and efficiency to the global carbon market.

8.7 Conclusion

The urgent need for absolute GHG emissions reductions can be realized in a cost-effective manner while supporting the development of new technological pathways. To do so, we must take advantage of the power of the market. The path towards a mature global carbon market, which is evolving today, seems complicated but not impossible to navigate. Patience and enhanced understating of this policy approach by political and business leaders, as well as regulators and taxpayers, around the world is necessary. Agreement among climate experts may be necessary, but it will not be sufficient.

Key governments beyond the more risk-averse EU and EEA partners need to take action that gives a clear signal about their commitment to emissions reduction targets supported by environmental commodities markets. The development of ETSs by a diverse set of climate jurisdictions at the national and sub-national level points towards the expansion of the carbon market. However, regulatory overlay can be counterproductive in terms of cost effectiveness. Governments that take climate action must also provide a predictable regulatory pathway that offers a long-view perspective to the private sector. The top-down, all-or-nothing approach of the UNFCCC will take time and is not currently working. Consequently, an enhanced, multi-track process that produces advancements in national, regional, and sub-national climate action should be supported and rewarded by expanding the cost-minimizing opportunities that an integrated and expanding global carbon market presents.

Historically, these advances have been stalled by politicians representing special interests. In the US, the primary strategy used to delay the implementation of new environmental regulations has been to require further research, as illustrated by the case of acid rain. As described in chapters 4 and 5, the lengthy policy cycle of the Acid Rain Program, which took several decades to implement, illustrates the potential impacts of this strategy on policymaking. Once scientists confirmed the existence of the environmental threat posed by acid rain, interests groups debated the potential health, economic, and environmental implications. Government, pressured by organized interest groups and lobbies, initiated its own research program to assess claims and potential fiscal and compliance costs. In the meantime, a focusing event occurred that prompted politicians to act to address the environmental threat. The focusing event, the damage to Northeastern US and Canadian agriculture and forestry from transport SO_2 emissions, triggered action on acid rain. More recently, the impact of a climate-related event in the US—Hurricane Katrina—prompted the George W. Bush administration to acknowledge the issue and jump-start a technology-driven policy approach to address climate change.

These experiences in the US reveal that the media plays a key role in putting a face on the potential risks by documenting evidence of the dangers posed by environmental problems. Governments are then pressured to react, as the impacts of environmental problems are more visible and closer to home. The choice then is between possibly burdensome and costly reactive regulation applied late and which could threaten economic development or the implementation of more flexible, innovative, and appropriate policy approaches customized to each problem.

This policy evolutionary pattern occurs frequently with environmental problems that may imply potentially large compliance costs for polluters. Through active participation in the policy formulation process, these groups may manage to delay regulatory action for years or even decades. The difference between acid rain and climate change is that the latter can bring about worst-case scenario catastrophes—though considered to be a low probability—that could have a major impact on humanity, our economies, and our habitat. Moreover, longer time-lags in the stock flow system will make delay much more costly, requiring sharper GHG emissions cuts later. Also, potential non-marginal and irreversible impacts make insurance against risk a key part of the price of action. However, opposing views about the economic effects of climate change on industrialized countries constantly feed the debate. The struggle continues to identify and implement cost-effective strategies that appropriately deal with the uncertainties surrounding the impact of climate change and the investments required to mitigate it.

Continuing with the US example, a new era in climate change policy was expected after the election of Barack Obama on November 2008. The first indication of this came when President-elect Obama spoke at the Governor's Global Climate Summit organized by Governor Arnold Schwarzenegger of California. In a taped message to this gathering, Obama stated the following just a few days after winning the election:

> Washington has failed to show the same kind of leadership. That will change when I take office. My presidency will mark a new chapter in America's leadership on climate change that will strengthen our security and create millions of new jobs in the process. That will start with a federal cap and trade system. We will establish strong annual targets that set us on a course to reduce emissions to their 1990 levels by 2020 and reduce them an additional 80 percent by 2050.
>
> (Change.gov 2010)

Before Obama's election, the collapse of Lehman Brothers in September 2008 marked in the US the beginning of the greatest financial and economic crisis since the Great Depression of the 1930s. This economic crisis became the first priority on the new president's agenda. Public health reform came next. While a national cap-and-trade system was also proposed to launch climate action in the US, the full auctioning design feature helped kill the proposed system from the start. It became a political target used to attack the new administration as the suggested ETS became a fiscal measure as well. *Cap-and-tax* has become the anti-Obama climate policy sound bite. For instance, the conservative grass-roots group known as the Tea Party Movement in its Contract From America has as its second priority after "Protect the Constitution" to reject cap-and-trade (Contract From America 2010). The policy formulation process in support (or against) significant US climate action has been characterized by observers and activists as a political war (Pooley 2010).

After the November 2010 mid-term elections in the US, in which the Republican Party gained ground in Congress, *The Financial Times* (2010) stated in an editorial, "If the paralysis in Capitol Hill does worsen, the implications will be global. Forget progress on climate change for instance, at least along the lines previously envisioned: the chances now for cap and trade in the US are zero." However, as the history of the ETS concept in the US shows, this policy approach was an innovative environmental regulatory solution introduced by a Republican administration and touted as the most business-friendly regulatory program for air pollution control at the time. It embodied the American principle of harnessing the market for efficient allocation of resources. The pendulum of politics seems to have reached the other extreme. While it may take time to come back to the center, the new realities that climate change will bring upon us will accelerate the search for pertinent policy solutions.

Congress has been given the task of reframing the issue (for instance, to focus on energy security instead of climate policy) and coming up with a compromise on policy solutions. Several bills have been presented to committees, but little has been achieved. However, despite the polarized political environment in Washington, DC, the financial and health reforms were dealt with and advanced. After his re-election in November 2012, President Barack Obama stated that he favors an agenda that creates jobs and advances economic growth while making "a serious dent in climate change". In the years to come, the dangers of climate change will become more salient and pervasive. Facing a low-probability, high-cost focusing event is a reality (Trexler 2010). Moreover, the issue of energy security and the loss in competiveness in environmental technology markets are emerging as sources of pressure for policy action in Washington, particularly from business lobbies. For instance, the American Energy Innovation Council (AEIC), formed by some of the most influential business leaders in the country, has been arguing since 2010 that there is a high price to pay for inaction in this area. More recently, in September 2011, AEIC sent a strong message to lawmakers that focused on the issue of competitiveness based on findings from a report sponsored by this group:

> If the U.S. fails to invent new technologies and create new markets and new jobs that will drive the transformation and revitalization of the $5 trillion global energy industry, we will have lost an opportunity to lead in what is arguably the largest and most pervasive technology sector in the world.
>
> (American Energy Innovation Council 2011)

Pricing carbon is essential to stimulating such transformational efforts; the carbon market can also help spur technological and managerial innovation to address the climate and energy policy challenges while freeing financial resources to enable a prosperous green economy. If the history of market-based solutions for environmental control in the US can teach us anything, we may say this: despite contentious policy formulation processes that can take a long time to yield a consensus in America's complex democratic system, practical policy solutions will ultimately emerge. Better understanding of the issues and the involvement of all stakeholders are important to furthering this fractious process.

To sum up, in 1973, the oil embargo triggered a search for more cost-effective environmental policies. The imminent reality of a carbon-constrained world and the search for new environmental technology markets may force a similar process in the US in the near future. Today, as recently suggested by Keith Johnson in *The Wall Street Journal*, the world is searching for "a new energy future that makes sense, both environmentally and economically. That's because, if new policies set out to tackle those externalities once and for all, the environmental answer will quite often become the economic answer. Everything has its price—and its cost" (2010).

Without a doubt, the stabilization of GHG emissions will come at a cost to nations around the world in the near future, but this transformational effort can also generate prosperity as we develop new, cleaner sources of energy and more sustainable production and consumption systems. Careful policy design and implementation processes will be essential for addressing climate change in a cost-effective manner. A market-based approach to climate policy should provide industrial and research groups with the incentives to innovate and develop the clean technology paths necessary for making a low-carbon future a reality.

As pointed out in Aldy and Stavins (2011), "the US political response to possible market-based approaches to climate policy has been and will continue to be largely a function of issues and structural factors that transcend the scope of environmental and climate policy." However, the possible future development of a US carbon market that integrates and harmonizes current efforts in the region (i.e., WCI, RGGI, and other regional collaborative efforts) could lead to the creation of a NA ETS. In turn, that institutional development could solidify the emergence of a global carbon market in combination with the existing EU ETS that could be worth at least a trillion dollars. China, the other key player in global climate policy, is exploring the implementation of an ETS that could eventually be linked with the EU ETS. This will take time. But China is clearly aware that delay on climate policy action risks missing out on clean technologies and markets and also, ultimately, presents the possibility of facing trade measures and tariffs from those key nations and regions already committed to these policies and the carbon market.

In the meantime policy analysis can continue to identify the design parameters that make the ETS approach perform at its best: ensuring the environmental integrity of the program while enhancing cost-minimization opportunities in addressing the dangers and risks of climate change. Less politics, more credible commitments from governments around the world to climate action, and high technical standards for validation and mutual recognition of ETS program design features, in particular for MRV, will allow for a smooth transition to integrating existing and emerging environmental markets into a more global system in the near future. Ultimately, a well-functioning global carbon market represents only one of many policy solutions necessary to support the transition to a green, low-carbon, resource-efficient economy.

Notes

1 Introduction

1 See for instance, Ellerman, Denny A., et al. *Markets for Clean Air, the US Acid Rain Program*. London: Cambridge University Press (2000).
2 Chan, Gabriel, Robert Stavins, Robert Stow and Richard Sweeney. *The SO₂ Allowance Trading System and the Clean Air Act Amendments of 1990: Reflections on Twenty Years of Policy Innovation*. Cambridge, MA: Harvard Economics Program (January 2012).
3 Sandor, Richard L. *Good Derivatives: A Story of Financial and Environmental Innovation*. Hoboken, NJ: John Wiley & Sons, Inc. (2012), p. 27.
4 For instance, a regulation to enclose a facility constructs an imaginary "bubble." Rather than regulating each source of emissions individually, the environmental agency regulates the total pollution in the bubble. Targets must be met for annual emissions reductions.
5 http://unfccc.int/meetings/cancun_nov_2010/meeting/6266txt.php.
6 See for instance on path dependence: Arthur, Brian W. *Increasing Returns and Path Dependence in the Economy*. Ann Arbor, MI: University of Michigan Press (1994); on history's relevance, Paul David. "Clio and the Economics of QWERTY," *American Economic Review*, Vol. 75, No. 2 (1985), pp. 332–337, and Neustadt, Richard E. and Ernest R. May. *Thinking in Time*. New York: Free Press (1986); on transaction costs economics, Williamson, Oliver. *The Economic Institutions of Capitalism*. New York: Free Press (1985), on transaction costs politics, Dixit, Avinash K. *The Making of Economic Policy: A Transaction-Cost Politics Perspective*. Cambridge, MA: The MIT Press (1996); and on institutional environment, North, Douglas C. *Institutions, Institutional Change and Economic Performance*. London: Cambridge University Press (1996).

2 Theoretical foundations

1 For instance see: Chay, Kenneth Y. and Michael Greenstone. *Does Air Quality Matter? Evidence from the Housing Market*. Working Paper 6826. Cambridge, MA: National Bureau of Economic Research (December 1998).
2 Marginalism is a tradition in which marginal concepts are used in economics. Marginal concepts are associated with a specific change in the quantity used (of a good or service), as opposed to a measure of general use (of a good or service) or the percentage of the total used.
3 The adjective "technological" is introduced in order to differentiate it from pecuniary external economies.
4 When a producer accounts for external damage by reducing the level of output including the marginal cost function in his/her decision, the response is to decrease output until the marginal benefit equals the sum of the private and social marginal costs.

5 Weitzman (1974) explains the comparative advantage between quantity and price mechanisms based on introducing uncertainty in estimating benefit and cost functions. The implication of not having cost and benefits independently distributed is that decisions on the preferred policy approach depend on the correlation term. When marginal costs are positively correlated with marginal benefits *ceteris paribus*, the comparative advantage of the quantity mode (e.g., permits) is increased. If prices (e.g., charges or penalties) are used as a control policy, the producer will tend to cut back output at high marginal cost levels. At the same time, marginal benefits will tend to be high, so that a cutback may not be in order. In such situations, the quantity mode has better properties as a stabilizer, other things being equal. This relation is proportionally inverted when correlation is negative. In this case high marginal costs are associated with low marginal benefits, and therefore the price approach (which decreases output for a high marginal cost) seems to be a better prescription.

6 Regulators cannot clearly identify original sources of discharge and their damage cost. There is still too much uncertainty about the fate-and-transport systems that move pollution emissions through alternative media (e.g., air mantle and water bodies) to allow accurate estimates on the physical impacts on human health and environmental damage. However, new technologies (i.e., nanotechnology) may soon be able to accurately pinpoint sources and measure emissions.

7 This is a situation where there is a risk of "moral hazard," where economic agents do not bear the full cost of their actions and are thus more likely to take such actions.

8 The Coase theorem states that when trade in an externality is possible, and there are no transaction costs, bargaining will lead to an efficient outcome regardless of the initial allocation of property rights. In practice, ill-defined property rights and other barriers can prevent Coasian bargaining.

9 Here, we understand the definition of "developing countries" and "the developing world" to include Brazil, Russia, India, China (the BRICS), Mexico (G8+5 group), and South Korea, as well as all other non-OECD countries.

10 On the policy recommendation to implement a broad-based carbon tax uniform to all sources of GHG based on the Norwegian experience, see for instance: Bruvoll, A. and B. M. Larsen. "Greenhouse Gas Emissions in Norway: Do Carbon Taxes Work?" *Energy Policy*, Vol. 32 (2004), pp. 493–505.

11 The greenhouse gases considered to be controlled by the UNFCCC are: carbon dioxide (CO_2), methane, nitrous oxide, perfluorocarbons, hydrofluorocarbons, and sulfur hexafluoride. However, CO_2 is the main precursor of the greenhouse effect.

12 The general problem of organization is to be able to choose the operating rules or instructions to command or direct certain behavior of the individual agents involved and an enforcement mechanisms (some form of incentives, either rewards or penalties) to control or induce individuals to follow the operating rules.

13 Even though these are two very different "costs" – the unanticipated implementation costs are inherent in the functioning of the system and the second is a choice variable to build political support for the scheme—both need to be considered.

14 An example of this is the Vivkrey–Clarke–Groves game-theoretic model auction. As described in Rothkopf (2007), "In theory, the mathematically elegant Vickrey–Clarke–Groves process offers perfect efficiency with dominant truth-revealing strategies. However, it has many serious practical problems."

15 Organizational theory explains that one way that institutional learning occurs is through the mechanism of organizational search. Radner (1975) suggests "that an organization draws from a pool of alternative routines, adopting better ones when they are discovered. Since the rate of discovery is a function of search, it depends on the history of success and failure" of the institution.

16 As defined by the United Nations Development Program, human development refers to the process of widening the options of persons, giving them greater opportunities for education, health care, income, employment, etc.

3 Creating efficient environmental commodities markets

1 A spot market is a market in which goods are sold for cash and immediately delivered ("on the spot"). Currently most of these exchanges take place electronically.

2 A futures market is a market in which parties agree on a contract to buy specific quantities of a commodity at a pre-specified price to be delivered at a specific future date.

3 An options market is a market in which parties agree on a contract that entitles (but does not require) the buyer to buy an asset at a pre-specified price at a later time.

4 For a discussion of this topic see: Friedman, Lee S. and Jeff Deason. (2009) "Should the Regulator or the Market Decide When to Reduce Greenhouse Gas Emissions?" *The Economists' Voice*, Vol. 6, No. 13, Article 1.

5 On this issue see for instance: Rowland, F.S. and Molina, M.J. "Ozone Depletions: 20 years after the alarm," *Chemical and Engineering News*, Vol. 72 (1994), pp. 8–13.

6 The Member countries of the OECD are: Australia, Austria, Belgium, Canada, Chile, the Czech Republic, Denmark, Finland, France, Germany, Greece, Hungary, Iceland, Ireland, Italy, Japan, Korea, Luxemburg, Mexico, the Netherlands, New Zealand, Norway, Poland, Portugal, the Slovak Republic, Slovenia, Spain, Sweden, Switzerland, Turkey, the United Kingdom, and the United States.

7 For a technical discussion on such debate see: Emanuel, K. "The Hurricane-Climate Connection," *Bulletin of the American Meteorological Society*, Vol. 89 (2008), pp. ES10–ES20.

8 Deason and Friedman (2010) suggest three-year compliance for GHG to enhance the flexibility of the ETS regulatory approach.

9 For instance see: Groth, Lars. *Future Organizational Design. The Scope for the IT-based Enterprise*. New York: John Wiley & Sons, Ltd (1999).

4 The first generation of air pollution trading systems

1 Air pollution aggravates a variety of health problems ranging from eye, nose, and throat irritation to bronchitis, emphysema, and other serious lung diseases. Air pollution may also impair visibility; damage crops, forests, and lakes; and cause historic buildings and monuments to deteriorate. Given the negative externalities of air pollution on society, regulators began to take legislative action.

2 A Clean Air Act was passed in 1963 authorizing research and hearings to develop conference systems to deal with interstate pollution problems. It also authorized federal grants to states to develop state and local air pollution control programs. Other investigative acts were later passed in 1966.

3 "Social" regulation seeks to achieve social goals with respect to safety, health, employment fairness, and related issues. Industry rarely demands social regulation, rather support is derived mainly from non-industry interest groups such as consumer advocacy groups and environmentalists. The technical justification for social regulation is that "market failures" impede the correct functioning of markets. Furthermore, "economic regulation" is traditionally aimed at specific industries and economic sectors in order to offset the problems of monopoly and abusive market practices. Social regulation, however, cuts across economic sectors and broad classes of industrial activities as in the case of environmental policy. Cook, Brian J. *Bureaucratic Politics and Regulatory Reform: The EPA and Emissions Trading*. New York: Greenwood Press (1988), p. 5.

4 These standards specify an acceptable level of selected substance concentration in ambient (i.e., outdoor) air. Primary standards are intended to "protect human health," and secondary standards are intended to protect public welfare, crops, property, and plant and animal life.

5 In situations where the regulation of discharges and emissions is not sufficient, the EPA also undertakes efforts to restore the environment to its original condition through waste treatment and the removal and disposal of hazardous wastes. Insecticides and chemicals are also within the agency's jurisdiction. Moreover, the environmental problems being addressed by the EPA range from imminent health hazards to long-term climatic effects that may not be apparent until well into this century. See: Viscusi, W. Kip, John M. Vernon, and Joseph E. Harrington Jr., *Economics of Regulation and Antitrust.* Lexington, MA: Heath and Company (1992), p. 653.

6 For example, while the Clean Air Act allows the EPA to set nationally uniform ambient quality standards, the state or local air quality control region areas are required to set source-specific emission limitations in order to achieve the national standards in each air basin.

7 For instance, see the description of the "Connecticut Enforcement Project" in Drayton, William, "Economic Law Enforcement," *Harvard Environmental Law Review* Vol. 1, No. 4 (1980), pp. 1–40. William Drayton and Douglas Costle were appointed by President Carter to the positions of EPA administrator and assistant administrator, respectively, after working in the Connecticut State Government. Later, the document published by the Offices of Sen. Timothy Wirth and Sen. John Heinz titled Project 88, issued in 1988, also shows congressional interest in harnessing market forces to improve environmental control.

8 Several proposals were introduced by the Nixon administration, all introducing taxes or fees with slight variations to control air pollution. Parking surcharges, gasoline additives, and sulfur dioxide emissions were the main incentive-base policy designs proposed. However, as recounted by Cook (1988), "The proposals never got out of the House Ways and Means Committee. The opposition in the committee especially from Chairman Wilbur Mills (D-AR) was to the concept of using a revenue-rising devise to control pollution. Mills objected to any use of the tax code other than raising revenue."

9 The basic criteria on type of polluting sources are: (1) size (major and minor); (2) location (attainment and non-attainment areas); and (3) age in relation to new regulations (existing and new sources).

10 This model is supported by the notion that regulation plays a positive role to dissuade potential law violators; therefore it should be enforced with considerable vigor. Without strict enforcement, it is expected that those subject to the law would freely break the law. See, for instance, Viscusi and Zeckhauser (1979), and Freeman and Haveman (1972).

11 See the legal case discussions over "netting" in the smelting industry in Asarco vs. EPA.

12 Hot spots only apply when the EPA's definition of an air basin is too broad and there is a concentration of a pollutant in a specific subsection. In the current Acid Rain Program this possibility has not become a major issue.

13 Markets are continuous when prices are determined continuously throughout a trading period as buyers and sellers submit their orders.

14 This is important in the US (and most OECD countries), as the Fifth Amendment of the US Constitution protects private property from being confiscated or affected in value because of regulatory action, also known as inverse condemnation.

15 Williamson (1985) described transaction costs in an economic system as the counterpart of frictions in a mechanical one.

16 For instance, local AQMDs in California created exemptions (or "thresholds") for entire categories of small facilities and for modifications that resulted in relatively small increases in emissions. See: Dwyer (1993), p. 109.

5 State-of-the-art market-based environmental policy

1 See for instance: Chan, Gabriel, Robert Stavins, Robert Stow, and Richard Sweeney. (2012). *The SO₂ Allowance Trading System and The Clean Air Act Amendments of 1990: Reflections on Twenty Years of Policy Innovation*. Cambridge, MA: Harvard Economics Program.

2 On March 13, 1991, an Air Quality Agreement was signed between Canada and the United States. Canada promised to reduce SO_2 emissions by 1994 to 2.4 million tons from sources in the seven eastern provinces and to impose a national cap of 3.2 million tons by the year 2000. During the negotiation of the treaty, the US Congress had already authorized the 1990 Clean Air Act Amendments, which implicitly set the US SO_2 reduction goals for the bilateral agreement.

3 For instance, *The New York Times* (June 1, 1987) "Acid Rain Lobby Led 1986 Spending" reported that in 1986 the acid rain proposal had more lobbying money directed against it than had any other legislation at the time.

4 OECD (1999) reports that in the United States approximately 3.5 percent of national investments go to pollution abatement and control activities. This figure excludes other private control efforts, such as household control activities.

5 In addition to EPA's own efforts to strengthen the case for acid rain policy action, Congress had mandated studies from the Congressional Research Service, the Congressional Budget Office, the Government Accounting Office, and the Congressional Office of Technology Assessment.

6 1990 CAA, Section 405(g)(6) exempts sources that are utility units such as "qualifying small power production facilities" or "qualifying cogeneration facilities" or "independent power production facilities."

7 These sources encompass combustion sources, such as those located at hospitals, universities, or residences that are not related to the production of physical products.

8 As defined in Section 402 of the 42 US C. 7651a, "The term affected source means a source that includes one or more affected units."

9 A unit is defined as combustion sources. Combustion sources are boilers, turbines, and internal combustion engines used to power electric generators.

10 As of the end of 1994, operable capacity of US electric utilities totaled 702,229 megawatts, of which coal-fired capacity represented 43 percent (301,098 megawatts) and petroleum 10 percent (69,919 megawatts).

11 By 1999 the existing capacity of US electric utilities totaled 639,324 megawatts, and based on primary energy source, coal-fired capacity represented 43 percent (277,789 megawatts), and petroleum 8 percent (49,153 megawatts).

12 The long-term goals of the Acid Rain Program are: a 10 million-ton reduction in SO_2 emissions and a two million-ton reduction in NO_X emissions.

13 The major health effects associated with high exposures to SO_2 in the ambient air include problems with breathing, respiratory illness, alteration in the lungs' defenses, and aggravation of existing respiratory and cardiovascular disease.

14 SO_2 produces foliage damage on trees and agricultural crops. SO_2 and NO_X in the air cause acidic deposition that damages forests, accelerates corrosion of buildings and monuments, and causes acidification of lakes and streams. Also, sulfates and nitrates in the atmosphere can significantly impair visibility.

15 Listed criteria pollutants currently include the following substances: sulfur oxides, particulate matter, hydrocarbons, and photochemical oxidants (i.e., nitrogen oxides and lead).

16 Brokers are middle-persons who bring buyers and sellers together for a fee. Also, individuals and civil society entities may buy allowances and retire them permanently.

17 Section 403(f) of the Clean Air Act specifically states that an allowance does not constitute a property right.

18 The act of government taking private property or expropriation. Legally defined in the US as Eminent Domain, it is the power granted to the government indirectly, by the Fifth Amendment to the Constitution, which states, in part, that "private property [shall not] be taken for public use, without just compensation."

19 The Clean Power Act of 2001 (S.556) sponsored by Senators Jim Jeffords, Joseph Lieberman, and John McCain was introduced as the first congressional attempt to reduce current emissions standards from power plants. The so-called "three-pollutants bill" proposed drastic new cuts in utility emissions of sulfur dioxide (SO_2), nitrogen oxides (NO_X), mercury, and carbon dioxide (CO_2). The proposal has been highly contested. Opponents argue that, according to the Energy Information Administration (EIA), S.566 would reduce the US gross domestic product by 0.8 percent, or about $100 billion, in 2007, with a loss of about one million jobs. Most of the increased cost would come from fuel switching from coal to natural gas. By 2020, the EIA estimates electricity prices would rise by 33 percent and natural gas prices by more than 20 percent. Therefore, changes to emissions standards are not impossible but difficult to implement. See for instance, National Center for Policy Analysis. S.566: A Backdoor Attempt to Implement the KP. Brief Analysis No. 386. (December 18, 2001).

20 The 1991 EPA proposed rules were: the Permits Rules (40 CFR, Part 72), the Allowance system Rule (40 CFR, Part 73), the Continuous Emission Monitoring Rule (40 CFR, Part 75), and the Excess Emissions Rule (40 CFR, Part 77).

21 Hot spots can be defined as localized levels of pollution that exceed safe standards.

22 EPA does have the authority to establish new ambient quality limits under the National Ambient Air Quality Standards, Title I of the 1990 CAA, Section 109. However, the SO_2 emissions cap is legislated, and Congress would have to pass new legislation to make it more stringent under Title IV.

23 The NAPAP was created in the context of the acid rain policy debate. Its inventory consisted of different databases. Therefore, some inconsistencies were found initially. In 1985 the inventory was improved to provide detailed estimates of plant-specific emissions from states and the private sector. The EPA Trends Report uses aggregate fuel data; production data and fuel sulfur content data collected by the Department of Energy and the Bureau of Mines; and other published references. At times the discrepancies between these two sources were around 2.7 million tons. In the end, the improved NAPAP was used for plant-by-plant calculations and the Trend Report for non-utility estimates.

24 A published source, Department of Energy's DOE Form 767 (which EPA had co-sponsored and helped pay for as part of the NAPAP research) contains emissions data the utilities had previously submitted.

25 Thus, given a 1980 baseline estimate for utility SO_2 emissions of 17.4 million tons minus the required reduction of 8.5 million tons, the amount left over after a 10 million-ton reduction is achieved was 8.9 million tons of allowances in the market.

26 For a description of this policy formulation process, see: Raymond, L. (2003). Private Rights in Public Resources: Equity and Property Allocation in Market Based Environmental Policy. Washington, Resources for the Future.

27 These rhetorical criteria translated into including in Phase I all units whose 1985 emission rates exceeded 2.5 lb/MMBtu and whose generation capacity exceeded 100 MW.

28 Title IV allows 3.5 million extra "bonus" allowances to be allocated in Phase I as an incentive for utilities to choose to build scrubbers that reduce SO_2 emissions by 90–95 percent. Some bonus allowances (530,000) will continue to be allocated in each of the years from 2000 to 2009. Bonus allowances will not exist from 2010 forward.

29 These measures do not add up to the 8.9 million tons overall emissions cap. These basic allowances are then supplemented by various bonus allowances, specified in Sections 405 (b),(c), (d), and (h) and 406, and taken from a Phase II reserve. The bonus allowances are allocated for the first ten years of Phase II. In addition, EPA is required to allocate 50,000

bonus allowances annually above the cap to units listed in Table A and located in ten Midwestern, Appalachian, and Southern states. Certain units in high-growth states also receive bonus allowances, pursuant to Section 405(i). See: Martineau, Robert J. Jr. and David P. Novello. Clean Air Act Handbook (1997), pp. 374–375.

30 Section 405 of the CAA establishes an emissions rate of 1.2 lb/mbBtu multiplied by the baseline fuel consumption.

31 Section 401 of the CAA states that the purpose of Title IV is to reduce SO_2 and NO_X emissions from "affected sources" in the contiguous United States. Section 402 establishes that an "affected source" is a source comprised of one or more "affected units." There are "existing utility units" and "new units." A "unit" is a fossil fuel-fired combustion devise, and an "existing" unit is one that commenced commercial operation before November 15, 1990, the enactment date of the CAA amendments. Likewise, a new unit is one that commenced operations after this date.

32 Cogeneration is the production of heat energy and electrical or mechanical power from the same fuel in the same facility. A typical cogeneration facility produces electricity and steam from industrial process use. As defined in Smeloff, Ed and Peter Asmus. Reinventing Electric Utilities. Washington, D.C.: Island Press (1997).

33 For a complete description, see http://www.epa.gov/airmarkets/arp/optin/index.html.

34 Voluntary participation is profitable to companies outside the program scope when the revenues from selling extra allowances derived from emissions reductions exceed the combined cost of the emissions reductions and the costs of participating in the Opt-in Program. Non-affected units participating in the program are subject to comply with the same or similar provisions of the allowance trading program.

35 For detailed information see http://www.epa.gov/airmarkets/auctions/factsheet.html.

36 Exchanges establish a fully functioning marketplace for commodity trading. They usually require standard contracts for transactions, which facilitate trades.

37 Because EPA delegated the administration of auctions to the Chicago Board of Trade, as opposed to contracting with CBOT, CBOT was not compensated by EPA for its services nor allowed to charge fees. CBOT's service was delivered pro bono. Moreover, CBOT was not allowed to bid for allowances in the auctions nor transfer allowances in the EPA Allowance Tracking System. Only the administrative functions of the auction program were delegated to CBOT; all other aspects of the auctions remained with EPA, as did all allowance transfer functions.

38 The Chicago Board of Trade, established in 1848, was the world's oldest derivatives (futures and futures options) exchange, until it merged with the Chicago Mercantile Exchange (CME) in 2007 to become the CME Group. For more information about CBOT see http://www.cmegroup.com/.

39 For more information see: http://nymex.greenfutures.com/notices/ntm138.html.

40 EPA lists most of the brokers in the ARP market at: http://www.epa.gov/airmarkt/trading/buying.html.

41 See: http://camddataandmaps.epa.gov/gdm/index.cfm?fuseaction=iss.progressresults.

42 According to EPA quality assurance rules on CEMS, the operator must perform periodic performance evaluations of the equipment, including daily calibration tests, daily interference tests for flow monitors, and semi-annual (or annual) relative accuracy test audits (RATA) and bias tests. The owner or operator must develop and implement a written quality assurance/quality control plan for each system. The quality control plan must include complete, step-by-step procedures and test operations to check calibration adjustments and to perform preventive maintenance, audits, and record-keeping and reporting. The quality assurance plan must include procedures for conducting periodic performance tests.

43 See EPA FAQ on the Acid Rain Program's allowance trading: http://www.epa.gov/airmarkets/trading/factsheet.html. For a common classification of allowance trades, see:

Bailey, Elizabeth M. Allowance trading activity and state regulatory rulings: Evidence from the US Acid Rain Program, Working Paper 96–002, Massachusetts Institute of Technology, CEEPR (March 1996).

44 Some price information sources are EPA's Annual March auction, Emissions Exchange Corporation (EX), Cantor Fitzgerald (CF), and Fieldstone (EATX), trade press reports such as Point Carbon, *The Wall Street Journal*, and Energy Daily.

45 Measurements are expressed in pounds per million British thermal units (lbs/Btu), pounds per hour (lbs/hr), or such other form as EPA may prescribe by regulations under Section 412 of the CAA.

46 This term was first introduced by Hagel III, John and Marc Singer in Net Worth: Shaping Markets When Customers Make the Rules. Cambridge, MA: Harvard Business School Press (1999).

47 See: http://www.epa.gov/airmarkets/business/industry/cbs.html.

48 At the time, some observers believed that the discriminatory pricing feature of the annual auction created a misleading downward bias. However, as allowance prices in the private market and the auction evolved, it was shown that this was not the case.

49 See for instance: Carlson, Curtis et al., Sulfur-Dioxide Control By Electric Utilities: What Are the Gains from Trade? Resources for the Future: RFF Discussion Paper 98–440 REV (July 1998), Ellerman, A. Denny et al. Emissions Trading under the US Acid Rain Program: Evaluation of Compliance Costs and Allowance Market Performance, Center for Energy and Environmental Policy Research, MIT Cambridge, MA. (1997); and Lange, Ian and Allen S. Bellas. "The 1990 Clean Air Act and the Implicit Price of Sulfur in Coal," The B.E. Journal of Economic Analysis and Policy, Volume 7, Art. 1 Issue 1 The Berkeley Electronic Press (2007), pp. 1–23.

50 See for instance: www.cleanairconservancy.org, www.usm.maine.edu/~pos/arrf.htm, www.adirondackcouncil.org and www.ert.net.

6 Local market-based environmental policy

1 Chemicals that evaporate easily and contain hydrogen and carbon (with the exception of methane) are known as volatile organic compounds (VOCs). Hundreds of these compounds are present in the atmosphere. In the presence of sunlight and nitrogen oxides (NO_X), volatile organic compounds react to form ground-level ozone (O_3), a component of smog. Fossil fuel deposits, including oil sands, volcanoes, vegetation, and bacteria are all sources of VOCs. Man-made volatile organic compound emissions come from transportation, solvent use, industrial processes, and gasoline evaporation. Gasoline evaporation can occurs when vehicles are being filled at service stations or when transfers of gasoline are made. Other VOCs are released when oil-based paints or cleaning solvents are used.

2 This decision led to the indefinite reinstatement of command-and-control regulation for VOC sources (SCAQMD 1993, EX-14). Public discussions on how to implement the VOC component of the program continued. In 1995, SCAQMD released a proposal to incorporate VOCs into RECLAIM. Business groups strongly opposed the proposal given the lack of regulatory precedent. Environmental groups, opposed for different reasons, believed that excessive VOC emissions allowances would have been created due to the lack of information on emission rates and control technology. The VOC RECLAIM project was ended in January 1996 (http://www.aqmd.gov/news1/Archives/vocr.html).

3 For an in-depth discussion of the technical and political arguments behind establishing the initial baselines for RECLAIM, see: Hall, J.V. and A.L. Walton. "A Case Study in Pollution Markets: Dismissal Science vs. Dismal Reality," *Contemporary Economic Policy*, Vol. 14 (1996), pp. 67–78.

4 For more on how the emissions rates were established, see: Fromm, O. and B. Hansjürgens. "Emissions Trading in Theory and Practice: An Analysis of EPA's

Emissions Trading Program," *Environment and Planning C—Government and Policy*, Vol. 14, No. 3 (1996), pp. 367–384.

5 South Coast Air Quality Management District. "Over a Dozen Years of RECLAIM Implementation: Key Lessons Learned in California's First Air Pollution Cap-and-Trade Program." June 2007, p. 2.

6 RECLAIM, White Paper, 2001, p. 23

7 For more on the initial steps taken to implement RECLAIM, see: Carlson, D. and Anne Scholtz, "RECLAIM: Lessons from Southern California for Environmental Markets," *Journal of Environmental Law and Practice*, Vol. 1, No. 4 (1994), pp. 15–26.

8 Annual RECLAIM Audit Report for the 2006 Compliance Year (March 7, 2008).

9 See Cantor and Fitzgerald's website http://environmental-center.com/consulting/auction.htm and www.justice-assoc.com.

10 See for instance: Business Wire, "Business industry groups cite harmful effects of SCAQMD's RECLAIM program on region's economy" (August 17, 1993).

11 See for instance: Abate Technologies Internationals, Inc., http://abatech.com/services.htm.

12 RECLAIM fees apply to the following subdivisions: Facility Permit, Facility Permit Amendment, Change of Operating Condition, Change of Operator, Annual Operating Permit, Transaction Registration, RECLAIM Pollutant Emissions, Duplicate Permits, Reissued Permits, RECLAIM Breakdown Emissions, and Non-Tradable Allocation Credit Mitigations.

13 California Health & Safety Code, Section 42400 et seq. and Section 42402 et seq.

14 New source rules allow for instance new independent power producers (IPPs) or other industries to build, modify, or expand their plants.

15 SCAQMD, Annual RECLAIM Audit Report for the 2006 Compliance Year (March 7, 2008).

16 The California Health and Safety Code (HSC) Section 39620 (c)(1) and (c)(4) requires that market-based permitting programs "result in equivalent emission reductions while spending fewer resources and while maintaining or enhancing the state's economy when compared with the command-and-control system." The law specifically requires that the emissions trading programs should result in fewer costs and "will not result in a greater loss of jobs or more significant shifts from higher to lower skilled jobs, on an overall district wide basis." Therefore, HSC Section 40728.5 (b)(1), (b)(2), and (b)(3) required SCAQMD to perform an assessment of socioeconomic impacts of the proposed and/or amended rule. Moreover, the assessment included affected industries, the range of probable costs to these industries, and the impact of the rule on employment to the affected economy as stated in Section 40440.8. California State Assembly Bill 1054 (1992).

17 For instance, EXELE Information Systems, Inc. offers its software "EXELE RECLAIM" to more than 200 sources at several RECLAIM facilities. The features highlighted to promote its information management product are reliability, flexibility, auditability, functionality, accessibility, and compliance. See http://www.exele.com/cems/cems.htm.

7 Interstate market-based environmental policy

1 Connecticut, Delaware, Maine, Maryland, Massachusetts, New Hampshire, New Jersey, New York, Pennsylvania, Rhode Island, Vermont, Virginia, and the District of Columbia.

2 Virginia rejected the 1994 MOU primarily for political reasons – analysts believe there wasn't a political desire in the state to commit to making the reductions proposed under the OTC program. Read the MOU here: http://www.dep.state.pa.us/DEP/DEPUTATE/airwaste/aq/transport/otc/noxmou.pdf

3 See the Clean Air Markets Division web page for more info: http://www.epa.gov/airmarkets/basic.html.

4 A GIS computer application is used for mapping and analyzing geographic data. GIS combines different types of data through a "layering" technique. This approach allows spatial analysis of data. GIS can help validate theories and explore trends and patterns of pollution using emissions, plant monitoring locations, and demographic/health data. For example, a policy analyst could buffer all plant locations by specified distances to examine how emissions relate to health in surrounding populations. For more information, see http://www.epa.gov/airmarkt/maps/c-map.html.

5 Selective catalytic reduction is a post-combustion NO_X reduction technology in which ammonia is added to the flue gas, which then passes through layers of catalysts. This technology is capable of reducing NO_X emissions by 80–90 percent.

6 Open Access is the ability of electricity generators to gain access to the nation's transmission and distribution system so as to compete with other generators (including owners of the transmission and distribution networks) for customers.

7 For authorization power, see CAA 40 CFR Sections 1504.1–1504.3 and NEPA 42 USC Section 7609(b).

8 63 Federal Register Section 57356 (October 27, 1998). The full name of the ruling: "Finding of Significant Contribution and Rulemaking for Certain States in the Ozone Transport Assessment Group Region for Purposes of Reducing Regional Transport of Ozone." The entire rulemaking history of the SIP Call can be found here: http://www.epa.gov/ttn/naaqs/ozone/rto/rto.html.

9 EPA. Finding of Significant Contribution and Rulemaking for Certain States in the Ozone Transport Assessment Group Region for Purposes of Reducing Regional Transport Ozone. Rule, 63 Federal Register Sections 57356–57538 (October 27, 1998).

10 64 FR Section 28250 (May 25, 1999).

11 65 FR Section 2674 (January 18, 2000).

12 For the history of the NO_X Budget Trading Program and the NO_X SIP Call (2003–2008) see: http://www.epa.gov/airmarkets/progsregs/nox/sip.html.

13 Once Massachusetts submits an SIP that achieves the same level of reduction as the 126 action, and from the same set of sources, EPA removes the 126 finding for all sources under this rule.

14 See: SO_2 Market Slumps on EPA Plan, Environmental Finance (July 8, 2010) http://www.environmental-finance.com/news/view/1230.

15 See: First trades complete replacement SO_2 and NO_x market (September 5, 2011) http://www.environmental-finance.com/news/view/1953.

8 International market-based environmental policy

1 Pacala S. and R. Socolow. "Stabilization Wedges: Solving the Climate Problem for the Next 50 Years with Current Technologies." *Science*, Vol. 305, No. 5686, pp. 968–972 (13 August 2004)

2 International Energy Agency. *World Energy Outlook*. 2011

3 Austen, Ian. Canada is Slow to Act on Emissions, Audit Warns. *The New York Times*. Green, A Blog About Energy and the Environment. Posting. May 8, 2012, 6:30pm. http://green.blogs.nytimes.com/2012/05/08/report-upbraids-canadian-government-on-emissions/?pagemode=print.

4 New Zealand Press Release. Tim Groser, Minister of Climate Change Issues, Minister welcomes South Korea ETS and Linking Study (May 4, 2012). http://www.scoop.co.nz/stories/PA1205/S00093/minister-welcomes-sth-korea-ets-and-linking-study.htm.

5 Australia–New Zealand Joint Media Release (December 5, 2011): http://www.climatechange.gov.au/~/media/Files/minister/combet/2011/media/december/MR2011 1205B. pdf.

6 http://op.bna.com/env.nsf/id/thyd-873n4z/$File/India%20Clean%20Energy%20Cess %20Rules%202010.pdf.

7 Oral Statement by Chris Huhne, Secretary of State for Energy and Climate Change, on the outcomes of Durban COP17 to the UK Parliament, (12 December 2011).

8 Hsiang Solomon, Kyle C. Meng and Mark A. Cane. "Civil conflicts are associated with the global climate," *Nature*. Vol. 476, (25 August 2011), pp. 438–441.

9 Oserkes, Naomi and Eric M. Conway. "Merchants of Doubt: How a Handful of Scientists Obscured the Truth on Issues from Tobacco Smoke to Global Warming. Bloomsbury Press (2010), p. 272.

10 Halons are defined as bromofluorocarbons.

11 See: United Nations, http://unfccc.int/essential_background/items/6825.php.

12 An EU Directive is a regional policy instrument. It is a legal instruction which is binding on all Member States but which must be implemented through national legislation within a prescribed time-scale.

13 Several studies indicated some stimulus to the economy and modest job creation from climate policy action in California. See for instance: Roland-Holst, David. "Energy Efficiency, Innovation, and Job Creation in California," Center for Energy, Resources and Economic Sustainability. Research Papers on Energy, Resources and Economic Sustainability. University of California, Berkeley (October 2008).

14 Mary Nichols. Chairman. California Air Resources Board. Statement to the California Senate Select Committee on Environment. March 27, 2012.

References

Ackerman, Bruce A. and William T. Hassler. *Clean Coal/Dirty Air*. New Haven: Yale University Press (1981).

Aldy, Joseph E. and Robert N. Stavins. *Using the Market to Address Climate Change: Insights from Theory and Experience*. Faculty Research Working Paper Series. Harvard Kennedy School of Government. RWP11–38. Cambridge, MA (September 2011), p. 1.

American Energy Innovation Council. *Top Business Leaders Issue New Report on Critical Role of Government Investment in Energy Tech Innovation*, Retrieved from: http://www.american energyinnovation.org/catalyzing-press-release (accessed on September 22, 2011).

Anderson, Barry and Corrado Di Maria. "Abatement and Allocation in the Pilot Phase of the EU ETS," *Environmental Resource Economy*, Vol. 48, No. 1 (2011), pp. 83–103.

Annex I. *Expert Group on the UNFCCC. Workshop on: International GHG Emission Trading*. Supported by the OECD and the IEA Secretariats. Szentendre, Hungary (April 17–18, 1997), p. 4.

Argus. *Lawsuit filed against California cap-and-trade offsets*. (March 28, 2012). Retrieved from: http://www.argusmedia.com/pages/NewsBody.aspx?id=791786&menu=yes.

Arrow, K. "Control in Large Organizations," in *Essays in the Theory of Risk-Bearing*. Chicago: Markham Publishing Co. (1971).

Aulisi, Andrew, et al. *Greenhouse Gas Emissions Trading in the US States, Observations and Lessons from the OTC NOX Budget Program*. Washington, D.C.: World Resources Institute, (2005), p. 1.

Bakken, Henry, H. "Futures Trading—Origin, Development and Present Economic Status," in Gaumnitz, Erwin A. (ed.), *Futures Trading Seminar, Vol. III, A Commodity Forum for College Teachers of Economics*. Madison, WI: Mimir Publishers, Inc. (1966), pp. xv+264

Bardach, E. and R. Kagan. *Going by the Book: The Problems of Regulatory Unreasonableness*. Philadelphia, PA: Temple University Press (1982).

Barker, T., P. Ekins, and T. Foxon, "Macroeconomic Effects of Efficiency Policies for Energy-Intensive Industries: The Case of the UK Climate Change Agreements, 2000–2010," *Energy Economics*, Vol. 29, No. 4 (2007), pp. 760–778.

Baron, Richard, R. Lacombe, P. Quirion, J. Reinaud, R. Trotignon, and N. Walker. *Competitiveness under the EU Emissions Trading Scheme*. Working paper. Association for Promoting Research into the Economics of Carbon. London, UK (2008).

Baumol, W.J. and W.E. Oates. "The Use of Standards and Prices for Protection of the Environment," *Swedish Journal of Economics*, Vol. LXXXIII (March 1971), pp. 42–54.

Baumol, W.J. and W.E. Oates. *The Theory of Environmental Policy*. Cambridge, UK: Cambridge University Press (1993), pp. 177, 257, 279.

Baumol, W.J. and W.E. Oates. *The Theory of Environmental Policy*. 2nd Edition. New York: Cambridge University Press (1988).

Baylor, Jill S. "Acid Rain Impacts on Utility Plans for Plant Life Extension," *Public Utilities Fortnightly*, Vol. 125, No. 5 (March 1, 1990), p. 24.

Benedick, Richard E. *Ozone Diplomacy, New Directions in Safeguarding the Planet*. Boston, MA: Harvard University Press (1998).

Bloomberg. (2012). Retrieved from: https://www.bnef.com/PressReleases/view/206.

Bohi, Douglas R. and Dallas Burtraw. "Avoiding Regulatory Gridlock in the Acid Rain Program," *Journal of Policy Analysis and Management*, Vol. 10, No. 4 (1991), p. 676.

Bohm, Peter and C.S. Russell. "Comparative Analysis of Alternative Policy Instruments," in A.V. Kneese and J.L. Sweeney (eds.) *Handbook of Natural Resource and Energy Economics*, Vol. 1. Amsterdam, New York, Oxford: North Holland (1985).

Bollier, D. and J. Claybrook. *Freedom from Harm: The Civilizing Influence of Health, Safety and Environmental Regulation*. New York: Public Citizen (1986).

Bowen, Alex and James Rydge. *Climate-Change Policy in the United Kingdom*. Economics Department Working Papers, No. 886. Organisation for Economic Co-operation and Development (August 2011).

Bravender, Robin. "Acid rain credits nosedive on CAIR concerns," *Greenwire* (March 27, 2009). See www.eenews.net/public/Greenwire/2009/03/27/4?page_type=print.

Brealey, R.A. and S.C. Meyers. *Principles of Corporate Finance*. 5th Edition. New York: McGraw Hill (1996), p. 711.

Broder, John M. "'Cap and Trade' Loses Its Standing as Energy Policy of Choice," *New York Times* (March 25, 2010), p. 13A.

Brown, L., et al. *The State of the World 2001*. New York: Worldwatch Institute (2001).

Browner, Carol. *Common Sense Strategies for Public Health and Environmental Protection*. San Francisco, CA: Remarks to Commonwealth Club, (March 29, 1996).

Bruce, J.P., H. Lee, and E.F. Haites. *Climate Change 1995: Economic and Social Dimensions of Climate Change. An Intergovernmental Panel on Climate Change Publication*. Cambridge, UK: Cambridge University Press (1996).

Bruvoll, A. and B.M. Larsen. "Greenhouse Gas Emissions in Norway: Do Carbon Taxes Work?" *Energy Policy*, Vol. 32 (2004), pp. 493–505.

Bryner, G.C. *Blue Skies, Green Politics*. Washington, D.C.: Congressional Quarterly Press (1995), pp. 101, 115–169.

Buchner, B., C. Carraro, and A.D. Ellerman. *The Allocation of European Union Allowances: Lessons, Unifying Themes and General Principles*. Discussion papers, no. 5843. London, UK: Centre for Economic Policy Research. (2006).

Burtraw, D., D.A. Evans, A. Krupnick, K. Palmer, and R. Toth. "Economics of Pollution Trading for SO_2 and NO_x," *Annual Review of Environment and Resources*, Vol. 30 (2005), pp. 253–290.

Burtraw, Dallas. "Innovation Under the Tradable Sulfur Dioxide Emission Permits Program in the US Electricity Sector". Discussion Paper 00–38, Washington, D.C.: Resources for the Future (September 2000), p. ii.

Burtraw, Dallas. Retrieved from: http://www.rff.org/rff/documents/rff-dp-98-28-rev.pdf (1998).

Burtraw, Dallas. "The SO_2 Emissions Trading Program: Cost Savings Without Allowance Trades," *Contemporary Economic Policy*, Vol. XIV (April 1996), pp. 79–94.

Burtraw, Dallas. "Written Testimony to the Subcommittee on Energy and Air Quality," *Senior Fellow, Resources for the Future. For Committee on Energy and Commerce*. Washington, D.C.: US House of Representatives (March 29, 2007).

Burtraw, Dallas and Sarah Jo. Szambelan "US Emissions Trading Markets for SO_2 and NO_X," Discussion Paper. RFF DP 09–40. Washington, D.C.: Resources for the Future (2009). Retrieved from: http://www.rff.org/RFF/Documents/RFF-DP-09-40.pdf.

Burtraw, Dallas, et al. "The Impact of Electricity Restructuring on NOx Emissions Affecting the Environment in Maryland," *Draft Final Report Resources for the Future*, Washington, D.C. (September 25, 1998).

Bush, George, H.W. *Announcement of the Clean Air Proposal*. Washington, D.C.: The White House (June 12, 1989).

Bush, George, H.W. *Letter to Congressional Leaders on Legislation to Amend Clean Air Act*. Washington, D.C.: The White House (September 26, 1990).

Bush, George, W. *The Clear Skies Initiative Announcement*. Office of the Press Secretary. Washington, D.C.: The White House (February 14, 2002).

Caisse dés Depôts. *Closing the door to fraud in the EU ETS*. Climate Brief. CDC Climate Research. No. 4. (February 2011). Retrieved from: http://www.cdcclimat.com/IMG//pdf/11-02_climate_ brief_4_-_closing_the_door_to_fraud_in_the_eu_ets.pdf.

Calel, Raphael. "Market-Based Instruments and Technology Choices: A Synthesis," Grantham Research Institute on Climate Change and the Environment, Working Paper No. 57 (August 2011).

California Air Resources Board. California's Climate Plan. (2010a). Retrieved from: http://www.arb.ca.gov/cc/cleanenergy/clean_fs2.htm.

California Air Resources Board. Offset Program Update. (2010b). Retrieved from: http://www.arb.ca.gov/cc/capandtrade/meetings/062210/offset_program_update.pdf.

California Air Resources Board. Supplement to the AB 32 Scoping Plan Functional Equivalent Document (2011). Retrieved from: http://www.arb.ca.gov/cc/scopingplan/document/Supplement_to_SP_FED.pdf.

California Office of the Governor. Gov. Schwarzenegger Signs Executive Order to Advance State's Renewable Energy Portfolio Standard to 33 Per cent by 2020. *Press Release*. (September 15, 2009). Retrieved from: http://gov.ca.gov/press-release/13273.

California Secretary of State. Qualified Statewide Ballot Measures. (2010). Retrieved from: http://www.sos.ca.gov/elections/ballot-measures/qualified-ballot-measures.htm.

Carbon Trust. *The European Emissions Trading Scheme: Implications for Industrial Competitiveness*. London (2004).

Carlson, Ann. Legal Planet The Environmental Law and Policy Blog [Internet]. University of California Berkeley/Los Angeles. (August 5, 2011). Retrieved from: http://legalplanet.wordpress.com/2011/08/05/epa-to-continue-emissions-trading-in-place-of-clean-air-interstate-rule/.

Carlson, L. *NESCAUM/MARAM NOX Budget Model Rule*. Boston, MA: Northeast States for Coordinated Air Use Management (1996).

Center for American Progress. *The Proof is in the Pudding. Regional Greenhouse Gas Initiative Shows Pollution Pricing Works* (2010). Retrieved from: http://www.americanprogress.org/issues/2010/03/rggi_roadmap.html.

Centre for Global Studies. *Lessons from the Montreal Protocol. Colloquium on the 10th Anniversary of the Montreal Protocol. University of Victoria*. Advisory Committee and National Organizing Committee, Canada. (1997). See summary prepared by the Centre of Global Studies at http://www.globalcentres.org/cgcp/english/html_documents/ads/coll-e.htm.

Chan, Gabriel, Robert Stavins, Robert Stow and Richard Sweeney. *The SO2 Allowance Trading System and the Clean Air Act Amendments of 1990: Reflections on Twenty Years of Policy Innovation*. Cambridge, MA: Harvard Economics Program (2012).

Change.gov. (2010). Retrieved from: http://change.gov/newsroom/entry/president_elect_obama_promises_new_chapter_on_climate_change/.

Change.gov. *President-elect Obama Promises* "New Chapter" on Climate Change. (November 18, 2008). Retrieved from: http://change.gov/newsroom/entry/president_elect_obama_promises_new_chapter_on_climate_change/%20target=.

Channon, A. "Journalist Gelbspan Addresses Reality of Climate Change," *The Brandeis Hoot* (April 18, 2008). Web.

Charles River Associates. *Analysis of the California ARB's Scoping Plan and Related Policy Insights* (2010). Retrieved from: http://www.crai.com/uploadedFiles/analysis-of-AB 32-scoping-plan.pdf.

Chartier, Daniel. "Trading NOX in the North-east USA," *Environmental Finance* (December 1999/January 2000), p. 23.

Chazan, Guy. "Shale gas boom helps slash US emissions," *Financial Times* (May 23, 2012). Retrieved from: http://www.ft.com/cms/s/0/3aa19200-a4eb-11e1-b421-00144feabdc0.html#axzz1wqjxsk7n.

Chestnut, L. and D.M. Mills. "A Fresh Look at the Benefits and Costs of the US Acid Rain Program," *Journal of Environmental Management*, Vol. 77, No. 3 (2005), pp. 252–266.

Chicago Climate Futures Exchange. *The Sulfur Dioxide Emission Allowance Trading Program: Market Architecture, Market Dynamics and Pricing* (2004). Retrieved from: http://www.ccfe.com/education_ccfe/SO2_Background_Drivers_Pricing_PDF.pdf

Climate Action Reserve. *About Us.* (2010). Retrieved from: http://www.climateaction reserve.org/about-us/.

Clinton, William J. *Meet the Challenge of Global Warming.* Office of the Press Secretary. Washington, D.C.: The White House (November 11, 2000).

CME. Retrieved from: http://cmegroup.mediaroom.com/index.php?s=43&item=2879& pagetemplate=article (accessed on May 13, 1997).

Coase, H.R. "The Problem of the Social Cost," *The Journal of Law & Economics*, Vol. III (October 1960), pp. 1–44.

Committee for the National Institute for the Environment. *Air Quality II: EPA's Revised NAAQS for Ozone* (April 2002). Retrieved from: http://www.cnie.org/nle/air-16a.html.

Congress of the United States. *Acid Rain and Transported Pollutants, Implications for Public Policy. Office of Technological Assessment.* Washington, D.C.: Congress of the United States (1985), p. 140.

Congressional Record. S. Rep. No. 228, 101st Cong., 1st Session 319 (1989).

Congressional Research Service. "Carbon Tax and Greenhouse Gas Control Options and Considerations for Congress" by Jonathan L. Ramseur and Larry Parker. CRS 7–5700, R40242. (March 10, 2009).

Contract from America. *Contract from America.* (2010). Retrieved from: http://www.thecontract.org/the-contract-from-america/.

Cook, B.J. *Bureaucratic Politics and Regulatory Reform: The EPA and Emissions Trading.* New York: Greenwood Press (1988), pp. 35, 38–39, 45.

Crocker, T. "Structuring of Atmospheric Pollution Control Systems," in H. Wolozin (ed.) *The Economics of Air Pollution.* New York: W.W. Norton (1966).

Dales, J.H. *Pollution, Property and Prices.* Toronto, Canada: University Press (1968).

Dao, James. "Acid Rain Law Found to Fail in Adirondacks," *The New York Times.* Front Page (March 27, 2000).

Davis, L.E. and D. North. *Institutional Change and American Economic Growth.* Cambridge, MA: Cambridge University Press (1971), pp. 5–6.

Deason, Jeffrey A. and Lee S. Friedman. Journal of Policy Analysis and Management, Vol. 29, No, 4 (2010), pp. 821–853.

Demetz, P. *Marx, Engels und die Dichter. Ein Kapitel deutscher Literaturgeschichte.* Frankfurt/M., Berlin: Ullstein (1969).

Dixit, A.K. *The Making of Economic Policy: A Transaction-Cost Politics Perspective.* Cambridge, MA: The MIT Press (1996), pp. 10, 31.

Doolittle, D. "Underestimating Ozone Depletion: The Meandering Road to the Montreal Protocol and Beyond," *Ecology Law Quarterly,* Vol. 16 (1989), p. 407.

Downs, Anthony. "Up and Down with Ecology: The Issue-Attention Cycle," *Public Interest,* Vol. 28 (Summer 1972), p. 27.

Drury, Richard, Michael E. Belliveau, J.Scott Kuhn, and Shipra Bansal. "Pollution Trading and Environmental Injustice: Los Angeles' Failed Experiment in Air Quality Policy," *Duke Environmental Law & Policy Forum,* Vol. 9, No. 232 (Spring 1999), pp. 231–289.

Dudek, Daniel. "Emissions Trading: Environmental Perestroika or Flimflam?" *Electricity Journal,* Vol. 2 (1989), pp. 32–43.

Dwyer, J.P. "California's Tradable Emissions Policy and Greenhouse Gas Control," *Journal of Energy Engineering,* Vol. 118, No. 2 (August 1992), p. 59.

Dwyer, J.P. *Lessons from California's Tradeable Emissions Policy and Its Application to the Control of Greenhouse Gases.* Berkeley: Institute of Governmental Studies, University of California (1992), p. 60.

Dwyer, J.P. "The Use of Market Incentives in Controlling Air Pollution: California's Marketable Permits Program," *Ecology Law Quarterly,* Vol. 20 (1993), pp. 104, 106, 109–112.

Editorial. "Apostle of Change Returns to Earth," *Financial Times.* (November 4, 2010), p. 10.

Ekins, Paul and Ben Etheridge. "The Environmental and Economic Impacts of The UK Climate Change Agreements," *Energy Policy,* Vol. 34, No. 15 (2006), pp. 2071–2086.

Ellerman, A.Denny. "The US SO2 Cap-and-Trade Program". *Proceedings of the OECD Workshop on Ex Post Evaluation of Tradable Permits: Methodological and Policy Issues.* Paris: OECD (January 21–22, 2003).

Ellerman A.D. and B.K. Buchner. "Over-Allocation or Abatement? A Preliminary Analysis of the EU ETS Based on the 2005–06 Emissions Data," *Environment Resources of Economy,* Vol. 41, No. 2 (2008), pp. 267–287.

Ellerman, A.D., and Paul L. Joskow. (2008). Retrieved from: http://www.c2es.org/doc Uploads/EU-ETS-In-Perspective-Report.pdf

Ellerman, A.D., Frank J. Convery and Christian de Perthuis. *Pricing Carbon: The European Union Emissions Trading Scheme.* Cambridge, UK: Cambridge University Press (2010), p. 20.

Ellerman A. D., Mort D. Webster, John Parsons, Henry D. Jacoby and Meghan McGuinness. (2008). Retrieved from: http://web.mit.edu/ceepr/www/publications/DDCF.pdf.

Ellerman, A.Denny, et al. "CO2 Emissions Limits: Economic Adjustments and the Distribution of Burdens," *The Energy Journal,* Vol. 18, No. 3 (1997), pp. 5–48.

Ellerman, A. Denny, et al. *Markets for Clean Air: The US Acid Rain Program.* Cambridge, UK; New York: Cambridge University Press (2000).

Emissions Trading Education Initiative. (1999). Retrieved from: http://www.wbcsdcement. org/pdf/tf1/eteihandbook.pdf.

Energy Information Administration. *Derivatives and Risk Management in the Petroleum, Natural Gas and Electricity.* Report SR/SMG/2002–01. US Department of Energy. Washington, D.C. (October 2002).

Environmental Defense. *From Obstacle to Opportunity: How Acid Rain Emissions Trading is Delivering Cleaner Air.* Washington, D.C.: Environmental Defense (September 2000), pp. 1–4.

Environmental Defense. *Solutions*, Vol. 36, No. 3 (2005), p. 1.

Environmental Finance. (September 5, 2011). Retrieved from: http://www.environmental-finance.com/news/view/1953.

European Commission. (2011). Retrieved from: http://europa.eu/rapid/pressReleasesAction.do?reference=IP/11/581

European Commission. (2012). Retrieved from: http://ec.europa.eu/clima/news/articles/news_2012082801_en.htm.

European Commission. *Emissions Trading: EU ETS Emissions Fall More than 11% in 2009.* (May 18, 2010). Retrieved from: http://europa.eu/rapid/pressReleasesAction.do?reference=IP/10/576.

European Commission. *Green Paper on Greenhouse Gas Emissions Trading within the European Union*, COM(2000) 0087 final. Brussels (August 3, 2000), p. 4.

European Community. *Directive 96/61/EC on Integrated Pollution Prevention and Control* (2009). Retrieved from: http://ec.europa.eu/environment/air/pollutants/stationary/ippc/index.htm.

European Parliament and Council. *Amending Directive 2003/87/EC Establishing a Scheme for Greenhouse Gas Emission Allowance Trading within the Community, in Respect of the Kyoto Protocol's Project Mechanisms.* Directive 2004/101/EC (October 27, 2004).

European Parliament and Council. Directive 2009/29/EC of the European Parliament and of the Council of 23 April 2009 amending Directive 2003/87/EC so as to improve and extend the greenhouse gas emission allowance trading scheme of the Community (June 25, 2009).

European Parliament. *EU Emission Trading Scheme: Use Permit Revenues to Fund Climate Change Protection* (July 2008). Retrieved from: http://www.europarl.europa.eu/sides/getDoc.do?pubRef=-//EP//TEXT+IM-PRESS+20081006IPR38798+0+DOC+XML+V0//EN.

European Parliament. *Greenhouse Gas Emission Allowance Trading System I - P6_TA(2008)0610.* (2008) Retrieved from: http://www.europarl.europa.eu/sides/getDoc.do?pubRef=-//EP//TEXT TA P6-TA-2008-0610 0 DOC XML V0//EN>.

Evolution Markets website. Retrieved from: http://new.evomarkets.com/index.php?page=Emissions_Markets-Markets-NOx_Seasonal_Allowances. Information updated on (February 8, 2009).

Evolution Markets. *Annual SO$_2$ Allowance Auction Clears at Record Low.* New York: White Plains (2012). Retrieved from: http://new.evomarkets.com/desks/emissions/post/412/.

Evolution Markets. *Southern California NO$_X$ RECLAIM Trading Credits Program* (2002). Retrieved from: http://evomarkets.com.

Evolution Markets. *The New RECLAIM* (2012). Retrieved from: http://new.evomarkets.com/index.php?page=Emissions_Markets-Markets-Regional_Emissions_Credits-California_Emissions-New_RECLAIM.

Fabozzi, F.J. and F. Modigliani. *Capital Markets, Institutions and Instruments.* Upper Saddle River, NJ: Prentice Hall (1996), pp. 11, 146.

Farrell, Alex. "The NOX Budget: A Look at the First Year," *Electricity Journal*, Vol. 13, No. 2 (2000), pp. 83–93.

Farrell, Alex. Talk at the University of California at Berkeley's Energy Resources Group Seminar Session (April 18, 2000).

Farrell, Alex and M. Granger Morgan. *Multilateral Emission Trading: Lessons from Interstate NOX Pollution.* Pittsburgh: Carnegie Mellon University (2000).

Farrell, Alex, Roger Raufer, and Robert Carter. "The NOX Budget: Market-Based Control of Tropospheric Ozone in the Northeastern United States," *Energy and Resource Economics*, Vol. 21, No. 2 (1998), pp. 103–124.

Federal Energy Regulatory Commission. (1995). *Annual Report*. Washington, D.C.: FERC.

Fomler, H. and E. van Ierland. *Valuation Methods and Policy Making in Environmental Economics*. Studies in Environmental Science 36. Amsterdam, The Netherlands: Elsevier Science Publishers (1989), pp. 109–110.

Foster, V. and R. Hahn. *ET in LA: Looking Back to the Future*. ENRP Project 88/Round II. Project Report P-94–01. Harvard University. MA: HKSG (January 1994), p. 21.

Franciosi, R.I., et al. "An Experimental Investigation of the Hahn-Noll Revenue Neutral Auction for Emissions Licenses," *Journal of Environmental Economics and Management*, Vol. 24 (1993), pp. 1–24.

Freeman, A.M. *The Measurement of Environmental and Resource Values: Theory and Methods*. Washington, D.C.: Resources for the Future (1993).

Friedman, L. "Peanuts Envy?" *Journal of Policy Analysis and Management*, Vol. 18 (Spring 1999), p. 217.

Friedman, L. *Microeconomic Policy Analysis*. New York: McGraw Hill (1984), pp. 561–562.

Friedman, L.S. *The Microeconomics of Public Policy Analysis*. Oxford and Princeton: Princeton University Press (2002), pp. 641, 648.

Friedman, Lee S. and Deason, J. "Intertemporal Regulatory Task and Responsibilities for Greenhouse Gas Reductions," *Journal of Policy Analysis and Management*, Vol. 29, No. 4 (2010), pp. 821–853.

Gelbspan, Ross. *The Heat is On: The Climate Crisis, the Cover-up, the Prescription*. Cambridge, MA: Perseus Books (1998).

Gildas De Muizon et Matthieu Glachant. "Climate Change Agreements in the UK: A Successful Policy Experience?" in R.D. Morgenstern A. Pizer (eds) *Reality Check: The Nature and Performance of Voluntary Environmental Programs in the United States, Europe and Japan*. Washington D.C.: RFF Press (2007), pp. 64–85.

Gillis, Justin. British Panel Clears Scientists. *New York Times* (July 8, 2010), p. A9.

Goulder, L.H. "Environmental Taxation and the Double Dividend: A Reader's Guide," *International Tax and Public Finance*, Vol. 2 (August 1995), pp. 157–183.

Goupille, Sylvan. *Interview*. London, UK: Deputy Head of Carbon Finance, BNP Paribas (November 28, 2008).

Green, K.P., S.F. Hayward, and K.A. Hassett. *Climate Change: Caps v. Taxes, Environmental Policy Outlook*. No. 2 (2007), Washington, D.C.: American Enterprise Institute for Public Policy Research. Retrieved from: http://www.aei.org/files/2007/06/01/20070601_EPOg.pdf.

Greenstreet, David. *Impacts of Phase II SO_2 Emission Restrictions on West Virginia's Economy*. Bureau of Business and Economic Research. Working Paper. College of Business and Economics, West Virginia University (December 1999).

Grossman, G.M. and A.B. Krueger. *Environmental Impacts of a North American Free Trade Agreement*. Working Paper No. 3914. Cambridge, MA: National Bureau of Economic Research, Inc. (1991), p. 15.

Hahn, R. "Economic Prescriptions for Environmental Problems: How the Doctor Followed the Doctor's Orders," *Journal of Economic Perspectives*, Vol. 3, No. 2 (Spring 1989), p. 111.

Hahn, R.A. *Primer on Environmental Policy Design, Fundamentals of Pure and Applied Economics*. Reading, UK: Hardwood Academic Publishers (1990), p. 18.

Hahn, R.W. "Economic Prescriptions for Environmental Problems: How the Patient Followed the Doctor's Orders," *Journal of Economic Perspectives, American Economic Association*, Vol. 3, No. 2 (1989), pp. 99–111.

Hahn, R.W. and G.L. Hester. "EPA's Market for Bads," *Regulation*, Vol. 3, No. 4 (1987), pp. 48–53.

Hahn, R.W. and G.L. Hester. "Where Did All the Markets Go? An Analysis of EPA's Emissions Trading Program," *Yale Journal of Regulation*, Vol. 6, No. 1 (1989), pp. 109, 136, 148, 377–379.

Hahn, R.W. and R. Noll. "Designing a Market for Tradable Emission Permits," in W. Magat (ed.) *Reform of Environmental Regulation*. Cambridge, MA: Ballinger Publishing Co. (1982), pp. 119–146, 132–133.

Hammitt, James K. The Successful International Response to Stratospheric Ozone Depletion. *Weekly Policy Commentary*. Resources for the Future. (2009). Retrieved from: http://www. rff.org/Publications/WPC/Pages/09_06_01_Successful_International_Response.aspx.

Hanemann, M. "Willingness to Pay and Willingness to Accept: How Much Can They Differ?" *American Economic Review*, Vol. 81 (1991), pp. 635–647.

Hanley, N. and C. Spash. *Cost-Benefit Analysis and the Environment*. Aldershot: Edward Elgar (1993).

Hanley, N., et al. *Environmental Economics in Theory and Practice*. New York: Oxford University Press (1997), pp. 93, 154.

Harvey, Fiona. "Climate scientists feel heat in e-mail probe," *Financial Times*. (February 6–7, 2010). Retrieved from: http://www.ft.com/cms/s/0/4a8f0038-12be-11df-9f5f-0014 4feab49a.html.

Hausker, Karl. "The Politics and Economics of Auction Design in the Market for Sulfur Dioxide," *Journal of Policy Analysis and Management*, Vol. 11 (1992), pp. 553–572.

Helm, Dieter. "Climate-Change Policy: Why so Little has been Achieved?," *Oxford Review of Economic Policy*, Vol. 24, No. 24 (2008), pp. 211–238.

Hepburn, C. and N. Stern. "A New Global Deal on Climate Change," *Oxford Review of Economic Policy*, Vol. 24, No. 2 (2008), p. 272.

HM Government. *Building A Low Carbon Economy. Unlocking Innovation and Skills*. Department for the Environment, Food and Rural Affairs. p. 13. (2008). Retrieved from: http://www.defra.gov.uk/environment/business/innovation/commission/documents/ cemep-response.pdf.

Hobbs, Benjamin F., James Bushnell, and Frank A. Wolak. *Upstream vs. Downstream CO_2 Trading: A Comparison for the Electricity Context*. Energy Institute at Haas, University of California, Berkeley. Working Paper 203. Berkeley, CA (March 2010).

House of Commons. *The EU Emissions Trading Scheme: Lessons for the Future*. Environmental Audit Committee, Second Report of Session 2006–07. London, UK: The Stationery Office Limited (2007), p. 17.

House of Commons. *The Role of Carbon Markets in Preventing Dangerous Climate Change*. Environmental Audit Committee. Fourth Report of Session 2009–10. London, UK. The Stationery Office Limited (February 8, 2010). pp. 3, 20.

IER. *Abundant Natural Gas Means Low Prices, Increased Trade Potential*. Washington, D.C.: Institute for Energy Research. Retrieved from: http://www.instituteforenergyresearch. org/2012/04/19/abundant-natural-gas-means-low-prices-trade-potential/

International Energy Agency. "Global Carbon-Dioxide Emissions Increase by 1.0Gt in 2011 to Record High" (May 24, 2012). Retrieved from: http://iea.org/newsroomandevents/ news/2012/may/name,27216,en.html.

International Energy Agency. *World Energy Outlook*. (2011).

IPA Energy Consulting. *Implications of the EU ETS for the UK Power Generation Sector* (November 2005).

Johnson, Keith. "Who's Afraid of a Clean-Energy Future? Environmental Capital," *Wall Street Journal* (January 14, 2010).

Joskow, Paul L., Richard Shmalensee, and Elizabeth Bailey. *Auction Design and the Market for Sulfur Dioxide Allowances*. Working Paper. Cambridge: MIT University (1996).

Joskow, Paul L., Richard Schmalensee, and Elizabeth M. Bailey. "The Market for Sulfur Dioxide Emissions," *The American Economic Review*, Vol. 88, No. 4 (September 1998), p. 669.

Jotzo, Frank. "Communication. Developing Countries and the Future of the Kyoto Protocol," *Global Change, Peace & Security*, Vol. 17, No. 1 (February 2005), p. 3.

Karousakis, Katia. *E-mail communication. Policy Analyst. EPA Clean Air Markets Division* (August 6, 2001).

Keating, Terry J. and Alex Farrell. *Transboundary Environmental Assessment: Lessons from the Ozone Transport Assessment Group. Office of Air Quality Planning and Standards*. Washington, D.C.: EPA (1999), pp. 29–30.

Kelman, S. *What Price Incentives?: Economists and the Environment*. Boston: Auburn House Publishing Co. (1981).

Keohane, Nathaniel. *Testimony before the Committee on Energy & Commerce*. Director of Economic Policy and Analysis, Environmental Defense, to United States House of Representatives. Washington, D.C. (April 22, 2008).

Kete, Nancy. "Air Pollution Control in the United States: A Mixed Portfolio Approach. US Mission to the OECD, Paris, France," in Ger Klaassen and Finn R. Førsund (eds.) *Economic Instruments for Air Pollution Control. International Institute for Applied Analysis*. Dordrecht, The Netherlands: Kluwer Academic Publishers (1994), p. 124.

Kette, N. *The Politics of Markets: The Acid Rain Control Policy in the 1990 Clean Air Act Amendments*. Thesis/Dissertation, 172, 239 (1993).

Klier, Thomas, Richard H. Mattoon, and Michael A. Praeger. "A Mixed Bag: Assessment of Market Performance and Firm Trading Behaviour in the NO_X RECLAIM Programme," *Journal of Environmental Planning and Management*, Vol. 40, No. 6 (1997), p. 753.

Kraft, M. and V. Norman. *Environmental Policy: New Directions for the Twenty-First Century*. 4th Edition. Washington, D.C.: CQ Press (1999), p. 20

Krowlewski, Mary Jo and Andrew S. Mingst. *Recent NOX Reduction Efforts: An Overview. ICAC Forum* (2000), p. 9.

Kruger, J. *Market Policy Chief, EPA Clean Air Markets Division*. Interview, Washington, D.C. (May 2000).

Kruger, J. and M. Dean. "Looking Back on SO_2 Trading: What's Good for the Environment is Good for the Market," *Public Utilities Fortnightly*, Vol. 135, No. 15 (August 2, 1997), pp. 30–37.

Kruger, J., Brian McLean, and R.A. Chen. "A Tale of Two Revolutions: Administration of the SO2 Trading Program," in R.F. Kosobud, et al. (eds.) *Emissions Trading: Environmental Policy's New Tool*. New York: Wiley (2000), pp. 1–10.

Lancaster, Robin. *Along Expectations. Trading Carbon*. London, UK: Point Carbon Publication (May 2010), p. 17.

Latin, H. "Ideal Versus Real Regulatory Efficiency: Implementation of Uniform Standards and 'Fine-Tuning' Regulatory Reforms," *Stanford Law Review*, Vol. 37 (May 1985), pp. 1270–1271.

Leman, C. "How to Get There from Here: The Grandfather Effect and Public Policy," *Policy Analysis*, Vol. 6, No. 1 (1980), pp. 90–116.

Lindblom, C.E. *Politics and Markets*. New York: Free Press (1977).

Lindblom, C.E. and D.K. Cohen. *Usable Knowledge, Social Science and Social Problem Solving*. New Haven: Yale University Press (1979).

Linowes, Lisa. *Regional Greenhouse Gas Initiative (RGGI) A Cap-Tax-Spend Model to NOT Follow* (July 19, 2010). Retrieved from: at http://www.masterresource.org/2010/07/rggi-cap-tax-spend-model/#more-11108.

Liroff, R.A. *Reforming Air Pollution Regulation: The Toil and Trouble of EPA's Bubble.* Washington, D.C.: Conservation Foundation (1986), pp. 3, 10–13, 15–18, 21–25.

Low, P. *International Trade and the Environment.* Washington, D.C.: The World Bank (1992).

Majone, G. *Evidence, Argument, and Persuasion in the Policy Process. Changing Institutional Constraints.* London: Yale University Press (1989), pp. 117, 166.

Margolis, J. and R. Langdon. *In the RECLAIM Trading Pit—Progress, Problems, and Prospects.* 95-TP65.04. Larkspur, CA: Cantor Fitzgerald Environmental Brokerage Services (1995).

Marshall, C. Lord, Chair. *Economic Instruments and Business Use of Energy.* London, UK: HMSO. Government Task Force on the Industrial Use of Energy (1998).

Martin, Ralf, Ulrich J. Wagner and Laure B. de Preux. "The Impacts of the Climate Change Levy on business: Evidence from Microdata," CEP Discussion Papers dp0917, Centre for Economic Performance, London School of Economics and Political Science (2009).

Martineau R. and D. Novello. *The Clean Air Act Handbook.* Chicago, IL: American Bar Association (1997), Vol. 8, pp. 375–377.

Martinez, Alier J. and J. Roca Jusmet. *Apuntes de Economia, Recursos Naturales y Medio Ambiente.* Facultat de Ciències Econòmiques i Empresarials. Universitat de Barcelona. Curs (1998–1999), p. 93.

McGinty, Kathleen. Retrieved from: http://www.epa.gov/ttn/rto/otag/finalrpt/chp8/final.htm (1996).

McLean, B. *Director of the Clean Air Markets Division (CAMD), US EPA.* Interview, Washington, D.C. (May 2000).

McLean, Brian. *Interview.* Director of the Clean Air Markets Division. Washington D.C.: EPA. (May 2000).

McLean, Brian. *US EPA Sulfur Dioxide (SO_2) Allowance Trading Program: The First Five Years* (January 19, 1996).

McNeil, Ben I. and Richard J. Matear. "Southern Ocean Acidification: A tipping point at 450-pmm atmospheric CO_2," PNAS, Vol. 105, No. 48 (December 2, 2008), pp. 18860–18864. Retrieved from: http://www.pnas.org/content/105/48/18860.full.

Melnick, R. Shep. *Regulation and the Courts: The Case of the Clean Air Act.* Washington, D.C.: The Brookings Institution (1983), p. 31.

Montero, J.P. "Optimal Design of a Phase-in Emissions Trading Program," *Journal of Public Economics*, Vol. 75, No. 2, (2000), pp. 273–291.

Montgomery, D.W. "Markets in Licenses and Efficient Pollution Control Programs," *Journal Economic Theory*, Vol. 5 (1972), pp. 395–418.

Morris, K. and A.M. Siegel. *The Wall Street Journal Guide to Understanding Money & Investing.* New York: Lightbulb Press (1993), p. 124.

Moser, Susanne C, and Lisa Dilling. *Creating a Climate for Change: Communicating Climate Change and Facilitating Social Change.* Cambridge: Cambridge University Press (2007).

Murray, Brian C., Richard G. Newell and William A. Pizer. *Balancing Cost and Emissions Certainty: An Allowance Reserve for Cap-and-Trade*, National Bureau of Economic Research: Working Paper 14258, Cambridge, MA (August 2008).

Nash, Jonathan Remy and Richard L. Revesz. "Grandfathering and Environmental Regulation: The Law and Economics of New Source Review," *Northwestern University Law Review*, Vol. 101, No. 4 (2007), pp. 1677–1734.

National Acid Precipitation Assessment Program. *National Acid Precipitation Assessment Program Report to Congress 2011: An Integrated Assessment.* US Geological Survey, Troy, NY (2011). Retrieved from: http://www.whitehouse.gov/sites/default/files/microsites/ostp/2011_napap_508.pdf.

National Aeronautics and Space Administration (NASA). *Ozone Trends Panel* (March 1988), Summary.

Navarro, Mireya. "Christie Pulls New Jersey from 10-State Climate Initiative," *The New York Times.* (May 26, 2011). Retrieved from: http://www.nytimes.com/2011/05/27/nyregion/christie-pulls-nj-from-greenhouse-gas-coalition.html.

Needham, David and Robert Dransfield. *Business Studies.* Cheltenham, UK: Stanley Thomes (1994), p. 723.

Neustadt, R. and E. May. *Thinking in Time: The Uses of History for Decision-Makers.* New York: Free Press; London: Collier Macmillan (1986), p. 2.

Newell, Richard G. "The Role of Markets and Policies in Delivering Innovation for Climate Change Mitigation," *Oxford Review of Economic Policy*, Vol. 26, No. 2 (2010), pp. 253–269.

Newnet. *UK Government Holds First Carbon Emissions Auction. NewNet – New Energy World Network* (November 19, 2008). Retrieved from: http://www.newenergyworldnetwork.com/renewable-energy-news/by-technology/energy-efficiency-by-technology-renewable-energy-news/uk-government-holds-first-carbon-emissions-auction.html.

Nobel Foundation. "The Nobel Peace Prize 2007" (February 14, 2010). Retrieved from: http://nobelprize.org/nobel_prizes/peace/laureates/2007/.

Nogrady, B. "Southern Ocean Close to Acid Tipping Point," *ABC Science* (November 11, 2008). Retrieved from: http://www.abc.net.au/science/articles/2008/11/11/2415539.htm.

Nordhaus, William D. (2005). Retrieved from: http://www.nber.org/papers/w11889.pdf?new_window=1.

North, D.C. "A Transaction Cost Theory of Politics," *Journal of Theoretical Politics*, Vol. 2 (1990), pp. 355–367.

Nussbaum, Barry D. *Phasing Down Lead in Gasoline in the US: Mandates, Incentives, Trading, and Banking. Climate Change: Designing a Tradable Permit System.* Paris: Organisation for Economic Co-operation and Development (1992).

NYMEX. "CME: Clearport, Sulfur Dioxide (SO_2) Emissions Futures" (2009). Retrieved from: http://www.nymex.com/RS_spec.aspx (accessed on December 24).

OECD. *The Distributive Effects of Economic Instruments for Environmental Policy.* Paris: OECD (1994a).

OECD. *Emissions Trading: Taking Stock and Looking Forward.* Paris: OECD (1998a).

OECD. *Environmental Policy: How to Apply Economic Instruments.* Paris: OECD (1991), p. 9.

OECD. *Evaluating Economic Instruments for Environmental Public Policy.* Paris: OECD (1997), pp. 9–26.

OECD. *International Greenhouse Gas Emissions Trading. Annex I Expert Group on the United Nations Framework Convention on Climate Change.* Working Paper No. 9. OCDE/GD(97) 76 Unclassified Document. Paris: OECD (1997), pp. 8–11, 22–23.

OECD. *Key Issues in the Design of New Mechanisms Under the Kyoto Protocol: Scoping Paper.* OECD/IEA Forum on Climate Change. Paris: OECD (March 12–13, 1998), p. 8.

OECD. *Lessons from Existing Trading Systems for International Greenhouse Gas Emission Trading. Annex I Expert Group.* Paris: OECD (1998b), p. 25.

OECD. *Lessons from Existing Trading Systems for International Greenhouse Gas Emissions Trading. Annex I Expert Group on the United Nations Framework Convention on Climate Change.* ENV/EPOC(98). Paris: OECD (August 1998c), p. 11.

OECD. *Managing the Environment: The Role of Economic Instruments.* Paris: OECD (1994b).

OECD. (2008). Retrieved from: http://www.fao.org/ag/againfo/programmes/en/lead/toolbox/grazing/epoc9813.pdf.

Olsen, J. "Scientists Warn Seas To Rise Faster Than Expected," *Sci-Tech Today* (March 10, 2009). Retrieved from: http://www.sci-tech-today.com/news/Seas-To-Rise-Faster-Than-Expected/story.xhtml?story_id=00100003LZXA&full_skip=1.

Ozone Transport Commission, States Working Together to Reduce Ground-Level Ozone in the North East. Retrieved from: http://www.sso.org/otc/publications/GENINFO.htm. Document retrieved on March 24, 2002.

Pacala S. and R. Socolow. "Stabilization Wedges: Solving the Climate Problem for the Next 50 Years with Current Technologies," *Science*, Vol. 305, No. 5686 (2004), pp. 968–972.

Pace Energy and Climate Center. *Analysis of Surplus Emission Allowances in the Regional Greenhouse Gas Initiative (RGGI) and State Control of the Surplus.* Pace Law School (December 2011). Retrieved from: http://www.pace.edu/school-of-law/sites/pace.edu.school-of-law/files/PECC/RGGI_Policy_Brief.pdf.

Pachauri, R.K. and A. Reisinger (eds.) *Climate Change 2007: Synthesis Report Contribution of Working Groups I, II and II to the Fourth Assessment Report of the Intergovernmental Panel on Climate Change.* Geneva, Switzerland: United Nations IPCC (2007) p. 30.

Palmer, Karen. and David A. Evans. "The evolving SO_2 allowance market: Title IV, CAIR, and beyond," *Resources for the Future Weekly Policy Commentary.* (July 13, 2009). Retrieved from: http://www.rff.org/Publications/WPC/Pages/090713-Evolving-SO2-Allowance-Market.aspx.

Parker, L. and J. Blodgett. *Air Quality EPA's Ozone Transport Rule, OTAG, and Section 126—A Hazy Situation?* Retrieved from: http://www.cnie.org/nle/air-16a.html (May 7, 2002), p. 4.

Parker, Larry B. and Donald W. Kiefer. *Implementing SO_2 Allowance Trading: Implications of Transaction Costs and Taxes. Congressional Research Service.* Washington, D.C.: The Committee for the National Institute for the Environment (March 12, 1993).

Pasurka, C. "Perspectives on Pollution Abatement and Competitiveness: Theory, Data, and Analyses," *Review of Environmental Economics and Policy*, Vol. 2, No. 2 (2008), pp. 194–218.

Pennock, J. Roland and D.G. Smith. *Political Science. An Introduction.* New York: The Macmillan Company (1964), p. 669.

Pérez Henríquez, Blas. "Information Technology: The Unsung Hero of Market-Based Environmental Policies," *Resources.* Washington, D.C.: Resources for the Future (Fall/Winter 2004).

Petrillo, Kathryn. *Senior Policy Analyst, the EPA's Clean Air Markets Division E-mail Communication* (April 12, 2002).

Pigou, Arthur C. *The Economics of Welfare.* 4th Edition. London: Macmillan (1932).

Pirrong, Stephen. *Market Oversight for Cap-and-Trade: Efficiently Regulating the Carbon Derivative Market.* Washington, D.C.: Energy Security Initiative. Brookings Institution (2009).

Pizer, William. (1999). Retrieved from: http://www.rff.org/rff/Documents/RFF-CCIB-17.pdf.

Point, Carbon. "US Offset supply grows 13% in '09," *Thomson Reuters* (March 1, 2010). Retrieved from: http://www.pointcarbon.com/news/1.1418893.

Pooley, Eric. *The Climate War. True Believers, Power Brokers, and the Fight to Save The Earth.* New York: Hyperion Books (2010).

Popp, David. "Pollution Control Innovations and the Clean Air Act of 1990," *Journal of Policy Analysis and Management*, Vol. 2, No. 4 (Fall 2003). pp. 641–660.

Porter, Michael. "America's Green Strategy," *Scientific American*, Vol. 264, No. 4 (1991), p. 168.

Porter, Michael. *The Competitive Advantage of Nations.* New York: Free Press (1998), p. 70.

Radner, R. "A Behavioral Model of Cost Reduction," *Bell Journal of Economics*, Vol. 6 (1975), pp. 196–125, summarized in Levitt, Barbara. Organizational Learning.

RECLAIM. *Over a Dozen Years of RECLAIM Implementation: Key Lessons Learned in California's First Air Pollution Cap-and-Trade Program* (June 2007), p. 2.

Reilly, William K. "The Greening of EPA," *EPA Journal* (July/August 1989).

Reuters, "CME Group Announces the Launch of New Sulfur Dioxide Futures and Options Contracts." (2009b). Retrieved from: http://www.reuters.com/article/pressRelease/idUS199486+29-Jun-2009+PRN20090629. (accessed on June 29).

Reuters. "EPA's 2009 SO$_2$ Auction Proceeds Slump to $9.6 Million," (2009a). Retrieved from: http://www.reuters.com/article/GCA GreenBusiness/idUSTRE52N6PQ20090324. (accessed on March 24).

RGGI. Regional Greenhouse Gas Initiative. (2010a). Retrieved from: http://www.rggi.org/docs/MM_2009_Annual_Report.pdf.

RGGI. Regional Greenhouse Gas Initiative. (2010b). Retrieved from: http://www.rggi.org/docs/Auction_8_NewsRelease_MMReport.pdf.

RGGI. Regional Greenhouse Gas Initiative. (2010c). Retrieved from: http://www.rggi.org/rggi_benefits (accessed on September 21, 2010).

RGGI. Regional Greenhouse Gas Initiative. (2012). Retrieved from: http://www.rggi.org/docs/PR031612_Auction15Results.pdf.

Roberts, M.J. and S.O. Farrell. "The Political Economy of Implementation: The Clean Air Act and Stationary Sources," in Ann F. Friedlaender (ed.) *Approaches to Controlling Air Pollution*. Cambridge, MA: MIT Press (1978), p. 156.

Rose-Ackerman, Susan. *Controlling Environmental Policy*. New Haven: Yale University Press (1995), p. 9.

Rothkopf, Michael H. "Thirteen Reasons Why the Vickrey-Clarke-Groves Process Is Not Practical," *Operations Research*, Vol. 55, No. 2 (March–April 2007), pp. 191–197.

Salzman, James and J.B. Ruhl. "Currencies and the Commodification of Environmental Law," *Stanford Law Review*, Vol. 53 (2000), pp. 607–694.

Sandbag. (2011). Retrieved from: http://www.sandbag.org.uk/site_media/pdfs/reports/Sandbag_2011-06_fatcats.pdf.

Sandor, R. "Implementation Issues: Market Architecture and Tradable Instrument (In Search of the Trees)," in *Combating Global Warming. Study on a Global System of Tradable Carbon Emission Entitlements*. Geneva: UNCTAD (1992), pp. 15, 160, 153–157.

SCAQMD & Ecoteck, MST Solutions, Inc. *Improved Point Source Inventory Through Validation and Audit of the Reported Data* (2001), p. 1.

SCAQMD. (1996).

SCAQMD. *Annual RECLAIM Audit Report for 2010 Compliance Year*. Retrieved from: http://www.aqmd.gov/hb/attachments/2011-2015/2012Mar/2012-Mar2-025.pdf. (March 2, 2012).

SCAQMD. *AQMD Annual Report* (1995).

SCAQMD. *Board Meeting* (March 10, 1999).

SCAQMD. *Board Meeting Date* (March 13, 1998). Agenda No. 42, Annual RECLAIM Audit Report for the 1996 Compliance Year. Retrieved from: http://www.aqmd.gov/hb/980342a.html.

SCAQMD. *Board Meeting Date* (March 2, 2012). Agenda No. 21, Report to Stationary Source Committee. Retrieved from: http://www.aqmd.gov/hb/attachments/2011-2015/2012Mar/2012-Mar2-021.pdf.

SCAQMD. *Board Meeting, Meeting Agenda* (November 9, 2001).

SCAQMD. *Board Meeting. Annual RECLAIM Audit Report for the 2007 Compliance Year*, Agenda No. 37. (March 6, 2009).

SCAQMD. *Budget & Work Plan, Fiscal year 2009–2010*. Diamond Bar, CA (2009), p. 95.

SCAQMD. *Over a Dozen Years of RECLAIM Implementation: Key Lessons Learned in California's First Air Pollution Cap-and-Trade Program* (June 2007).

SCAQMD. Retrieved from: http://www.aqmd.gov/news1/1999_smog_season_end.htm (accessed on October 12, 1999).

SCAQMD. Retrieved from: http://www.aqmd.gov/news1/2000_smog_season_2000.htm (accessed on October 27, 2000).

SCAQMD. Retrieved from: http://www.aqmd.gov (accessed June 23, 2011).

SCAQMD. Retrieved from: http://www.aqmd.gov/news1/RECLAIM_market.htm (accessed on August 16, 2000).

SCAQMD. Retrieved from: http://www.aqmd.gov/rules/html/r301_reclaim.html (accessed on May 8, 2002).

SCAQMD. *RECLAIM, Development Report and Proposed Rules*, Revised Draft. (July 1993), p. EX–5.

SCAQMD. Retrieved from: http://www.aqmd.gov/news1/Governing_Board/BS3_16_01.htm (accessed March 16, 2001), pp. 1–2.

SCAQMD. "Twelve-Month Rolling Average Price of Complianced Years 2011 and 2012 NOx RTCs," *Quarterly Report to Stationary Source Committee*. Retrieved from: http://www.aqmd.gov/reclaim/docs/2012-7_Avg_NOx_Price.pdf (July 2012).

SCAQMD. *White Paper on Stabilization of NOX RTC prices* (January 11, 2001). p. 4.

Schakenbach, John T. "Use of Calibration Gases in the US Acid Rain Program," *Accreditation and Quality Assurance: Journal for Quality, Comparability and Reliability in Chemical Measurement*, Vol. 6, No. 7 (2001), p. 301.

Schennach, Susanne M. *The Economics of Pollution Permit Banking in the Context of Title IV of the 1990 Clean Air Act Amendments*. Cambridge, MA: MIT CEEPR (May 1998).

Schmalensee, Richard et al. "An Interim Evaluation of Sulfur Dioxide Emissions Trading," *Journal of Economic Perspectives*, Vol. 12, No. 3 (1998), pp. 53–68.

Schwarze, R. and Zapfel, P. "Sulfur Allowance Trading and the Regional Clean Air Incentives Market: A Comparative Design Analysis of Two Major Cap-and-Trade Permit Programs?" *Environmental and Resource Economics*, Vol. 17, No. 3 (2000), pp. 279–298.

Schwarze, R. and Zapfel, P. "Sulphur Allowance Trading and the Regional Clean Air "Incentives Market: A Comparative Design Analysis of Two Major Cap-and-Trade Permit Programs?," in *Environmental and Resource Economics.*, Vol. 17, Dordrecht, The Netherlands: Kluwer Academic Publishers, Vol. 17, (2000), Vol. 17, p. 287.

Shelling, T. "What Makes Greenhouse Sense? Time to Rethink the Kyoto Protocol," *Foreign Affairs*, Vol. 81, No. 3 (May/June 2002), pp. 6–8.

Sijm, Jos, Karsten Neuhoff, and Yihsu Chen (2006). Retrieved from: http://www.eprg.group.cam.ac.uk/wp-content/uploads/2008/11/eprg0617.pdf.

Smith, Stephen and Joseph Swierzbinski. "Assessing the Performance of the UK Emissions Trading Scheme," *Environmental and Resource Economics*, Vol. 37, No. 1 (2007), pp. 131–158.

South Coast Air Quality Management District. Regulation XIII, Rule 1309(a). Amendment (June 28, 1990).

Stavins, R.N. "Clean Profits. Using Economic Incentives to Protect the Environment," *Policy Review*, No. 48 (Spring 1989), pp. 58–63.

Stavins, R.N. *The Problem of the Commons: Still Unsettled After 100 Years*, Working Paper 16403. National Bureau of Economic Research. Cambridge, MA. (September 2010).

Stavins, R.N. "Significant Issues for Environmental Policy and Air Regulation for the Next Decade," *Environmental Science and Policy*, Vol. 1 (1998), pp. 143–147.

Stavins, R.N. "Transaction Costs and Markets for Pollution Control," *Resources*, Vol. 119, No. 9 (1995), p. 145.

Stavins, R.N. "Transaction Costs and Tradable Permits," *Journal of Environmental Economics and Management*, Vol. 29, No. 2 (1995).

Stavins, R.N. and R. Hahn. "Trading in Greenhouse Permits: A Critical Examination of Design and Implementation Issues," in Henry Lee (ed.) *Shaping National Responses to Climate Change: A Post-Rio Policy Guide*. Cambridge: Island Press (1995), pp. 177–217.

Stavins, Robert N. "Transaction Costs and Tradable Permits," *Journal of Environmental Economics and Management*, Vol. 29 (September 1995), pp. 136–146.

Stavins, Robert N. Market-based Environmental Policies, in Paul R. Portney and Robert N. Stavins (eds.) *Public Policies for Environmental Protection*. Washington, D.C.: Resources for the Future (2000), pp. 31–76.

Stern, N.H. *The Economics of Climate Change: The Stern Review*. Cambridge, UK: Cambridge University Press (2007).

Sterner, T. *Economic Instruments for Environmental Management in Developing Countries*. Paris: OECD (1992), p. 53.

Susskind, Lawrence E. *Environmental Diplomacy, Negotiating More Effective Global Agreements*. London: Oxford University Press (1994).

Tapscott, Don, David Ticoll and Alex Lowy. *Digital Capital: Harnessing the Power of Business Webs*. Boston: Harvard Business School Press (2000), pp. 46–47, 160.

Tesoriero, Paul. "Should the SO_2 Market Be Saved?" *Environmental Finance* (2010). Retrieved from: http://new.evomarkets.com/pdf_documents/evo/envirofinance_may2010_pault_article.pdf

Tesoriero, Paul and Margaret Watson. *New Clean Air Rules Take Markets on a Detour*. Executive Brief. Evolution Markets. Edition 39. (August 10, 2010), p. 1.

Thompson, Dale H. "Political Obstacles to the Implementation of Emissions Markets: Lessons from Reclaim (May 13, 2011)," *Natural Resources Journal*, Vol. 40, No. 3, (Summer 2000), p. 653.

Tietenberg, T.H. *Emissions Trading: An Exercise in Reforming Pollution Policy*. Washington, D.C.: Resources for the Future (1985).

Tietenberg, T.H. *Economics of the Environment: An Overview. Environmental and Natural Resource Economics*. New York: Harpers Collins Publishers (1992), pp. 16, 39.

Tietenberg, T.H. *Emissions Trading: Principles and Practice*. 2nd Edition. Washington, D.C.: Resources for the Future (2006), pp. 31–32.

Tietenberg, T.H. *Environmental Economics and Policy*. 2nd Edition. Reading, MA: Addison-Wesley (1998), pp. 5–6, 272.

Tietenberg T.H. and H. Folmer. *The International Yearbook of Environmental and Resource Economics 1998–1999: A Survey of Current Issues*. Cheltenham, UK; Northampton, MA: Edward Elgar Pub. (1998), pp. 19–20.

Tietenberg, T., et al. *Greenhouse Gas Emission Trading, Defining the Principles, Modalities, Rules and Guidelines for Verification Reporting & Accountability*. Geneva: UNCTAD, United Nations Conference on Trade and Development (1998), pp. 1–3, 21–32, 135.

Tietenberg, Tom. "Tradable Permits for Pollution Control When Emission Location Matters: What Have We Learned," *Environmental and Resource Economics*, Vol. 5, No. 2 (1995), pp. 95–113.

Tietenberg, Tom. *Emissions Trading Principles and Practice*. Washington, D.C.: Resources for the Future Press (1996).

Tirole, J. *The Theory of Industrial Organization*. Cambridge, MA: MIT Press (1988), p. 4, 49.

Trexler, Mark. "A Gathering of Black Swans," *Environmental Finance*, Vol. II, No. 10 (September 2010), pp. 22–23.

US Code. "Monitoring, Reporting, and Recordkeeping Requirements" Title 42, Chapter 85, Subchapter IV-A, § 7651k(a). (1990). Retrieved from: http://www.law.cornell.edu/uscode/html/uscode42/usc_sec_42_00007651—k000-.html November 4, 2010.

US Department of Energy. *Energy Information Administration*. Retrieved from: http://www.eia.doe.gov (accessed on January 10, 2000).

US Environmental Protection Agency (1994), See http://www.epa.gov/airquality/urbanair/sipstatus/reports/ky_elembypoll.html (59 Fed. Reg. 60, § 960).

US Environmental Protection Agency. "Letter from the Director in EPA," Update No. 4, The Next Generation. Office of Air and Radiation. Acid Rain Program. EPA-430-R-98–006 (May 1998).

US Environmental Protection Agency. Acid Rain and Related Programs: 2008 Emission, Compliance and Market Analysis. (2009b). Retrieved from: http://www.epa.gov/airmarkt/progress/ARP_2008_ECM_Data.pdf (accessed on December 24, 2009). 5.

US Environmental Protection Agency. Acid Rain Program 2007 Progress Report. (2009d). Retrieved from: http://www.epa.gov/airmarkets/progress/arp07 (January 2009).

US Environmental Protection Agency. *Acid Rain Program 2008 Progress Report*. (January 2009c). Retrieved from: http://www.epa.gov/airmarkt/progress/ARP_1.html. (accessed on October 23, 2009).

US Environmental Protection Agency. *Acid Rain Program, Update No. 3, Technology and Innovation*. Office of Air and Radiation. Acid Rain Division. EPA-430-R-98–004 (May 1996).

US Environmental Protection Agency. *Acid Rain Program*. Retrieved from: http://www.epa.gov/airmarkets/progsregs/arp/basic.html (accessed on October 4, 2009).

US Environmental Protection Agency. *CFC Regulatory Impact Analysis*, Vol. 2 (1988).

US Environmental Protection Agency. *Documentation for the 2005 mobile National Emissions Inventory*, Version 2.ftp://ftp.epa.gov/EmisInventory/2005_nei/mobile/2005_mobile_$nei_version_2_report.pdf (2008).

US Environmental Protection Agency. *Emissions Trends 1900–1998*. Office of Air and Radiation. EPA-454/R-00–002. (May 2000).

US Environmental Protection Agency. *Federal Acid Rain Program: Notice of Annual Adjustment Factors for Excess Emissions Penalty*. Federal Register 74:50962–50963, Oct. 2. (2009a).

US Environmental Protection Agency. *Measuring Air Quality: The Pollutant Standards Index*. *Office of Air Quality Planning and Standards*. EPA 451/K-94–001, 73 (1994).

US Environmental Protection Agency. *Office of Policy, Planning and Evaluation, Environmental Investments: The Cost of a Clean Environment*, EPA-230–11–90–083 (November 1990).

US Environmental Protection Agency. *Progress Report on the EPA Acid Rain Program. Office of Air and Radiation. Acid Rain Program*. EPA430-R-99–011. (November 1999).

US Environmental Protection Agency. *Rule to Reduce Interstate Transport of Fine Particulate Matter and Ozone (Clean Air Interstate Rule)*, Federal Register. 70:25162 (May 12, 2005).

US Environmental Protection Agency. *Update No. 2, Partnership for Cleaner Air. Office of Air and Radiation*. Acid Rain Program, EPA 430-N-95–012 (July 4, 1995).

US General Accountability Office. *Report to the Chairman, Committee on Energy and Commerce, House of Representatives: Air Pollution. Difficulties in Implementing a National Air Permit Program. Resources, Community, and Economic Development Division. GAO/RCED-93–59*. Washington, D.C.: GAO (February 23, 1993).

US Senate Committee on Environment and Public Works. (November 15, 1993)., p. 69.

UK Department for Environment, Food and Rural Affairs. (UK DEFRA). *Appraisal of Years 1–4 of the UK Emissions Trading Scheme. A Report by ENVIROS Consulting Limited.* London, UK (December 2006).

UK Department for Environment, Food and Rural Affairs. (UK DEFRA) (2010a), Retrieved from: http://www.decc.gov.uk/en/content/cms/what_we_do/change_energy/tackling_clima/ccas/uk_ets/uk_ets.aspx.

UK Department for Environment, Food and Rural Affairs. (UK DEFRA) (2010b), Retrieved from: http://www.defra.gov.uk/environment/climatechange/trading/index.htm.

UK Department of Energy and Climate Change. (UK DECC) (2010c). Retrieved from: http://www.decc.gov.uk/.

UK HM Revenue & Customs. (2001). Retrieved from: http://www.legislation.gov.uk/uksi/2001/662/contents/made

UK HM Revenue & Customs. *Finance Act 2000 Part II, clause 30 and in Schedules 6 and 7.* Retrieved from: http://customs.hmrc.gov.uk/channelsPortalWebApp/channelsPortalWebApp.portal?_nfpb=true&_pageLabel=pageExcise_ShowContent&propertyType=document&id=HMCE_CL_000290.

UK Legislation. *Climate Change Act of 2008 § 27* (2008). Retrieved from: http://www.opsi.gov.uk/RevisedStatutes/Acts/ukpga/2008/cukpga_20080027_en_2

UNEP. "Celebrate the Montreal Protocol 20th Anniversary," *Ozone Action.* Paris: United Nations Environment Program. (2007). Retrieved from: http://www.unep.fr/ozonaction/information/mmcfiles/3139-e-oanspecial20thanniversary.pdf.

United Nations (UN). *Glossary of Environment Statistics,* Studies in Methods, Series F, No. 67. New York: United Nations (1997).

United States Clean Air Act (US CAA). (1970), 42 US CAA sec 7401(a).

United States Clean Air Act. US C.A. (1990). Section 126.

United States. Tradable Emissions Hearing Before the Joint Economic Committee, Congress of the United States, 105th Congress, 1st Session, July 9, 1997. Washington, D.C.: US G.P.O. (1997).

Ury, W. *Getting Past No. Negotiating Your Way from Confrontation to Cooperation.* New York: Bantam (1993).

US Congress. *Environmental Policy Tools, a User's Guide.* Office of Technology Assessment. OTA-ENV-643. Washington, D.C.: US Government Printing Office (September 1995), p. 111.

US EPA. *1997 Compliance Report Acid Rain Program.* Office of Air and Radiation. EPA-430-R-98-012. Washington, D.C.: EPA (1998).

US EPA. *2001 OTC NOX Budget Program Compliance Report.* Clean Air Markets Division, Office of Air and Radiation. Washington, D.C.: EPA (March 26, 2002).

US EPA. *Acid Rain Program Model NOX Cap and Trade Program: Elements of Model NOX Cap and Trade Rule.* Draft Working Paper. Acid Rain Program (December 7, 1997), p. 1. Document retrieved from EPA's web site (June 6, 1999).

US EPA. *Air Transport,* www.epa.gov/airtransport/ (accessed August 22, 2011).

US EPA. *Finding of Significant Contribution and Rulemaking for Certain States in the Ozone Transport Assessment Group Region for Purposes of Reducing Regional Transport Ozone.* Rule, 63 Federal Register Sections 57356–57538 (October 27, 1998).

US EPA. *The NOX Budget Trading Program: 2008 Highlights.* EPA-430-R-09-026, Washington, D.C. (October 2009).

US EPA. *Questions Being Explored Using C-MAP and GIS.* (June 26, 2001).

US EPA. *Rule To Reduce Interstate Transport of Fine Particulate Matter and Ozone (Clean Air Interstate Rule); Revisions to Acid Rain Program; Revisions to the NOX SIP Call; Final Rule*, Washington, D.C. (May 12, 2005).

US EPA. *Transport Rule (CAIR Replacement Rule)*. Retrieved from: http://yosemite.epa.gov/opei/rulegate.nsf/byRIN/2060-AP50 (accessed May 26, 2010).

US EPA. *The United States Experience with Economic Incentives to Control Environmental Pollution*. EPA-230-R-92-001 (1992), pp. 14–15.

US EPA and OTC. (2002). Retrieved from: http://www.epa.gov/airmarkt/progsregs/nox/docs/otcreport.pdf.

US Senate. *Testimony of Brian McLean, Director, Acid Rain Division, US Environmental Protection Agency Before the Subcommittee on Clean Air, Wetlands, Private Property and Nuclear Safety of the Committee on Environment and Public Work*. Washington, D.C.: The Congress of the United States (October 6, 1998).

USA Today. *Report Says Global Warming Very Likely Man-Made, to Continue for Centuries*. (September 03, 2009). Retrieved from: http://www.usatoday.com/weather/climate/global warming/2007-02-01-ipcc-report_x.htm.

Velders G.J.M., S.O. Andersen, J.S. Daniel, D.W. Fahey, and M. McFarland. "The Importance of the Montreal Protocol in Protecting Climate," *PNAS*, Vol. 104 (March 20, 2007), pp. 4814–4819.

Victor, D.G. *The Collapse of the Kyoto Protocol and the Struggle to Slow Global Warming*. Princeton, NJ: Princeton University Press (2001), p. xi.

Vogel, David. *Kindred Strangers: The Uneasy Relationship between Politics and Business in America*. Princeton, NJ: Princeton University Press (1996).

Vogel, David. *Trading Up, Consumer and Environmental Regulation in a Global Economy*. Cambridge, MA: Harvard University Press (1997).

Wagner, Janice K. Interview, Chief, Market Operations Branch, CAMD. Washington, D.C.: US EPA (August 2001).

Warren, L. *American Environmental History*. Malden, MA: Blackwell Pub (2003).

Waxman, Henry A. "An Overview of the Clean Air Act Amendments of 1990," *Environmental Law*, Vol. 2 (1991), pp. 1721–1816.

Wed-Works. *AB 32 Proposed Implementation Plan Summary. Workforce and Economic Development*. (2008). Retrieved from: http://www.wed-works.org/pdfs/2008/AB%2032%20one-page%20summary.pdf.

Weimer, David L. *The Craft of Policy Design: Can it be More Than Art? Report delivered at the 1989 Annual Research Conference for Public Policy Analysis and Management*. Washington, D.C. (November 4, 1989), p. 20.

Weitzman, M.L. "Prices Versus Quantities," *Review of Economic Studies*, Vol. 41 (October 1974), pp. 477, 480.

Wenders, John T. "Methods of Pollution Control and the Rate of Change in Pollution Abatement Technology," *Water Resources Research*, Vol. 11 (1975), pp. 393–396.

The White House. Statement by the President on the Ozone National Ambient Air Quality Standards. Retrieved from: http://www.whitehouse.gov/the-press-office/2011/09/02/statement-president-ozone-national-ambient-air-quality-standards (accessed on September 2, 2011).

Williamson, O.E. *Organizational Theory: From Chester Bernard to the Present and Beyond*. New York: Oxford University Press (1995).

Williamson, O.E. *The Economic Institutions of Capitalism: Firms, Markets, Relational Contracting*. Free Press: New York and London (1985), pp. 211, 426.

WindAction Editorial. RGGI: A cap-tax-spend model to NOT follow (July 19, 2010). Retrieved from: http://www.windaction.org/faqs/28358.

Wirth, Timothy and John. Heinz. *Project 88: Harnessing Market Forces to Protect Our Environment: Initiatives for the New President, a Public Policy Study.* Washington, D.C.: Environmental Policy Institute (1988).

Yandle, B. *The Political Limits of Environmental Regulation: Tracking the Unicorn.* New York: Quorum Books (1989), Preface. 66.

Yang, Trent, Kira Maus, Sergey Paltsev, and John Reilly. *Economic Benefits of Air Pollution Regulation in the USA: An Integrated Approach.* Report No. 113, Joint Program on the Science and Policy of Global Change, Massachusetts Institute of Technology. Cambridge, MA (January 2005).

Zaelke, Durwood, Paul Orbuch and Robert F. Housman. *Trade and the Environment, Law, Economics, and Policy.* Washington, D.C.: Center for International Environmental Law (1993).

Zeckhauser, Richard. "Preferred Policies Where There is a Concern for Probability of Adoption," *Journal of Environmental Economic Management,* Vol. 8 (1981), pp. 215–237. In Stavins (1995), 146.

Zerefos, Christos, Georgios Contopoulos, and Gregory Skalkeas (eds.). *Twenty Years of Ozone Decline: Proceedings of the Symposium for the 20th Anniversary of the Montreal Protocol.* Berlin, Germany: Springer (2009).

Index